Essays in memory of Peter Nettl

# Imagination and Precision
# in the Social Sciences

Edited by T. J. Nossiter, A. H. Hanson, Stein Rokkan

Faber & Faber · 3 Queen Square · London

First published in 1972 by
Faber and Faber Limited
3 Queen Square London WC1

Printed in Great Britain by
Robert MacLehose & Co. Ltd.
The University Press, Glasgow

ISBN 0 571 09572 0

© 1972 Faber and Faber Ltd.

# Imagination and Precision
in the Social Sciences

**Books by Peter Nettl**

*The Eastern Zone and Soviet Policy in Germany.*
London–New York 1950

*Rosa Luxemburg* (2 vols.). London–New York 1966

*Political Mobilization.* London–New York 1967

*The Soviet Achievement.* London 1967

*International Systems and the Modernisation of Societies*
(with R. Robertson). London–New York 1968

# Contents

# Contents

# Preface and Acknowledgements

The variety in the subject-matter of the essays is a reflection of Peter Nettl's own width of interests. He was a historian, political scientist, sociologist and man of affairs. His published work ranged from the most down-to-earth to the most abstract—and he took the whole world for his province.

The title we have chosen reflects another of Peter's outstanding characteristics. He brought to all his work an imagination that never failed to illuminate whatever it touched upon; but he was deeply conscious of the scholar's duty to achieve the greatest possible precision in both exposition and analysis. If he sometimes failed in this respect—as we all do—it was the failure of a man who could never remain content with the merely pedestrian. In him there was a tension between imagination and precision which, although often frustrating, was essentially creative.

This work is addressed primarily to scholars who share Peter Nettl's interests and who are concerned, as he was, with vigorously pushing forward the boundaries of their subjects. Each essay, we hope, is an original contribution to learning. Many of them display an iconoclasm which we are sure he would have enjoyed. Their division between 'Sociology', 'Politics' and 'History' is necessarily somewhat arbitrary, since their authors are characterised, like Peter himself, by an impatience with disciplinary boundaries.

Our best thanks are due to them for their willing response to our appeal for contributions to this volume. We also wish to thank the New York *Review of Books* for permission to reprint Hannah Arendt's review of *Rosa Luxemburg*, and *Political Studies* for permission to reprint Richard Rose's essay on 'The Variability of Party Government'. Finally we are grateful to Lewis Minkin for the use of his bibliography of Peter Nettl's publications.

**T.J.N., A.H.H., S.R.**

A. H. Hanson

# Peter Nettl: A Memoir

I have made a few small corrections of fact to this memoir as Professor Hanson died shortly before the galleys were received (Ed.)

This volume is a tribute to an extraordinary man by fellow-scholars who knew and admired him. Why Peter Nettl was so extraordinary as to deserve this kind of memorial, will, I hope, emerge from my attempt briefly to delineate his character and to assess his intellectual impact. But even the bare facts about his short life show that we are here doing homage to one who had a touch of genius.

He was born in the Sudetenland at Liberec (Reichenberg) in 1926. His parents, of the Viennese middle class, were prosperous. He attended the local elementary school until 1936, when his parents decided to transfer the family home to England. As by this time his father's woollen business had already established strong connections with Bradford, emigration presented no serious problems.

Sent to a preparatory school called Fernden, near Haslemere, Peter was confronted by the dual assignment of learning English and adjusting himself to an unfamiliar way of life. He worked hard at both, and succeeded in winning a major scholarship to Marlborough.

In 1944, at the age of eighteen, he joined the British army as a private in the King's Royal Rifles. Commissioned in the following year, he was transferred to Intelligence and posted to Berlin, where he became occupied with the interrogation of prominent German prisoners. The youngest staff officer in the British army, he now for the first time showed that capacity for the utilisation of experience that never left him; for his intelligence work provided him with much of the knowledge which he eventually incorporated in *The Eastern Zone and Soviet Policy in Germany 1945-50* (OUP 1950) and in the essay on 'The Economy of the Soviet Zone of Germany' which he contributed to Professor Carl Friedrich's symposium,

*Totalitarianism* (Harvard U.P. 1953), as well as several articles.

On demobilisation he went with an Open Scholarship to St. John's College, Oxford, where he took the shortened post-war finals, in which he predictably obtained a First. In 1950 he married Marietta Lux, a Hungarian ballerina from Budapest.

Offered a joint teaching post by St. John's and Brasenose, he might now have embarked on an academic career, which he preferred to any other. His father, however, wanted him to enter the family business. Eventually, they agreed that Peter should accept a tutorship for a year and then become a 'wool man' in Bradford. Peter kept to his bargain and went north, to an environment which he cannot have found very pleasant. Old hands in the Bradford woollen industry were understandably sceptical about the capacity of this brilliant young Oxford graduate to adjust himself to the traditions of an extremely traditional trade, and advised his father to keep his nose to the grindstone in the warehouse for as long as possible. After six months, however, he seems to have learnt all that he needed to know.

During the next ten years he devoted himself to building up the business, without ever abandoning his academic interests. He travelled extensively in all continents and exploited his linguistic gifts for purposes of salesmanship. He not only made a lot of money but gained a first-hand knowledge of a variety of countries, particularly in the 'developing' world, which subsequently proved of the greatest value when he abandoned his business career to become a political scientist.

In 1961, sated with business, he took up a visitor's position at Nuffield College, Oxford, in order to work on a biography of Rosa Luxemburg. It was at this time, when he was devoting fantastic energy to research in several languages, that I first met him. In 1963 he secured an appointment as Lecturer in Politics at the University of Leeds. Very soon afterwards, *Rosa Luxemburg* (OUP 1966) was completed and published to an acclaim by the scholarly world which was recognised by his promotion to a Readership in 1967; but by this time he had transferred most of his abundant energies from political history to political sociology. In a prolific period of writing he quickly produced *Political Mobilization* (Faber 1967) and, in collaboration with Roland Robertson, *International Systems and the Modernisation of Societies* (Faber 1968); and yet could still find time for his little classic of popularisation, *The Soviet Achievement*, and several articles. After a period of leave of absence in the United States, he accepted an appointment as Professor of Political Sociology in the University of Pennsylvania; but almost as soon as he and Marietta had settled in Philadelphia, he was tragically killed on 25 October, 1968, in an air crash on his way to a conference. Marietta, who was accompanying him, escaped with minor injuries. Peter was only 42 when he died.

Such, in brief, is the story of his life. What kind of man was he, to encompass so much in so few years? In the more obvious ways, he was a fortunate man—so fortunate as to inspire both admiration and envy. By the standards accepted by most of us, he was very rich. (Stories of tutorials interrupted by telephone calls from his broker were not entirely apocryphal.) He was also handsome, healthy, and physically as well as intellectually vigorous. The amenities of a cultured, elegant and varied life were well within his reach, and he took full but discriminating advantage of them. Culturally, he was both knowledgeable and discerning. There was no element of dilletantism in his connoisseurship of paintings, which he bought for enjoyment as well as for profit; and if his taste in music was (at least in my view) a little less secure, his knowledge of his favourite composers—particularly Wagner—was very detailed and his appreciation of them exceptionally intense. Moreover, he was an accomplished pianist.

Enormously talented and versatile, he had an intelligence that brought a sharp cutting edge to everything to which it was applied. He also possessed the ability to 'get up' a subject in a remarkably short time, and then to move among its complexities with apparent ease and confidence. Sometimes—particularly in his youth—he used this simply to show off, as when he accepted and won a bet that he would secure publication in a legal journal of an article on a subject of which he had no previous knowledge; but he also took advantage of this extraordinary capacity to bring to fruition, within two or three years of intense work, a historical masterpiece, *Rosa Luxemburg*, which in the breadth and detail of its scholarship might pass for the product of half a lifetime.

He not only read at great speed; he had the ability to absorb, by what looked like an osmotic process, the essence of an author's message and rapidly to extract from a book or document precisely what seemed relevant to his current intellectual preoccupation. Moreover, he could use these absorptive and perceptive talents in several languages. He was thoroughly familiar with French, German, Russian, Italian, Spanish and Hebrew, and could learn other languages, at least for reading purposes, very quickly and without apparent effort.

He chose, in the end, to be a scholar, and hindsight suggests that this choice was predestined. But his versatility was such that he could have achieved success in almost any field of activity calling for intelligence, initiative, energy and self-confidence. He fully proved his ability as a businessman, and few of those who knew him would doubt that, had he applied himself to business single-mindedly, he could have become a distinguished industrialist or financier. Had he been so minded, he could have been equally successful as administrator or politician—although it must be admitted that either of these occupations would have presented him with problems of temperamental adjustment perhaps even more serious than those he experienced in the woollen trade. Had he devoted himself full-time to art or to music, he might well have distinguished himself as a critic or pianist. Nor did he lack the capacity for literary work. Admittedly, none of his four novels, published under the pseudonym of 'Paul Norwood', is first-rate (although one is very good); but it must be remembered that all of them were produced, largely by way of relaxation, in the interstices between more important, or at least more demanding, activities.

One had the impression that he would have liked to achieve mastery of every field of thought and action. He was a belated Renaissance-type man to whom the achievements of others always presented a challenge. Perhaps he never said, even to himself, anything so vulgar as 'Whatever you can do I can do better', but he undoubtedly had a great faith in his own capacity to excel. One of his sources of frustration—and he had many—was the need for specialisation imposed on him by the conditions of twentieth-century life. He tried to escape from it by moving restlessly from one field to another, with an apparent (but only apparent) loss of interest in the old one in his enthusiasm for the new. Having 'done' business, he became an academic. Having succeeded as a historian, he moved on to political sociology, taking, of course, the whole world for his province. Having switched to this new subject, he had to aim at quickly becoming one of its top-level practitioners, and at securing recognition of his mastery of it by the award of a professorship. And he did indeed get his Chair. Had he lived longer, it is almost certain that he would have moved on to something else—probably quite different but equally challenging and as successfully mastered that.

Such undisguised ambition, particularly when successful, is no recipe for universal popularity, and it is not surprising that Peter found critics and even made enemies. He tended to 'use' people; and they did not like it. His contempt for mediocrity was obvious, as was his impatience with those whose minds were slower than his own. As a colleague, he could be rather difficult; as a teacher, he tended to produce a series of *tours de force* which were barely intelligible to any but the really able students. Not surprisingly, the practice of 'catching Peter out' acquired a certain vogue; for his speed of work sometimes led him into error, while his intellectual fertility could give birth to foolishness as well as to brilliance. A distinguished scholar once said of him, 'Mr. Nettl has at least three ideas a day, some of them good.'

Of such faults, however, he was sublimely unconscious until they happened to be brought to his notice. Fundamentally of a generous nature, he could be almost pathetically anxious to make amends once he realised that he had given offence. One of the contradictions of his character was that he simultaneously wanted to outshine everyone else and yet to be loved by those he had all-too-conspicuously outshone. But there were much deeper contradictions than this—of a kind that only psychological investigation could have attempted to unravel. For all his obvious success and appearance of abounding self-confidence, he remained arguably something of a displaced person, able to cope with almost any kind of social environment yet nowhere fully at home. With an established position, a beautiful house, a delightful and infinitely understanding wife, and three much-loved children, he still experienced the kinds of tensions said to be characteristic of the wandering Jewish intellectual. His cosmopolitan background and restless critical intelligence prevented him from entering the way of life of the English establishment, for which his parents—not without some justification, in the light of their own experiences—had apparently destined him. Yet he found the 'cosmopolitan' establishment, as exemplified by the habitués of a Sardinian summer resort, even less acceptable. As an intellectual with strong Marxist leanings, his natural sympathies were with the working-class movement; yet of the real world of the working classes he knew very little. The 'solid' middle class he knew much better, from his business experience, but he had no wish whatever to enter it or to identify himself with it, since its way of life was totally alien to his tastes. Even among university colleagues, who were his most natural companions, he tended to be the odd man out. A few he respected, and a very small handful he positively venerated, but the majority he tended to dismiss as pedestrian. This intense and proud individualism was incompatible with repose. Only through perpetual activity, physical and mental, could he find temporary satisfaction—and he drove his Jaguar as furiously as he wrote his books.

It seems probable, however, that during his later years he was discovering a centre of emotional commitment with which no European country, no political party, and no social class or interest group could provide him. His Jewishness, on which George Steiner perceptively comments in his article in this symposium, was reasserting itself, and with it came a loyalty towards the state of Israel. This must have been a difficult evolution; for Peter, as far as I could discover, had no religious beliefs, and he was certainly far more aware than most of his fellow Jews of the political ambiguities and incoherences involved in Israel's very existence. It was not a subject about which he often talked, and only at the time of the Six Days' War did I begin to understand the depths of his feelings. Even when he was expounding what appeared to be a toughly objective analysis of these events, his elation at Israel's victory could not be concealed. It may be, therefore, that in the long run Israel would have provided him with a much-needed home, physical and spiritual. But how far he had actually travelled towards a militant Zionism is difficult to say.

Even when all these facets of his character have been noted, it is still hard to 'place' Peter; for he refuses to be type-cast. The image of restless individualism and acerbic intellectualism is too unidimensional. It omits his poignantly human qualities: a personal warmth, a generosity, a determination (when he remembered) to be helpful, a delight in shared enthusiasms, a peculiar *gaucherie* of a most disarming kind, and an extraordinary capacity, in his rare moments of relaxation, for self-revelation, together with a ready appreciation of such capacity in others. The fact is that Peter not only wanted to be loved; he was actually loved, with peculiar intensity, by those who knew him well. One must therefore emphasise that this volume is more than a tribute of intellectual respect.

What of his scholarly work? How important is it, and what impact has it had on the fields of study within which it is located?

One thing may be said about it with certainty: that it is a significant individual contribution to the current trend towards an amalgam of the various social science disciplines. Trained as a historian, Peter acquired a capacious knowledge of economics, sociology, political science and organisation theory, and used all of them (sometimes a little indiscriminately) to illuminate whatever subject was currently attracting his attention.

It is as a historian, however, that his reputation is likely to be most secure. Here he was on the home ground. History gave him little opportunity to display the methodological originality on which he placed so high a value, but it was undoubtedly the thing he did best. Probably no-one in this country had a deeper knowledge, based on a wide and intensive reading of original sources, of the history of the labour movement in central Europe during the late nineteenth and early twentieth centuries. This knowledge he displayed not only in his *chef d'oeuvre*, *Rosa Luxemburg*, but in a series of scholarly and deeply-pondered articles, of which the best is probably the essay he contributed to *Past and Present* on the German Social-Democratic Party during the years immediately preceding the First World War (April 1965). Both there and in the great biography one finds a stimulating combination of scrupulous scholarship with a sense of commitment. Precisely to what he is committed may be open to discussion, but he always succeeds in communicating a sense of the importance, for our own day, of the historical events he is narrating and analysing. Writing as a Marxist, of however individual a kind, he is on a level with Eric Hobsbawm, Edward Thompson or E. H. Carr in his capacity to make history 'relevant'. In the work of a genuine scholar this fusion of objectivity and commitment produces history of the most compulsively readable kind.

In *Rosa Luxemburg*, his most distinguished work, the commitment takes the form both of a critical sympathy for the doctrines preached by the great socialist and of a deep personal understanding of her that is obviously the product of intellectual and emotional affinity. Precisely why he became involved with Rosa at the time when he was making the transition from the business to the university world I do not know. What is obvious is that, as a historian of the labour movement, he was bound to take her on sooner or later. For she was one of his sort: Jewish, central European, cosmopolitan, bold, intellectually adventurous and with a contempt for mediocrity. It is true that Peter never gave himself to the socialist movement with the fervour that Rosa did, but he would almost certainly have done so had the times been more propitious and the issues better defined. He also shared with his subject an artistic sensitivity, a personal fastidiousness, and an anxiety to keep the personal life in a separate compartment from the public. The result of this meeting of minds across the years is a portrait of unusual depth and intimacy. It is this that maintains the reader's interest through the many pages that are overloaded with detail, where Peter, intent on telling the whole truth, has failed to jettison material of a peripheral or repetitious kind. It is this that transforms what might have been a merely scholarly work into one of the great biographies. During the composition of this book, Marietta may well have wondered whether Rosa was the 'other woman' in Peter's life.

The strength of *Rosa Luxemburg* lies in its historical narrative and psychological penetration. When Peter turns to the analysis of Rosa's theoretical work, his touch is a little less sure. After reading the manuscript, I pointed out what seemed to me weaknesses in this area, spelling out my disagreements and criticisms at some length. With the characteristic good humour with which he confronted his critics, Peter said that my few pages of scribble had given him a 'bad night'; it did not have any other effect, nor did I really expect it to have. For to say 'What I have done I have done' was both his virtue and his vice. It was also his reaction, later, when I levelled more serious criticisms at *Political Mobilization*—in this case after publication; for he had decided, perhaps rightly, that I was disqualified by lack of sociological knowledge to vet the manuscript of that ambiguous work.

His decision to focus his attention on political sociology, although like all his decisions a rapid one, was not quite the *volte-face* that the record of his published work might suggest. A turning of his mind in this direction is reflected in many of the footnotes, both learned and provocative, to *Rosa Luxemburg*. The precise moment at which he decided to become a different kind of academic is unknown to me, but by the time he took up his appointment as Lecturer in Politics at the University of Leeds the transformation was well under way. By then he was immersing himself, with growing excitement, in the works of the American sociologists. The first major product of this new interest was *Political Mobilization*, a book that fared as ill at the hands of the reviewers as *Rosa Luxemburg* had fared well.

This *tour de force* is one of the most difficult books I have ever had occasion to read. After a second reading much of it remains unintelligible to me, and I am still uncertain, as I was when I reviewed it for the TLS, whether its unintelligibility is the product of muddled thought or of obscurity of expression or of a bit of both. Had Peter really acquired a sure grasp of the conceptual framework, largely derived from Talcott Parsons, that he had chosen to use? Had he genuinely absorbed and understood the great mass of sociological literature from which he so freely quoted? I still do not know. What I do know is that he did not take enough trouble to make himself clear, even to the sociologically-knowledgeable reader; that he was far too often careless with his factual information; and that he showed an alarming tendency—strange in so reputable a historian—to look to the empirical record for a confirmation rather than for a test of his fine-spun hypotheses. Even the most sympathetic readers of this book tended to feel that as a political sociologist Peter was jumping the gun.

In a long discussion of my criticisms of the book, Peter freely admitted, in his usual frank and disarming manner, that it was marred by serious defects. I think he more than half-realised that his anxiety to make a fresh reputation had betrayed him into premature publication, before he had given himself adequate opportunity to test, clarify and refine his ideas. But although obviously disappointed with the hostile or exasperated reviews the book received (mine was in the latter category), he was quite prepared to dismiss it as *juvenilia* and to try again. He did indeed try again, in collaboration with Roland Robertson, a thoroughgoing professional in the field of sociological theory. Their book of essays, although variously assessed, made a much more favourable scholarly impact than *Political Mobilization*, as a result of what one reviewer called the admirable way in which they demonstrated 'the relevance of a great many sociological concepts, drawn primarily but not exclusively from Parsons' Theory of Action, to the analysis of international phenomena'. In any case, by 1967 Peter had already made a sufficient impression on the minds of reputable sociologists to be offered at least two Chairs. It may well be that he would have become as brilliant a sociologist as a historian.

Nevertheless, I still hold—although more tentatively than I used to do—to my belief that in political sociology he had chosen a field in which his mind moved with rather less than its accustomed confidence and flexibility. He had it in him to become one of the greatest historians of the late twentieth century, but I am less sure that as a sociological theorist he would have reached the standards set by—say—Parsons, Smelser, Merton, Bendix or Etzioni—and nothing less than this would have satisfied him. That he would have become a distinguished sociologist there is little doubt; but in my view he could have accomplished much greater things as a sociologically-minded historian.

Perhaps he would never have totally abandoned history for sociology. It was during the period when he was reading sociological works most furiously that he produced, to order, his brilliant little history of the Soviet Union, entitled *The Soviet Achievement*. As an introduction to post-revolutionary Russia, this could hardly be bettered. It is a well-proportioned, well-written and extremely perceptive interpretation of events which he knew mainly from secondary sources. Again, as in *Rosa Luxemburg*, one is carried along by the feeling that here is a narrative that *must* be understood if one is to make sense of the modern world. Unlike many of his other writings, it displays an admirable tautness—clearly the result of his being confined, by the nature of the series for which he was writing it, to a limited number of words. In common with many other writers, he greatly benefited from this discipline. Yet, characteristically, he attached little importance to *The Soviet Achievement*. He wrote it very quickly indeed (and largely, I believe, with the help of dictation) and seemed mainly concerned that it should sell successfully—which it deservedly did. For him, it was no more than an *oeuvre de vulgarisation*, incidental to his sociological pursuits. One could only envy the good fortune of a man capable of producing a veritable little classic 'on the side'.

What political attitudes emerge from his historical and sociological works? For the most part they are implicit rather than explicit. As I have said, he was a Marxist of some kind. He and Eric Hobsbawm, one of his closest friends, certainly talked the same language and shared similar interests. But he was never a communist, nor, to my knowledge, did he ever attach himself to any political party of the extreme left. If he had a clear commitment, it was—at least during the final years of his life—to Israel; if he had a major interest, it was in the development of the underdeveloped countries, many of which he knew at first hand. His contribution to Colin Leys' symposium, *Politics and Change in Developing Countries*, seems to me the clearest and most perceptive of the essays he wrote during his 'sociology' period. Combined with an impatient temperament, this interest led him to look favourably on the more efficient of the authoritarian regimes in the developing countries, whether communist or non-communist. It is significant that he chose to call his history of the Soviet Union 'The Soviet Achievement'. He admired Ayub Khan and (with rather more reservations) Gamal Abdul Nasser. He was prepared to give the Great Proletarian Cultural Revolution in China rather more than the benefit of doubt. I never heard him express any particular affection for parliamentary democracy, and he once told me that he 'did not understand' British politics—what he meant, of course, was that they did not interest him. He found it inexplicable that I, his colleague, should be working simultaneously on parliamentary government in Britain and on economic development in India.

Yet he was anything but starry-eyed about authoritarian regimes. He knew only too well the price they charged for their problematical services. In *The Soviet Achievement* the account of collectivisation and the purges, lapidary as it is, makes no effort to minimise their horrors, while *Political Mobilization* contains little that could give conspicuous comfort to dictators. Always conscious of his obligation to scholarship, he preferred analysis to prescription; and if the trend of his analysis did less than justice to democratic ways of life, that was partly a consequence of his temperament and far more of his consciousness that twentieth-century humanity, particularly in the developing countries, was confronted with harsh political choices.

Peter Nettl was a great scholar and a great human being. Even his faults, when seen in perspective, become an inseparable part of a dynamic and fundamentally attractive personality. If this introductory memoir has 'mentioned his virtues, it is true, but dwelt upon his vices too', the intention is to do him the justice that, in his quieter moments, he might have meted out to himself. He would not have wished it otherwise; for he hated hypocrisy and would have loathed a conventionally congratulatory memorial notice. I can only add that all his friends felt diminished as well as saddened by the news of his death.

# Herminio Martins

# The Kuhnian 'Revolution' and its Implications for Sociology

For reasons of space Mr Martins' original contribution to this symposium has had to be considerably shortened. The excision and rewriting involved were undertaken editorially, with Mr Martins' approval.

Looking back at the development of sociological thought between the English language publication of *Ideology and Utopia* (1936) and the sixties a certain persistent disjunction must strike future intellectual historians as rather odd—the disjunction between the 'sociology of knowledge' and the sociology of science. The sociology of science has used as its chief analytical tools those of structural-functionalist sociological theory and has had comparatively little use for the characteristic concepts of the 'sociology of knowledge'—myth, ideology, utopia, 'false consciousness', etc. One might recall that Mannheim emphatically excluded logico-mathematical and natural-scientific knowledge from the purview of the 'sociology of knowledge'. The 'sociology of knowledge' as a general theory of ideology dealt with such thought—or belief—systems as philosophy, the social sciences, the humanities, political, moral and educational theory, law and jurisprudence, etc. Mannheim formulated a scheme[1] in terms of which the fine arts were chiefly characterized by a pattern of Gestalt transformation, and ideological phenomena by a 'dialectical' pattern, while the natural and technological showed linear cumulative development. The 'Mertonian' development of the sociology of science also contributed to the bifurcation of the sociology of knowledge and the sociology of science.

The most successful attempt so far to look at scientific and mathematical knowledge from a sociological perspective has come

---

[1]    Karl Mannheim, *Essays in the Sociology of Knowledge*, London, 1952, pp. 109-124.

from outside sociology: Kuhn's *The Structure of Scientific Revolutions*
(1962)[2] which has reopened a whole range of problems which sociologists themselves seemed determined to avoid. Part of the shock
value of Kuhn's theory of science stems from his adoption of terms
like consensus, authority, dogma, tradition, faith, conversion—
whole array of 'irrationalist' symbols—in a serious, tightly argued
theory of science and scientific knowledge. Consensus theories of
science are no novelty: Comte too taught the 'necessity of dogma' in
science and pointed out the absurdity of *libre examen* in, say,
astronomy. More recently Polanyi[3] outlined a social theory of
scientific knowledge in which terms like consensus, authority and
faith played an important part. The original formulation of the
theory however grew out of a polemic against the rationality of
attempting to plan science—a theme which lost its topicality in the
West after the end of the Second World War; while the later formulations of Polanyi's consensus theory of science were embedded in a
vast intellectual edifice from which this particular strand was not
easily retrieved. Moreover Polanyi's historical analysis of science
left much to be desired.

Kuhn's general picture of science has become familiar in its main
outlines. His starting point is the perception that most of the time
scientists carry out research which is very closely circumscribed in
conceptual, methodological, experimental and other ways. The bulk
of fundamental research, or 'normal science', consists of 'puzzle-

---

2      In addition see Thomas S. Kuhn, 'The essential tension: tradition and
       innovation in scientific research', in C. W. Taylor and F. Barron (eds.),
       *Scientific creativity: Its recognition and development*, New York 1963,
       pp. 341-54, reprinted in Liam Hudson (ed.), *The ecology of human
       intelligence*, London, 1970, pp. 342-356 and henceforward cited as
       'Tension'; 'The function of measurement in physics', *Isis*, 1961, pp.
       161-193 and henceforward referred to as 'Measurement'; 'The function
       of dogma in scientific research' in A. C. Crombie (ed.), *Scientific
       Change*, London, 1962, and henceforward referred to as 'Dogma'. *The
       Structure of Scientific Revolutions* was first issued as a monograph in
       *The international encyclopaedia of unified science*, Chicago, 1962, but
       the edition used is the most widely available one in Phoenix Books,
       Chicago, 1964: it will be cited as *SSR*.

3      Michael Polanyi, *Science faith and society*, London, 1946: 'The republic
       of science', *Minerva I*, 1962, pp. 54-73; *Personal Knowledge*, London,
       1958; *Knowing and Being*, London, 1969.

solving': it is not oriented so much to the pursuit of fundamental novelties of fact or theory, or indeed to the testing of theory, as to the ingenious production of expectable or expected solutions to prescribed problems according to standardized procedures. These standardized procedures are not those of logic or methodology or epistemology: indeed they vary over space and time. Although Kuhn has used a variety of terms for them—dogma, theory, paradigm, exemplar—the term that has really jelled is 'paradigm'. Paradigms are the 'universally recognised scientific achievements that for a time provide model problems and solutions to a community of practitioners'.[4] Far from being simply theoretical systems, they 'include law, theory, application and instrumentation'. Nor can they be construed as logically equivalent to rationally reconstructible bodies of knowledge: for they are the 'accepted examples of actual scientific practice . . . which . . . provide models from which spring particular coherent traditions of scientific research'.[5] Moreover, a paradigm is rarely an object for replication. Instead, 'like an accepted judicial decision in the common law, it is an object for further articulation and specification under new or more stringent conditions'.[6]

Within paradigm-guided normal science there are only three foci for investigation: the determination of that class of facts that the paradigm has shown to be particularly revealing of the nature of things,[7] the matching of facts with the paradigm theory, and the articulation of the paradigm theory. Normal science research is 'esoteric', a highly technical, 'subtle' pursuit, only fully intelligible to those who share the paradigm. Under these conditions, cumulative growth, or 'rapid and consequential advance', may be expected. Indeed, it is only through this type of procedure that science can flourish: 'since in the absence of a paradigm or some candidate for a paradigm, all of the facts that could possible pertain to the development of a science are likely to seem equally relevant',[8] and consequently the discipline and focus required for the pursuit of normal science could not be attained.

---

4   SSR, p. X.
5   SSR, p. 10.
6   SSR, p. 23.
7   SSR, p. 25.
8   SSR, p. 15.

In any scientific research process there are always 'anomalies' or 'violations of expectation'. Most of the time anomalies are ignored; sometimes they are the object of successful resolution into 'puzzles'; and on occasion they trigger off a major scientific crisis. Most crises are overcome within normal science. But from time to time the loosening of the rules of normal science goes too far and a revolutionary situation arises, in which the previous paradigm is replaced by a new one and another cycle of normal scientific research starts. Note that paradigms are psychologically exclusive (since the same scientist cannot entertain both with respect to the same field), socially monopolistic (since men 'whose research is based on shared paradigms are committed to the same rules and standards for scientific practice'), historically discrete (since each epoch of normal science is a tolerably clearly delimitable period). They are also logically and epistemologically incompatible, incommensurable, and non-cumulative. Major scientific progress takes place through scientific revolutions; these profound transformations *destroy* the previous paradigms each time they occur. Hence a given paradigm cannot be seen as incorporating, or subsuming, the truth-content of previous paradigms or even of the antecedent stock of scientific knowledge.

Normal science is manifest in codifications which contain all that a budding scientist needs to know formally about the history and the logical structure of the field. Thus Kuhn emphasises a 'socialization' pattern of science[9] which, psychologically restrictive or 'convergent',[10] structurally authoritarian and culturally dogmatic, is a marvellous engine for the production of paradigm-bound and even paradigm-shifting researchers. This, for him, is more important than the more obvious mechanisms of social control, such as those inherent in the system of journal editing and refereeing, or in the more subtle processes of recognition and reward allocation. Indeed,

---

9     Particularly in 'Tension', 'Dogma' as well as in some sections of *SSR*, pp. 80, 166, 167, 172 (cp. fn. 6).

10     'Tension', p. 342. The conceptions of 'convergent' and 'divergent' thinking have become particularly associated with the work of L. Hudson on English grammar school children's psychological orientations: *Contrary imaginations*, London, 1966, and *Frames of Mind*, London, 1968.

it may well be that he overestimates the efficacy of science pedagogy *per se* in achieving full internalization of relevant scientific norms and standards.

This account of the production of scientific knowledge has been both commended and attacked as 'sociological', 'sociologistic', or 'Durkheimian'. To bring out the 'normality' of cognitive consensus in science and at the same time to show that this is not simply the result of a logic of scientific inquiry, but rather of the authoritative maintenance of rules and standards by a discrete collectivity of specialists, does indeed involve some form of sociologism. Nevertheless the sharp contrast between 'normal' and 'revolutionary' science would appear to run counter to Durkheimian principles, although a Kuhnian might argue that both are sociologically homogeneous in that in neither is there a criterion superior to the assent of the community. This sociological homogeneity of paradigm-bonded and paradigm-shifting scientific communities would seem wholly consonant with Durkheim's theorems concerning moral change: ' . . . The principle of rebellion is the same as that of conformity. It is the true nature of society (i.e. "scientific community") that is conformed to when the traditional morality is obeyed and yet it is also the true nature of society which is being conformed to when the same morality is flouted'[11] (i.e. through paradigm change). Yet Kuhn neither seeks nor effects a sociologically monistic account of paradigm change: for psychological (and even generational) variables are brought into the explanatory scheme of scientific revolutions. It should also be noted that Durkheim's theory of scientific knowledge, in however inconsistent and erroneous a fashion, was a veristic one, since he professed belief in an increasing approximation to an 'ideal' truth. It was also a rationalist one, in that he believed in the invariance to social and historical change of the fundamental categories of thought. Moreover, he drew a sharp distinction between two types of collective representations: those maintained by mechanical solidarity (mythological beliefs) and those maintained by organic solidarity (scientific or rational beliefs).[12] It will not, therefore, do to

11    E. Durkheim, *Sociology and Philosophy*, London, 1953.
12    E. Durkheim, *Pragmatisme et Sociologie*, Paris, 1955, partially translated in K. Wolff (ed.): *Emile Durkheim—essays on sociology and philosophy*, New York, 1967.

praise or condemn Kuhn's theory of scientific knowledge on a basis of vaguely Durkheimian criteria.

The following discussion will first take up the concept of paradigm and then Kuhn's model of scientific change. I shall advance arguments tending to show that the concept of paradigm is not satisfactory as the basic epistemological isolate of science, as a major tool for the periodization of scientific history or as the unique sociological category for the analysis of scientific culture. Secondly, I shall deal with the structure of scientific 'revolutionary episodes', with the triadic scheme of normal science-revolution-normal science and with the Kuhnian model of large-scale, long-term cognitive change in science.

Kuhn's theory of scientific knowledge, although arising in part out of the contrast between the conflict-ridden and fissiparous social sciences and the consensual natural sciences, raises the possibility and even the desirability of a general, systematic *cognitive sociology*. Although it is possible that cognitive sociology, like the classical 'theorie sociologique de la connaissance' or *Wissenssoziologie*, may be doomed to failure, I shall nevertheless try to show that the *damnosa hereditas* of epistemological relativism may not be a permanent incubus.

'Cognitive psychology' and 'cognitive anthropology' are well established branches of human scientific inquiry which have developed at least in recent years without arousing philosophical hostility or bitter attacks from defenders of reason and from crusaders for freedom and the open society. Admittedly there *was* a time when 'psychologism' was a major target of epistemologists and critics of irrationalism: but 'cognitive psychology' did not it appears inherit the stigma of 'psychologism'. Although it is part of my purpose to bring about a more rational atmosphere for the discussion of the sociological claims involved in what used to be called and no doubt will still be called the 'sociology of knowledge', a mere terminological change is hardly likely to bring about a 'gestalt switch'. Nevertheless such a change can help, and I wish to suggest that such a cognitive sociology can befriend and assist epistemological rationalism. Of course one should not disguise the fact that cognitive sociology may continue to be involved with epistemological relativism and with irrationalism: the tension between sociology and epistemology is likely to continue. But to claim that cognitive sociology is necessarily and uniquely conducive to epistemological relativism and irrationalism is quite unwarrantable. Just as the ecology[13] of knowledge in society changes so do the interconnections between sociology and epistemology. These must be restated with every major development in culture and institutions. The genetic fallacy argument cannot simply be reiterated *ad nauseam*: philosophical thought must really be stimulated.

Kuhn's theory of science is a theory of pure or fundamental scientific research. It is also mainly developed in connection with physics, neglecting, at least for the sake of economy of presentation, both the formal sciences and the 'life' sciences. Although the scope of the theory is not temporally restricted it seems best to treat it as if it applied almost exclusively to the period since the seventeenth century 'scientific revolution'. Moreover the account deliberately holds constant 'external' societal factors, not because of their irrelevance to a comprehensive sociology of science, but because of their irrelevance to *The Structure of Scientific Revolutions*. We shall accept these restrictions for most of the time; due warning will be given when they are being lifted.

## PARADIGMS

*Span*

Paradigms pertain to fields like the study of heat, optics, mechanics, etc.; there are not and cannot be paradigms of physics or chemistry. In other words paradigms are not discipline-wide but sub-disciplinary. Their span is likely to be coterminous with that of specialties; conversely, specialties will be paradigm-bonded social systems. The specialty moreover is 'the primary locus of social control in the sciences'.[14] Within it the pressure of the scientific peer group and the weight of shared scientific opinion will be maximal. Often small enough for all the members of the collectivity to be acquainted with one another, and for informal communication networks to be highly effective, it does indeed constitute the optimal site for the crystallisa-

---

13    Cp. Ernest Gellner, *Thought and change*, London, 1964.
14    W. Hagstrom, *The Scientific Community*, New York, 1965, p. 163. I would like to acknowledge my debt to Hagstrom's most stimulating discussion of social control in science.

tion of cognitive consensus, for the maintenance of 'mechanical solidarity', and for the 'carrying' of Kuhnian paradigms.

Nevertheless, the Kuhnian model of science appears to commit what one might call a fallacy of misplaced discreteness; for although the specialty as a social control agency is relatively self-contained and exclusive, it is not the sole locus of social control in the sciences. Information and recognition flow between specialties as well as within them, both at the disciplinary and at the cross-disciplinary levels. This interdependence of functionally distinct structures creates what Durkheim called 'organic solidarity' in addition to the 'mechanical solidarity' obtaining within the specialty. Polanyi's 'principle of overlapping neighbourhoods'[15] is very pertinent here. The mutual control of adjacent specialties throughout the entire range of academic science brings about, however diffusely and in the long run, the control of each specialty by all and of all by each, 'from astronomy to medicine'. Indeed Polanyi goes so far as to say that this chain or network of overlapping neighbourhoods 'is the seat of scientific opinion'.[16] This is obviously in sharp contrast with the view that the specialty is 'the primary locus of social control in the sciences'. Both statements, however, may be accepted if they are taken to refer to two sociologically distinct types of solidarity and social control—the 'mechanical' and the 'organic'—and correlatively to two different levels of the socio-cultural organisation of science. Clearly the consensus that obtains at the level of the specialty is far more compact and directly enforced than the relatively diffuse 'overlapping neighbourhoods'.

We may summarise the foregoing argument schematically as follows:

### SOCIAL CONTROL IN SCIENCE

| Unit or Level of Social Control | Solidarity Type | Consensus Type |
|---|---|---|
| Specialty | Mechanical | Direct (or 'paradigmatic') |
| Supra- or Cross-Specialty | 'Organic' | Indirect |

This indirect consensus, or 'state of scientific opinion', is not a

---

15    M. Polanyi, *Personal Knowledge*, pp. 216-8; 'The republic of science'; *Knowing and Being*, pp. 73-86.
16    M. Polanyi, 'The republic of science', p. 59.

Kuhnian consensus because it is not 'paradigmatic' in his sense. It would seem, therefore, that Kuhn understates the consensus that effectively obtains by limiting himself to the discrete normative complexes he calls 'paradigms'. Admittedly the indirect consensus appears more precarious than the direct, in that it is not maintained by an immediate peer group which is the *locus* of social rewards, facilities and sanctions, but by a network of comparatively diffuse social relations and of contacts with other cognitive scientific subcultures. To focus attention exclusively on the former consensus type is to repeat the old sociological mistake of regarding concrete, primary groups and relations as uniquely and completely determining effective social control. It is, moreover, to neglect the scientific division of labour and the unity of science that is maintained through extensive culture contact. Science is more than the sum of paradigm obtaining at any point of time; for a mechanical aggregate of discrete paradigms or specialties would bear only a very partial resemblance to the total social organisation of science.

The components of this totality need not be shared by every specialty and sub-discipline, nor need they consist of coherent and systematic complexes of cognitive beliefs. Not only do scientists accept on trust the 'paradigms' of other fields; they participate to varying degrees in the diffuse cognitive orientations that pervade a number of otherwise distinct scientific fields. These include a number of great historic importance: the Platonic faith in the geometrisation of the world, the belief in the simplicity of natural laws, the ideal of unrestricted universality, the Laplacian programme of universal mechanics, the statistical view of nature, Baconian inductivism, etc. Such cognitive orientations have been called 'intellectual passions', 'metaphysical programmes', 'ideals of natural order', 'generalised intellectual commitments', 'regulative principles', 'absolute presuppositions', etc. One could argue that these cognitive orientations, however important to science, are not themselves part of science; but such a distinction completely misses the essential function of 'metaphysical' research programmes in the development of mathematical physics and other mature sciences. Such beliefs are labelled as 'metaphysical' only after the exhaustion or failure of the research programmes to which they have given rise—and not necessarily even then—or, as in the case of the complementarity principle in con-

B

temporary quantum mechanics, by those who refuse to accept them.

To describe them as 'metaphysical' does in fact point to their utility in linking scientific thought with general philosophical and cosmological ideas. They are often linked to what one might call philosophical *logotopias*:[17] visions of complete, perfect, and final knowledge and the criteria and procedures involved in the search for it. Baconian inductivism, Cartesian rationalism, Platonic geometricism are good examples of influential and fertile logotopias; and there are plenty of others. Insofar as they are 'encoded' in working programmes and actual achievements of a 'paradigmatic' sort they are part of the cognitive culture of the scientific community. A Kuhnian might regard them simply as epiphenomena of paradigm formation, as by-products of paradigmatic achievements; but even if the influence of these cognitive orientations and logotopias is enhanced by the paradigms that seem to embody and implement them, they may in turn act as stimuli to paradigm-formation. Such cognitive orientations may thus be a means of transmitting paradigm-formation from one area of inquiry to another, with results which may or may not be fruitful.

## Parity

The foregoing considerations also throw doubt on an implicit assumption of the Khunian model, that of parity between contemporaneous paradigms. Given organic solidarity through overlapping neighbourhoods, as in all complex social systems, there will be an inherent tendency towards cognitive stratification;[18] for some paradigms will be more prestigious and *ceteris paribus* more influential than others. The cognitive orientations associated with them (however wrongly, e.g. the association of Machism with the special relativity theory) will tend to enjoy a greater presumption of heuristic fertility, explanatory power, elegance, etc. Similar con-

---

17      If 'eutopias' and 'dystopias' (C. Walsh), 'heterotopias' (used in different senses by Henri Lefebvre and M. Foucault), and 'pornotopias' (S. Marcus) why not 'logotopias'?

18      As well as a system of social stratification in terms of authority ranks or levels. On the whole a kind of 'functional theory of stratification' is—surprisingly—accepted by even bitter critics of that theory as a general sociological explanation of societal stratification.

siderations apply if we introduce the concept of scientific revolution. (Since revolutions are parasitic on logically and historically prior paradigms, the argument will apply to mature sciences only.) Scientific revolutions in the Kuhnian sense are spectacular occurrences and hence will increase the visibility and perhaps also the prestige of the fields in which they occur.

*Autarky*

In criticising the assumption of the parity of paradigms we have also criticised by implication the assumption of paradigm autarky, i.e. the assumption that each paradigm develops almost exclusively by endogenous change. In so far as organic solidarity obtains in the scientific community, this is *prima facie* incorrect.

There is a curious parallel here between the Kuhnian stance and that of functionalism. One of the standard functionalist arguments against diffusionism was that no matter how many cultural traits were imported into a social system, their selection and persistence could be accounted for solely in terms of immanent structural constraints and requisite functions. Similarly, a Kuhnian might argue that it is the paradigm that dictates which cognitive beliefs will be added to the consensus, regardless of origin. This type of argument is not easily refutable since it promulgates a methodological rule rather than a historical generalisation. Nevertheless it is highly questionable.

Pantin[19] has drawn an important distinction between 'unrestricted' and 'restricted' sciences which has a close bearing on this issue. The 'unrestricted' sciences are those that require that their practitioners 'must be prepared to follow the analysis of their problems into every other kind of science', whilst in the 'restricted' sciences no such requirement obtains. This distinction corresponds very roughly with that between the physical sciences and chemistry on the one hand, and biology on the other. If this distinction is at all valid and illuminating, in what sense can we speak of autonomous paradigms in the 'unrestricted' sciences? We might here make a further distinction between *mono-paradigmatic* fields (or fields with self-sufficient autarkic paradigms) and *poly-paradigmatic* fields where

---

19    C. F. A. Pantin, *The relations between the sciences*, Cambridge, 1968, chs. 1 and 5 and *passim*.

paradigms are complementary and lacking in individual self-sufficiency. Alternatively one might refuse to regard these ostensibly poly-paradigmatic fields as constituents of mature science; but this would be rather implausible as they include a number of important branches of biology and geology, which may reasonably be considered to have acquired paradigms during the nineteenth century. Again, it would be possible to speak of *degrees* of maturity or degrees of paradigmaticness which would involve a drastic modification of the very concept of paradigm—perhaps more drastic than the admission of poly-paradigmatic sectors. Any of these alternatives is bound to create difficulties for the Kuhnian model.

Genetically, of course, some mature scientific fields emerge not from an inchoate 'natural history' stage or from a revolutionary shift away from a single anterior paradigm but from the cross-fertilisation of two different paradigms pertaining to different sectors of scientific inquiry. The rise of molecular biology out of biochemistry and crystallography provides an example of a striking success story in which the rule of one paradigm leading to one successor, and of each paradigm (after the first) having only one predecessor does not apply. Although such cases are not ruled out completely by the Kuhnian model, they are marginal to it. Generally, Kuhn emphasises the autonomy of paradigm succession, and does not systematically study the mutual interaction of contemporaneous paradigms in different fields. Yet one question, among others, that must obviously be asked is whether revolutions in prestigious scientific fields do not reinforce the revolutionary potential of neighbouring regions of scientific inquiry.

Another feature of the Kuhnian model is the lack of autonomy or semi-independent variability of paradigm components:[20] the basic complex of law, theory, instrumentation and application is an integral unity capable of articulation and consolidation but not of significant qualitative change short of a full-fledged revolution. This is tantamount to a paradigm holism, in which the chief components of paradigms are linked by logically internal relations. Even if one

---

20    The paradigm is 'a fundamental unit for the student of scientific development, a unit that cannot be fully reduced to logically atomic components that might function in its stead', *SSR*, p. 11.

regards cognitive beliefs as part of the normative culture of scientific collectivities, the resultant model does not entail that cognitive norms even in 'mature' sciences always and necessarily cluster in quasi-organic, tight, discrete complexes.

If one does subscribe to a holistic model then change must necessarily bring about wholesale upheavals—'revolutions'—of a sharply discontinuous, 'all-or-nothing' kind. A more moderate view would allow for various 'degrees of organicity', or of systemic clustering of scientific beliefs, norms and values. (Toulmin's[21] distinction between 'compact' and 'diffuse' traditions is an improvement upon the Kuhnian contrast between paradigmic order and natural history chaos, although even here 'compactness' may be too easily equated with the paradigmatic.) Although, as we have seen, at the level of the specialty there will be strong pressures towards convergence, consensus and 'mechanical solidarity', such pressures do not necessitate the kind of paradigm holism posited in the Kuhnian model, which is logically stronger than anything sociologically required.

To cast doubt on paradigm holism is not necessarily to subscribe to an atomistic model of cognitive norms in science. Nevertheless important cognitive norms do not appear to be paradigm-specific and paradigm-bound, but rather common to a multiplicity of contemporaneous or successive paradigms. For instance, Polanyi[22] has drawn attention to an important norm that has prevailed in chemistry for over a hundred years—a period which has surely by Kuhnian as by other criteria witnessed a number of revolutions or paradigm shifts in this field: the norm that no contributions to chemical journals be accepted which not do contain new experimental findings. This long-lasting norm cannot of course by itself constitute a whole paradigm, yet it has remained invariant to whole epochs of chemical research, involving changes in theory, procedures and accredited empirical beliefs. Generalised cognitive orientations have undergone modification, yet this lower-level norm has persisted. Another example (from a field which may perhaps be regarded as

---

21    S. Toulmin, 'Conceptual revolutions in science', *Boston Studies in the Philosophy of Science*, vol. III, Dordrecht, 1967 and 'The evolutionary development of natural science', *American Scientist*, 55, 4, 1967, pp. 455-471.

22    M. Polanyi, *Personal Knowledge*, p. 156.

pre-paradigmatic) is the requirement of field work[23] as a necessary condition for membership of the professional collectivity of anthropologists. The norms pertaining to any given paradigm do not all succumb at the same time, the time of paradigm-shifting: they may well enjoy widely varied life spans. We still know very little about the differential vulnerability of cognitive norm complexes in science histories.

More trivial than multi-paradigm norm-constancy is the phenomenon of fashion in science, which may well be regarded in Kuhnian terms as irregular, inconsequential change within a paradigm history. Alternatively the sensitivity to fashion[24] in a scientific field may be regarded as inversely correlated with the strength and extent of consensus. In so far as fashions have reality, they may perhaps be regarded as examples of paradigm-contained fluctuations not conforming to the 'pattern of rapid and consequential advance' expected of 'normal science'.

*Univariance*

Every philosophy of science and indeed every theory of knowledge contains or implies a classification and evaluation of different types of knowledge and of different categories of scientific discipline. The explicit elaboration of such classificatory schemes flourished from the time of Comte and Ampère to that of Ostwald, often but not always linked to the 'encyclopaedic' conception of philosophy as the systematisation of the main findings of the sciences. This systematic classification of the sciences has become unfashionable, partly because of the withering away of the encyclopaedic conception of philosophy. Of course specific cleavages and ostensible dichotomies (e.g. formal/empirical, nomothetic/idiographic, natural/cultural) have been the subject of wide and protracted discussion; but the main schools of the philosophy of science have concentrated on transdisciplinary, invariant themes—theories, laws, models, verification, confirmation, falsification procedures, explanation, etc.—and often on the relatively isolated and discrete analysis of these. The sharp distinction sometimes drawn between epistemology and methodology

---

23    I. C. Jarvie, 'On theories of field work and the scientific character of social anthropology', *Philosophy of science; The revolution in anthropology*, London, 1964.
24    On 'fashion' in science see W. Hagstrom, *op. cit.*

provides another example of the disinclination to engage in the systematic study of the differential logics of disciplines or sub-disciplines: as if methodology were not detailed epistemology and epistemology the system of methodologies.

But even when the primary concern is with invariant schemata of scientific knowledge, a classification of the sciences may be sketched. Popper,[25] in presenting what is now widely called the covering law model of scientific explanation (purporting in effect to show the similar logical structure of explanation, prediction and testing) suggests that the pure theoretical sciences aim at the discovery and testing of general laws, the pure historical sciences at the delineation of initial conditions, and the applied sciences or technologies at eliciting the initial conditions which, in conjunction with known laws, will yield desired final conditions. General laws and theoretical systems being the hallmark of pure science, there is little doubt as to the cognitive value-hierarchy underlying this classification of inquiries. Kuhn's model of science departs from this received mode of 'metascience' in taking as his key isolate not the usual analytical items, like law or theory or 'coordinating definitions', but complexes therof, 'package deals' of a holistic character, comprising law, theory, instrumentation, application combined in a single cognitive system. But the paradigm schema is invariant with respect to cross-disciplinary variations within the genus of 'mature' science. Neither degrees of paradigmaticness nor even different types of paradigm structures are recognised; so it would appear that all 'mature' sciences conform to the Procrustean schema of paradigm normality. But, just as in other cases of formally univariant schemata of scientific cognition, a barely implicit scale of scientific value is involved: branches of mathematical physics like mechanics and thermodynamics embody the paradigm ideal to near-perfection in the strength, extensiveness and resilience of their mechanisms for con-sensus formation and re-formation, and in their frequently-recurring crises and revolutions. Thus Kuhn concurs in effect with logical empiri-cism in selecting physics as the 'paragon science'.[26] The implied cogni-

---

25   The poverty of historicism, pp. 133-34; and 'Naturgesetze und Wirklichkeit' in Gesetz und Wirklichkeit, ed. S. Moser, Innsbruck, 1949, pp. 43-60.

26   To use the expression coined in a similar context by G. Radnitzky, Contemporary schools of metascience, 2 vols, Göteborg, 1968.

tive value hierarchy is nothing but the familiar prestige hierarchy, with selected branches of physics at the top and most of the life and earth sciences as second-class citizens. The presence of this hierarchy is masked by the fact that the basic distinction is between mature, consensual, paradigmatic science on the one hand, and immature, natural-historical, paradigm-lacking sciences on the other. Certainly Kuhn does not consider the possibility that physics does not necessarily maximise all the criteria of cognitive value. Yet Polanyi, whose consensus model of science anticipated some of Kuhn's general theses, argues that scientific consensus involves a threefold scale of reliability, relevance, profundity (together constituting systematic interest) and intrinsic human interest—the three criteria applying conjointly 'so that deficiency in one is largely compensated for by excellence in the others'.[27] To challenge the prevalent monohierarchical view is not to suggest that we should aim at complete parity of cognitive esteem. But there are many alternatives to the 'paragon complex' in the evaluative classification of the sciences, to the exclusive concern with transdisciplinary schemata of scientific investigation, and to the simple univariant (or at best bivariant) standards of scientific maturity.

In addition to the 'paragon complex', other factors have contributed to the inhibition of science classification studies: their historical association with 'polymathy' and with the defunct synoptic conception of the role of philosophy. It is noteworthy that the most ambitious attempt at a systematic classification of the sciences in recent times has come from outside the ranks of professional philosophers of science: Piaget's 'genetic epistemology'. One important and novel feature of his systematisation of the sciences is his abandonment of the traditional hierarchical principle for the 'circle' principle.[28]

---

27     M. Polanyi, *Personal Knowledge*, p. 136.
28     J. Piaget, *Introduction a l'epistemologie génétique*, 3 vols., Paris, 1950. The Piagetian theory of the sciences has of course undergone considerable further elaboration in subsequent work, much of it in collaboration. It is regrettable that so little notice has been taken of Piaget's work by epistemologists, metascientists, sociologists and historians of science in the English-speaking world. Although references to Piaget's work abound (cf. *SSR* also) they are usually far too casual and perfunctory and often twenty to thirty years out of date. See, however, W. Mays, 'The epistemology of Professor Piaget', *Proceedings of the Aristotelian Society*, 1953, pp. 49-76 and M. Harvey, 'The structure of dialectics', London University Ph. D. thesis, 1969.

Inter-science relations are seen as partially symmetric, involving complex relations of epistemological as well as ontological interdependence. However this 'circle' of the sciences still takes as units big disciplinary fields like logic, mathematics, psychology, sociology and the like, even though no longer ordered in terms of a single hierarchy of epistemological worth and authority. What is now required from the standpoint of a cognitive sociology of science is the comparative as well as the 'clinical' study of intra- as well as inter-disciplinary variations in scientific knowledge situations and of the cultural constraints they generate. Such distinctions as that between 'unrestricted' and 'restricted' sciences throw new light on familar facts and can afford some guidance, but nothing less than the orientation of metascientific studies towards a 'differential' epistemology of the sciences is really adequate. To call for such a morphology of scientific cultures is not to disparage 'generalising' metascientific inquiries; it is rather to call for the removal of the idol of a single linear hierarchy of scientific cognitive value which has hindered the study of science. However revolutionary Kuhn's theory of science may be it has not departed from this outmoded tradition.

*Independence*

Yet although Kuhn's theory of science implies a 'paragon science', so that 'maturity' involves a growing resemblance to physics, particularly in consensus-strengthening mathematisation, it does not seem to entail reducibility to physics. Kuhn's criticisms of the conventional wisdom concerning the *historical* unity of science (i.e. linear cumulative scientific growth) seem applicable *mutatis mutandis* to analogous beliefs in its *systematic* unity. If the meaning of key terms in physical theories (such as 'mass', 'force', 'simultaneity') changes drastically through historical paradigm-shifts, as in the transition from Newtonian to Einsteinian mechanics (so that the ostensibly more inclusive theoretical system does not in fact 'contain' the predecessor system), the same considerations would appear to apply to 'reductionism'.[29] The widely-accepted argument against reductionist claims is that the meaning of the key terms of a macro-theory shift drastically when they appear in the micro-theory, with the

---

29    As P. Feyerabend has shown, terms change meaning when they function in the context of another theory. (Radnitzky, *op. cit.*, p. 80.)

result that the reductions are spurious. Although at least some trans-ordinal laws[30] enabling macro-theories to be reduced to micro-theories have been recognised as scientific achievements, the general point, that the terms themselves cannot remain invariant to level-shifts in theoretical statements, remains strongly supported. It may be closely linked with the Kuhnian critique of the cumulative growth of physical theory and, by extension, of the natural sciences generically.

Is the thesis of the autonomy of sociology therefore safeguarded by a Kuhnian view of the structure and growth of science? Only partly so: for in sequential terms collectivist models of human behaviour could be replaced by individualistic ones and a Kuhnian would still say that there had been no genuine reduction but only a paradigm shift. This would be a poor consolation for present day defenders of the autonomy of sociology. It would also mean the relinquishment of the cumulative model of scientific growth. Fortunately the 'no cumulation, no reduction' argument does not commit one to the converse thesis; it is not necessary to cleave to the Kuhnian non-cumulative model of science to avoid reductionism.

*Ideology*
To speak of scientific cognitive culture inevitably raises in a socio-logical context the relationship of science and ideology. If an ideology is defined as a cognitively distorted belief-system, and if the standard of cognitive adequacy is provided solely by the current state of scientific knowledge, then it would seem self-contradictory to speak of 'scientific ideology' or of the 'ideology of science'. However, the scientific community, like all collectivities, generates shared beliefs about the moral cultural and social implications of its activities which may be described as the moral values and norms of science; but since values and norms are closely related to ideologies, we face the paradoxical conclusion that science both provides the standard in terms of which 'ideologies' are determined and is itself ideologically laden. Must we therefore, in Parsonian terms, accept the existence of an 'ideology of natural scientists' but reject that of an 'ideology of science'?

---

30    C. D. Broad, *The mind and its place in nature*, London, 1925, pp. 76 ff.

That 'functionalism' generates a conception of 'ideology' relevant to science, although frequently overlooked by sociologists, clearly emerges in the following passage from a standard Parsonian text.

'There is a special significance of the content of scientific knowledge in the *ideology of scientists* [italics mine—H.M.] as members of professional collectivities. Tentativeness is of course, an essential part of the value system which governs the role of the investigator. But equally the acceptance of evidence in accord with the canons of investigation, and of the implications of such evidence, is part of that same value system. Hence, in a special sense, subject of course to the ultimately tentative character of all scientific findings, there is an *obligation* on the scientist to accept the validity of scientific findings and theories which have been equally demonstrated. The extreme skeptic of the variety who when faced with the direct evidence stubbornly insists that "there ain't no such animal" cannot be a good "citizen" of the collectivity of scientists. Thus not only is there in the value-system of science commitment to the canons of scientific procedure, but there is commitment to a system of belief-content which is part of the obligation of the role of scientist. The fact that the beliefs may be modified in the light of new scientific evidence does not alter this'.[31]

Thus the ideology of scientists comprises not only a series of reflexive beliefs about science as a social enterprise but also the whole corpus of scientific beliefs, in that subscription to it is binding on the scientist *qua* member of a professional collectivity. However, Parsons implies that science ideology is in a sense epistemologically contingent, because the social system of science specialises in the maximally isolated pursuit of the cognitive interests of scientists. Moreover, he regards 'the canons of scientific procedure' as epistemologically autonomous and invariant to scientific change. To speak of the ideology of scientists, therefore, is almost to reify a given cross-section of scientific cognitive culture and to isolate it from the epistemologically autonomous regulative principles which in the process of scientific research will co-determine the continual revision and enrichment and deepening of that culture. Note also that Parsons regards scientific cognitive change not merely as extensive, incremental and linear but also as involving structural reorganisations and discrete levels of advancement. Obviously his

---

31    T. Parsons, *The social system*, New York, 1951, pp. 353-4.

conception of 'canons of scientific procedure' must be revised in the light of the change in standards of explanatory force, mathematical proof and experimental adequacy brought about by scientific revolutions. Allowing for this revision his account could be combined with an epistemologically rational theory of scientific growth.

## THE DIACHRONIC MODEL

That science does not uniformly proceed by the stockpiling of discrete quanta of information or through minute advances is now part of the conventional wisdom. A historiography of science that laid primary emphasis on cognitive cultural continuity was given extreme expression by scholars like Duhem,[32] who were in effect trying to demolish the notions, then current, about the chasm between medieval and modern science. Now that such notions no longer hold sway, continuism and 'adumbrationism'[33]—the tendency to see anticipations of subsequent scientific achievements in fragmentary conceptions bearing the vaguest resemblance to them— have been shown to be methodologically sterile. Although a good deal of the debate aroused by Kuhn's work concerns the depth and scope of the cognitive transformations brought about by scientific revolutions, there is general agreement that relatively large-scale conceptual displacements do actually take place, and that these occur at the level of cognitive culture. Much of the debate revolves round the opposition between what we may call the 'episodic revolutionists' like Kuhn, for whom scientific revolutions, although inevitable, indispensable and decisive, are 'episodes' of comparative rarity, and the 'permanent revolutionists'.[34]

The latter can reasonable argue that the distinction between 'normal' and 'revolutionary' science raises difficult problems of periodisation. Periods of 'normality' in science are as difficult to isolate as those in cultural or social history. Kuhn himself points out that crises in the history of science, although frequent, are usually

32    J. Agassi, *Towards an historiography of science*, Beiheft 2 of *History and theory*, The Hague, 1963.

33    R. K. Merton, *On theoretical sociology*, New York, 1967, pp. 20-26.

34    P. Feyerabend's contribution to S. Morgenbesser (ed.), *Philosophy of science*, New York, 1967.

resolved within the bounds of the ascendant paradigm. Only rarely do they result in revolutionary upheavals.[35] But this is to take an *ex post* stance: for the scientists actually experiencing the crisis cannot say whether it is a 'normal' or a 'revolutionary' one. Kuhn, of course, points out that normal science typically neither seeks nor encounters fundamental novelties of fact or theory; but again this is a retrospective appraisal. The scientist cannot know his future knowledge and his conduct must therefore be oriented to the permanent possibility of 'revolutionary' occurrences, even though he may be aware that they are less frequent than revolution-averting reconstructions. The distinction between 'normal' and 'revolutionary' science is a retrospective reconstruction, emphasizing the spectator's rather than the player's standpoint.

This distinction is something like that between risk-taking and uncertainty-facing in economics. In 'normal' scientific research, the paradigm-pattern so closely structures the field or relevance and acceptability that the scientific investigator has to take only risks; for although the outcome of research is not known in advance, it falls within prescribed limits and need not occasion any surprise.[36] In 'revolutionary' science situations, however, uncertainty has to be faced; for fundamental novelties of fact and theory are both expected and sought. Yet economic theory operates with a conception of uncertainty which is too weak for the epistemologist. Uncertainty for the conventional economist refers to particular events against a background of sure knowledge:[37] in Kuhnian terms, the breakdown of a paradigm need not affect other paradigms. A stronger conception of uncertainty is that of fallibilist epistemology, which states that all scientific decisions are reversible in principle, that all cognitive beliefs are corrigible and that we cannot ever know the truth. Normal science as much as revolutionary science is subject to this kind of 'uncertainty'[38]. Hence the distinction between risk-taking and uncertainty-facing, although useful in economics, does not yield

---

35    *SSR*, p. 82.
36    G. S. Shackle, *Decision, order and time in human affairs*, Cambridge, 1961.
37    A. Downs, *An economic theory of democracy*, New York, 1957.
38    R. Dahrendorf, *Essays in the theory of society*, Stanford, 1968.

the kind of information we need about the epistemological structure of scientific problem-situations.

If the two-fold categorization becomes rather strained as a result of the foregoing considerations, this does not mean that one should simply opt for the 'permanent revolutionary' as against the 'episodic revolutionary' model. The very concept of scientific revolution must be considered afresh. Kuhnian revolutions are postulated as rare partly because they are so wholesale and 'catastrophic'. Such complete breaks with the past do not have extra-scientific historical counterparts, certainly not in the universe of socio-political revolutions. In societies, massive cultural continuities—of language, law, primary socialization patterns, ethos, etiquette, etc.—bridge the gap between the *ancien* and the revolutionary regime. Conversely, large-scale societal transformations may be brought about without conscious design as a result of convergence of unintended, unforeseen and unwanted consequences of human actions, as in the transition from feudalism to capitalism or in the first 'industrial revolution'. But in the Kuhnian model of science, large-scale changes are brought about, at least initially, through conscious and deliberate action. This should at least give pause for further thought.

In ordinary socio-political revolutions Newthink does not completely supersede Oldthink.[39] Indeed, revolutionary regimes are deeply concerned with the persistence of 'pre-revolutionary' survivals long after the consolidation of the new order. Kuhnian science, however, faces no such exigencies. Like anthropological and sociological functionalism, it considers that 'survivals' or 'vestigial remains' from earlier cultural epochs do not present serious theoretical problems, since the old paradigms are too effectively destroyed for them to remain of any importance. Yet the question of their obstructive persistence has been widely raised in connection with relativity theory and quantum mechanics. It is often and convincingly argued by metascientists that deep-seated sensory and imaginative proclivities hinder the full comprehension and heuristic exploitation of new theoretical systems. The contention is not simply that belated converts to the new physical theories cannot entirely shake off the hold of the old paradigms, but that even the 'Young

---

39    To use Toulmin's terminology: cf. fn. 21.

Turks' and their successors, knowing the old paradigm only through the old textbooks, are affected. The internalization of new cognitive norms, in fact, appears as a much more protracted, partial and precarious process than in the Kuhnian model of paradigm-destruction and paradigm-creation.

This type of argument can be presented in two different ways. One is that these sensuous-imaginative proclivities are natural psychological ones, and that the tension between them and novel theoretical concepts has always been present, to some degree, since the breakdown of the Aristotelian natural philosophy. The other is that the clash is really the product of our 'Newtonian-Euclidean background'. To deal with this, Bachelard[40] has outlined a programme for a 'psychoanalysis of knowledge' which would 'unmask' our Newtonian-Euclidean cognitive subconscious (or 'tacit knowledge' in Polanyi's sense) and thereby facilitate the internalization of new cognitive norms.

Kuhn himself points out that old paradigms can and do persist outside the 'revolutionizing' specialty and outside pure science as such. Thus Newtonian mechanics and ray optics are still widely utilized in applied science and technology.[41] This consideration, however, does not count against his model of pure science, for obviously the utilisation of old scientific paradigms for purposes other than fundamental scientific investigation involves a change in paradigm-function. This kind of persistence is of less importance than the sedimentation of old paradigms in the latent cognitive culture of pure science itself, a circumstance which does not seem to be taken into account in the Kuhnian model.

'Permanent revolutionists' in the theory of science do not hold, of course, that all revolutions in science are alike in scale or depth of cognitive change; some writers have distinguished between 'micro' and 'macro'[42] revolutions according to the sweep of conceptual

40    G. Bachelard, *La formation de l'esprit scientifique—contribution a une psychanalyse de la connaissance scientifique*, Paris, 1967. M. Capek, *The philosophical impact of contemporary physics*, Princeton, 1961, pp. XV, 181, 264, 300, 333.

41    M. Bunge, 'Technology as Applied science', *Technology and Culture*, 8, 1967, pp. 329-347.

42    S. Toulmin, *op. cit.*

transformation. One might go further and suggest that the distinction between 'normal' and 'revolutionary' and between 'macro' and 'micro' is as vicious as that between change *within* the system and change *of* the system offered by synchronic-consensus models in sociology and anthropology. The fundamental unit of analysis should be the scientific innovation; to ask whether the innovation falls within the compass of a paradigmatic tradition or involves a paradigm shift begs the question of whether such discrete and stable complexes of norms and exemplars are really characteristic of science. But to elaborate an 'innovation' model of scientific change generally involves a shift from the Kuhnian analogies to biological, evolutionary ones, in the manner of Toulmin.[43] This meets with opposition from those who would rule as extra-epistemological all inquiries into the origins of cognitive (as of other) beliefs, and would condemn exponents of the 'genetic fallacy' as victims of 'psychologistic' or 'sociologistic' illusions.[44] Popper, for instance, has often stressed the epistemological irrelevance of the 'pedigree' of ideas[45], particularly in the context of his polemics against the sociology of knowledge, while Logical Positivists have drawn a sharp distinction between the 'context of discovery' and the 'context of justification' (or, in Popperian terms, of 'refutation'). The latter is the province of rigorous logical and epistemological inquiries; the former is epistemologically irrelevant. Philosophers, in fact, have decided that inquiries into the genesis of ideas are fitting only for psychologists and sociologists; while sociologists, in their turn have decided to focus on the social selection rather than the social determination of ideas, passing the buck presumably to psychologists or metaphysicians.

But another approach is now emerging both in the theory of knowledge and in the human sciences. It takes invention, innovation, discovery and creation as constituting something more than a mere 'residual' problem. Logical gaps have been found even in the most apparently rigorous of hypothetico-deductive models.[46] Polanyi's

---

43    S. Toulmin, *op. cit.*
44    P. Kurtz in S. Hook (ed.), *Language and philosophy*, New York, 1969, p. 168.
45    *Conjectures and Refutations*, Introduction.
46    S. Körner, *Experience and theory*, London, 1966.

concern with the general 'heuristics'[47] involved in routine scientific procedures, such as mathematical proof, hypothesis-finding, and verification/corroboration techniques as well as in spectacular upheavals of the Kuhnian type, is perhaps the most outstanding example of the new approach, which may be termed 'creationist'.[48] As Agassi[49] has so forcefully argued, the belief in an algorism of verification (or corroboration, or falsification) is both mistaken and incompatible with a genuinely fallibilistic epistemology. (It is also based on a quite misplaced fear of imagination.) The asymmetry between conjectures and refutations is somewhat misleading, in that it presents refutations as mechanically, quasi-algorismically determined, and conjectures as springing from goodness knows where. Yet refutations are as imaginative, non-algorismic and corrigible as conjectures. These considerations show how misguided is the usual derogation of certain theories and methods as 'mere heuristic devices'; for discovery cannot be taken for granted or relegated to extra-epistemological folklore.

All this, of course, arouses fears of irrationalism. It is precisely on these grounds that Kuhn's analysis of paradigm change has been most strongly criticized. The cleavage between 'episodic' and 'permanent' revolutionism in the theory of science is thus cross-cut by the 'rationalist'-'irrationalist' cleavage.

That Kuhn's account of scientific revolutionary episodes is irrationalist is now almost taken for granted. One should note, however, that he claims that scientists never abandon a paradigm unless and until an alternative is available; that there is always an overlap between the old paradigm and the new paradigm[50] (at least in the sense that concrete problem-solving ability is never lost in the transition); that the decision to change paradigms 'involves the comparison of both paradigms with nature *and* with each other'; and that a paradigm is never abandoned unless there is general dis-

---

47    *Personal Knowledge.*

48    H. Barnett, *Innovation*, New York, 1953. D. A. Schon, *Displacement of concepts*, London, 1963.

49    J. Agassi 'The confusion between science and technology in the standard philosophy of science', *Technology and Culture*, 8, 1967, pp. 348-366.

50    *SSR*, pp. 84, 168.

satisfaction with paradigm-saving expedients. These seem to be the accepted norms of large-scale cognitive change. But Kuhn also outlines the process of change, starting with the new paradigm-pioneer and the individual psychology of paradigm-shift, continuing with the cultural diffusion of the new paradigm to a first wave of new paradigm-followers, and proceeding (if the process is not aborted) to the eventual near-complete adherence of the relevant scientific collectivity to the new paradigm. There is a resemblance here to sociological models of innovation-diffusion and value change; but this does not necessarily establish a presumption of irrationality.

It is particularly Kuhn's use of the terms 'Gestalt switch' and 'conversion'[51] coupled with his strongly argued case for the existence of logical as well as psychological gaps between the old and the new paradigm that has triggered criticism. When using such terms Kuhn appears to be giving a psychological account of paradigm change rather than a sociological one. When he writes, elsewhere, that in scientific as in socio-political revolutions there is no standard higher than that of the relevant community, he appears to suggest that a sociological account is the more pertinent. But in so far as he emphasizes the diffusion of pioneering paradigm-shifts, through something like charismatic leadership, to a first circle of new paradigm-followers ('disciples') he again eliminates sociological considerations in favour of psychological ones. Of course psychological and structural variables may be combined in an account of cultural change, but their systematic articulation requires a more fully elaborated conceptual scheme than he provides.

In fact the Kuhnian account has eclectic and ambiguous characteristics which can be understood as a result of his attempt to give a 'total' account of some of the most extraordinarily complex phenomena of culture history.[52] 'Crisis' is a cultural category, since it denotes the failure to match the cognitive cultural complex of the paradigm with recalcitrant 'anomalies'; 'Gestalt switch' is a phenomenon of perceptual psychology; the reception of a new paradigm for its intellectual elegance and beauty is a cultural phenomenon;

---

51    Also used by G. Bachelard, *La philosophie du non*, Paris, 1940, p. 8, and M. Polanyi, *Personal Knowledge*, p. 151.

52    *SSR*, p. 86: 'Often a new paradigm emerges, at least in embryo, before a crisis has developed far.'

'conversion' is a matter of interpersonal psychology; the pressure of community opinion is an expression of 'mechanical solidarity'. Moreover the Kuhnian account is partly sequential, partly logical. Like sociological models of collective innovation, it oscillates between a pattern of natural sequence and the logic of 'value-added'. In his version, a natural sequence in paradigm-change, crisis precedes the creation of new paradigm-candidates; but both in fact and in logic new paradigms may *precede* crises, or, if contemporary with their incipient phases, only enter the life of scientific community if and when the crisis escalates. If paradigm-candidates historically precede crises of normal science in more than a small minority of cases, then scientific collectivities are not normally as homogeneous or as culturally constricting as the Kuhnian model claims.

The rationality-irrationality issue is complicated by the circumstance that social and cultural variables cannot be placed in the same genus as psychological ones if situational logic and the rationality principle are taken seriously. For according to situational logic,[53] sociological explanation (in terms of institutions and traditions) is or should be 'rational', in contrast with psychological explanation (in terms of instincts, drives, impulses, passions and the like). If situational logic is valid, explanations of scientists' conduct in terms of institutional constraints and cultural beliefs and norms cannot be 'irrational' in the same sense as explanations of their conduct which use terms like 'conversion', 'faith', 'credulity', 'attachment to peers', 'inertia' and 'charismatic attraction'. It has been claimed that one of Popper's achievements is to have shown that the 'basis of science is social, not psychological'.[54] But the Popperian account of the social structure and cultural traditions of the scientific community stresses such features as freedom of communication, freedom to publish and teach, the moral obligation and situational pressures compelling scientists to be receptive to criticism, and the institutionalised requirements of individualism and autonomy, etc. Such cultural norms and values and such institutional constraints are conducive to epistemological rationality.

---

53    There are somewhat different versions of 'situational logic' theory. See K. Popper, *The poverty of historicism*, and *The open society and its enemies*, London, 1945; and I. C. Jarvie, *The revolution in anthropology*.

54    J. Agassi, 'Sensationalism', *Mind*, 75, 1966, pp. 1-24, at p. 23.

This sociology of science is not strictly compatible with other sociological accounts, such as Kuhn's, which show the pressures for conformity inherent in specialist collectivities, in the dynamics of information-exchange, and in the quest for 'recognition'. In the Popperian account sociological and epistemological rationality converge rather than coincide; in the Kuhnian account scientific behaviour is neither rational in the situational sense nor wholly rational in the epistemological sense;[55] in other, strictly sociological, accounts situational logic explanations make scientific behaviour rationally intelligible but not necessarily conformable with epistemological rationality.[56]

We may summarize the foregoing argument in the following schematic arrangement:

TYPES OF SCIENTIFIC BEHAVIOUR

|  | *Explanation of Scientific Behaviour* | |
|---|---|---|
|  | *Sociological* | *Psychological* |
| Rational (situational logic) | + | — |
| Rational (epistemological) | + or — | — |

(Rational: +. Irrational: —)

(Sociologically explicable behaviour is rational in the sense of situational logic: it *may* be rational [or irrational] in the epistemological sense. Psychologically explicable behaviour is irrational in *both* the sense of situational logic and the epistemological one.)

For example a scientist who is socially constrained to entertain criticism of his theory is acting rationally in terms of situational logic (i.e. his behaviour is explicable in terms of the logic of his professional situation, not in terms of any disposition to be hyper-critical); and he is also being epistemologically rational, for criticism

---

55    I. Lakatos, 'Criticism and the methodology of scientific research programmes', *Proceedings of the Aristotelian Society*, 1968, pp. 149-186.
56    One might argue that epistemological rationality is essentially an appraisive concept whilst situational logic rationality pertains to *explanation* within social science. There has, however, been a good deal of controversy on the epistemological import of 'rational' explanations —see the articles in S. Hook (ed.), *Philosophy and history* and W. Dray (ed.), *Philosophical analysis and history*.

is essential to epistemological rationality. A scientist who is socially constrained to accept the current paradigm is acting rationally in terms of situational logic (cf. the Velikovsky affair);[57] but he is not necessarily acting rationally in the epistemological sense, for he may not come to appreciate the rational case to be made for the paradigm in terms of its ability to meet logical and empirical criticism. A scientist who accepts the cultural tradition of maximum criticism is acting rationally in both senses. A scientist who is converted to a new paradigm through the charismatic leadership, the magisterial authority, or the persuasive powers of another scientist, is behaving irrationally in both senses. A model of scientific behaviour which stresses psychological variables (particularly motivational and personality syndromes) may be regarded as 'irrational'; whereas one which stresses the sociological variables is not necessarily so, at least on the assumption that the institutions and traditions of science really demand maximum criticism and permanent revolution. Under such conditions scientific behaviour would be both rational by both situational-logical and epistemological criteria.

The most important attempt at a rational reconstruction of scientific behaviour that tries to meet the Kuhnian challenge is that of Lakatos.[58] His account disposes of the somewhat futile disputes between episodic and permanent revolutionists by showing under what conditions the retention of a theoretical system is epistemologically rational and under what conditions it is not. One cannot stipulate the inevitability or necessity of permanent revolution: it depends on whether the research programme adhered to is still bearing fruit, and one cannot say whether its fertile life-span will be long or short. By rationally distinguishing between 'progressive' and 'degenerative' problem-shifts, it becomes possible both to identify genuine crises and to vindicate the rationality (within limits) of paradigm-retention. The tenacity of the 'normal scientific' research tradition is thus given a rational reconstruction. All theories would be stillborn if the availability of counterexamples were sufficient for their rejection on falsificationist principles. This theory of scientific growth meets some of the most important Kuhnian contentions concerning the 'irrational' explicability of scientific revolutions.

---

57    Alfred de Grazia (ed.), *The Velivoksy affair*, New York, 1966.
58    I. Lakatos, *op. cit.*

But although the postulation of a 'Third World'[59] of ideas in terms of which criteria can be formulated for an 'ideal' history of epistemologically-rational scientific growth may be philosophically justified, some of the arguments advanced for it are not sociologically cogent. The category of 'culture'[60] (i.e. systems of meanings, values and norms) has long been in currency in sociology precisely because purely psychological categories are inadequate for the understanding of human behaviour. It is odd that the Popperian distinction between persons, traditions and institutions should not be reflected in his ontology; yet it corresponds, however roughly, with the sociological distinction between personalities, cultural systems and social systems respectively. To claim that Kuhn must necessarily construe his account of science in terms either of individual or collective psychology seems to me doubly wrong: he could reformulate his account more in terms of roles and institutions or of patterns of cognitive culture and 'configurations of cultural growth'.

In fact, a model of large-scale long-term scientific change, bearing considerable resemblance to Kuhn and yet wholly depsychologized, can be found in Kroeber's *Configurations of Cultural Growth.*[61] Kroeber, like Kuhn, tries to show that scientific change does not proceed by accumulation: it more resembles an 'ecological succession' of theoretical systems, in which the later systems do not in any simple sense contain the former as special cases. Each phase or burst of scientific growth is oriented to the resolution and exploitation of a distinctive problem complex: it rises to a climax of superlative achievement and eventually declines with the exhaustion of the heuristic potentialities of its distinctive pattern. In the subsequent phase, scientists turn to a different problem-complex, not simply to an enlarged, modified or enriched version of the previous one. In this way, Kroeber argues, the basic rhythm of scientific change resembles that of the fine arts (with their style shifts) rather than that of applied science.

---

59     K. Popper, 'Epistemology without a knowing subject', in *Proceedings of the Third International Congress for Logic, Methodology and Philosophy of Science*, Amsterdam, 1968, pp. 333-73.

60     A. Kroeber and T. Parsons, 'The concepts of culture and the social system', *American Sociological Review*, 23, 1958, pp. 582-3 and D. Bidney, *Theoretical Anthropology*, New York, 1953.

61     Berkeley, 1944.

This non-cyclical, non-linear, 'successional' model of change does not hinge on mysterious 'conversions'; it is determined by the cultural exigencies of scientific discovery and invention—by the nature of the scientists' knowledge and work situation. Believing in the autonomy of cultural systems, Kroeber tries to show that this 'ecological succession' is largely independent of social conditions and of psychological variables. One of his chief concerns is with the nature of genius. Since the supply of highly gifted individuals may be regarded as inelastic, or largely invariant to race, ethnicity, historical period and the like, how do we account for the rarity of superlative achievement and the high incidence of the *clustering* in time and space of high achievers in all fields of culture? His answer is in terms of the inherent possibilities of cultural pattern—styles, scientific problem situations, philosophical idea-systems, etc. This account would seem to be couched in terms that resemble and overlap with those of the 'Third World'. No concessions are made to psychology or to the spirit of the scientific community or to the social organ-ization of science.[62] However, Kroeber does not formulate a concept of scientific revolution involving in the Kuhnian manner a clash between rival visions of reality, as he is more concerned with the construction of 'configurations of cultural growth'. Such a construct is different from that of normal science in that it is climactic rather than parasitic on an exemplar of scientific achievement.

Kroeber cautions against grand generalizations about the duration of cultural rhythms. Kuhn, however, suggests that the three phases 'normal science-revolution-normal science', are typically 'long-short-long'. There seems little reality in such a pattern: consider, for instance, the conceptual explosions in microphysics of 1901, 1905, 1911, 1913, 1915, 1924-30.[63] A pattern of frequent revolutionary upheavals separated by relatively short 'peaceful' intervals may be characteristic of long periods of mature science history. The longevity of a paradigm may also depend on 'external' factors. For instance, Ptolemaic astronomy's long reign could hardly survive the invention of printing.

Kuhn's account of science may be 'irrationalist' and 'sociological'

---

62　Kroeber regarded social process—within and outside culture-creating collectivities—as largely irrelevant to his analysis.

63　N. R. Hanson, *Patterns of discovery*, Cambridge, 1958, p. 2.

(or partly so) but it holds 'external' variables constant. It is 'internal' in the sense that its only explanatory variables pertain to the culture of science and the psychology of scientists. The social system of science—its modes of communication and of reward allocation, its 'invisible colleges'—is not 'external' in the sense that, for instance, the distribution of political power or the overall system of social stratification are 'external'. Commonly, the broad internal/ external dichotomy has obscured the need to make much finer distinctions in the social analysis of science, which may be schematized in the following table:

SCIENCE SOCIOLOGIES[64]

|  | Culture | Social Structure |
|---|---|---|
| Science | internal<br>cultural | internal<br>structural |
| Wider Society | external<br>cultural | external<br>structural |

Each box contains bundles of variables that may impinge on the life of science. 'Social' theories of science may be 'external-structural' (like, at least, some versions of historical materialism), 'external-cultural' (as in some versions of the primacy of values or 'implicit dominant ontologies' or 'major cultural premises' in social life as a whole), 'internal-structural' (as in some accounts of the differentiation of the scientific role and of the importance of competition amongst scientific institutions)[65] or 'internal-cultural' (as when metaphysical commitments or the exigencies of cognitive problem-situations are emphasized). Each set of variables may be combined with the others in various ways, according to the type of problem under con-

---

64    This table was presented with the original version of this paper read at a meeting of the British Sociological Association in 1969. A similar 'property space' pertaining to the case of religion-society relations appears in R. Robertson, *A sociological interpretation of Religion*, Oxford, 1970, p. 66.

65    J. Ben-David, 'The scientific role: the conditions of its establishment in Europe', *Minerva*, 4, 1965, pp. 15-54; 'The universities and the growth of science in Germany and the United States', *Minerva*, 7, 1968-9, pp. 1-35.

sideration. For instance, one may explain variations in the level of scientific productivity or innovation in terms of the prevalence of competition in science, and yet account for discontinuities in theoretical system-change in terms of immanent cognitive-cultural determinations. Most recent sociological accounts do not emphasise only the 'quantitative' aspects of scientific knowledge-production, regardless of truth value, epistemological rationality or cognitive potency. The Mertonian sociological theory of science focuses on the culture, values and norms of science (e.g. universalism, organized scepticism, community of intellectual property, etc.), not because these determine the truth-value of scientific knowledge but because they provide the optimal moral environment for the pursuit of truth. More recently this internal cultural emphasis has been partly superseded by an internal structural one, using the factors of competition and role hybridization. In both cases the autonomy of epistemology as against sociology is accepted.

Considered in these terms, Kuhn's theory combines social-structural, cultural and psychological variables without reference to their relative potencies. Consensus is both a cultural imperative for cumulative growth and a social imperative for cohesive specialisms. The charismatic leadership of paradigm-makers is stressed, yet paradigm-shifts are also the product of crises in the cognitive-cultural system. Yet the 'autonomy' norm implies that even when intra-disciplinary communication virtually breaks down and intellectual tensions are maximal, moral consensus is maintained. Hence, when scientific social systems temporarily cease to be paradigm-bonded, they remain moral norm-bonded.

One sociological feature of scientific revolutions that Kuhn emphasises is the tendency for paradigm-clashes to coincide with generational divides. If science advances through multiple intergenerational paradigm-shifts in which old paradigms are 'destroyed', how do we account for the historical continuity of science as a social system? The social identity of the scientific role has persisted through many revolutionary upheavals. As Polanyi has put it: 'Science has a most closely knit professional tradition; it rivals the Church of Rome and the legal profession in continuity of doctrine and strength of corporate spirit'.[66] It is not obvious how the

66      M. Polanyi, *The logic of liberty*, London, 1951, p. 39.

Kuhnian 'catastrophist' model can be reconciled with this. Kuhn himself advances four arguments. First, there is the 'false consciousness' argument, which indicates mechanisms that ensure that the illusion of cumulativeness is maintained through paradigm shifts. Second, there is the argument to the effect that certain moral values and norms are invariant to all mature sciences, irrespective of historical change: this is essentially the Mertonian argument. It derives its force from the fact that many social systems outside science are multi-bonded and that consequently there is nothing anomalous in a social system being both cognitively and morally consensual. Third, there is an argument based on the cultural sedimentation of superseded paradigms in applied science and technology. Fourth, it can be argued that, although scientific change is not accumulative across paradigm-shifts, there are certain massive, overall 'secular' trends in science history. The most important arguments are the first and fourth, to which we now turn.

One of the most reliable signs of a paradigm-shift is the rewriting of textbooks. The re-writers naturally regard the newly-achieved paradigm as the culmination of scientific thought, embodying all that was valid in previous theory. Scientific socialization being almost completely monopolized by textbooks, the socialisee will receive both the new science and the vision of science as cumulative growth of knowledge. The process of transmitting a cumulative growth picture of the history of science is facilitated by the fact that terminological continuities, like 'mass' and 'force', mask the real depth of the cognitive transformations. The 'visibility' of the scientific revolution is thereby reduced.

It is pertinent at this point to ask whether the cumulative model is not a necessary scientific myth or rationally defensible regulative belief. Is not the cumulative growth model of science psychologically necessary, in view of the strategic importance of eponymy in the reward system and the communality of intellectual property? This, of course, is not an epistemological or logical question, but it is hardly fitting for a Kuhnian to draw a sharp line of demarcation between the logic and the psychology of discovery. It may also be argued that a quasi-catastrophist view of long-term scientific change 'pragmatically implies' the pointlessness of scientific endeavour. The quasi-catastrophist view is more congruous with a futilitarian evaluation of science than with an affirmative or meliorist one. But before we pursue this matter further we must return to Kuhn's trend model of long-term scientific change.

## The trend model

There are important directionalities in Kuhn's account of science. First, once a field of inquiry acquires its initial paradigm it goes on acquiring paradigms through recurrent revolutionary crises. Considering how extraordinarily arduous is the road to the acquisition of the first paradigm, it is strange that subsequent paradigm-acquisition is managed so smoothly.[67] Itwould seem that with its first paradigm a field of scientific inquiry also acquires an irreversible disposition towards paradigm-acquisitiveness. A paradigm may not have predecessors but it almost always generates successors. As the concepts of paradigm and revolution are correlative, it would seem that a field that does not experience revolution cannot be said to possess a paradigm (yet economics, a science which has not experienced revolutions on the Kuhnian scale, has a long and rich history and is certainly not dead in terms of research).[68]

Second, once a paradigm is replaced it is never restored. In socio-political history counter-revolutions sometimes succeed; in scientific life, never. Indeed, as we have seen, Kuhn does not even allow for the covert persistence of old paradigm by-products (as in the case of our 'Newtonian-Euclidean subconscious background'). Paradigm-shifts are irreversible: this is another element of linearity in the Kuhnian model of long-term scientific change. Each paradigm is wholly new: alternations, replications and cumulations are ruled out.

Third, the time intervals between consecutive periods of normal science tend to get shorter with scientific advance (at least in the history of the various branches of mathematical physics). In other

---

67    *SSR*, ch. IV.
68    J. J. Spengler, whose views are briefly noted by Kuhn in 'Measurement', p. 191. Cp. A. W. Coats: 'Economics has been dominated throughout its history by a single paradigm—the theory economic equilibrium via the market mechanism.' 'Is there a "structure of scientific revolutions" in economics'? *Kyklos*, 22, 1969, pp. 289-95 at p. 292.

words, this is a progressive contraction of inter-paradigmatic interregna.

Fourth, more and more fields are crossing the great divide into the first period of paradigm-controlled normal science. The overall trend is towards the 'normalization' of an increasing number of fields.

Thus although Kuhn repudiates any teleological or orthogenetic view of science, he stresses the directionality and irreversibility of scientific change. This he seems to construe both as a description of actual scientific history and as a criterion of scientific maturity. But unlike most theories of scientific growth, Kuhn's is not couched in conventional epistemological terminology, whereby upward shifts in parameters of cognitive value coincide with the growth of 'truth', 'verisimilitude', 'simplicity', 'economy of thought', 'ontological and epistemological depth', etc. Implicitly, however, the mechanisms that ensure rapid paradigm shifts are deemed to be carriers of scientific 'maturity', and a 'paragon science' is selected. It may be argued that in the Kuhnian model the criteria of cognitive validity, relevance and excellence themselves change; but it is not clear whether a Kuhnian would allow an upper limit or logical ceiling to change in cognitive norms. Even if he did he might claim that such trans-paradigmatic, trans-cultural invariants allow so much effective variation in research-directing cognitive norms at the level of para-digmatic normal science—*the* privileged site of live scientific inquiry —that such formal invariants may be safely ignored or discounted. Alternatively he might come perilously close to a kind of polylogism, by construing the history of logic as a succession of paradigms: here again invariants might be allowed yet their relevance belittled.[69]

Even if we reject the concept of paradigm as a category of the historiography or epistemology of science in any strict Kuhnian sense, we must—'permanent revolutionists' no less than others— grant that not only do scientific beliefs change but also procedural norms, criteria of acceptability, and thought-forms. The standards

---

69    Of course one can speak of a 'multiplicity' of logics in a fairly innocuous non-relativist sense; the law of the excluded middle has been challenged by intuitionist metamathematics; but the issue of 'polylogism' in a stronger sense remains.

of mathematical proof themselves have undergone historical change. It does seem implausible, however, to regard all scientific revolutions as equally and uniformly destructive of antecedent paradigms, as if the logical gaps involved were all of the same width, and as if the transitions from the phlogiston theory, geocentrism and Newtonian dynamics to their successors were of the same epistemological type. If in Lakatosian terms each revolution can be shown to be rationally defensible then the ensemble of revolutions cannot be irrational either.

It does not seem possible to me to elaborate a Kuhnian position without eventually endorsing certain epistemological growth vectors or alternatively going even further in the direction of 'symmetrical epistemological relativism' (Gellner),[70] with each paradigm as a distinct world-perspective, precluding any common scale of cognitive evaluation for the succession of paradigms in time.

The most satisfactory position seems to me to be that of a meliorist epistemology. Taking science not only as an epistemological system but also as a socio-cultural complex, it may be feasible to establish *levels of cognitive development*, including social-structural thresholds such as the differentiation of the scientific role, the growth of the scientific division of labour, and even the invention of printing. In the terminology of a critic of scientific catastrophism, we must distinguish between 'constituted reason', the system of cognitive norms and ideals at a given moment, and 'constituting reason',[71] the rational processes involved in even the most revolutionary 'paradigm-shifts'. At any rate we may regard the conception of levels of scientific development and of 'constituting reason' as regulative ideals.

Sociologically, the mechanisms determining the 'collective memory' of science do not satisfactorily account for the persistence of science as one of the most massive socio-cultural continuants of Western civilization, despite the quasi-catastrophist procession of paradigms. The hypothesis of meliorism would at least not impede

70    E. Gellner 'The new idealism—cause and meaning in the social sciences', in Lakatos and Musgrave (eds.), *Problems in the philosophy of science*, Amsterdam, 1968, pp. 377-406.

71    A. Lalande, *La raison et les normes*, Paris, 1948.

our attempt to comprehend the sociological problems set by the continuity of scientific roles and institutions.

The phenomenon of 'multiples'[72] (i.e. multiple independent discovery and invention) may be partly explained both by Kuhn's and by Merton's rational-cultural models. According to the Kuhnian model, 'multiples' occur as a result of the convergent expectations of 'normal science', by which 'anomalies' will be recognized by independent (yet paradigm-sharing) scientific workers. Yet by no means all of Merton's lists of 'multiples' are drawn from 'paradigm' sciences. In these lists there appears no systematic discrepancy between 'mature' and 'immature' sciences, yet the common recognition of 'anomalies' is regarded by Kuhn as a merit of 'normal science', for only where firmly institutionalized expectations exist will attention be focused on community-relevant problems. If the Keynes-Kalecki 'multiple' is more than a curiosity, it suggests that even in economics a shared paradigm is not a necessary condition for convergence in respect of major theoretical achievements: for, in contrast to Keynes, Kalecki knew no 'bourgeois' neoclassical economics and was trained as an engineer.

Regardless of the foregoing criticisms, a minimum gain from the Kuhnian impact on the philosophy of social science and on cognitive sociology should be the enhanced recognition of the paramount importance of the problem of scientific *growth*. The exclusive concern with the master-keys, the diacritics of scientificness, empiricalness or positive knowledge that was so characteristic of the logical empiricist epoch of the philosophy of scientific knowledge can at last be relegated to a humbler sphere. No matter how different Popper's criteria for distinguishing science from other idea-systems may have been from the criteria of empirical meaning, such as verifiability and confirmability, it did partake of the same diacritical and rather atemporal concern. Fallibilism is certainly more conducive to a theory of scientific growth than classical rationalism, but the general philosophical climate shared by both logical empiricism and early Popperism was in effect inimical to a historical and genetic approach to metascience. This is of course in some ways rather odd if one recalls

---

72     R. K. Merton, 'Singletons and multiples in scientific discovery: a chapter in the sociology of science', *Proceedings of the American Philosophical Society*, 107, 1961, pp. 470-85.

Comte's historical theory of science[73] and the contribution of positivism to the institutionalization of the historiography of science, as well as the character of Mach's contribution.

Both Mach and Duhem were creative scientists, outstanding philosophers of science and eminent historians of science. This treble role is even more unusual now than it was in their days, and even the dual role of scientist-historian of science or scientist-philosopher of science is not conspicuous. The historiographical role became differentiated at first through the medium of highly idiographic, archival, annalistic specialization, as in the case of scholars like Sarton. At the same time philosophy of science was cultivated with a primary concern for logical reconstruction and axiomatization through formal syntactics, semantics and pragmatics. However, changes in the historiography of science through the 'Koyréan revolution' have turned it into a major source of philosophical inspiration. The historicization of late Popperism partly reflects, partly converges with, such trends towards the intellectualization of the history of science and the shift to a more historical interest in the philosophy of science.

## KUHN AND SOCIOLOGY

The influence of Kuhn's theory of science on social scientists has grown rapidly in recent years. There is something paradoxical in Kuhn's appeal to sociology, for Kuhn's work *combines sociologism with anti-sociology*, thus simultaneously satisfying two mutually incompatible idols of the age. It is sociologistic in that it presents something like a social theory of natural-scientific knowledge and stresses the importance of cognitive consensus as against cognitive individualism. On the other hand, it can be used as an ideological tool of anti-sociology, in so far as sociology appears to be lacking in the diagnostic criteria of scientific maturity—paradigmaticness and revolutions. Theoretical, methodological and value conflicts are

---

73  It was under Comtist influence that the first Chair of the history of science was created in France: for the story see G. Canguilhem, 'L'histoire des sciences dans l'oeuvre epistemologique de Gaston Bachelard', *Annales de l'Université de Paris*, 1963, pp. 24-39 at p. 25.

according to Kuhn the marks of the pre-history (or 'natural history') stage of science, valuable only as part of the subconscious gestation period of the first paradigm.

It is primarily Kuhn's conception of normal science that has impinged most directly on social scientists, especially in the 'softer' social sciences like sociology, political science, anthropology and their offshoots.[74] The concept of long-run non-cumulativeness of scientific change, although running counter to deep-seated convictions, can be safely ignored if the pre-requisite of revolution is a stage of para-digmatic normal science. Curiously enough, the cognitive consensus model is likely to converge with the objectivist or positivist view of science as both consensual and accumulative, since 'in the long run we are all dead', and an initial stretch of consensual accumulation is also part of the Kuhnian stage model of scientific history. In this respect something like a 'self-fulfilling prophecy' might occur, with the Kuhnian model reinforcing positivist, objectivist and socio-technological demands for convergence and coordination, particularly of 'methodological' norms and standards. Cognitive consensus may come to be seen as a pre-requisite of scientific advance and 'forced' into being rather than awaited as the unintended, crescive, confluent by-product of problem-directed inquiries. Although Kuhn's theory of science is clearly incompatible with logical empiricism's at the epistemological level, its influence on the social sciences is only too likely to reinforce that of logical empiricist canons. Formalization, quantification, extrusion of 'soft' data, social behaviourism, 'ethical neutrality', the discouragement of epistemological debate and close links between systematic theory and history of thought—all these prescriptions, prohibitions and preferences can be justified on standard neo-positivist grounds, such as intersubjective agreement, extrusion of extra-scientific valuations, predictive power. But if they can be justified on such plain, naive, rational or veristic grounds, they can also be argued on sophisticated, indirectly-legitimating grounds such as the necessity to maximize consensus-formation and

74    Cf. in geography, Peter Haggett and Richard J. Chorley, 'Models, paradigms and the new geography' in the authors' *Models in Geography*, 1967, pp. 19-42. In political science, S. Wolin 'Paradigms and political theories' in P. King and B. C. Parekh (eds.) *Politics and experience*, Cambridge, 1968, pp. 125-152.

unitary, monopolistic paradigm-control for the take-off into self-sustaining scientific growth. Kuhnianism in social science is beginning to act as a functional equivalent and substitute for philosophical positivism. To some extent this 'Kuhn effect' is the result of the reception of Kuhn in a milieu saturated with positivism, but it also partly reflects the substance of Kuhn's analysis.

However, even within a strictly Kuhnian framework, one must note a widespread confusion concerning the proper application of the model. It is sometimes claimed by the Kuhnians of social science that sociology and political science suffer from an embarrassment of paradigm riches: action theory, structural-functionalism, symbolic interactionism, existential phenomenology, 'actionalism', conflict theory, behaviouralism, 'genetic structuralism', etc. It is also claimed that the besetting sin of the prevalent style of sociological work is eclecticism: the indiscriminate, *ad hoc* borrowing of concepts, models and theories from a variety of these systems—the 'cannibalization', as it were, of the available 'paradigms'. Thus the same piece of work may conjoin the Marxist theory of alienation, the Durkheimian theory of anomie, the Parsonian pattern variables, the Malinowskian theory of tissue-needs, the Smelserian theory of collective behaviour, etc. Such claims indicate that the diffusion of the Kuhnian model to the social sciences has resulted in its corruption. First, of all Kuhn's 'paradigms' are, virtually by definition, monopolistic, hegemonic and exclusive for a stretch of time. It is therefore practically a contradiction in terms to speak of a *plurality* of coexisting, incompatible, competing paradigms except in an aberrant and in a revolutionary situation (where the conflict is between a paradigm in crisis and a paradigm-candidate rather than between competing paradigms *stricto sensu*). What the Kuhnian sociological anti-sociologists have in mind when they voice their complaint is the co-availability of multiple, competing *paradigm-candidates*, not that of paradigms proper. But the properties of paradigm-candidates are not simply attenuated versions of those of paradigms proper: they are different in principle, and not just in degree—just as 'natural history' science and mature science are separated by a logical gulf and historical threshold of the first importance. Therefore the 'sin' of eclecticism is really no sin, for we do not know and cannot know whether and to what extent genuine (i.e. monopolistic) sociological

c

paradigms will emerge out of any one of the existing paradigm-candidates or out of some perhaps unforeseeable conflation of several of them. There appears to be no Kuhnian rationale for condemning eclecticism in a pre-paradigmatic field. All one can say is that a bid for paradigm status is and must be *ex vi termini* a bid for monopoly status for whatever theoretical system one is advocating.

A more important weakness of the 'overabundance of paradigms' claim is that it involves a category-mistake in its Kuhnian exegesis. Typically Kuhnian paradigms are *not* discipline-wide but confined to segments of disciplines. But none of the above-mentioned perspectives is less than discipline-wide. Sometimes, indeed, it is more than discipline-wide, as in the case of historical materialism, behaviouralism or action theory. The growth points of paradigmatic potentiality must therefore be in narrowly-focused problem-areas.

There is also another distorted version of Kuhnianism that is gaining ground in social science. It is the advocacy of methodology as the generator and custodian of consensus, particularly in sociology. This would place 'methodology' as the central core of a sociologist's formal education. However, this is quite remote from Kuhnianism; for the 'normal science' model does not imply that consensus on methods alone is a sufficient condition for scientific advance nor that it can be logically, historically or psychologically separated from a wider concurrence on other cognitive norms and ideals. There is nothing in Kuhn to suggest that methodological consensus comes about more easily or rationally than 'substantive' consensus. To posit an asymmetry between methodological and extra-methodological components of scientific cognitive culture, on the grounds that the former constitute the cutting edge of objectivity in social science, or are more secure and less controversial than the latter, is ill-founded—and also dubiously Kuhnian. It is odd how easily critics of 'grand theory' adopt a consensual mode of argument, construing methodology as a generalised facility for the attainment of collectively and distributively valid cognitive goals. This line of argument overlooks that methods of research are not theory-free or epistemologically neutral.

It is also odd that so many partisans of consensus in social science believe in the irrelevance of metaphysics to science and simultaneously hold that a strong dose of Hempel, Braithwaite or Nagel (severally or in conjunction) could be extremely beneficial for young social scientists. '*The*' philosophy of science[75] for such consensualists means simply logical empiricism. In a sense, such consensualists are right in that exclusive exposure to one philosophy of science, presented as 'the' philosophy, may act in an intellect-binding way. Once mono-philosophical consciousness and quasi-monopolistic methodology have become entrenched in a non-natural science, Kuhnian revolutions seem rather unlikely.[76]

Despite corruptions and misunderstandings, the Kuhnian model of science is indubitably a consensus model: it therefore converges with other pressures against epistemological controversy in the social sciences. Logical empiricism is somehow regarded as 'unphilosophical' or 'uncontroversial' in the same way as a Conservative allegiance used to be regarded in Britain as unpolitical. To suspend epistemological debate, however, is not equivalent to declaring epistemological neutrality. To apotheosize instrumentalities like regression equations, graph theory, and deontic logic involves a characteristic ambiguity. The constraints involved in commitment to such techniques are regarded as a necessary cost of progress—but of progress towards what? A Kuhnian would say, 'Towards "normal science" paradign-bonding'. The underlying intellectual passions, however, readily emerge from a little epistemological psychoanalysis: positivistic logotopia-building, phenomenalistic reductionism, deductivism—even vestiges of unrestricted universalism and Laplacean mechanism.

Moreover, to advocate that sociologists should be spared learning from the 'classics' is neither to successfully emulate the distinctive 'collective memory' system of the natural sciences nor to bring about a neutral orientation to the history of sociology; for amnesia is not tantamount to a Baconian-Cartesian elimination of preconceived ideas. The kind of historical perspective associated with methodolatry involves a naive origin myth: that sociometrics, social physics and behaviouralism are new to this generation. In some ways they are as

---

75   For this tendency, see L. Laudan, 'Theories of scientific method from Plato to Mach', *History of science*, 7, 1968, pp. 1-63.
76   Cf. S. Koch, 'Psychology and emerging conceptions of knowledge as unitary' in T. Wann (ed.), *Behaviourism and phenomenology*, Chicago, 1965, pp. 1-42.

old as 'speculative' sociology, and they have not always been associated with research programmes comparable with the current ones, although they have often been linked with its precursors. Those who tell us that the 'Hobbesian problem of order' is old hat often enjoin us in the same utterances to adhere to a metaphysical programme substantially similar to Hobbes' 'physicalistic' one!

It is a little paradoxical, too, that so many of our 'consensualists'—particularly those who have responded with enthusiasm to Kuhn's theory of science—should be severe critics of sociological consensus models and partisans of 'conflict theory'. The adoption of a consensus model in methodology, combined with that of an anti-consensus model of social systems, appears at least logically odd. Indeed, it involves a logical inconsistency; for if the social system of science is a member of the general class of social systems, there is at least *one* social system which is consensual in fact and disposition, for the social system of science comprises paradigm-bonded collectivities. Obviously consistent conflict theorists tend to adopt a fallibilistic epistemology. Less consistent ones apparently do not recognise the cognitive dissonance between the rejection of consensus models in sociological theory and the adoption of Kuhnian views. It is not clear whether a theory of 'scientific exceptionalism' is here vaguely at work, in the form of a belief to the effect that the logic of scientific knowledge-production *uniquely* requires consensus and that in some sense the social system of scientific disciplines is therefore asymmetric to all other social systems.

One by-product of the historical rule of amnesia is the futilitarian view of sociological controversies. But controversy even in the 'soft' social sciences does not occur randomly nor is its incidence uniquely determined by 'external' circumstances (i.e. societal variables). Some sociological theories, such as the 'functional theory of stratification', have engendered controversy that often spills over into questions of epistemology. The shame and guilt attached to such dissensus are evidence of how deep-rooted infallibilistic epistemological prejudices are. 'Disagreements in belief', it is held, must be fairly easily resoluble, and any protracted intellectual conflict must be basically non-cognitive in character.

The view that intellectual conflict is somehow epistemologically unclean is tenable, at least for a non-Kuhnian, only if stemming from some logotopia of conclusively verifiable or highly probable knowledge. Even a Kuhnian must be interested in cognitive conflict, in so far as it is involved in the clash between rival visions of reality during scientific revolutions: and if one is neither an infallibilistic logotopian nor a Kuhnian there seems no reason to take the view that conflict must necessarily stem from ignorance or error and be epistemologically contingent or redundant. Nor need one restrict the sociology of knowledge to erroneous or irrational beliefs or to some other residual category, after a 'master criterion' of cognitive value has been applied to distinguish certain (or highly probable) knowledge and 'rational' belief.

The analysis of verbal conflict situations has been pursued philosophically mainly in the context of moral or evaluative discourse rather than in that of the theory of knowledge or the philosophy of science. Admittedly, the analytical or critical philosophy of history has undertaken studies of non-scientifically resoluble intellectual conflict, but again the 'appraisive' or 'evaluative' coefficients of historical explanation have been much to the fore. In any case, concern has usually been limited to the vindication of the autonomy of historical explanation rather than expanded to take in wider considerations of cognitive conflict (with important exceptions such as the work of W. B. Gallie).[77] As a result of such studies, modes of inference have been 'discovered' which, although claimed as 'reasonable' or 'rational', are neither inductive nor deductive, and forms of implication weaker than 'logical implication' have been disclosed, such as 'contextual implication'[78] and 'pragmatic implication'. Concepts have been elicited the cognitive rationality of which systematically requires the aggressive and defensive presentation of alternative formulations. Indeed, some enthusiasts of 'informal logic' have gone further, as in the claim that every 'form of life' is characterized by 'its own logic'. Their concern with the 'pragmatic' dimensions of explanation sometimes ends in a complete relativization of explanatory standards.[79]

---

77    W. B. Gallie, *Philosophy and the Historical Understanding*, London, 1964.
78    P. Nowell-Smith, *Ethics*, London, 1954.
79    For a work which shares the 'logical' or 'semantical' polymorphism in moderation but provides a balanced account see L. J. Cohen, *The diversity of meaning*, London, 1956.

Such studies of reasonable discussion need to be generalised rather than restricted to *ad hoc* issues or, in the analytic manner, to topics of moral philosophy. The theory of 'agonistics'—of cognitive conflict in its wide and in some ways open-ended variety—must be extended to social science. It is indeed difficult to see how the philosophy and sociology of agonistics can be other than correlative throughout every phase of inquiry, if indeed in the sociology-epistemology debate there is a Gordian knot which defies the standard solutions of both *social epistemology* and *epistemological sociology*. A fallibilist should not believe in the cutting of Gordian knots; but he may reasonably put forward the controversial claim that the study of cognitive agonistics can illuminate the study of sociological controversy as well as contribute to the understanding of cognitive-conflict-ridden Kuhnian scientific revolutions. This, indeed, even a Kuhnian might be glad to acknowledge.

Roland Robertson

# The Sociocultural Implications of Sociology: A Reconnaissance

This essay has been conceived as a tribute to Peter Nettl in a very definite, self-conscious sense. While it says very little about his work it does relate directly to it. Indeed, some of the themes which I discuss were the objects of debate between Peter Nettl and myself in informal discussions and more visible collaborations. Peter Nettl was acutely interested in the general cultural significance of sociology in the modern period, as was appropriate to someone who cared so much about the quality of human societies. And he was, in turn, deeply concerned about the relationship between the technical-scientific and the intellectual segments of the sociological role.

Peter Nettl was above all else a *daring* intellectual, one who took risks in the pursuit of 'truth'. I would like to think that this essay echoes and celebrates this characteristic, the characteristic of a man whose early death has left an acutely-felt void in my life.

I am concerned in this essay with sociological purpose and action.[1] Traditionally, sociologists have conceived of their discipline in one-dimensional terms—the *substance* of their arguments, findings, propositions and theories has been related to the *logic* of their procedures and methodologies. Two other dimensions have not received sufficient attention: the relationship between sociology and general cultural characteristics of the societies in which it is located; and the relationship between sociology and trajectories of social change. In brief, I address myself to the sociocultural significance of sociology; not only because such a theme is itself of *sociological* interest, but also, and more particularly, because it bears very much

---

1    This essay draws on papers previously given at the Universities of Mannheim, Essex and Lancaster. It also rests in part on general ideas expressed in J. P. Nettl and Roland Robertson, *International Systems and the Modernization of Societies*, London, New York, 1968, esp. Part I. It should be said that I have particularly enjoyed discussing some of the themes presented here with Burkart Holzner, Geoffrey Guest and Thomas Fararo. (The essay was completed in March, 1970.)

on the *practice* of sociology. Once the question of *sociological identity* has been raised in this way the individual sociologist has but two, broadly conceived, choice-alternatives: either to embrace his self-consciousness, or to insulate himself from it. The first alternative clearly leads to a further choice-point: what should the content of that consciousness be? Much of what follows is devoted to considering this question. I will suggest at various points that the insulative posture is becoming increasingly difficult to sustain—not so much through logical weaknesses of the arguments which can be advanced in its favor, but through sociocultural and psychological circumstances. The distinction between *logic* of argument and inquiry and the *circumstances* of argument and inquiry is critical to what follows—but *not* in the sense that the distinction is virtuously upheld. Quite the opposite. The distinction is analytically necessary; but, I argue, the two are so compellingly indissoluble in empirical and ontological terms that it is high time that we fully embraced this compulsion. A long line of philosophers and analysts of sociocultural life have in one way or another argued for this. Marxian epistemology clearly falls in this category, as does the work of those in the modern period—outstandingly Polanyi (certainly no Marxist) —who have either directly or indirectly maintained the artificiality— in a significant sense, the impossibility—of separating the philosophy of science from the sociology and psychology of science.[2] There is evidently an emergent agreement (which needs further crystal-lization) that sociology has little to gain from reverential deference in the direction of 'hardline' philosophy of science, much of which is

---

2    Among the many contributions which relate to these themes I can cite
     the following, somewhat arbitrary, list: Henri Lefebvre, *The Sociology
     of Marx*, London, New York, 1968; Michael Polanyi, *Personal Know-
     ledge: Towards a Post-Critical Philosophy*, New York, 1964 (revised,
     paperback edition); Ernest Gellner, *Words and Things*, London, 1959;
     Ernest Gellner, *Thought and Change*, London, 1964; Thomas Kuhn,
     *The Structure of Scientific Revolutions*, Chicago, 1962; Abraham
     Maslow, *The Psychology of Science*, New York, 1966; Amitai Etzioni,
     *The Active Society*, New York, 1968, esp. pp. 21-93; Eugene J. Meehan,
     *Explanation in Social Science: A System Paradigm*, Homewood,
     Illinois, 1968; Thomas A. Langford and William H. Poteat (eds.),
     *Intellect and Hope: Essays in the Thought of Michael Polanyi*, Durham,
     North Carolina, 1968; Robert G. Colodny (ed.), *Mind and Cosmos*,
     Pittsburgh, 1966.

based at best on an idealized reconstruction of the logical procedures of physicists.[3] This attitude has, of course, been promulgated
continuously by action-oriented, descriptivistic and intuitivistic
sociologists. What *is* new is the attenuation of positivism and scient-
ism among the more analytically-minded members of the sociological
community.

Whether we like it or not, the sociological community has become
increasingly self-conscious in the modern period, initially in the
U.S.A. through the mere assertion of professional protectiveness
and expansiveness. More recently, however, self-consciousness has
begun a new turn. More is being written about sociological 'self-
images', while sociology has been made especially conspicuous
through its prominence in crises in institutions of higher education
and reactions to that prominence—exampled dramatically by the
French government's attempt to limit the teaching of the discipline
and the Vatican's censorial statements about sociology. Neil
Smelser has called sociology the new 'psychoanalysis—without the
mystique',[4] while Andreski speaks of sociology as being sorcery-

---

3    See, *inter alia*, Phillip E. Hammond (ed.), *Sociologists at Work*, New
York, 1964; Irving Louis Horowitz (ed.), *Sociological Self-Images*,
New York, 1969. In a more continuous respect, see the concern with
sociological identity in the journal *Sociological Inquiry*, which publishes
a regular autobiographical-type section on work in progress. (Cf. the
journal, *The History of the Behavioral Sciences*. At the more or less
purely professional level see the journal, *The American Sociologist*.
Cf. the fun-poking *Subterranean Sociology*.) See also the arguments for
sociological histories of sociology in Robert K. Merton, *On Theoretical
Sociology*, New York, 1967, pp. 1-37; and Alvin Gouldner, *Enter Plato*,
London, 1967. For debates about the uses of sociology, see *inter alia*,
Paul F. Lazarsfeld *et. al.* (eds.), *The Uses of Sociology*, New York, 1967;
Irving Louis Horowitz (ed.), *The Rise and Fall of Project Camelot*,
Cambridge, Massachusetts, 1967; Gideon Sjoberg (ed.), *Ethics, Politics,
and Social Research*, Cambridge, Massachusetts, 1967; and Maurice
Stein and Arthur Vidich (eds.), *Sociology on Trial*, Englewood Cliffs,
1963. See also John R. Seeley, *The Americanization of the Unconscious*,
New York, 1967. Autobiographical accounts by social scientists,
notably anthropologists, are also relevant here—as are novels about
social scientists. See, *inter alia*, Claude Lévi-Strauss, *Triste Tropiques*,
Paris, 1955; Alison Lurie, *Imaginary Friends*, New York, 1967.

4    *New York Times*, January 5, 1970, p. 39.

like.[5] And it would be simple to produce many similar statements. This paper in part explores the implications of both the self-consciousness and the visibility of sociology—the implications which these have for sociological practice. In principle, however, the latter theme could be, indeed needs to be, tackled quite independently of such considerations.

The mode of discussion which I will adhere to most closely is indicated well in Bellah's analysis of the evolution of religious symbol systems. Bellah points out that his own analysis is 'a symptom of the modern religious situation as well as an analysis of it'; and he locates this observation in the view that in the modern period life has become 'an infinite possibility thing'.[6] Men can now to a large extent choose their forms of symbolization. Or, as Germani puts it, action is being interpreted increasingly as *elective*, as opposed to prescriptive.[7] Such statements clearly have important implications for sociology itself.

Auguste Comte's ideas about the cognitive and ethical superiority of sociology have rarely been viewed very favorably. Nevertheless, the major point of this essay is to consider what are basically Comteian themes. There were in fact two major dimensions of Comte's program.[8] The one which has been taken least seriously was

---

5     Stanislav Andreski, *Sociology as Sorcery*, London, forthcoming.

6     Robert N. Bellah, 'Religious Evolution', *American Sociological Review*, XXIX (June 1964), p.358-74.

7     Gino Germani, 'Secularisation, Modernisation, and Economic Development', in S. N. Eisenstadt (ed.), *The Protestant Ethic and Modernization*, New York, London, 1968, pp. 346-50.

8     For a highly relevant extract from Comte's work see Auguste Comte, 'Plan of the Scientific Operations Necessary for Reorganising Society', in Philip Rieff (ed.), *On Intellectuals*, Garden City, New York, 1969, pp. 248-82. (For the most succinct and perspicacious critique of Comte with which I am familiar, see Raymond Aron, *Main Currents in Sociological Thought*, Vol. I, New York, 1965.) The full extent of the relationship between the work of Comte and Saint-Simon, on the one hand, and of Marx and Engels, on the other, is really only now becoming fully realised—a point which is relevant to later sections of the present paper. (As far as the themes of the present essay are concerned it is clear that Engels was 'the Saint-Simon' of the Marx-Engels duo. Cf. Theodore Roszak, *The Making of a Counter Culture*, New York, 1969 (paperback edition), pp. 99 ff.)

that which he elaborated in the later years of his life, namely his conception of sociology as a 'religion of humanity'. (I have the impression, however, that during the last few years social scientists have become more fond of discussing this aspect of Comte's work.)[9] It is Comte's presentation of the institutional structure of such a 'religion' in terms of the structure of the Catholic Church which has been the focus of most ridicule; partly, of course, since in adumbrating his well-known 'law of the three stages' Comte had emphatically insisted upon the evolutionary demise of religious thought-styles and their replacement by scientific modes of thought, at the apex of which was placed sociology. It is this latter theme which comprised the second and most salient dimension of Comte's thoughts on the significance of sociology; that is, the evolutionary cultural ascendancy of science, to be crowned by the most complex science, sociology.

It is not my purpose either to evaluate or explicate the minutiae of Comte's writings. I have started with Comte mainly because I suspect that it is the negative response that his work has generally elicited which has functioned as a block against investigation of the problem of the cultural significance of sociological styles of thought. It is, however, of much more than passing interest to note that the ideas of Comte's major intellectual predecessor, Saint-Simon, have come to be more readily accepted.[10] It is in respect of solutions to technical, administrative and programmatic issues that many now argue, either implicitly or explicitly, for the exceptional importance

9    Cf. Louis Schneider, *Sociological Approach to Religion*, New York, 1970, pp. 148-50.
10   I do not enter here into the problematic relationship between sociology and ethics in Comte's work. The relationship between the views of Saint-Simon and Comte has long been an issue of controversy. My remarks are based on: (a) Comte's insistence on the autonomy of social science in contrast to Saint-Simon's tendency to treat social science as an application of mathematics; (b) The disjunction in Saint-Simon's work between scientific administration and his vision of a 'New Christianity'—in contrast to Comte's *attempt* to integrate logically both the culture and the organisational principles of the emergent societal pattern. See the very useful introduction by Markham to Henri de Saint-Simon, *Social Organization; the Science of Man and Other Writings* (ed. and trans. by Felix Markham), New York, 1964, pp. xi-xlix.

of social science. As is widely known, at the end of the 1950's and in the early 1960's a group of sociologists and social observers proposed that modern industrial societies had been to all intents and purposes divested of ideological cleavages and that the major problems of industrial societies henceforth were to be essentially administrative ones—problems to be tackled in terms of the norms of social science.[11] The over-riding problem was how to implement and sustain 'the good society'. The last few years have in fact witnessed a remarkable growth in the degree to which social scientists have become involved in central and local government and in advisory positions generally. Given the greater efforts put into the professionalization of sociology in America and given also the pragmatic optimism of American culture it is not surprising that it is in the U.S.A. that this tendency is most manifest.[12] Sociologists, political scientists, psychologists and economists have become key factors in major sectors of American society—notably, of course, in the areas of foreign policy and so-called urban problems. There are intimate links between the end-of-ideology movement and many of the sociologists and political scientists working closely in, for or in reference to American governmental agencies—most generally in terms of intellectual continuity, but also in terms of personnel.[13]

11  For a partial survey of the end-of-ideology thesis, see Chaim I. Waxman (ed.), *The End of Ideology Debate*, New York, 1968.

12  Merton's famous statement on the differences between American and (continental) European sociology should still be regarded as the major backdrop to this: Robert K. Merton, *Social Theory and Social Structure*, Glencoe, 1949, pp. 440 ff. On the more general theme of anti-intellectualism in America, Richard Hofstadter, *Anti-Intellectualism in American Life*, New York, 1962; and Christopher Lasch, *The New Radicalism in America 1889-1963*, New York, 1967, esp. pp. 286-349. Etzioni's *The Active Society* (*op. cit.*) would be an important book *simply* in terms of its combination of American and European perspectives.

13  Notably in the case of Daniel Bell. See Bell, *The End of Ideology*, New York, 1960; and Bell (ed.), *Toward the Year 2000: Work in Progress*, New York, 1967. Bell is also an editor of the journal *The Public Interest*. (This is not of course the first time that a sociology of knowledge argument has led a sociologist into a policy-oriented position. Karl Mannheim's transition is probably the best example of the twentieth century. See also n. 78. Marx of course combined the two throughout his work.)

The pathetic elements of the end-of-ideology thesis as we consider it in retrospect and with hindsight are very obvious.[14] Racial crises in America and elsewhere and a resurgence of militant politics, notably but not exclusively among the young, have risen to a crescendo since the original flowering of the end-of-ideology viewpoint. In a way which is more ironic than anything else we can also see that there were traces of suicidal prophecy in the end-of-ideology thesis. For it is clear that much of what is central, and indeed innovative, about the ideological formulations of the last five years or so, consists in an ideological response to the existing and projected realities of the bureaucratized and rationally administered society. Thus the end-of-ideology prognosis has in fact been, at least partially, responsible for its own partial negation.[15]

Notwithstanding the prestige of and demand for sociological expertise at the present time, it is also true, almost dramatically so, that sociology is very much on trial. The tendency for modern governments and other agencies to draw increasingly upon the intellectual resources of sociologists should not be regarded too readily as a sign that the sociologist is genuinely regarded by his clients as a kind of 'know-all' or a fount of modern wisdom. For there

---

14  It should be pointed out that one of the men most closely involved with the end-of-ideology thesis, Edward Shils, has written one of the few penetrating analyses of the general cultural significance of sociology in the modern period. In spite of my disagreement with some of the details of Shils' argument, I nevertheless regard it as an extremely stimulating contribution. See Edward Shils, 'The Calling of Sociology', in *Talcott Parsons et. al.* (eds.), *Theories of Society*, Vol. II, New York, 1961, pp. 1405-1448.

15  Space precludes discussion of a notable sense in which the end-of-ideology theorists have perhaps turned out to be correct: There is a conspicuous *anti-ideological* thrust in many of the left-wing radical movements of the modern period. The latter are in a Mannheimian sense frequently more *utopian* than ideological. (Karl Mannheim, *Ideology and Utopia*, New York, 1936. Cf. Clifford Geertz, 'Ideology as a Cultural System', in David Apter (ed.), *Ideology and Discontent*, New York, London, 1964, pp. 47-76.) However, such a concession to the end-of-ideology position does not obviate the point that they seriously underestimated the range of potential dislocations of modern societies—mainly due to their 'Marxian' focus on economic-class variables.

are many indications that the sociologist may be utilized by various agencies as a symbol of taking a problem seriously and /or a scapegoat to be invoked should the occasion arise. Thus we should be sensitized to the applicability of the distinction between the cases in which the sociologist is used *ritually* as a fount of wisdom and those in which he is used *substantively* so. There is, however, a more serious respect in which sociology is on trial: The great visibility of sociology in crises in institutions of higher learning has made the general community of sociologists, as opposed to the relatively small elite who have become involved in practical affairs, highly vulnerable and has placed it in a defensive position—although, there is, of course, societal variation in this respect. The split within the sociological community which is emerging as a consequence of this is a profound one.

The last few years have seen some rather dramatic changes within the sociological community. Only a few years ago there was a widespread feeling that in some sense sociology had come of age and that the tasks which had to be performed were fairly obvious; and, concomitantly, there set in a surge of interest in methodological and technological issues. (In saying this I readily acknowledge that men like C. Wright Mills stood firmly against this mainstream tendency.)

Now in the context of the still bewildering crises (even, I believe, to the Marxists who expect them) which have afflicted most industrial societies,[16] more and more sociologists are becoming concerned about the nature and purposes of their discipline. And so they should. For it is clear that the social sciences (but particularly sociology) have become a crucial *site of cultural tension* in a number of modern societies. The recent drift in intellectual preference away from the natural and physical sciences among school, college and university students almost certainly involves a challenge to many of contemporary sociology's most salient, professionally prescribed, attributes. The 'analytical rationality' of much of sociology is precisely that which is more generally under challenge by many of

---

16   I attempt to put these in a broader comparative context in Roland Robertson, "Modern Societies, the Maintenance of National Boundaries and International Relations", in Victor Lidz *et. al.* (eds.), *Explorations in General Theory*, New York, 1972.

the discipline's undergraduate and graduate students.[17] It should quickly be established that this writer certainly does not thereby suggest a capitulation in favor of emergent cultural demands. But sociologists do have to look critically at their analytic styles and substantive pre-occupations in the light of cultural changes of possible major significance.[18]

There are profound dangers in talking of sociology as a self-contained discipline. It is, of course, a highly amorphous and blurred science—it is not a *normal* science. It is this writer's conviction that there *is* a core sociological perspective (which is a normative judgment about the sociological task) and that there are core sociological problems (which is a proposition about the themes to which analysts of sociocultural life have traditionally addressed themselves, and a claim as to continuity between sociology past and present). One of the great psychological difficulties in 'being a sociologist' is that it not only shares with more normal sciences the problem of attending to new information in the sense of sheer quantity, but it also has greater problems of *relevance assessment* and faces the phenomenon of *sociology in disguise*, by which I mean the fact that much of what is obviously relevant is frequently generated in distant intellectual contexts. From the points of view of both the generalist and the specialist, sociology is clearly a highly pluralistic discipline, but more so in a competitive, than in a division-of-labor sense; although one of the major tasks of the generalist is to attenuate the former characteristic in favor of establishing a division-of-labor situation.

---

17    Cf. the classic debate about analytical *versus* dialectical rationality between Sartre and Lévi-Strauss. See Claude Lévi-Strauss, *The Savage Mind*, London, Chicago, 1965, pp. 245-69.

18    The literature relevant to this is growing at a tremendous rate. For various aspects see, *inter alia*, Daniel and Gabriel Cohn-Bendit, *Obsolete Communism: The Left-Wing Alternative*, London, New York, 1969; Roszak, *The Making of a Counter Culture*, *op. cit.*; Norman, Birnbaum, *The Crisis of Industrial Society*, London, Oxford, New York, 1969; Alain Touraine, *Le Mouvement de mai ou le communisme utopique*, Paris, 1968; and Alexander Cockburn and Robin Blackburn (eds.), *Student Power*, London, 1969. For a highly suggestive description of some particularly American trends, see Gary Wills, 'The Making of the Yippie Culture', *Esquire*, LXXII (November 1969), pp. 135 ff.

Bearing such difficulties in talking about sociology as a whole very firmly in mind, it is still possible, I believe, to delineate and pinpoint the more thrustful tendencies within the sociological field at any given point in time. My concern at this stage is to attempt such an exercise, be it all very briefly; although it should be strongly emphasized that the two developments I pick here both relate closely, and deliberately so, to my major immediate concern; that is, the sociocultural significance of sociology.

### Planning, Prediction and Control

This development is closely bound-up with the increasing involvement of social scientists in governmental affairs which I have already mentioned. But aside from the mere growth in number of what Chomsky has aptly called 'The New Mandarins'[19] we should also note that the whole question of the relationship between social-scientific analysis and the course of social change has been given more attention in recent years. (Much less has been done in reference to *cultural* change.)[20] A few sociologists have again raised the basically Durkheimian theme concerning the implications which can be drawn from within sociology itself for the shape of the good society—something which clearly goes well beyond the 'politically-

---

19    Of course the mandarinate attributes of social scientists were noted long ago. The 'savant syndrome' has been strongly continuous in France from Saint-Simon to Raymond Aron. Institutionalised social science in Britain was conceived under the 'planist wisdom' of the Webbs—in the form of their brain-child, the London School of Economics. In America Edward Ross denounced (on grounds echoing Marx very strikingly) philosophy and all but highly specialised, administrative thought around the same time. See Edward A. Ross, *Social Control*, New York, 1901. See also discussion of Ross's anti-intellectualism in Lasch, *The New Radicalism, op. cit.*, pp. 17-77.

20    I take up the theme of sociological change and cultural change in relation to the sociology of knowledge below, pp. 87 ff. At this juncture the relevance of the following should be noted: Robert N. Bellah, 'Religious Evolution,' *op. cit.*; Shils, 'The Calling of Sociology,' *op. cit.*; Perry Anderson, 'Components of the National Culture,' in Cockburn and Anderson, *Student Power, op. cit.*, pp. 214–84; Talcott Parsons, 'Social Science and Theology', in William A. Beardslee (ed.), *America and the Future of Theology*, Philadelphia, 1967, pp. 136–57.

given' approach of the New Mandarins, and which puts sociology as philosophy (in an anti-Winchian sense) in a superior relation to sociology as technique.[21] Closely related to this development we may note also the growing importance of varieties of evaluative research—a stance which involves the sociologist in simultaneously analyzing and evaluating the performance of the collectivities upon which he or she focuses.[22] Generally, developments such as these are predicated in one way or another upon sociology becoming 'locked-into' societal change. Sociology becomes both a mode of analysis *of* and a critical component *in* the course of change in human societies.

It is noteworthy that interests in large-scale planning have occurred in social science in spite of what appeared to be only a few years ago an 'establishment' kind of social philosophy proscribing such activities, associated in particular with the name of Popper. Popper labelled attempts at large-scale planning and prediction as forms of holistic historicism—combining 'Plato's will to arrest change' with 'Marx's doctrine of its inevitability'. His arguments

---

21    Peter Winch, *The Idea of a Social Science*, London, New York, 1958. Cf. A. R. Louch, *Explanation and Human Action*, Berkeley, Los Angeles, 1966; Alasdair MacIntyre, 'The Idea of a Social Science', *Aristotelian Society, Supplementary Volume*, LXI (1967), pp. 95-114; Ernest Gellner, 'The Entry of the Philosophers', *Times Literary Supplement*, April 4, 1968, pp. 347-9. For combination of social-scientific analyses and philosophic prescriptions see, *inter alia*, W. G. Runciman, *Relative Deprivation and Social Justice*, London, 1966; and Peter Laslett and W. G. Runciman (eds.), *Philosophy, Politics and Society*, Third Series, Oxford, 1967. See also Robert L. Heilbroner (ed.), *Economic Means and Social Ends*, Englewood Cliffs, 1969. In recent sociology Etzioni's *The Active Society* (*op. cit.*) remains the most daring and fertile attempt to combine prescription and analysis—although the logical structure of the relation is not clearly explicated or consistently maintained. See Roland Robertson, review of Amitai Etzioni, *The Active Society*, in *British Journal of Sociology*, XX (March 1969), pp. 92-95.

22    See in particular Edward Suchman, *Evaluative Research*, New York, 1967. See also Etzioni, *op. cit.* Work of the Etzioni type is very much informed by cybernetic principles. Probably the most influential book of a *general* kind has been Karl W. Deutsch, *The Nerves of Government*, Glencoe, 1963.

have apparently not had much long-run impact;[23] although an ironic aspect of this situation is that acceptance of Popperism in *this* respect has been particularly conspicuous among Marx-inspired students. What the Popperians in their ultra-rationalism have failed to understand is that in secular modern societies man cannot apparently make do without some kind of integrated image of the future, that is, without some kind of eschatological and theodical notions. The Popperian view is predicated on an essentially Kantian belief in an incontestable estate of reason, unguided by anything but highly abstract conceptions of freedom, tolerance and the like. It should be stated, nevertheless, that Popper grants an 'irrational' basis to faith in rationality.[24]

Even though many social-scientists of the various planning and prediction schools may eschew interest in cultural matters *per se* they do nevertheless *by their own activity* clearly assist in the construction of a future-oriented culture—a culture which is in principle as analyzable in terms of its dimensions of meaning, as is any religious belief system or ideology; they have to make assumptions, however naive, about the course of cultural change in order to explicate their predictions and prescriptive plans. In this connection it should be added that *some* social scientists, particularly those working in the field of what might be called phenomenal anticipations do clearly entertain a very crucial cultural variable—namely the future-oriented reality constructions of the individuals and groups in the populations with which they deal.[25]

One of the major points of significance about the growth of interest in planning and prediction as far as the present essay is concerned is that it can (and should) be related sociologically to such phenomena as interest in science fiction and developments in the field of theology.[26] (Sometimes, in fact, predictors, such as Herman Kahn,

---

23     K. R. Popper, *The Open Society and Its Enemies*, London, 1962 (fourth edition), Vol. II, p. 212.

24     Cf. W. W. Bartley, III, 'Karl Barth', *Encounter*, March 1970, pp. 46-49.

25     See Jiri Nehnevajsa, *Anticipations Theory*, Los Angeles, 1972. Cf. Kurt Baier and Nicholas Rescher (eds.), *Values and the Future*, New York, 1969.

26     See pp. 78-85.

are called 'new theologians'.) We may view these kinds of endeavors as providing functionally necessary images of a future which is no longer accessible in terms of traditional religious conceptions or tension-management mechanisms. (Although clearly the apparent rapid growth in interest in the occult and astrology is an important modern adaptation to the uncertainty of the future.) But we should also realize that apart from the purely extrapolative kind of endeavor or the one which inquires into images of the future held by respondents to survey inquiries, many of the predictions, speculations and conjectures about the future[27] are no less than *competing* scenarios—in the sense that social scientists have it largely in their power within certain quasi-factual limits to persuade others (and each other) that certain things are *just short* of being inevitable. And those who work in reference to political agencies clearly have an interest in painting bleak images of the future precisely in order that the 'prophecy' should be a suicidal one—i.e., the prediction is made deliberately in the hope that its statement will bring about its refutation. Good examples are provided by the extremes of demographic pessimism.

The prediction-planning phenomenon is an excellent case in which there is a crying need for thorough 'sociological transcendence'. By this I mean that so central to societal reality construction is the work of social scientists operating in this field that we need comprehensive explorations of the phenomenology of their endeavors. Their work is so 'locked into' societal change, so close to the very course of social and cultural change itself, that it is rapidly becoming a part of the reality which sociologists typically study. If one of sociology's main tasks is to comprehend—and ideally account for—the beliefs and values by and in terms of which societies operate then it has to move to a level of discussion in which all those who image the future—those who predict and plan, those who sketch fictional possibilities, those who anticipate—are treated as engaging in a fundamentally similar process.[28]

---

27    See Daniel Bell, 'Twelve Modes of Prediction', *Daedalus* (Summer, 1964), pp. 845-80.

28    Among the more important books on concrete prediction are: Robert Jungk and Johan Galtung (eds.), *Mankind, 2000*, London, 1969; Victor C. Ferkiss, *Technological Man: The Myth and the Reality*, [over

Moreover, we need to know much more about the degree to which people live under the weight of the future and the adjustments made to that burden where it is perceived as being excessively heavy. Sociologists only serve to enhance the significance and worthwhileness of illuminating these basic cultural features of conceiving of the future, or of alternative futures, by involving themselves in such tasks. There may, to take a major aspect of the problem, be a limit to the extent to which people can 'live in the future'—reflected in those science fiction novels which are addressed to the theme of the problems of populations possessing unconditional immortality. We also need to know more about the orientation to the future which has crystallized so strongly among revolutionary students—partly under the intellectual tutelage of Marxist thinkers, notably Rosa Luxemburg and Mao Tse Tung. This orientation basically consists in the idea that a society, or any sociocultural system, can only be understood experientially and analytically (the two are closely fused together) through engaging with its most fundamental characteristics. Future possibilities and probabilities can, so the argument goes, only be grasped at the moment of full 'revelation' of the system. In fact this posture is based on the sensible sociological insight that oppositions are *by definition* always to a significant extent cognitive victims of that which they oppose.[29] The stranglehold of the oppositional target can only be prised open—and then never completely—by pressing it so hard that in the very process of its collapse a future emerges which is dictated not solely by the denigrated system but by the process of overcoming it.[30]

It seems likely that the technical discovery of the future will

---

*cont'd.*   London, 1969; Herman Kahn and Anthony J. Wiener, *The Year 2000*, New York, 1967; C. S. Wallia (ed.), *Toward Century 21*, New York, 1969. Cf. Andrew M. Greeley, *Religion in the Year 2000*, New York, 1970.

29      The symbiotic relations between dominant and counter-cultures have been illustrated considerably in the development of black militancy in America. See for example, Lewis M. Killian, *The Impossible Revolution?*, New York, 1968; Charles Keil, *Urban Blues*, Chicago, 1966; cf. Nettl and Robertson, *International Systems . . . op. cit.*, Part II.

30      Further aspects of this orientation and its tactical and strategic correlates have been dramatically illustrated in the trial of the 'Chicago 7-8'.

frequently come into conflict with the orientation which I have just described. In fact I would argue that they are, in a small part at least, reactions to each other.

### Inner Layers of Sociocultural Life

A second development worthy of note is on the face of it very different and covers a wide variety of more or less independently pursued sociological activities. It can best be described as a fairly generalized concern with the deeper layers of social relationships and social experience. Whereas sociology originally studied what to us now seem to have been the more manifest and intuitively visible aspects of social interaction and social structure, many of its modern practitioners seem to be concerned with going more and more deeply into the very core of social life—a 'questioning' of the very fabric of the assumptions upon which social life is based. Such explorations range from the detailed analysis of the ways in which individuals present themselves in social life to a probing of the underpinnings of conventionally accepted everyday realities. Insofar as sociology has traditionally been a 'debunking' science there is nothing new about this, especially in the light of the fact that sociologists have for a long time insisted upon the importance of distilling and explicating the latent as opposed to the manifest, being as conscious of objective function as of subjective meaning, and so on. But in the main sociologists have conventionally performed these exercises in relation to what one might call the 'outer layers' of sociocultural life— that is, to such areas as the social and cultural bases of economic, political and religious belief and practice.[31] As it is, we know that sociology has been regarded with much suspicion and distrust solely on these grounds. And sociologists themselves have been what now appears to be excessively nervous about their debunking role in this respect.[32]

---

[31]  Prior to modern manifestations of this orientation one of the most subtle advocates was Rosa Luxemburg. See J. P. Nettl, *Rosa Luxemburg* (2 vols.), Oxford, 1966.

[32]  As has been particularly evident in the sociology of religion. See Roland Robertson, *The Sociological Interpretation of Religion*, Oxford, New York, 1970, esp. chs. 2 and 7. See also Roland Robertson, 'Factors Conditioning Religious Belief', *Cambridge Opinion*, 49 (1967), pp. 13-15.

Nineteenth-century sociology tended to rely—although there were a few exceptions, such as Comte—on the idea of there being some extra-sociocultural force underlying the operation of social life, e.g., the cunning of reason, the hidden hand, the dialectic, and so on. Durkheimian sociologism heralded the first major break into a conception of sociocultural reality as *the* reality (under Comteian inspiration). It was not until the middle of the twentieth century that sociologists became widely and thoroughly interested in 'the problem of reality'. Polanyi has tentatively linked a phase-movement in physical science (numericism and geometricism; mechanicism; emphasis upon systems of mathematical invariance) to artistic change (Byzantine mosaicism; Impressionism; Surrealism).[33] These individual phases are, as Polanyi himself cogently states, *visions* of *ultimate reality*. Without fully attending here to the problem of whether analysis of sociocultural life has proceeded in a similar way, I think it can be safely said that sociology has developed significantly in the direction of 'mathematical surrealism' in the modern period.[34] The mathematical side of this is exhibited best in abstract sociology in general. (The mere application of mathematics to data is, in the present context, irrelevant.) The 'surrealist' aspect is to be witnessed in the questioning of 'the reality of reality' (about which I shall say more shortly). To date there has been relatively little effort displayed in linking these developments; but in the field of ethnomethodology[35] we may glimpse a significant degree of recognition of the importance of the linkage—while the great revival of interest in the philosophy of Whitehead, notably among theologians,[36] provides an obviously relevant basis for exploration of the linkage, concerned as he so deeply was with the phenomena of reality and scientific analysis.

Exploration of these deeper layers of the social condition to which I have referred has, I think, the effect of making precarious not only

33    Polanyi, *op. cit.*, p. 164.
34    Cf. T. J. Fararo, 'The Nature of Mathematical Sociology: A Non-Technical Essay', *Social Research*, 36 (Spring 1969), pp. 75-92.
35    See Harold Garfinkel, *Studies in Ethnomethodology*, Englewood Cliffs, 1967.
36    See, for example, Norman Pittenger, *Alfred North Whitehead*, Richmond, Virginia and London, 1969; Ralph E. James, *The Concrete God*, New York, 1968.

the existence of the everyday world taken-for-granted, in the sense
that sociology makes most facets of sociocultural life seem fragile,
but also in the even more profound sense of making the individual's
own social existence seem fragile. In brief, whereas sociology has
traditionally functioned as questioning the general fabric of structures
and grounds of belief—in Berger's phrase, *plausibility structures*[37]—
in human societies, *i.e.*, the 'field' in which the individual operates,
it is now entering a phase in which many of its practitioners are
laying bare even more secret and taken-for-granted realities of
everyday existence; such as reality construction, language and
non-verbal communication, in increasing order of 'interference with
the world'.

The phrase 'interference with the world' demands elaboration.
The basic idea involved here is the degree of penetration of taken-
for-grantedness. It is almost certainly the case that close and comprehensive inspection on a comparative basis would show that
what is taken-for-granted varies significantly from one cultural
context to another. Another dimension of variation concerns the
disposition of the society to turn *the exposure* of taken-for-grantedness
(including hiddenness) into an inner-directed therapy and/or an
other-directed instrument of social-relational manipulation. Aspects
of this cluster of problems get further attention later on.

The inner layers of social life have been tapped in a particularly
vivid way by recent sociologists of knowledge.[38] Recent developments in the sociology of knowledge are crucial to the present
discussion for two major reasons. First, a sociological concern
with fundamentals of reality construction by social individuals and
groups—the pivotal theme of modern sociology of knowledge—takes
as its basic focus extremely elemental cognitive and perceptual

---

37    Peter L. Berger, *The Sacred Canopy*, Garden City, New York, pp. 45 ff.
38    See, *inter alia*, Burkart Holzner, *Reality Construction in Society*,
      Cambridge, Massachusetts, 1968; Peter L. Berger and Thomas
      Luckmann, *The Social Construction of Reality*, Garden City, New York,
      1966; Thomas Luckmann, *The Invisible Religion*, New York, 1967;
      Peter L. Berger and Thomas Luckmann, 'Sociology of Religion and
      Sociology of Knowledge', *Sociology and Social Research*, 47 (1963),
      pp. 417-27.

assumptions.[39] It is probably more 'challenging' to the social order than purely psychological inquiries into cognition and perception, in that it connects with inter-personal beliefs and modes of communication. And, ideally, it is not content with illuminating what Berger calls the 'fictive' realities by and in terms of which social systems operate. As Holzner argues, a sociological approach to the construction of reality acknowledges above all that such construction 'occurs in a social context'. We must therefore 'transcend the phenomenology of it until we reach a sociology of reality construction'.[40] That is, we should attend analytically and explanatorily to the dynamics of reality construction. It can be readily seen that this type of sociology of knowledge is far more 'threatening' to the social order than the classical sociology of knowledge which dealt with ideologies, grand systems of belief and *weltanschauungen*, precisely because of its focus on more elemental and basic modes of cognition; *i.e.*, those which are more continuous and vital to all individuals or groups. It is both more personal *and* more general. Furthermore its epistemological implications, as I shall try to show, are more profound. By emphasizing the precariousness of reality, by pointing-up the plurality of subjective realities, and, I suggest, *hierarchies* of reality conceptions, it introduces a relativistic and indeed a *solipsistic* problem of a much greater kind than that posed by most classical sociologists of knowledge.[41] In pointing to the notion of precariousness it is, however, important to emphasize two

---

39     This is particularly true of the difference between the old and the new sociologies of knowledge. We should not, however, ignore the important bridges between the two provided above all by Alfred Schutz. Retrospective significance within the domain of the sociology of knowledge has been accorded in particular to George Herbert Mead. Moreover Marx's early attention to these 'inner layers' should not be missed. See Peter Berger and Stanley Pullberg, 'Reification and the Sociological Critique of Consciousness', *History and Theory*, V (1965), pp. 198 ff. One could also say that the modern sociology of knowledge is 'simply' a sociologization of phenomenology.

40     Holzner, *Reality Construction in Society, op. cit.*, p. 15.

41     Cf. Talcott Parsons, 'An Approach to the Sociology of Knowledge', in Parsons, *Sociological Theory and Modern Society*, New York, 1967, pp. 139-65; Peter L. Berger, *A Rumor of Angels*, Garden City, New York, 1969.

things—which apply particularly to Berger's and Luckmann's sociology of knowledge. First, it can be viably argued that the diagnosis of precariousness *per se* relates not so much to first-order, phenomenal features of everyday social life but rather to a sociological, second-order and analytical level. That is, precariousness is diagnosed on the basis of *comprehending from an analytic distance* the nature of 'everyday matter-of-factness'. It seems a kind of 'miracle' that something which is open to analytic perusal and, by that very act, desacralization can survive and persist.[42] But this is a *sociological* judgment and not a statement as such about the subjective, phenomenal character of social life; which leads us to a second point: the diagnosis of precariousness—in effect, the prising open of the sociocultural order—probably does *indirectly* have the *consequence* of making the social world seem *phenomenally* precarious. But (as is further indicated below, pp. 80–81) we have to be sensitized to the likelihood that the form of this phenomenal precariousness differs from society to society. There may be a parallel here with the relationship between psychoanalysis as scientific diagnosis and psychoanalysis as phenomenal life-style.[43] In its latter form people selfconsciously live *in terms of* the principles of psychoanalysis—their lives are governed by the interpretive norms of psychoanalysis. At the social level we are familiar enough with popularized presentations of game theory and exchange theory.[44] Again, there is a crucial difference between saying 'these are the principles which govern social behavior' and 'this is the way in which I can cope socially'.

The second major reason for the importance of the new focus in the sociology of knowledge is the light which it casts on *sociological*

42    The idea of there being a sacred, 'untouchable', center of societies is an old and persistent one in sociology. See Robert A. Nisbet, *The Sociological Tradition*, New York, 1966, pp. 221-63. See also Edward Shils, 'Charisma, Order and Status', *American Sociological Review*, XXX (April 1965), pp. 199-213. Cf. Roland Robertson, *The Sociological Interpretation of Religion*, Oxford, New York, 1970, pp. 196 ff.

43    See Peter L. Berger, 'Toward a Sociological Understanding of Psychoanalysis', *Social Research*, 32 (Spring 1965), pp. 26 ff. See also Philip Rieff, *The Triumph of the Therapeutic*, London, New York, 1966; and Seeley, *The Americanisation of the Unconscious, op. cit.*

44    See, for example, Eric Berne, *Games People Play*, New York, 1964.

culture. Classical sociology of knowledge itself turned very much on the epistemological relationships between sociology and the wider society; in fact it became obsessed by them. But we can see rather easily that the newer focus on reality construction has added to this a formidable ontological problem. Seen in the perspective of the theme of the social construction of reality, sociology is 'merely' a specialized mode of reality construction. The very statement of this proposition bears profoundly upon a problem which beset Mannheim's sociology of knowledge. As has been noted on numerous occasions, Mannheim trapped himself by making propositions about the social determination of knowledge—the principles of which when applied to the propositions themselves, and logically they had to be so applied, violated those same propositions. The sociological perspective was used as a springboard for making statements about the social determination of knowledge; and yet the comprehensive application of such statements obviously included the sociological perspective itself.[45]

### Sociology as Social Eidos

It is as well to be mindful at this stage of the fact that all human societies have always had some form of *social eidos*—the stock of ideas which relate to social institutions and activities.[46] Social science is in this sense but one type of social eidos. Historically, religion has been, almost certainly, the major form of social eidos; and the analytic side of religion—namely, theology ('the queen of the sciences')—can clearly be regarded as *functionally* similar to some behavioral sciences, notably sociology and psychology. In the modern period theology has been increasingly secularized in the sense that it has come to lean on secular philosophies and sociologies.[47] Death-of-God Theology, The Theology of Hope and Process Theology are excellent

---

45    For an interesting discussion of the lack of reflexivity in many post-Cartesian theories of knowledge see Edward Pols, "Polanyi and the Problem of Metaphysical Knowledge", in Langford and Poteat (eds.), *Intellect and Hope, op. cit.*, pp. 58-90. The conventional notion of reflexivity relates very closely to my idea of sociological transcendence.

46    See Charles Madge, *Society in the Mind: Elements of Social Eidos*, London, 1964.

47    See Robertson, *The Sociological Interpretation of Religion, loc. cit.*

examples. But theology of course still concerns itself with basically metaphysical questions. To this extent it can in some respects clash with social and behavioral science; *and* ask very basic questions of the latter.

One of the most conspicuous cases in which a tension between theology and sociology appears is in the work of Peter Berger. It may be instructive to look at the problem in the terms which Berger has posited.[48] Two of Berger's major concerns have been to establish an appropriate relationship between sociology and theology and to inquire into the limitations of sociological consciousness. Although some aspects of these themes are only tangentially related to the present discussion, the claims which Berger makes for his particular theological and religious perspectives, and the disadvantages of the sociological consciousness which he depicts by way of comparison, assist in throwing the problems with which I am directly concerned into sharp relief. In any case, as I argue subsequently, the sociology of religion, especially in its wider range of reference, is particularly facilitative in gaining sensitization to the general nature of the sociocultural significance of sociology.

In his essays which are most clearly oriented towards theological, religious and philosophical issues Berger sees sociology as performing an essentially unmasking function. Sociology exposes the social dimension of belief. On the other hand, Berger explicity contends, along grounds very close to the orthodox functionalist position, that the 'fictions' of sociocultural life are fundamental to the operation of human society: 'For most of us, as we grow up and learn to live in society, its forms take on the appearance of structures as self-evident and as solid as those of the natural cosmos. Very likely society could not exist otherwise. Nor is it likely that socialization could take place if this were not the case.[49] For Berger the everyday realities, the self-evident structures, in terms of which 'normal'

---

48  See especially Peter L. Berger, *The Precarious Vision*, Garden City, New York, 1961; Berger, *The Sacred Canopy, op. cit.*; Berger, *A Rumor of Angels, op. cit.* Cf. David Martin, *The Religious and the Secular*, London, 1969, esp. chs. 3, 5, 6 and appendix. See also David Martin, *A Sociology of English Religion*, London, 1967, concluding chapter; and Berger, *Invitation to Sociology*, Garden City, New York, 1963.

49  Berger, *The Precarious Vision, op. cit.*, pp. 10-11.

people live are functionally necessary. He speaks very much of social fictions and social fictitiousness, and yet maintains very firmly that 'to take fictions as reality can become a moral alibi. It then becomes possible to avoid responsibility for one's actions. To live in unperceived fictions is morally dangerous because it leads to inauthenticity'.[50] It is in these terms that Berger once expressed the view that social science is a 'profane auxiliary to Christian faith'.[51]

Berger's self-confessed conservatism[52] comes through very clearly in these remarks. His view of socialization is of the fairly conventional sociological kind—that is, socialization consists in induction into the normative thoughtways of a given sociocultural order. Such a view suggests that sociocultural systems depend upon constant generational re-confirmation of their norms and values—that uninstitutionalized youthful deviance constitutes a failure of the socialization process. Nothing seems more destined to make sociology redundant than an insistence upon this way of looking at socialization processes. Our conceptions of socialization might much more usefully and realistically be re-shaped by acknowledging the *electiveness* (as opposed to the prescriptiveness) which is clearly evident in many modern societies. Viewed in this light socialization becomes a process of learning *how to elect*, and not how to follow traditional or rational-legal prescriptions (or indeed charismatic ones). This is not, I emphasize, an open embracing of 'do-your-own-thing' principles—as I hope my concluding comments will show.

Berger's position may be compared to that of Dahrendorf who poses the question of the ontological status of what he calls 'sociological man'.[53] Like Berger, Dahrendorf sees sociological analysis as viable only in terms of regarding individuals as acting and responding in the phenomenal world in terms of *social roles*. But whereas for Berger role-playing is an ontological characteristic of the

---

50     *Ibid.*, p. 85.

51     *Ibid.*, p. 204. Cf. Martin's emphasis on religion *versus* sociology (n. 48, supra.).

52     See Peter L. Berger and Richard J. Neuhaus, *Movement and Revolution*, Garden City, New York, 1970.

53     Ralf Dahrendorf, *Essays in the Theory of Society*, Stanford, London, 1968, pp. 19-106.

phenomenal world Dahrendorf argues that it is only for the analytic purposes of sociology that we should regard the phenomenal world as consisting in individuals-in-role. Dahrendorf maintains that sociologists erect a fictional man, sociological man, who is seen in terms analogous to the way in which economists erected an analytic-fictional type of economic man. Beyond, or behind, this analytic fiction lies a 'real' man—to whose wellbeing, Dahrendorf contends, sociology should be morally committed. Thus, whereas Berger proposes that social individuals have in the main to live a fictional, inauthentic existence, Dahrendorf is saying that the sociologist in order to be genuinely scientific has to speak *as if* social individuals live in terms of the fictions associated with role playing. The complexities of this particular theme cannot be resolved here. Much of the problem has to do with the nature of the societal context to which the sociologist makes reference; for it is no accident of the differential development of sociology and social psychology that role analysis has been developed mainly in the U.S.A. Whereas Dahrendorf's essay on this problem created much controversy in Germany, American reception of the idea of seeing society as made-up of roles, and man as essentially a role-playing being, has apparently been unproblematic. Thus we have to recognize fully the possibility that although the language and conceptual apparatus of sociology has been widely transnationalized, the relationship between concept and analytic mode, on the one hand, and phenomenal referent, on the other, differs from society to society. We can say that whereas in American sociology the role concept has been *phenomenally emergent*, in Germany it has been *analytically imposed*. Such an observation clearly assumes considerable significance in the context of conceiving of sociology as a mode of reality construction—and the examples could be multiplied. A more central point, however, is that both Berger and Dahrendorf, in their different ways, seem to get caught in a three-part dilemma: sociology, society and philosophical-ideological preference constitute, respectively, three *competing* attachments.[54]

---

54 Cf. John R. Seeley, 'Thirty-Nine Articles: Toward a Theory of Social Theory', in Kurt H. Wolff and Barrington Moore, Jr. (eds), *The Critical Spirit: Essays in Honor of Herbert Marcuse*, Boston, 1967, pp. 150-171.

Berger's attitude towards society is basically, as he himself puts it, not 'ultimately serious'. To be ultimately serious about society, he argues, 'means *ipso facto* to be caught within it'.[55] We have already glimpsed, however, that one's analysis of society hinges crucially on the image of society which one erects in the first place. Berger having depicted society as essentially based on myths and fictions cannot afford, given his own moral and religious commitments, to embrace 'ordinary' social life with any enthusiasm. In these terms sociology emerges for Berger as having profound limitations. According to him, sociology takes the world seriously and therefore suffers from a kind of worldly encapsulation. Only a stance which does not see the humor of social life, its fragility, in a sense its absurdity, can gain sufficient transcendence to see the world for what it is—or, to put it the other way round, only a transcendence of social life can yield the perception that the world is basically humorous, fragile and absurd. It should be noted that in Berger's work there has been a shift from a concern with existentialist themes—manifested in the emphasis upon humor, absurdity, and particularly the search for authenticity—to an emphasis upon the significance of the supernaturally transcendent. In his most recent works Berger has tried to relativize sociology, as he puts it; since according to him sociology has done enough relativizing.[56] Indeed, he says, it is perhaps the very relativizing proclivity of sociology which has enabled us to see the simplicity of relativizing sociology itself. Thus from proclaiming that sociology, or rather social science generally, is a major supplement to Christian faith, Berger has moved to a position in which he claims that sociology is essentially dismal and pessimistic, and that its immanentism, its lack of transcendence, is an inadequate perspective on the significance of human life.

But no more than Mannheim could escape relativization by relationalization, can Berger escape relativization (which, as we have noted, he has crystallized into solipsism) by his style of transcendentalizing. For the very arguments which he generates in

---

55　　Berger, *The Precarious Vision, op. cit.*, pp. 216-7.
56　　Berger, *A Rumor of Angels, op. cit.*

support of the supernatural presence are sociological—they are based on *sociocultural* 'signals' of supernatural transcendence.

I have said that I am not directly concerned here with the theological and religious considerations which inform the contributions of Peter Berger to our understanding of sociological consciousness. But it may be worthwhile to illustrate further the links between discussions of religion and sociology. Historically the links have been emphatically clear. Comte, Marx, Weber and Durkheim—all of them—related sociology to religion in their distinctive ways. In Weber's famous piece on science as a vocation the question of the relation between a scientific commitment and the fundamental problems of personal meaning is perhaps most piquantly stated.[57] The importance of Durkheim's thesis about religion being the means by which primitives thought about society needs no elaboration. In the modern period it is precisely the broader issues of meaning which are engaging the attention of sociologists of religion; and it has become increasingly obvious, as we have seen, that social science is a major part of the meaning pattern of modern society. The sociology of religion—in its broadest frame of reference—is thus inherently concerned with *two* major sources of meaning; indeed, as I have argued elsewhere, pursuit of this sub-discipline involves a confrontation between these two general bases of cultural meaning.[58]

There are some important cognitive symmetries common to both the Christian and the sociological perspectives on sociocultural life.[59] These revolve around the basic Christian imperative about *being in but not of the world*. I would argue that the classical debates

---

57   For a suggestive exposition see Richard A. Fenn, 'Max Weber on the Secular', *Review of Religious Research*, 10 (Spring 1969), pp. 159-69. Cf. Raymond Aron, 'Max Weber and Michael Polanyi', in Langford and Poteat (eds.), *op. cit.*, pp. 341-63.

58   See Robertson, *The Sociological Interpretation of Religion*, *op. cit.* For a useful discussion of dimensions of meaning see Jan Loubser, 'Calvinism, Equality, and Inclusion: The Case of Afrikaner Calvinism', in Eisenstadt (ed.), *The Protestant Ethic and Modernization. op. cit.*, pp. 367-383, but esp. 369 ff.

59   Cf. Harold K. Schilling, *Science and Religion*, London, New York, 1963. See also Ian G. Barbour, *Issues in Science and Religion*, London, 1968.

about the differences between the natural and social sciences, notably in Germany, may fruitfully be seen in these terms. More broadly, the whole problem of involvement versus detachment is something which is culturally an Occidental one. As many social scientists from Weber onwards have taught us, this problem and the pristine Christian solution to it—*i.e.*, being in but not of the world— came to a head in the religious context with the rise of Protestantism. I am not arguing here for a direct historical continuity between the development of Protestantism and the development of sociology (although there probably are elements of such an idea worthy of exploration). What I am saying is that in ideal-typical form the required stance of the sociologist conforms to the 'in but not of' Christian dictum. As within the history of Christianity, so within the discipline of sociology there are acute versions of this requirement. A good example is that mode of inquiry known as participant observation—or its more subtle and demanding successor, eth- nomethodology (which is, of course, much more than a mode of inquiry).

There are, then, two different respects in which this characteristic of the sociological consciousness (being 'in-but-not-of') makes its appearance in modern social-scientific circles: the religious-cultural and the methodological. Lying mid-way between Christian ob- servations on what Martin calls the 'schizoid' stance of the soci- ologist[60] and the methodological strictures about scientific procedure in sociology are observations such as those of Chomsky, who speaks, in the context of linguistics, about the problem of 'psychic distance'. Although Chomsky is speaking specifically about the problems we encounter in grasping scientifically the principles governing such a fundamentally taken-for-granted phenomenon as language and linguistic ability, the notion of psychic distance—the capacity to distance ourselves psychologically from something which is ex- tremely familiar to us—is, of course, a common feature of the sciences of man. And yet we know relatively little about the foundations and nature of psychic distance. Undoubtedly Berger is correct, and very importantly so, in remarking that 'the social sciences have become so much part of the intellectual scene taken for

---

60    Martin, *A Sociology of English Religion, op. cit.*

granted that sometimes the sociological enterprise itself can become for an individual an excellent method of avoiding any existential encounter with the social reality within which he is located'.[61] The *degree* to which this is true is naturally a matter for empirical inquiry.

The phenomenon of 'sociological insulation' minimizes the problem of psychic distance in one major respect. For those sociologists who are insulated from encounters with existential reality in the sense intended by Berger—that is in confronting the basic issues of meaning in sociocultural life—will tend to have few problems connected with stretching psychic capacities, particularly if they have technical and methodological intellectual equipment to guide them 'through' (and insulate them from) the perceived surface of sociocultural reality. The phenomenal world is for them basically a field of *objects* to be studied, conceptually arranged, abstracted from, and so on. This kind of sociologist, again ideal-typically, manages to isolate his sociological role from his other role contexts in such a way that the phenomena he confronts sociologically are for him or her not of the same class as those which he confronts in his non-sociological roles, even though at a sociologically transcendent level they clearly are (an attribute which may be clearly recognized by the insulated sociologist). Sociological problems are located within specific cognitive settings, 'guarded', for example, by institutional and personal work routines—sociocultural experience is separated from sociological experience.[62] The degree to which this is a satisfactory solution to the problem of attaining psychic distance (more accurately, getting round it) depends very much on one's views about the goals and aims of sociological inquiry, and also the branch of sociology in which one is involved. This raises profoundly the question of what it *means* to be a sociologist.

It could be argued—indeed I would so argue—that sociology could not survive as such, even in its present amorphous and fuzzy condition, without the existence of those who are concerned with the

---

61    Berger, *The Precarious Vision, op. cit.*, p. 13.
62    Highly relevant to this part of the discussion is Nettl's distinction between those dealing with ideas of quality and those focusing upon ideas of scope. See J. P. Nettl, 'Ideas, Intellectuals, and Structures of Dissent', in Rieff (ed.), *On Intellectuals, op. cit.*, pp. 53-122.

D

notion of there being a core sociological perspective. This, I maintain, has three leading characteristics: First, it involves an interest in the phenomenon of *sociality*—which *may* be transmuted into a form of *sociologism*. Second, the core sociological perspective involves attention, as an ongoing preoccupation, to the problematic relationship between phenomena clustering, on the one hand, in a domain of subjective and cultural variables and, on the other hand, in a domain of objective, social-structural and environmental variables.[63] Third, the core perspective includes a fundamental concern with the problematic relationship between being in but not of the sociocultural order—a theme which clearly relates to an experiential dimension of sociological praxis. (Polanyi's conception of *personal knowledge*, mainly in reference to physical science, has an acutely significant relevance to this characteristic.)

One of the major problems of any science concerns that of attaining *ontological depth*. There are various conceptions of this. I characterize the attainment of ontological depth as a process of going deeper and further into sociocultural reality such that one finds 'ultimate' factors which account for the basic phenomenon in which we are sociologically interested. Thus some sociologists would argue that sociology suffers from so much conceptual confusion and fuzziness precisely because it has not cut deeply enough into sociocultural reality—that it has not got beyond or behind the readily observable and/or measurable. The main point I wish to make is that there are a number of socio-psychological ways of getting to this 'reality'. I will mention only two here. The first procedure essentially involves an (in principle) infinite series of abstractions from sociocultural reality. One proceeds in terms of a continuous search for underlying variables—on the basic principle that underlying one variable is always another. In principle, then, 'reality', be it all a highly abstract conception of reality, is obtainable through these processes of analytic regression. The hypothetical end-point of such an

---

63    See Roland Robertson, 'The Objective—Subjective and Social—Cultural Distinctions in Sociological Analysis', University of Pittsburgh, 1967 (mimeo). It is well known that these are precisely the questions which have most preoccupied philosophers of social science, see n. 21 supra.

endeavor is a two-fold sociological reality. One of these realities is, again in principle, at the very depths of man's ontic state—way 'underneath' the realities of everyday perceived reality. In great contrast the way in which this deep reality is expressed is in a highly abstract theoretical reality. To put it another way, the referents of this kind of sociology are deeply embedded in sociocultural reality, while the symbolic modes of expressing that reality are, so to speak, way 'above' phenomenal, sociocultural reality.

In contrast to this style there is an orientation to the problem of psychic distance which involves a very different tack. This involves what one might call ontological probing. A major example of this kind of approach is that of ethnomethodology—which may generally be regarded as a sophisticated extension of the principles of participant observation at the methodological level and in substantive terms an attempt to demonstrate that, while things are not what they seem, there are, nevertheless, universal principles of sameness about the apparent *lack* of sameness in everyday reality.

Manifestly the scientific goals of these approaches are not in principle ultimately dissimilar—but they are different in their procedures. The first, the abstractive, does not take everyday, phenomenal reality very seriously; whereas the second takes this reality as its very point of departure. In contrasting these two approaches—which are invoked merely to illustrate some extreme cases in contemporary sociology—we can, I hope, now see the problem of reality conceptions or, more important, the sociologist's contribution to reality conceptions as being far more complex than has been suggested by Berger.

## Sociology in the Future

What then can we say in more constructive vein about the stance of the sociologist at this point in historical time? Geertz has effectively argued that Mannheim's Paradox about the relationship between social science and the validity of ideologies should be circumvented, rather than tackled in its own terms—that we should eschew the problem. With this, I think we may safely agree (although my grounds for so doing are not the same as those of Geertz).[64] In

64    Clifford Geertz, 'Ideology as a Cultural System', in Apter (ed.), *Ideology and Discontent, op. cit.*

fact Mannheim himself said as much towards the end of *Ideology and Utopia* when he argued for an essentially pragmatic orientation to the problem of the relationship between 'sociology and society'. The interesting link between Mannheim's recommendation in this respect and the philosophical pragmatism of people such as Dewey and James has been neglected—Stark being a major exception.[65] We might also note that Simmel's justification for the 'validity' of sociology was based on not dissimilar grounds—that it was functionally effective.[66] Simmel's position in this respect does of course run counter to the widely-accepted recommendations of the Popperian school, approximating what Popper calls instrumental conceptions of theory and validity.[67] In many ways the obsession with empirical confirmation, or better, possibility of disconfirmation, which one finds in some prominent schools of contemporary philosophy of science may be seen as a very significant residue of the old philosophical position which posits a rationalistic notion of dualism—of a world out there to be analyzed, one which exists independently of the observer and the interpreter. (This in spite of deference to the Heisenberg principle.) Indeed the Mannheim Paradox itself may be seen as a victim of precisely this mode of thought.

I wish to suggest here that what we need right now is what can be best described as sociological *realism*—a sociology which in some way synchronizes sociological thought as a reality with 'the world(s)' which lies outside sociology as a reality (or realities). In such connections, as I have already hinted, I believe we can learn something from some developments in modern theology. (It is ironic to observe *en passant* that some sociologists of religion have become the leaders, be it all unwittingly, of a return to more conventional modes of theological thought—those who emphasize transcendent immediacy

---

65    Werner Stark, *The Sociology of Knowledge*, London, 1958, pp. 307-28. See also C. Wright Mills, 'Methodological Consequences of the Sociology of Knowledge', *American Journal of Sociology* (1940-41), pp. 316 ff.

66    See Nicholas J. Spykman, *The Social Theory of Georg Simmel*, Chicago, 1925.

67    See Karl A. Popper, *Conjectures and Refutations: The Growth of Scientific Knowledge*, 1965 (second edition), pp. 107 ff.

and supernaturalism and/or experientialism).[68] I suggest that in terms of the Mannheim-Scheler debate some contemporary theology leans very much in the Schelerian direction—in the direction of what one might call precarious, futuristic transcendentalism.[69] The so-called Theology of Hope argues very much in terms of hopes for the future based on trajectories of change inherent in the present.[70] This stance contrasts with the predictors and planners of the Bell, Kahn and Wiener type who tend to argue in terms of extrapolations, which we can by knowing in part control. To this I oppose the more precarious and conjectural view, which does *not*, as Kahn and Wiener predict of the future, entail *surprise freeness*. What I am saying amounts to a precarious synthesis of probabilities and possibilities—a synthesis which in fact puts a tremendous burden upon sociology.

The Theology of Hope rests considerably on Marxian ideas, notably those of Ernst Bloch. Epistemologically and gnosiologically, the key theme of Marx's work which bears on the present essay is that which is presented by Lefebvre as 'overcoming'. Marx maintained that in his time philosophy was overcoming religion and that philosophy in turn had to be overcome by a social-scientifically guided form of political action—the 'voluntaristic' elements of which were later spelled out more definitively by Lenin and Lukács.[71] Generally, by implication, much of Marxist thought has held to the position that the final phase in the series of cognitive overcomings appears in the genuinely socialist society—when interpretation and analysis of sociocultural life become fused with sociocultural life itself (or, better, the former 'disappears into the latter'). This, from a sociological standpoint, is essentially a scenario of a *tacit* society—one in which people merely *act*, and there is no functional need for

---

68  See for example Robert N. Bellah, 'Transcendence in Contemporary Piety', in Donald R. Cutler (ed.), *The Religious Situation 1969*, Boston, 1969, pp. 896-909. Cf. Berger, *A Rumor of Angels, op. cit.*

69  See Stark, *The Sociology of Knowledge, op. cit.*, esp. pp. 339 ff.

70  See in particular Jurgen Moltmann, *The Theology of Hope*, New York, 1967; Ernst Bloch, *Man on His Own*, New York, 1969; Martin E. Marty and Dean G. Peerman (eds.), *New Theology No. 5*, New York, London, 1968, esp. the papers by Braaten, Pannenberg, Metz and Cox.

71  A central theme of Etzioni's *The Active Society (op. cit.)* is the relationship between unfolding and epigenetic aspects of social change.

social science. (Somewhat mischievously one could say that this conforms to the philosophic implications of Simmel's brand of formalism: all is sociation; and there is no need for culturation. At least the latter is of no real significance.) In this scenario there is no need for social-science as *culture*; indeed there may be no room for any kind of culture—which ironically is precisely where—yet again—the end-of-ideology planners and predictors converge with the implications of certain features of Marxism. Although it should quickly be added that far more emphatic conceptions of a cultureless society are openly advanced by more 'anarcho-hippyist' schools of thought and their academic interpreters. Thus Roszak writes: '. . . (T)he primary purpose of human existence is not to devise ways of piling up ever greater heaps of knowledge, but to discover ways to live from day to day that integrate the whole of our nature by way of yielding nobility of conduct, honest fellowship and joy'.[72] Who could quarrel with this—*except* in the realization that the statement is made in the context of denigrating 'the myth of objective consciousness,' which for Roszak is almost synonymous with what he takes to be 'official' conceptions of scientific method (and which also includes the artistic visions of Antonioni, Godard and Pinter—among others)? Roszak goes on to argue that what is important is 'that our lives should be as *big* as possible, capable of embracing the vastness of those experiences which though yielding no articulate, demonstrable propositions, nevertheless awake in us a sense of the world's majesty'.[73]

As arguments along the one-dimensional plane of contention about scientific procedure there would of course be no need to take Roszak seriously, notwithstanding his attempt to seek intellectual legitimation through the invocation of Polanyi. *But* Roszak's views are, I fear, part of the reality which sociologists have to contend with and these same views suggest an attempt to de-mythologize science as a whole. The apparent seriousness of variants of this view in conjunction with other cultural tendencies which deny the validity of analysis and interpretation, which celebrate the virtues of irrationality (sometimes backed up misleadingly by appeals to

---

72    Roszak, *The Making of a Counter Culture, op. cit.*, p. 233.
73    *Ibid.*, p. 234.

*dialectical* rationality) pose to sociology one of its most formidable challenges. The other main challenges which emerge as being significant in the course of this essay are the technification of sociology and the 'therapization' of the reality which sociologists construct.

It seems clear that sociology has now to meet a challenge which is unavoidable. Insofar as societies are becoming increasingly future-oriented then sociology itself has to become more seriously so than heretofore. Insofar as there are shifts against the idea of there being *any* canons of scientific inquiry then sociologists have to adapt positively to the situation. I can only provide brief suggestions here as to what would be the implications for sociology if it fully embraced these challenges. In saying this it should be re-stated that in some areas of sociology the challenges *are* being confronted.

Cultural dynamics in the modern period involve, I suggest, forces emphasizing planning and therapizing, on the one hand, and those which stress experience and elective consummation, on the other. I believe the two sets stand in a symbiotic relationship. What does or can sociology offer in this situation? What would sociologists prefer to offer? My two main proposals are that sociology should be adequate to the task of comprehending the *becoming* sociocultural world *and* that it should be capable of maintaining *analytic distance* from its subject matter. In adumbrating these proposals I am particularly heedful of Parsons' application to the sociocultural field generally of Freud's maxim: 'where *id* was there shall *ego* be'.[74] This application implies that societies tend to become increasingly 'manifestful'. In turn social science, in order to maintain analytic distance has to keep ahead of long-term processes of sociocultural manifestation.

To advocate a *teleological* sociology may be dangerous—given that the word 'teleological' almost certainly evokes memories of the invocation of mysterious prime-movers in the work of nineteenth-century social scientists and that it was one of the major symbols

---

74    Talcott Parsons, 'Social Science and Theology', in Beardslee (ed.), *America and the Future of Theology, op. cit.*, p. 156. Parsons, however, seems to think that sociologists and psychologists have discovered 'order' in the world and his commentary does not appear consistent with the view of continuing processes of manifestation.

of attack on structural-functionalism in the 1950's and early 1960's. I use the term here, however, simply to convey the ideas of purposefulness and means-ends relationships.[75] Thus a teleological sociology is one which is concerned with routes to goals, goals which are preferably not ultimate, but always penultimate. A teleological sociology is one which is concerned with realistic possibilities. It is concerned with *end-constrained becoming.* Following Whitehead, I regard becoming as ontologically prior to being—as more real than being, which is essentially an abstraction from becomingness.[76] On the other hand, without getting too involved with exegetical problems of Whitehead's metaphysics, it seems clear that many contemporary interpretations of his work suffer from an immanentalist liability—that the emphasis upon the process of becoming yields an image of sociocultural unfolding, the directiveness of which inheres in the process itself.[77] Parsonian sociology is in large measure predicated upon such conceptions. If, however, we allow not only for phenomenal, voluntaristic becomingness, but also in our sociological practice—analytically, that is—for images of what man and sociocultural systems may become, images which are so to speak distanced from process itself, we add something crucial to the Whiteheadian-Parsonian viewpoint. Not only do we see the future as combinatorial—not solely unfolding—we also stipulate in sociological reality construction itself possibilities and in a sense hopes.[78] To be sure, as I have (critically) indicated, some sociologists are already doing this—but there are many, many areas where this conception does not obtain. And yet, I would argue, it is in principle possible for all of sociology to be like this.

---

75    Tendencies in the direction of teleological economics seem to have strengthened in recent years. See, for example, Heilbroner (ed.), *Economic Means and Social Ends, op. cit.*; Peter F. Drucker, *The Age of Discontinuity*, New York, Evanston, 1968, pp. 167-68.

76    I make no claim to a full understanding of Whitehead's work. See Alfred North Whitehead, *Process and Reality*, Cambridge, 1929; Norman Pittenger, *Alfred North Whitehead, op. cit.*

77    For immanentism in sociology and society see Robertson, *The Sociological Interpretation of Religion, op. cit.*, chs. 4, 7, and 8.

78    Cf. Mannheim's proposal that sociology be accommodated to societal needs. The position advocated here demands a greater analytic and psychic detachment than Mannheim advocated.

I doubt whether even an approximation to this latter condition could be reached without there being some broad paradigmatic conception of what sociology is about. In the history of the discipline there have probably only been three such sustained attempts to establish a master-paradigm of the sociological enterprise—those of Comte, Durkheim and Parsons.[79] Of these the last has *mainly* been confined to the internal analytic and institutional requirements of the discipline. Given what I have said in the preceding pages I am led inexorably to the conclusion that sociology *qua* sociology cannot survive without an attempt to do something of the kind which Comte and Durkheim did in their different ways. Since this essay has not been in any sense at all a *sustained* argument in favor of the sociological perspective (although I do believe such should be carried out) I do not intend to more than hint at what would be involved. Much more, I believe, is involved than mere statements as to the value of the 'sociological imagination'.[80] Mills' arguments provided us with no elaborations of what it means to be committed to sociality, for example. Moreover he mixed his arguments for the sociological imagination with ideological contentions in a very undisciplined manner. The thrust of the present essay is in pointing to the need for a fuller understanding of the implications of being a sociologist in our time and in the future. More directly I am concerned with the survival capacity of sociology and its adjacent intellectual pursuits in terms of epistemological stances and relationships to 'the world'. Thus it ought to be clear that what I have said comes close to being what I would call *the analytic orientation* of Marxism: my position approximates a Marxist analytic one insofar as it posits a delicate balance between being in but not of the world, between being 'locked into' but yet marginal to the sociocultural

---

79   Cf. Roland Robertson, review essay on Raymond Aron, *Main Currents in Sociological Thought*, Vol. I, in *History and Theory*, V (1966), pp. 191-98.

80   C. Wright Mills, *The Sociological Imagination*, New York, 1959. The general significance of Mills' plea and also of Lynd's classic statement is, however, willingly acknowledged. My main objection is that Mills never seemed to comprehend the potential of particular sociological approaches. In my view his was a case of 'throwing the baby out with the bath water'.

order. It departs from Marxist thought in these terms by being highly sceptical of utopian belief in the end of history and historicity—the end of surprise and the end of objective culture. Almost needless to say, the position I have adopted in this respect says nothing in itself about the substance of sociology. To be sympathetic to Marx on questions about the relation between thought and reality, between theory and practice, commits one in no way whatsoever to the substantive aspects of Marxist sociology.

There are, however, what might be called pre-substantive implications of the trend of the immediately preceding statements. These implications apply equally to, *inter alia*, 'architectural' sociological schemata (as in Parsons' work); empirical research; abstract sociology; comparative sociology and experimental sociology. Each of these *could* be pursued in the spirit which I have indicated. For example, abstract sociology could be pursued much more than it is in terms of what is socially *possible*,[81] as opposed to taking as its departure point the social relations with which we are most intuitively familiar—as could experimental sociology. To take another example, policy-oriented research could—and should—be much more explicitly concerned with its own sociocultural circumstances, with the sociocultural significance of its own activities.

I am arguing that the long-run, overall *raison d'être* of sociology *per se* is its *transcending* capacity. Much of what we generally and liberally include under the heading of 'sociology' would undoubtedly survive strongly without its practitioners being in the slightest bit concerned with most of the themes I have touched upon—in terms of pure intellectual curiosity, or moral commitment to specific values, or functional demand, etc. But I believe the discipline would have in a major sense failed human society if it did not reach to the limit of its potential.

That potential inheres, I argue, in its transcending capacities; that is, in its capacity to go beyond what already obtains, both in tem-

---

81    Johan Galtung, 'Rank and Social Integration: A Multi-dimensional Approach', in Joseph Berger, *et. al.*, *Sociological Theories in Progress*, Vol. I, Palo Alto, 1966, ch. 7. In this connection the potential inspiration of science fiction for sociological theorizing should be emphasized. See Richard Ofshe (ed.), *The Sociology of the Possible*, Englewood Cliffs, 1970.

poral and in situational respects. A reviewer of a previous attempt I made at dealing with the kind of problem which I have tackled here emphasized the dangers of getting lost in 'receding and distorting mirrors'. The fact that there is this danger is, I think, a challenge to sociology which at least a few of its practitioners ought to preoccupy themselves with. To be sure, many working within the sociology-of-knowledge tradition have done precisely this. But there is still much work to be done. I have attempted here only to bring a large cluster of problems into sharper focus. We now need to go beyond focusing—to the delineation of separate problems and the intensive pursuit of the more salient ones.

Philip Rieff

# Toward a theory of culture: with special reference to the psychoanalytic case

First read, in an earlier draft, as a lecture at the University of San Francisco, California.

'But in general we have no cause to deny the hostility of analysis to culture. Culture involves neurosis, which we try to cure. Culture involves super-ego, which we seek to weaken.'
—Gez Roheim, *The Riddle of the Sphinx.*

Among the absurd little difficulties that Freud carried patiently in his person was what amounted to a 'Rome' phobia. We know that, like others among us, he had anxieties about catching trains; taking a train to Rome was the most postponed, and yet desired, trip of his life. For years Freud wanted to visit Rome and yet could not bring himself there. He achieved northern Italy; he achieved Naples; he skirted Rome. As Freud himself fully understood, this failure of desire had its own significance. Finally, in September of 1901, his own life turned at last in its immortal direction; the *Interpretation of Dreams* achieved, Freud achieved Rome. It was a triumph about which he wrote to his confidant of those long years of interior struggle, the Berlin nosologist, Wilhelm Fliess:[1]

'My dear Wilhelm, I received your card a few hours before I left. I ought to write to you about Rome, but it is difficult. It was an overwhelming experience for me, and, as you know, the fulfilment of a long-cherished wish. It was slightly disappointing, as all such fulfilments are when one has waited for them too long, but it was a high spot in my life, all the same. But, while I contemplated ancient Rome undisturbed (I could have worshipped the humble and mutilated remnants of the Temple of Minerva near the forum of Nerva), I found I could not freely enjoy the

---

[1]     *Letters to Wilhelm Fliess, Drafts and Notes: 1887-1902.* Ed. by Maria Bonaparte, Anna Freud, Ernest Kris. Translated by Eric Mosbacher and James Strachez (New York, 1954), pp. 335-336.

second Rome. I was disturbed by its meaning, and, being in-capable of putting out of my mind my own misery and all the other misery which I know to exist, I found almost intolerable the lie of the salvation of mankind which rears its head so proudly to heaven. I found the third, Italian Rome hopeful and likeable.'

This letter, this personal manifesto against the second Rome, the Rome of faith, plunges us directly into Freud's response to one revolutionary condition of his time—and of ours. As a doctor, and, by 1901, as a therapist, Freud was responding, beyond his own misery, to historical conditions he saw carried unconsciously, by diverse people become patients, into his own consulting room. The grotesque inner lives of modern men were literally laid down before his averted eyes, demanding diagnosis and surcease; and yet his patients were unwilling to part precisely from their own profound wretchedness, that true counterpart of a false and superficial spirituality they could not claim truly as their own. The 'lie of salvation' no longer worked. First and foremost, the response of Freud to this historical condition consisted, in great measure, of analyzing that useless lie, in microcosm through the patient, in macrocosm through the culture in which the patient lived.

Much nonsense is talked about the special Viennese culture of Freud's time. In its main characteristics, Freud's culture bore all the marks that have grown more visible in our own. He too was a patient, even like ourselves, in a society that has come to resemble, more and more, one vast emergency ward. I shall be interested, here, not in the mind of Freud as revolutionary, but rather in the revolutionary character of the culture to which, for his own survival and ours, he created his immortal response. Freud's letter to Fliess introduces us directly, and most succinctly, to the culture that had failed and yet, remaining established, produced the condition to which a re-volutionary response became necessary, in Freud's mind, as therapy is the necessary response to neurosis. The 'lie of salvation' had become 'intolerable', not only to Freud but to significant numbers of others. A misery had developed which at once functioned, like a neurosis, as an escape from misery. My references to Freud's critical response are intended to illustrate some aspects of the revolutionary crisis of contemporary western culture.

I must say, briefly, how I intend the concept 'culture'. As individuals, we live, those of us who may be said to belong somehow together, as unique subscribers to a common symbolic. By a 'symbolic', I mean, first of all, a pattern of moral demands, a range of standard self-expectations about what we may and may not do, in the face of infinite possibilities. The great Western symbolics, Jewish and Greek, have been constituted by repressive, militant ideals opposing the destructive splendor of human possibility; those symbolics seemed to Freud embodied in the 'second Rome'.

Culture, our ingeniously developed limitations, is constituted by two motifs which are dialectically related. These two motifs, which have shifting contents, I call 'interdicts' and 'remissions' from interdicts. Every culture is so constituted that there are actions one cannot perform; more precisely, would dread to perform. (Despite the influence of Freud upon my discipline, sociology has not paid attention enough to what is not done, to the closed possibilities, to the negatives, the suppressed.) There are remissions specific to interdicts. These interdictory-remissive complexes are more or less compelling; human action is organized in their terms. To the degree that they are imperative, interdictory-remissive complexes are observable specially by those who do not feel compelled by them. For the imperative thrust of an interdictory-remissive symbolic is into character, the more imperative the deeper a thrust into the unconscious, beyond reason and capacity deliberately to change it.

A symbolic contains within itself that which one is encouraged to do and that which one is discouraged from doing, on pain of whatever animates the interdict. Permit me to cite a trivial example from the everyday life of an academic. At a certain faculty club I used to frequent, horse steak was served. It may be still on the menu, and considered by some a delicacy; why, then, did it provoke such anxieties in me? I could feel my gorge rising at the thought of eating a horse steak; yet horse steak was precisely what I came to eat. I was aware of that ambivalance which sometimes complicates and heightens pleasure. A certain tension had been created; excellent as they were, horse steaks were difficult for me to eat, just as some 'assimilated' Jews, for example, still find it difficult to eat shellfish. Crustaceans, not to mention pork or bacon, provoke certain anxieties. I think the 'culturological' fact is that inhibitions early installed prevent my enjoyment of the flesh of horses. Some significant time during my boyhood was spent reading books that were quite sentimental about horses and dogs; I recall Albert Payson Terhune and other authors of my boyhood, not to mention 'Black Beauty', a horse for which I used to care passionately. The interdict upon horseflesh, shaping my pleasure and pain in a remissive occasion in the Harvard faculty club, originated in the eighth century. Perhaps it was the great Boniface, himself from a family not long removed from the Roman ghetto, who enjoined a superficially Christian peasantry against killing or eating horses, the animals specially relevant to the power and status of aristocrats.

Of course, horse meat is eaten by other peoples. Thus, in what they may and may not do, on pain of feeling ill, the price of a transgressive breaking of a moral command (the remission thus became subversion) are members of one culture distinguished from another. Worse for me than eating horse meat would be the possibility of eating dog meat. In China dog meat is a common and acceptable delicacy. Anthropogical literature abounds in examples, equally elementary, that might provoke anxieties in members of other moral demand systems. In every culture, whether one does or does not cross a certain line, whether one does or does not eat dog meat or horse meat, shellfish, pork, fish on one day or another, in short, interdictory-remissive complexes, open and close the possibilities of ordinary life activities, differently or universally, to enactors of what is thus rendered a meaningful social structure.

Everything is possible to human beings; we are members of a culture in the sense that everything is not permitted to us, nor even conceivable by us. Every culture is constituted as a moral demand system of shifting interdictory and remissive contents. When significant, profoundly anxiety-producing shifts occur, then, at the most fundamental level, a society is undergoing revolutionary changes. Not all changes are equally significant; indeed, not even the most violent activity is necessary revolutionary.

As I understand the phenomenon, 'revolution' is a significant discontinuity in the moral demand system, an interchange in the relation of interdictory-remissive contents, by which men may well do what they have not done before—and do not as they have done. Contradicting the older, now archaic, meaning, a 'revolution' implies a definite break with the past. By the efficacy of revolution, the impossible becomes quite possible. In this sense, Hitler, with his dictum that 'the impossible is always successful', was a true revolutionary—a permanent revolutionary. On the other hand, most political 'revolutions' in Latin America, consisting in the displacement of one set of military politicians by another, are not revolutionary. Shifts of political authority may not transform the moral demand system, what can and cannot be done. A change in regime is not a revolution, no more than violence necessarily means revolution.[2] Freud, Darwin and Marx may be far more profoundly revolutionary than any mob on a rampage.

Is the 'negro revolution' a revolution? I doubt it. It may become so, when it is linked to a subversive symbolic, but it does not appear so now. The black American does not aim to transform the white moral demand system but only to find a larger place in it. The Negro still wants 'in', not 'out'. Even looting does not necessarily represent a radical break from the white moral demand system; looting may represent an ardent desire to enter and to share in that same American plenitude, to be full receivers in it. Yet, in the process of breaking into the American society more fully, the black American may create a fundamental break away from it; that eventually remains to be developed by blacks themselves, and by those whites who imagine they see among the blacks an erotic alternative to the ascetic traditions of western (white) culture. The white discovery of 'soul', the noble savage returned yet again to harass high culture, has a far more dangerous revolutionary potential than any of the fighting, politized gangs within the black ghettoes.

A 'revolution', then, refers to some radical and significant discontinuity[3] in the moral demand system; what is permitted, so to say, becomes interdicted and what is interdicted is permitted. Revolutions may be defined as reversals—violent or non-violent—of significant behavioral contents. The Christian movement in Roman culture was revolutionary, although non-violent in a culture

---

2    There is a question whether wars, terrorist activities and certain types of violence, are not always revolutionary, so far as they close the established distances and role relations between vastly different men, reducing them to a sameness. But this is a problem into which I cannot go in this paper.

3    Exactly reversing the classical meanings of *evolution* and *revolution*.

that encouraged official (state) acts of violence. With respect to sexual behavior, the early Christians appear remissive to the dominant establishment Romans. The established interdictory-remissive motifs of Roman culture were reversed in significant ways. In turn, the Christian motifs did not triumph without partially incorporating the defeated Roman motifs. Cultures rarely die; they merely marry.

There are two kinds of remissive motifs. First, those remissions which subserve—that is, support—the moral demand system of which they are a part; second, those same motifs, expanding their jurisdiction in the system of action, can become subversive of that system. This says nothing about any intrinsic meaning of a motif. The question of what an interdictory-remissive complex means can be elaborated empirically only with respect to its purposes and effects in a system; no complex means, intrinsically, one thing or another. Even as it functions within a system, an interdictory-remissive complex may be significantly differentiated. Thus, Bolshevism may remain in the realm of aesthetics, remarkably conservative. Oppositional elements in a culture are not uniformly conservative or revolutionary; none represent a universal break from what is and is not enactable.

A truly revolutionary movement must penetrate, through the symbolic and beyond it, to at least two other structures: first, the social order of privileges and deprivations; second, the intrapsychic order of character, of impulse and inhibition. Freud has helped sociologists understand the dynamics of change on all three levels, but in particular on the levels of culture and personality. He understood politics as the middle level, its shape and thrust mediated through the interplay of culture and personality; thus Freud conceived politics as a more dependent, or reactive, level. *Political* change interested Freud least of all, for theoretical reasons that should now be clear. What interested Freud much more than social structures was the degree to which a symbolic penetrates into the depths of character, organizing what men like and would be like. It may be said that for Freud the most fundamental politics are the politics of desire, always ambivalent, suppressed and suppressing.

To assess the depth at which a new set of moral demands penetrates character structure, in some specific ways altering it, is a task of great difficulty. Freud made efforts, on scattered occasions, to illustrate such assessments, the more to enlighten himself, I think, about what he was doing; for this was by no means always clear to him. For example, in Christian cultures, just beneath the surface where the Christian symbolic had been absorbed, there was lurking the particular organizations of impulse and the control of impulse that preceded Christendom—'pagan' behavior. In Freud's assessment of the quality of Christian life, the Christian symbolic had not penetrated Christian character deeply enough to prevent 'un-Christian' conduct. On the contrary, because the symbolic had not penetrated very deeply, so-called Christians were capable of the most un-Christian behavior, under a Christian institutional veneer.

On the other hand, we may note that within the Christian symbolic there were dominant particular interdictory-remissive motifs. By its original terms, for example, Christianity—more precisely the Christian symbolic or religion of love—encouraged hatred of Jews. In the illogic of Christian culture, there is an unresolved ambivalence towards those who were closest and yet remain furthest apart. Jew-hatred is thus a built-in remissive element of the Christian moral demand system. Here is an example of a remissive motif which has penetrated a variety of social structures; without this motif certain acts fall into disuse.

But my main interest, here, is not in elaborating upon the dynamics of Jew-hatred in Christian and post-Christian cultures. (In this culture, ironically, since the late nineteenth century, the Jew has been reassociated with the Christian system, which is itself under attack. This may help to explain the nature of Nietzsche's anti-Semitism.) My point is more general to the revolutionary potential in all cultures rather than to the relation between cultural and social structures. I suggest that interdictory-remissive complexes, like motifs of hatred in religions of love, can be found in all systems of culture. The normative structure of personal and social reality is characterized by *ambivalence*.

In its ambivalence, no moral demand system is static or unchangeable; no culture is immortal. It is the face of all cultures to fall victim to the particular ambivalences by which they are constituted. There appears to be a dialectical tension within the interdictory and remissive contents of every known moral demand system. Permit me to sketch, by way of illustration, one major shift in the moral demand system of seventeenth-century England, and, also the way that social structures have of absorbing those interdictory-remissive shifts and cognate shifts in privileges and deprivations.

When I was a student in high school, I was led to believe that Archbishop Laud was a villain; the Whig tradition of English historiography taught that the anti-Laudians were 'progressive', fighting for the liberty of the individual. Yet the events can well bear quite another interpretation. Laud and the Star Chambers can be understood as defending, among other things, not only church land but the traditional rights of peasants to use common pasture land, which, of course, the enclosure movements were destroying in the name of the right of private property. In that revolutionary confrontation, as I once learned about it, the 'good guys' were those who fought and argued for the rights of private property and individual liberty, while the 'bad guys' were the judges of the Star Chambers. Perhaps Laud and the church establishment were defending not only their own interests, which were clearly involved, Church lands, but also the common lands of England. Individual rights, civil liberty, and private property indivisibly intermingled in the moral demands of the rising bourgeois, for whom Locke composed 'charters' (in the Malinowskian sense).[4] In that cultural crisis of English history, a complex of demands we now call 'liberalism' and 'democracy' was subversively remissive, asserting a radical break in the way land tenure and personal relations was organized. Who and what was then the revolutionary force? It was the demands of worshippers of private property that became subversively remissive. In due course, a successful reinterpretation changes the structure of social reality. 'This demand to change consciousness', Marx and Engels observed, 'amounts to a demand to interpret reality in another way, *i.e.* to accept it by means of another interpretation'. By the time the Whig and Liberal historians had finished rationalizing events, the reverse had become the accepted fact: good (what men ought to do) was assigned to the private property advocates, and bad (what men

---

4    It is a charter proposition of liberalism that family and property are prior institutions to the State. Politics develop to protect us, in our private pursuits, from unwarranted interference.

ought not to do) was assigned to those who opposed the enclosures. When a remissive thrust is victorious, it becomes interdictory, while other remissive contents are produced by the transformed complex. In the Marxist idea of history, the bourgeois produced the proletariat, which would grow to subvert the entire capitalist system, which is not only economic and social but primarily a moral system, inducing men to realize themselves in certain possibilities and not in others.

Where and when a significant shift occurs in the moral demand system, there is implicit an incorporation of the contents of that shift into the social structure. Every radically significant shift in the contents of an interdictory-remissive complex transforms what is demanded of us and by us, transforms the distribution of goods, roles and statuses, transforms relations of deference in a given social order. In this sense, the Marxist movement was truly revolutionary; but so were the movements of the bourgeois, as Marx himself proclaimed. Revolutionary orders of moral demand animate social structures.

Every form or school of sociological, psychological or historical analysis implies a symbolic, not least where that symbolic does not assert any such aim to reanimate social structures; no more did the carriers of the early Christian symbolic assert such an aim. Moreover, a symbolic may be incorporated by certain groups having particular powers in the social structure. The comparative position and effect of the incorporating group is vital to any analysis of basic social change; for example, although low in the American social structure, the black lumpenproletariat is probably the single most influential social formation on the inner attitudes of certain sections of white youth. In effect, a shift of moral demand may bypass apparently protection strata of the social structure in its transformative effect upon character structures. Thus, the eroticizing of American life from the bottom up, through the influence of the blacks, as whites, in fear and envy, understand them,[5] represents, at least in its initial phase, no significant shift in the social structure.

Unlike Marx, who is supremely political, Freud appears apolitical

---

5    Further discussion of this influence involves the entire ambiguous question of racism in contemporary American society.

—even anti-political. Here, precisely, Freud made his great contribution to our revolutionary condition. He established again that knowledge the ancients possessed: that revolutions are, at once, a stirring of the depths, out of which new men are created, to act out once suppressed possibilities. Then, and only then, in the acting out of new possibilities, can there be truly new regimes.

The new man Freud tried to avoid imagining, lest he become too committed to his vision, would be capable of analyzing his own symptomatic behavior, in a culture at last free of its bankrupt inheritances of moral demand. As Freud wrote to Pfister, a Protestant pastor who was one of his more distant disciples, there could be no more the happier state of earlier times when religious faith stifled the neuroses. That way of disposing of the matter will no longer work, Freud thought. Thus, in Freud's own mind, it was the historic failure of the Christian (and Jewish) moral demand system that called forth his revolution. Freud confirmed a radical discontinuity; he did not invent one. It is from the *failure* of the repressions, not their success, and from the more general failure of the moral demand system to compensate men satisfactorily for the necessary deprivations imposed upon their impulse lives, that Freud thought to derive his revolutionary explanations of the modern translation of common faith into individual symptom.

Individual symptoms may be collectively creative; they may be the beginning of yet another generalization of faith. But because Freud pays relatively little attention to social structures, it is unclear how one symbolic succeeds another. He sees concentrated in individuals those symptomatic consequences of the systemic failures he has to treat. What can a therapist do in such a situation? Can he return men therapeutically, as Jung proposed, to the very moral orders which are the predicates of their symptoms? Freud cannot believe, as Jung did, that the cure lies hidden still in what has become the disease. What then remains to be done, by the therapist, self-proclaimed successor to the pastoral guide?

The revolutionary component in Freud's thought is precisely that through analytic insight men are to give up all thought of salvation. They will become new men the moment they cease sacrificing themselves, and others, to what has become an impossibility: salvation. Then real possibilities of living will open up, closed down as they have been by cultures that promise salvation. Like a neurotic, this failing culture hangs on desperately to the particular stabilities, created in its neurotic condition, through which faith neither can stifle impulse nor express it. Freud's hostility to 'religion' was due to the 'readiness' with which religions 'fit in with our instinctual wishful impulses,'[6] rather than oppose them, as Freud knew they must.

Patently, the therapist is no neutral. The very ground of his discipline is the failure of the social symbolic that produces the too lightly individual patient. Even profound revolutionary movements are caught up in structural failures truly and realistically to oppose the impulse life. Of Marxism Freud wrote, in a famous passage:[7] 'Theoretical Marxism, as realized in Russian Bolshevism, has acquired the energy and the self-contained and exclusive character of a *Weltanschauung*, but at the same time, an uncanny likeness to what it is fighting against . . . It has created a prohibition of thought which is just as ruthless as was that of the religion of the past . . . And although practical Marxism has mercilessly cleared away all idealistic systems and illusions, it has itself developed illusions which are no less questionable and unprovable than the earlier ones.'

Thus, in Freud's analytic, Marxism has become yet another repressive order of moral demands. Although he admires the power of the Marxist analytic, Freud marks it too, at least in its Russian form, as a symbolic. As yet another ideology of the super-ego, Marxism has not escaped the past. Offering an analytic that helps men think against all ideologies of the super-ego, Freud is truly revolutionary. He has opened the possibility of suspecting, in a diagnostic way, all symbolics: he has given us a mode of analyzing them. Finally, Freud leaves us with that most revolutionary attitude of all, the analytic attitude, which closes off in the resolution of the transference the ancient possibility of creating, by its success, yet another ideology of the super-ego—yet another moral demand system. In this sense Freud promises no politics but an anti-politics, no faith but an attendance to a shifting sense of well-being that marks, I suggest, a new man: the therapeutic. As a therapeutic

---

6    *New Introductory Lectures*, Standard Edition, Volume XXII (London, 1964), p. 175.

7    Ibid., pp. 179-180.

anti-creed, Freudianism denies that it is a symbolic—an ideology of the super-ego—at all. How can there be clinical evidence for the therapeutic when he is the clinician? As clinician to all ideologies of the super-ego, Freud may well be the most profound and trans-formative revolutionary of all.

Implicit in the Freudian analytic is the main lesson of a re-volution that runs deeper than politics. That main lesson is not easily or swiftly learned. Yet, in a growing capacity even among the officially devout, Christian and Communist, to ride loosely to all symbolics, there is a hint of Freud's victory, of his permanent revolutionary assault upon precisely what he (departing from many among his disciples) considered tragically necessary: a moralizing culture. Because he considered culture, as a moral demand system, a tragic necessity, Freud did not enjoy even the fantasy of a victory for his analytic. Rather, in his criticism of that tragic necessity, Freud, the revolutionary, also draws the limit within which all revolutions must play themselves out.

Amitai Etzioni

# Toward a Cybernetic Theory of Societal Processes

An earlier and substantially different version of this article was published in *Medical Opinion and Review*, vol. 4, num. 8 (Aug. 1968), pp. 22-29.

The sixties may be referred to as the domestic huff and puff period: we came; we huffed and puffed about desegregation, elimination of poverty, development of backward countries; and the problems stayed. Why can we not handle our domestic problems more expeditiously and effectively? The answer to this question varies according to the world view or theory of man, society, and history one holds. Some subscribe to a hydraulic theory of national efforts: if the level of effort is pushed up in one place, it will fall lower at all others. Specifically, they blame the war in Vietnam as having drained our resources and energies; but we must note that the country did not handle its domestic affairs much better before the war escalated and most observers do not foresee a major domestic effort once the fighting is finally terminated.[1]

Others subscribe to an *elite* theory and blame the leader—be it the President or the mayor. President Nixon is now under criticism for his lack of action on the domestic front. However, his pace can hardly be attributed solely to his personal (or his administration's) shortcomings, for Presidents Johnson, Kennedy and Eisenhower were all—quite justifiably—criticized from the same vantage point. In regard to at least one part of the country, New York City, the question is increasingly asked: Can it be managed at all?

Still others subscribe to a *class* (or economic interest) theory and fault the military-industrial complex, an elite which monopolizes

---

[1]    For typical forecast and analysis, see Charles L. Schultze, 'Budget Alternatives after Vietnam' in Kermit Gordon (ed.), *Agenda for the Nation* (Doubleday and Co., Garden City, New York, 1968), pp. 13-48.

privileges, speaks reforms, but does not really seek them. But we must note that countries said to be free of capitalist ruling classes are not realizing *their* domestic social goals effectively. The USSR's fifty-year-old endeavor to do away with economic differentiation, the state and religion can be characterized at best as moving two steps back for every one it moves forward. Underdeveloped nations form master plans but do not follow their plans. And, Israel, one of the most effective societies, rather than absorbing the immigrants, its top domestic goal, is slowly being absorbed by them.

In addition, there are the *rationalists* who blame our lack of 'know-how' and see at least partial salvation in greater investment in the social sciences and in the accumulation of social knowledge, especially the systematic collection and utilization of data on social processes[2] and various administrative reorganizations. Finally, there are the newly reinforced *naturalists* who believe that 'human nature' (instincts and genetic predispositions) prevents man from controlling his destiny, or provides him with all he needs to fulfill it. Some key representatives of this school believe we must cease to let our rational processes interfere, thereby losing the capacity to heed our animal base.

All these approaches, it seems to me, are mistaken in that they see one major force or factor as explaining our difficulties to marshal our efforts at societal self-surgery, while actually they are all correct in seeing *a* factor which is important. If we view the role of elites, classes, societal knowledge and organization, our biological limitations and opportunities (and other factors) as *partial* explanations, we may be on the way to eclectically building a theory of societal guidance, of the conditions under which societal processes may be guided toward the goals the membership seeks to realize. Progress in social science over the recent years allows us now to develop a Keynesian theory of *societal* processes, i.e., a theory of the factors which determine our capacity to manage society and of the conditions which will allow us to improve our guiding capacity. Of

---

2       See 'HEW Urges Annual "Social Report"', *Science*, Vol. 163, Jan. 31, 1969, p. 456; *Toward a Social Report* (Washington, D.C.: U.S. Government Printing Office, 1969); and 'Social Goals and Indicators for American Society', May and Sept., 1967 issues of the *Annals of the American Academy of Political and Social Science*.

course, even once we possess such a theory, however valid, this will only be the first step toward its effective use. At least a generation lapsed after Keynes published his seminal book before it became the basis for economic steerage. Hopefully, application of the theory will not be so long in coming this time around.

The nature of the theory of societal guidance we need can be indicated by drawing upon an *analogue* from cybernetics. (I stress 'analogue' because, to some of my colleagues, the term 'cybernetics' implies a mechanistic approach to social life; as will become evident below, this is not a necessary attribute of a cybernetic approach— surely not of ours.)[3] Cybernetics is still most developed in reference to guidance of mechanical and electrical systems. It assumes (a) one or more centers (command posts) that issue signals to the units which carry out the work; (b) communication lines which lead from the center(s) to the working units, carrying the instructions for what is to be done, and 'feedback' lines which carry information and responses from the subject units to the center (in short, two-way communication links). (c) While many cybernetic models omit the conception of power,[4] we see it as a main factor: if the steering units cannot back up their signals with rewards or sanctions, they will frequently be disregarded (i.e., the command post must be stronger than those who carry out its instructions). (d) A further subtlety is to distinguish, within the command centers, between sub-units which absorb and analyze the incoming information and those which make decisions (i.e., between knowledge makers and policy makers). When all these elements are available and function effectively, that is, communication lines are well linked and not overloaded, information and decision-making units have unimpeded access to each other, etc., we have an effective *control* system.

Some engineers and managers think that a social system, be it of a corporation or of a society, can likewise be managed this way. The government is viewed as the cybernetorial overlayer of society. The White House, Congress, state capitols and city halls provide the

---

3    For an earlier but fuller discussion of our approach see Amitai Etzioni, *The Active Society: A Theory of Societal and Political Processes* (The Free Press, New York, 1968).

4    Cf. Karl W. Deutsch, *The Nerves of Government* (The Free Press, New York, 1963).

command positions. Universities, research institutes, government experts and 'think-tanks'—the knowledge makers. The civil service and the media—the two-way communication lines. As we see it, when a cybernetic model is applied to a social system, one must take into account, for both ethical and practical reasons, that the citizens cannot be coerced to follow 'signals' unless those signals, at least to a significant extent, are responsive to their basic values and interests. If force is used, the system both violates their rights and generates increasing levels of resistance which become a major reason why the society is unable to manage its affairs effectively, whether the goals be collectivization of the farms or abolishing alcoholism. Effective *societal* cybernetics requires that the downward flow of control signals (from the government to the people) be accompanied by effective upward (from the people to the government) and lateral (among citizens) flows of signals, which express the citizens' values and needs. This may sound like a statement from a high school textbook in civics. And indeed this does approximate the textbook model of democratic processes. The reason this must be explicitly included, aside from the fact that an element cannot be left out of a theory just because it is well known, is that, recently—both in the social sciences and in the educated public—it has been widely held that the citizens can be manipulated by their government. If this is true, the mechanic model of cybernetics would suffice as a model for societal theory; downward flows could characterize the process of societal guidance, as policy and its public acceptance could be engineered jointly. It is our position, however, that the power of governments or the mass media to sway the citizenry has been grossly exaggerated. The majority of the citizens are not a mass of atoms, responding to the speeches by national leaders or the stimuli of their TV sets, but are guided chiefly by their biological needs, personalities formed in their youth, positions in the economic structure and positions in the community. It hence does not come as a surprise to us that practically all studies of the effects of manipulative efforts on substantive matters show little or no effect of either the national leadership or the mass media.[5] These can *temporarily* rally some segments of the public around a war which is

5     Bernard Berelson and Gary A. Steiner, *Human Behavior* (Harcourt, Brace and World, New York, 1964), pp. 574 ff.

against the national interest, but not for long; they can make the public shift from one consumer product to another which is at most marginally different. However, the public's political, religious, ethnic, racial or other more deeply rooted preferences cannot be significantly changed.[6] It is therefore necessary, in seeking to construct a theory of how societies move more effectively toward their own goals, to include *both* the downward flows (to which we refer as societal control) and the upward ones (consensus building) which jointly comprise a theory of societal guidance.

## THE ELEMENTS OF SOCIETAL GUIDANCE

The differences between active and passive societies, between those more and those less capable of handling their problems, are best studied by scrutinizing one factor at a time, although effective guidance requires their combination. The theory which emerges is eclectic in the sense that its various components can be seen as representative of those factors previous theories considered sufficient explanations in themselves. *One* such factor is the amount and quality of knowledge an acting social unit possesses. This 'represents' in our scheme the rationalist viewpoint.

*Knowledge-units*
Upon examination of the amounts of funds, the size of manpower and the extent of expertise devoted to the collecting and processing of knowledge as compared to other activities (e.g., production of goods and services), we gain an impression of how 'knowledgeable' a particular society, government, or federal agency is. Doing so, we are immediately struck with one reason societies often regulate themselves so poorly—they spend relatively very little on knowledge with most of the funds going into the production of knowledge earmarked for the natural sciences (for the study of the non-social environment). When societies deal with poverty, riots, and urban

6    Among the studies which demonstrated this point are, Elaine Cumming and J. Cumming, *Closed Ranks—an Experiment in Mental Health Education* (Harvard University Press, Cambridge, Mass., 1957); Albert D. Biderman, 'The Image of "Brainwashing"', *Public Opinion Quarterly*, Vol. 26 (1962).

problems, they often have little knowledge about the underlying factors, and may even incorrectly identify them. One instance of a policy based on insufficient knowledge is one that American society has followed for more than four decades, a highly punitive policy against the users of marijuana. The assumptions on which this policy is based, that the weed is detrimental to health or that it leads its users to the consumption of other, more dangerous drugs, have yet to be demonstrated. Another example of inadequate researching is provided by experts who urge reducing the relief rolls by sending the 900,000 mothers to work, with their children to be left in day-care centers. Nobody has established yet whether or not this would result in psychological problems for young children such as to create more social costs and human misery than that which the system tried to remove.

Blue ribbon commissions are appointed to study other issues, but these commissions tend to be composed of prestigious citizens rather than experts, citizens who can dedicate only a small part of their time to studying the issue at hand.[7] The President's Commission on Civil Disorder completed its work in about seven months. But its members held full time jobs 'on the side' including such as the mayoralty of New York City or the top position of the United Steel Workers. No wonder the members could devote only a few days to the study of the causes and cures of riots. The situation in the social sciences is not much better: most social scientists' work is not policy-oriented and not readily accessible to key decision-makers. Prestige and promotions go to those who work on theoretical subjects; applied research is discouraged.

The knowledge that is available to experts must be communicated to societal decision-makers before it can be effectively utilized. Even in corporations, the planning as well as the research and development units often have a hard time capturing the attention of key executives. In society, the social distance between the research centers, where many of the best experts work, and Washington, D.C. (let alone city hall and the state capitol) is often vast. 'Retired' scientists,

7        Daniel Bell, 'Government by Commission', *The Public Interest*, No. 3 (Spring, 1966), pp. 3-9; and Robert Blanner, 'Whitewash Over Watts', *Transaction*, Vol. 3 (March-April, 1966), pp. 3-9, 54.

academic statesmen frequently further lengthen the passage. Those federal agencies which have their own 'think-tanks', e.g., RAND for the Air Force,[8] tend to accomplish more, in terms of their respective goals, which shows the importance of systematic 'input' of information and analysis to policy makers. This may seem obvious, but little action has been taken to correct this situation on the domestic front.

*Decision-making*

The examination of how consequential are differences in decision-making styles or strategies, stands in our theory for the consideration of the role of elites and leadership. As we see it, Anglo-Saxon societies are inclined to be 'pragmatic', to 'muddle through', making one small decision at a time; they avoid longer-run overall planning.[9] This approach is quite effective when the environment is relatively stable and the system is basically sound. Then, minor revisions are sufficient. But when major change is required, something more than 'tokenism', these pragmatic societies have a harder time adapting. The war in Vietnam is a case in point. It was escalated gradually, step by step, following neither a 'dove' nor a 'hawk' policy, and it seems without genuine attempts at *basic* change of policy.

Totalitarian societies often err in the opposite direction. They tend to assume they have a much greater capacity to control the society from one center, over more matters, and for a longer period of time than they are actually capable of. Thus, they overplan and often launch major projects, 'Great Leaps', only to be forced to tone them down or revise them at tremendous economic and human cost.[10]

It would be tempting to state that the most effective decision-making strategy is a happy medium, between democratic under-planning and totalitarian over-planning. It seems more accurate to suggest that the capacity of both democratic and totalitarian societies

---

8    For a careful study see Bruce L. R. Smith, 'Strategic Expertise and National Security Policy: A Case Study', in John D. Montgomery and Arthur Smithies (eds.), *Public Policy*, Vol. 13 (1964), pp. 69-106.

9    See Charles E. Lindblom, *The Intelligence of Democracy* (The Free Press, New York, 1965).

10   For a recent study see James R. Townsend, *Political Participation in Communist China* (University of California Press, Berkeley, 1967).

to make encompassing and anticipatory decisions has increased with the improvements that have been occurring rapidly since about 1955 in the technology of communication, knowledge storage and retrieval, computation, and research. That is, we are rapidly gaining *tools* of societal guidance which were not available before. While no society can effectively manage all the matters which totalitarian states seek to control, we have now the capacity for more societal policy-making and guidance than democracies assumed—quite correctly until recently—is feasible.[11]

In addition, it may be said that, to some degree, each society has the decision-making pattern which best suits it. Decision-making strategies are not chosen in a vacuum but partially reflect the political structure of the society. Democratic societies tend toward 'muddling through' because there is no powerful central authority, including the presidency, that can impose a master plan, even if this were otherwise desirable. The policies formulated are the outcome of the give and take of a large variety of interest groups, civic groups, political parties, and varying trends in public opinion. Under these circumstances, straight sailing seems difficult; zig-zagging is the natural course. Totalitarian societies can more easily follow one course but are also much more likely to disregard the feelings and interests of most of their constituencies. A 'middling' policy-making —one deeper and more extensive than democratic decision-making, but also much more humane than totalitarian decision-making— requires not only new technologies of communication and control but also the proper power structure in society.[12]

*Power*
The study of the distribution of power in society and the uses to which it is put represents in our theory the class (or inter-group 'conflict') approach. All societies are composed of sub-groupings of members such as classes, regions, ethnic groups, which differ in the share of the societal assets and power they command. (In our society, obviously, farmhands, black Southerners and Spanish-Americans

---

11     This point has been made by Andrew Shonfield, *Modern Capitalism* (Oxford University Press, New York, 1965).
12     For illustration of this point see Etzioni, *op. cit.*, Chapter 12.

tend to have a smaller proportion of power than their share of the population.) The distribution of power in any one society significantly affects its capacity to treat its problems and to change its structure and policies, if it should be necessary. It is useful to consider the distribution of power from two vantage points: first, between the members of the society and the government and, second, among the members of the society.

The government, and more generally, the state, may overpower the society. This occurs when the state bureaucracies either themselves checkmate most other power centers (e.g., as in contemporary Egypt) or—more commonly—do so in conjunction with some other organization (the Party, in Communist China). On the other hand, the state may be overpowered by society, fragmented the way society frequently is. This has occurred in highly feudalistic societies (e.g., ninth-century France) and continues to occur in contemporary tribal societies (such as Nigeria).

When the state is overpowering, societal guidance tends to be unresponsive to most members' needs and values (as in Stalin's Russia); when it is overpowered, the major societal cybernetic over-layer is knocked out and the society drifts (as is the case in many underdeveloped countries). Only a tense balance between society and state, each one guarding its autonomy, is able to maintain a relatively responsive and active societal guidance. Democracy itself requires such a power constellation: *state power* which limits conflicts among member-groupings (such as classes and races) to non-violent give and take, and prevents the overpowering of some member grouping(s) by others; *autonomous power* of the citizens which maintains the capacity to change the government, i.e., to replace those in power if they cease to be responsive to the plurality of the citizens. The fewer the power differences among the member groupings the more democratic a government can be. As the needs of no member have a superior claim over those of any other, the only way to assure that a society will be responsive to the membership-at-large is to give all members comparable amounts of control over its guidance mechanisms. This means that not just the right to vote, but the socio-economic and educational prerequisites for its effective use, must be extended to all citizens before a democracy can be fully effective.

The special features of the war on poverty illustrate the effect of power relations on societal guidance. The 89th Congress was unusually liberal, due to the anti-Goldwater landslide of 1964, which elected Democrats and liberals where Republicans and conservatives had previously been chosen. This, plus heavy pressure from the President, facilitated passage through Congress of an anti-poverty bill. Its implementation was to rely heavily on 1050 Community Action boards, which would receive anti-poverty funds and manage their programs with 'maximum feasible participation of the poor'. Leaving aside the question whether this would ameliorate the plight of the poor, it surely did not fit the existing power structure, because it by-passed both city hall and the established welfare agencies. In 1966, a fair number of liberals were defeated, less than 3% of the eligible poor voted in elections for the Community Action boards, and by the end of 1967, the anti-poverty program was being restructured so as to bring it under control of the local authorities. Similar points could be made with reference to bussing of school children, attempts to control smoking, or efforts to help the farm-hands. A social program needs political backing; if this is not forth-coming, the program will sooner or later be modified or blocked.

The power relations among the groupings which make up a society shift over time due to a great number of processes, including technological changes, the extension of education, and a rise in the level of self-organization of some previously less organized groups (e.g., Negro-Americans).[13] As power relations change, new programs become feasible, and old ones are undermined. In other cases, new coalitions are formed; for instance, federal aid to education was initiated when a way was found to answer some of the needs of public *and* parochial schools.[14]

*Consensus Building*
Fortunately, societal guidance is activated not only by power but

13        For a good description of the Negro community in Chicago before mobilization see James Q. Wilson, *Negro Politics* (The Free Press, New York, 1960).

14        For a detailed report see Frank J. Munger and Richard F. Fenno, Jr., *National Politics and Federal Aid to Education* (Syracuse University Press, Syracuse, N.Y., 1962).

also by the moral commitments of the citizens. People are motivated not only by self-interest but also by their conceptions of patriotism, social justice, and freedom. Thus, American advocacy of foreign aid, the United Nations, or civil rights can be explained at best partly by the self-interest or power of their advocates. Such values as humanity, peace, and justice have a key role in American subscription to these policies. Now, there is less than full agreement among the people of any country with regard to the values to which they subscribe or the ways they believe those can be advanced. Nor are such positions unchangeable. A program's chances to be successful are greater assuming a given level of power backing, the more it is in accord with the values of the majority of the citizens (or the more it succeeds in obtaining their endorsement, if initially the policy conflicted with their values).

One of the great unanswered questions of our political life is what new or improved mechanisms for consensus building we will evolve. Elections are too infrequent, too indirect, 'mass' phenomena to satisfy the need, especially as more and more facets of the citizen's life are affected, ever more deeply, by the government. Participation in the control of 'private governments', such as those in charge of universities and hospitals, emerges as one intricate answer. *Peaceful* demonstrations, as a routine political tool, provides another. Neither of these is satisfactory; they serve mainly to illustrate the need for more avenues of 'upward' and 'lateral' participation, and attempts made to answer them.

### Active for What ?

Assuming a society developed more effective cybernetic systems— better knowledge, more effective decision-making, higher degree of power balancing for its programs and more consensus to endorse them—which values would it promote and what kind of society would it be?

Social philosophers have tried, at least since the days of Plato's academy and the biblical prophets, to answer these questions, to define the Good Society. The resulting Utopias sound attractive but also frequently leave the reader with an acutely frustrated sense of irrelevancy; these Utopias obviously cannot be realized.

The Utopian writers also tend to assume that the writer, philosopher or social scientist can speak for man, identify his values and needs and proclaim them in the form of an ordered platform. As I see it, such a task is both extremely presumptuous (the Utopia maker plays king if not God) and headed for failure.

The values a society effectively manages will have to be those *its* citizens will seek to advance. A Keynesian theory of societal processes informs the citizenry where to turn to get more of the values more fully and more rapidly realized; it does not tell them what their values ought to be. Actually, only as society becomes more active, both in pursuing its goals and in providing for all its citizens a chance of true and full participation, will many of the members and society, itself, discover what the deeper preferences are.

Social science's answer ought to be sheerly 'procedural'; we should point to ways man may be more in command of societal processes and less subject to his blind fluctuations, rather than spell out where precisely he will guide the processes once he is more involved in decision-making. That, by the way, is prescribed in the traditional conception of democracy as the best way for citizens to choose their government and to make it realize their values. True, an active society will promote several key values, without which it cannot be active, such as the greatest possible participation in its political life. This, in turn, requires a free and informed citizenry, and at least a measure of economic affluence so that the struggle for survival will not take up all their time and energies.[15] But all this put together provides only for a rather 'basic' Utopia; the rest will have to be filled in, by the citizens, acting together to make society more responsive to *their* needs and values. An effective theory of societal guidance cannot determine the goals toward which the system should be directed, any more than can the Keynsian theory tell us whether we ought to prefer economic growth over price stability, full employment over growth, etc. Such theories, can, at best, tell us how to achieve our goals once we formulate them and help us to see the available alternatives.

---

15    S. M. Lipset, 'Some Social Requisites of Democracy', *American Political Science Review*, Vol. 53 (1959), p. 71.

Stein Rokkan

# Models and Methods in the Comparative Study of Nation-Building

Originally presented as a background paper for the UNESCO Symposium, Aspenäs Studiegård nr. Gothenburg, Aug. 28-Sept. 2 1968, itself a revision and extension of a note presented at the preparatory meeting held in Brussels, Sept. 24-25 1967.

The extraordinary growth in the number of legally independent units of government during the 1950s and 1960s has prompted a wide variety of scholarly efforts toward description, analysis and theorizing. The literature generated through these efforts is voluminous and dispersed and has so far never been subject to systematic codification.[1] In this brief paper there can be no question of doing justice to the entire range of approaches to the comparative study of state formation and national development. Only a few lines of attack will be singled out for discussion and even these will not be evaluated in any great detail: the purpose is not to review the past literature but to define priority tasks for future cooperative data processing and interpretation.

*Imbalances in Current Research*

There are curious discontinuities in the history of the comparative study of national development. Karl Deutsch published his pioneering study of *Nationalism and Social Communication* in 1953 and focused all but one of his quantitative analysis of rates of as-

---

[1]    These are probably the most complete bibliographical listings: Koppel S. Pinson. *A Bibliographical Introduction to Nationalism.* (New York: Columbia University Press, 1935). Karl W. Deutsch. *An Interdisciplinary Bibliography on Nationalism. 1935-1953* (Cambridge: M.I.T. Press, 1956). Karl W. Deutsch & R. L. Merritt. *Nationalism and National Development: An Interdisciplinary Bibliography 1935–1956* (Cambridge: M.I.T. Press 1970). For a useful review of major writings from 1953 through 1965 see K. W. Deutsch, *Nationalism and Social Communication* (Second Edition, Cambridge: M.I.T. Press, 1966), pp. 1–14.

similation and mobilization on European nations. Two of these were post-World War I nations: Czechoslovakia and Finland. The third was a nation but not a sovereign state: Scotland. And only the fourth was a new nation of the underdeveloped world: India. These analyses appeared just a few years before the great onrush of new state formations in Africa and Asia: the UN added some fifty new states to its roster of members from 1953 to the end of 1966.

This extraordinarily rapid wave of decolonization and state formation deeply affected the priorities within the social science community from the mid-fifties onward: vast investments were made in research on the political and the economic developments in this 'third world' and a great phalanx of scholars were able to familiarize themselves with the intricacies of these many cases of state formation and initial nation-building. These efforts went beyond mere fact-finding: the great wave of 'third world' studies also triggered impressive efforts of theory construction.

Perhaps the most influential of these efforts of conceptualization and theorizing was the series of studies of political development organized by the Almond-Pye Committee of the American Social Science Research Council:[2] these studies represented a persistent and systematic endeavor to identify crucial variables in a generic process of change from the traditional tribal polity to the modern 'bureaucratic-participant' state and have exerted a great deal of influence on the structure and the style of current research on the politics of the developing countries.

But the very success of these efforts of research on the developing areas of the world threatened to disrupt the continuity of scholarly

---

2    The initial formulations appeared in G. A. Almond and James S. Coleman *eds. The Politics of the Developing Areas* (Princeton, Princeton Univ. Press, 1960). The Committee on Comparative Politics has so far published six volumes in the series *Studies in Political Development* (all with Princeton University Press): L. W. Pye, *ed. Communications and Political Development*, 1963. J. LaPalombara, *ed. Bureaucracy and Political Development*, 1963. R. E. Ward and D. A. Rustow, *eds. Political Modernization in Japan and Turkey*, 1964. J. Coleman, *ed. Education and Political Development*, 1965. L. W. Pye & S. Verba *eds. Political Culture and Political Development*, 1965. J. LaPalombara & M. Weiner, *eds. Political Parties and Political Development*, 1966.

concern with processes of state formation and nation-building: the theories of the late fifties and the early sixties tended to concentrate exclusively on the experiences and the potentialities of the polities just emerging from colonial status and showed only minimal concern with the early histories of nation-building in Europe and in the European-settled territories. The idea of the participant nation-state was European in origin and had been exported to the developing world through colonization and ideological diffusion: yet there was a great deal of reluctance to draw directly on the rich European experience in developing models for the explanation of the processes of change inherent in the growth of national polities. There were many reasons for this reluctance: the great complexity of the European developments, the linguistic difficulties, the low level of communication between historians and generalizing social scientists. It was easier to deal in comparative terms with the less history-burdened, less documented and less scrutinized countries of the developing world: the working languages were fewer because of the colonial inheritance, and there were fewer professional historians around to question the interpretations and the classifications of the social scientists.

There are many signs of uneasiness about this gap. A number of comparisons across the developed and the developing polities have been published in recent years and still more are under way and will help to pave the way for a *rapprochement*.[3] The Committee on Comparative Politics has itself given increasing attention to the peculiarities of the developments in Europe and has encouraged attempts to incorporate the variations within Europe in a broader model of political modernization.[4] A number of attempts have been made at comparisons across pairs or multiples of contrasting polities in the West and the East: among the most important of these are

---

3    Cf. especially J. LaPalombara 'Parsimony and Empiricism in Comparative Politics: an Anti-Scholastic View', R. Holt & J. Turner eds. *Methodology of Comparative Research* (N.Y. Free Press 1970).

4    Several of the publications flowing from the Committee or its individual members evidence interest in the theoretical implications of the variations within Europe and the West, see especially G. Almond and S. Verba. *The Civic Culture* (Princeton: Princeton University Press, 1963) and G. Almond and G. B. Powell, Jr. *Comparative Politics: a Developmental Approach* (Boston: Little, Brown, 1966).

Reinhard Bendix's work on aspects of nation-building in Germany, Russia, Japan and India,[5] Robert Holt and John Turner's paired comparisons of England and Japan, France and China,[6] Barrington Moore's analysis of the economic basis of political development in England, France, the United States and Germany, Russia, China, India and Japan.[7] Lipset's attempt at a comparison of the early stages of nation-building in the United States with the current efforts of integration and consolidation in the newest states of Africa and Asia[8] points in the same direction and so does Samuel Huntington's current work on contrasts in the timing of social and political modernization.[9] Karl Deutsch and his team at Yale, since 1966 at Harvard, have extended the programme of research implicit in the 1953 volume: Deutsch has not only deepened his analysis of conditions and varieties of nation-building through his work on the Swiss case[10] but he has also built up, with his colleagues, an important computer archive of data on the new as well as the old units of the expanding international system.[11]

These varied attempts at bridge-building across the great gap in the comparative study of political development have helped to clarify the priorities of further research but have barely scratched the surface of the vast masses of data to be processed in any serious and systematic effort to test alternative models and hypotheses.

---

5        R. Bendix, *Nation-Building and Citzenship* (New York: Wiley, 1964).

6        R. Holt & J. Turner. *The Political Basis of Economic Development* (Princeton: Van Nostrand, 1966).

7        Barrington Moore, Jr. *Social Origins of Dictatorship and Democracy: Lord and Peasant in the Making of the Modern World* (Boston: Beacon Press, 1966).

8        S. M. Lipset. *The First New Nation* (New York: Basic Books, 1963).

9        Samuel P. Huntington 'Political Development and Political Decay' *World Pol.* 17(3) April 1965 386-430; 'Political Modernization: America *vs.* Europe' *World Pol.* 18(3) April 1966: 378-414.

10       K. W. Deutsch and H. Weilemann 'The Swiss City Canton: a Political Invention' *Comp. Stud. Soc. Hist.*, 7(4) July 1965: 393-408 and *United for Diversity: The Political Integration of Switzerland*, forthcoming 1972.

11       B. Russett *et al. World Handbook of Political and Social Indicators* (New Haven: Yale Univ. Press, 1964), cf. the further discussion in R. L. Merritt & S. Rokkan *eds. Comparing Nations* (New Haven: Yale Univ. Press, 1966).

There are still marked imbalances in the ranges of cases and variables covered in comparative analysis of processes of political development:

(1) *The large-nation bias*
—most comparisons, whether within the West or with developing polities, have limited themselves to the larger and more influential units[12] and have tended to neglect the richly varied experiences of the smaller polities, particularly the many European 'secession states' after 1814, 1830 and 1918 and their histories of nation-building: these are, after all, the units most immediately comparable to recently formed states of the 'third world'.

(2) *The 'whole-nation' bias*
—most comparisons have been limited to institutional or aggregate statistical data for each nation as a unit and have tended to neglect highly significant variations in the rates of growth among competing

---

12    Cf. a typical remark by Barrington Moore, *op. cit.*, pp. XII-XIII: 'This study concentrates on certain important stages in a prolonged social process which has worked itself out in several countries. As a part of this process new social arrangements have grown up by violence or in other ways which have made certain countries political leaders at different points in time during the first half of the twentieth century. The focus of interest is on innovation that has led to political power, not only the spread and reception of institutions that have been hammered out elsewhere, except where they have led to significant power in world politics. *The fact that the smaller countries depend economically and politically on big and powerful ones means that the decisive causes of their politics lie outside their own boundaries. It also means that their political problems are not really comparable to those of larger countries. Therefore a general statement about the historical preconditions of democracy or authoritarianism covering smaller countries as well as large would very likely be so broad as to be abstractly platitudinous'* (our italics). Clearly, there are as good intellectual reasons for studying diffusion and reception as for analyzing conflict and innovation in major centres: after all, most of the units open to comparative research are 'follower' nations rather than leaders. But this surely is not always and exclusively a matter of size: Greece and Israel produced the greatest innovations of the ancient world and Sweden, the Netherlands and Switzerland can hardly be fruitfully studied as passive victims of exogenous pressures.

economic, political or cultural centres and between such centres and the rural peripheries.[13]

### (3)  The 'economic growth' bias
—most comparisons have limited themselves to the most easily accessible time series data from censuses and economic bookkeeping statistics and have neglected a wide range of less complete data series for levels and rates of social, educational and cultural mobilization, all processes of crucial importance in the study of nation-building.

This paper will discuss alternative strategies in coping with these deficiencies in the data bases for comparative developmental analysis:
—it will first review salient features of recently advanced *models of nation-building*
—it will pass on to a listing of *priority variables* for comparative data collation and analysis
—and it will wind up with some suggestions for *international action* to accelerate the development and testing of different models through a series of encounters between historians and social scientists.

### A Sample of Models
Models of political development vary along a variety of dimensions: in their logical structure and their openness to direct empirical testing, in the number and precision of the variables and in the possibilities of adequate matching with actual or potential data sources, in the ranges of historically given variations they seek to explain.

Let us, to simplify the mapping of variations in the organization of models, try to locate a few of the best-known ones within a two-dimensional diagram inspired by Talcott Parsons.[14]

---

13    For discussions of the 'whole nation' bias in the draft version of the Russett *et al.*, *World Handbook* see Part III of Merritt-Rokkan *eds. Comparing Nations, op. cit.* Also B. J. L. Berry, 'By What Categories May a State Be Characterized?' *Econ. Devel. and Cult. Change* 15(1) Oct. 1966, 91-94.
        This 'hierarchization' of the Parsonian *A—G—I—L* scheme of functional differentiation was first presented in the Introduction to S. M. Lipset and S. Rokkan *eds. Party Systems and Voter Alignments* [over

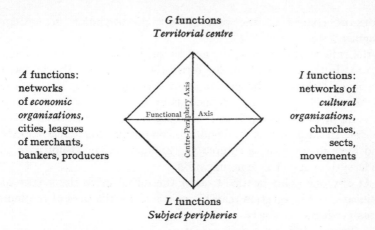

*G* functions
*Territorial centre*

*A* functions:
networks
of *economic*
*organizations,*
cities, leagues
of merchants,
bankers, producers

*I* functions:
networks of
*cultural*
*organizations,*
churches,
sects,
movements

*L* functions
*Subject peripheries*

Karl Deutsch focuses on the centre-periphery axis: his model is primarily designed to predict variations in the extent of territorial-cultural integration through the joint, but not necessarily parallel, processes of national standardization and social mobilization: his dependent variables bear on *nation-building* and his model simply assumes some initial level of state formation through inter-elite coalitions.

The Deutsch model is particularly appropriate in the study of the actual or potential breakup of multi-lingual empires: it is no accident that his four examples of quantitative analysis bear on such linguistically divided territories as Finland (Finnish vs. Swedish), Bohemia-Moravia-Silesia (Czech vs. German), Scotland (Gaelic vs. English) and India-Pakistan (Hindi vs. other vernaculars vs. English).

The model posits a *centre* and a *leading group of active 'nation-builders'* and seeks to specify the conditions for the development, within the territory controlled from this centre or reached by this group, of a *culturally cohesive, or at least complementary, community* clearly distinct from the surrounding populations.[15]

The core of the model explores the interrelations between two

cont'd (New York: Free Press, 1967). For a further utilization of this imagery in the study of the international system see J. P. Nettl and R. Robertson, *International Systems and the Modernization of Societies* (London: Faber, 1968) pp. 162-168.

15 Deutsch, *Nationalism*, 2nd ed. pp. 101-104.

rates of change in the process of nation-building or nation-fragmentation:

—the rate of *assimilation*, defined as an increase or decrease from $t_1$ to $t_2$ in the subset (A) of the territorial population (P) who have become speakers of the predominant ('nation-building') language;

—the rate of *mobilization*, defined as an increase or decrease from $t_1$ to $t_2$ in the subset (M) of P who are no longer exclusively tied to the traditional, locally-bounded communication environments and have in some sense entered the broader, urban, if not nation-wide, system of social communication.[16]

At any one point in time $t_i$ after the initial drive the extent of unification or integration may be measured by the sizes of the four cross-products of these two dichotomies:

the *mobilized and assimilated* ($M_A$)
the *mobilized but still differentiated* ($M_D$)
the *underlying but assimilated* ($U_A$)
the *underlying and differentiated* ($U_D$)

The rise and fall in these shares of the territorial population from one point in time to another will obviously be affected by the inter-action between the two processes of change but the character of this interaction will vary over time and as a function of the levels already reached on each variable. A number of extraneous variables will also affect the inter-relations of assimilation and mobilization: differential fertility and mortality, the economic or military strength of alternative centres or clusters of nation-builders, the extent of exogenous mobilization through economic, ecclesiastical or other cultural networks.

There is no attempt in *Nationalism and Social Communication* to spell out in any formal detail the consequences of this simple model: there is a brief mathematical appendix on the relationships between the principal rates of change distinguished[17] but there are no explicit

---

16    See the definitions *ibid*. Ch. 6. For a further elaboration of the concept of mobilization see Karl Deutsch 'Social Mobilization and Political Development', *American Political Science Review* 65(3) Sept. 1961: 493-514.
A similar listing of variables is discussed in S. Rokkan 'Electoral Mobilization, Party Competition and National Integration', in J. LaPalombara & M. Weiner, *op. cit.*

17    *Nationalism*, 2nd ed., Appendix V.

formulations of functional relationships between the rates of assimilation and mobilization and the finally generated national structure. There is a series of illuminating applications to concrete historical developments but no easily identifiable generalizations for empirical testing across a broad range of nations. Karl Deutsch's model is essentially heuristic: it suggests a priority in comparative data collation and then simply exhorts us to develop generalizations inductively through the processing of such materials.

The Deutsch model fired the imagination of a number of scholars: it was a first attempt to apply notions from information theory and cybernetics to the study of political development and it pointed to exciting possibilities of empirical testing through the construction of quantitative indicators from historical statistical data. But the core of the model limited itself to *mass effects*: the focus was primarily on the incorporation of peripheral populations within some form of national community, much less on the actual political or administrative measures of nation-building at the territorial centres or on the conflicts among competing elites and organizations over such policies.

A variety of difficulties, terminological, conceptual, empirical, confront the student of processes of centre formation. In this quick review we shall focus on attempts to cut across the historically inherited confusions of national terminologies through the identification of discriminating variables and through the development of models for the cross-classification of cases and the establishment of distinctive syndromes and configurations.

Much of the literature in this field focuses on single cases of centre formation and nation-building and offers only *ad hoc* comparisons: outstanding examples are Lipset's interpretation of the United States as *The First New Nation* and Ralf Dahrendorf's *Gesellschaft und Demokratie in Deutschland.*[18] Conceptually and empirically much more taxing, but of greater potential value in the development of systematic macro-theory, is the strategy of *paired comparisons* attempted in a number of recent writings. Such confrontations of

---

18    R. Dahrendorf. *Gesellschaft und Demokratie in Deutschland* (Munich: Piper, 1965), cf. the parallel analysis of central political institutions in K. D. Bracher, 'Staatsbegriff und Demokratie in Deutschland' *Pol. Vierteljahresschr.* 9(1) 1968: 2-27.

pairs of contrasting cases of centre formation and nation-building may not only offer opportunities for a deepening of insights into the dynamics of each system but also offer springboards for further model building across a broader range of cases.

This strategy is well-known in comparative economic history: consider Clapham's classic study of the French and the German economies,[19] Habakkuk's path-breaking study of technological developments in Britain and the United States,[20] Kindleberger's attempt at a systematic confrontation of data on society and economy in Britain and France.[21] Students of comparative political development have found the method of paired contrasts of great value, both as a device in the ordering and evaluation of data, and as a procedure in the generation of hypotheses and insights. Possibly the best example of a collective effort of this type is the symposium organized by the Almond-Pye Committee on contrasts in the development of the Japanese and the Turkish political systems.[22] Excellent examples of the use of this strategy in a broader context of theory development are Reinhard Bendix's work on the development of territorial systems of public authority in Prussia/Germany and Russia and in India and Japan[23] and Robert Holt and John Turner's[24] paired comparisons of two early industrializers, England and Japan, with two late industrializers, France and China. Both these works focus on variations in the distinctiveness, the strength and the cohesion of the centre-forming collectivities in each territory: the aim is to pinpoint contrasts in the characteristics of the agencies of territorial decision-making and control and to develop models for the explanation of such contrasts. Bendix's analysis focuses on the tactics of centre-forming collectivities, dynastic

---

19     J. H. Clapham. *The Economic Development of France and Germany* (Cambridge: Cambridge University Press, 1921).

20     H. J. Habakkuk. *American and British Technology in the 19th Century* (Cambridge: Cambridge University Press, 1962).

21     Ch. P. Kindleberger. *Economic Growth in France and Britain, 1851-1950* (Cambridge, Mass. Harvard Univ. Press, 1964).

22     R. E. Ward and D. Rostow eds. *Political Modernization in Japan and Turkey, op. cit.*

23     R. Bendix, *Nation-Building and Citzenship, op. cit.*

24     R. Holt and J. Turner. *The Political Basis of Economic Development, op. cit.*

bureaucracies and military organizations in breaking down local solidarities and creating direct links between the territorial nation and its individual subjects through the development of universalistic criteria of citizen rights and citizen obligations. The study by Holt and Turner is organized around a distinctive hypothetico-deductive model: it seeks to test a set of propositions about the likelihood of economic innovations under different conditions of administrative centralization.

These studies help to underscore the importance of the 'centre' variables for an understanding of contrasts in nation-building processes. Nationalization processes in the territorial peripheries are clearly conditioned by circumstances of cultural as well as physical distance and by the possibilities of concerted mobilization of local resources against the standardizing agencies but the *contents* of the communications spread through the actual or potential national territory are primarily determined by the centre-forming collectivities. No typology of nation-building processes can be developed without an analysis of variations in the structures and the functions of the territorial centres. Among recent attempts at classifications of such structures two deserve particular attention: Samuel Huntington's analysis of the contrast between the United States and what he calls 'Europe', in fact primarily England, France, Prussia and Sweden, and Peter Nettl's effort to identify dimensions of 'stateness'. Huntington's much-discussed article focuses on the origins of the marked differences in the speed of political modernization between England and France on the one hand and the United States on the other. This dependent variable is a composite of several indicators of organizational complexity: the extent to which traditional, familial, religious and ethnic authorities have been replaced by a single, secular, nation-centered political authority, the extent of differentiation within the political and the bureaucratic machinery, and the extent of the development of parties and interest associations for the channeling and mobilization of popular participation.[25] His explanatory variables are essentially social-structural: the higher levels of centralization and administrative differentiation characteristic of a number of European polities can only be understood

---

25     Huntington, 'Political Modernization', *op. cit.* p. 378.

against the background of long histories of feudal resistance and of secular-religious conflicts; the 'fusion of functions' and the 'division of power' characteristic of the United States could only emerge in a settler society freed from any legacy of feudalism and unencumbered by entanglements with a dominant supranational Church.[26] Peter Nettl goes one step further: relying heavily on Weber's analysis of the growth of bureaucratic organizations, he suggests a scheme for the rank ordering of historically given political systems on a number of dimensions of 'stateness'.[27] He does not attempt any detailed ordering of a wide range of polities along such dimensions but concentrates his attention on four significant cases: Prussia/Germany, France, Britain and the United States. The Continental polities were built up around increasingly autonomous bodies of territorial administrators, British polity around the coalitions of elite 'establishments' embodied in parties while the American polity stuck to what Huntington calls the 'Tudor constitution' in its heavier emphasis on the integrative role of the courts and the legal profession. Schemes of this type clearly have to be spelled out in greater detail before they can be subjected to tests against empirical indicators: among the most obvious ones would be time series data on the growth of full-time administrative personnel in each territory, on the economic resource bases of each category of administrators, their family and kin links to local power-holders, the distinctiveness of their education, the standardization of criteria of entry and promotion. The marked variations in administrative structures within the 'developed' world have never been adequately mapped: Huntington and Nettl tend to group together in their 'European-Continental' category markedly different cases of centre-formation. Clearly, we cannot expect much progess in the empirical testing of models of political development without some concerted action to organize confrontations between generalizing social scientists and students steeped in the administrative histories of pairs or triples of developed systems, smaller as well as larger.

The great merit of Nettl's analysis in this context is his systematic

---

26    *Ibid.*, pp. 401-408.
27    J. P. Nettl, 'The State as a Conceptual Variable', *World Politics* 20(4) 1968: 559–592. My own work in this field owes very much to Nettl's insight.

insistence on the logical and empirical independence of the variables 'state-ness' and 'nation-ness': there have been many examples of non-national states and there are a great number of national polities without any 'intrasocietal' state apparatus. A territorial nation need not be built around an autonomous state in the Weberian sense. 'What constitutes nations is surely the organized diffusion of common experience, and this may be structured and experienced by a King, leader, church, party, army *or* state—or all of them'.[28] In this style of conceptualization the term 'nation-state' is an unfortunate misnomer: 'If the entry of the third world onto the stage of modern socioscientific consciousness has had one immediate result (or should have had), it is *the snapping of the link between state and nation*'.[29] In the language of our Parsonian diagram the national centre can be organized around collectivities and coalitions varying markedly in power resources and styles of legitimation: the national centre need not constitute a 'state' except in the elementary sense that it is the locus of external representation.

This is the great thrust of Barrington Moore's path-breaking analysis of the centre-forming coalitions of the leading powers of the modern world[30]: he proposes a model of 'polity-building' options and seeks to substantiate a set of propositions about the consequences of such options for the structuring of the central institutions in each territory.

Moore's model posits four sets of actors in the historical process of change from traditional to modern society: the central dynasty and its bureaucracy, the trading and manufacturing bourgeoisie in the cities, the lords of the land, and the peasantry. None of these four sets of actors is strong enough to constitute a centre-forming collectivity on its own: the model forces them to enter into coalitions by pairs or triples and at least one set of actors will be left outside to form an opposition front against this 'nation-building alliance'.

Moore does not attempt any formalization of his model but the underlying combinations are easily spelled out. The system mathe-

---

28   *Ibid.*, pp. 565-566. Nettl's italics.
29   *Ibid.*, p. 560, my italics.
30   B. Moore, *The Social Origins, op. cit.*

matically allows six two-against-two and four three-against-one coalitions. Four of these are highly unlikely to occur in any historical situation: the likelihood of any form of bourgeois-peasant co-operation is very small and so is a direct landowner-peasant front against the others. Of the remaining six coalitions Moore singles out four for detailed study: these are the ones he uses in his attempts to explain the variations among seven of his eight leading polities and at the same time constitutes the alternatives he finds it most fruitful to concentrate on in his analysis of the one deviant case, India.

The four alliance options and their consequences in the seven empirical cases may be set out schematically as follows:

| Type of coalition | Cases | Decisive modernizing revolution | Consequences for structure of polity |
| --- | --- | --- | --- |
| Urban with Landed interests | Britain | Puritan Rev. 1640-1660: subordination of dynastic bureaucracy. | Weak, elite-dominated bureaucracy, rule through alternation of parties. |
| Urban with Landed interests | U.S. | Civil War 1860-65: defeat of Southern 'Junkers'. | Weak, dispersed bureaucracy; rule through pluralist bargaining between courts and established interests. |
| Urban with Landed interests and with Bureaucracy | France | Great Rev. 1789-1815: abolition of feudal privileges, but increased openings for bourgeois land ownership and strengthened peasantry. | Strongly centralized egalitarian-competitive bureaucracy; oscillation between plebiscitarian rule and fragmented multiparty bargaining. |

| Type of coalition | Cases | Decisive modernizing revolution | Consequences for structure of polity |
|---|---|---|---|
| *Landed* interests with *Bureaucracy* | Prussia German *Reich* | No 'bourgeois' revolution: failure in 1848. Modernization from above: alliance of bureaucracy, armed forces and Junker landowners. | Strong, elite-dominated bureaucracy, autocratic rule leading to mass dictatorship. |
| | Japan | No revolution: Imperial Restoration in 1868 through action of modernizing landowners. | Feudalized bureaucracy, autocratic rule leading to period of fascist-military domination. |
| *Bureaucracy* with *peasantry* | Russia | October Rev. 1917: temporary coalition of peasantry with party bureaucracy against the old 'agrarian bureaucracy', the landowners and the (weak) bourgeoisie. | Strong centralizing bureaucracy, single-party rule. |
| | China | Long March 1934: party-peasantry coalition against traditional gentry-scholar bureaucracy. | Single-party rule. |

This schema obviously cannot do full justice to Moore's richly faceted comparative analysis but it does help to bring out the structure of the argument. In the language of a Parsonian diagram the Moore model concentrates on variables on the $G$-$A$-$L$ side: on options on the economic front. Linguistic and religious variations enter only marginally into the discussion. True enough, Moore does analyze the weight of religious traditions in the structuring of elite coalitions and peasant reactions in his comparison of India, Japan and China, but he quickly comes to the conclusion that the inherited system of beliefs and ritual was less important than the style of centre-formation: in India continuous segmentation through the operation of caste codes, in Japan fragmentation of peasant oppositions through the feudal control system, in China a much higher level of vulnerability to peasant mobilization because of the heavy concentration of power in the 'agrarian bureaucracy'. Moore is anxious to keep his model free of redundancies: the merit of his analysis lies exactly in the parsimony of his selection of explanatory variables. But this leaves the question of the *range of variations to be accounted for* in any such model of centre-formation and nation-building. Moore argues strongly for a concentration of attention on leading nations: his model focuses on the variations among the eight economically and politically most powerful polities of the modern world and explicitly leaves out of consideration all the smaller and less influential units of the international system. He even goes so far as to the question the possibility of any general model of political development:'. . . a general statement about the historical preconditions of democracy or authoritarianism covering small countries as well as large would very likely be so broad as to be abstractly platitudinous'.[31]

Moore is probably right in questioning the possibility of constructing empirically models for cross-polity variations at all levels of size *across all cultural regions of the world*: this may work, as he so ably shows, for large and powerful units, but the smaller political systems tend to be so heavily dependent on their cultural contexts that there is likely to be very small payoffs in attempts at indiscriminate comparisons across distinctive cultural regions. This still

---

31    Moore, *op. cit.*, p. XIII.

leaves one important strategy open: the development of *region-specific models* for the explanation of variations in centre-formation and nation-building. Such regionally focused models cannot fruitfully be restricted to the large and powerful leader polities: on the contrary the purpose is to account for variations among *all* the distinctive polities in the region and this requires direct attention to the possible consequences of such factors as size, economic resource potential and location in the international power system.

A model of this type has been sketched out for one cultural region of the world: it differs markedly from Moore in its dependent variable but is astoundingly similar in its logical structure. Seymour Martin Lipset and I presented a first version of this model in our Introduction to the volume *Party Systems and Voter Alignments*:[32] we developed a scheme of successive 'option points' in each nation-building history to account for variations in the party systems which emerged in Western Europe with the extension of the suffrage to all adult men. In my further work on 'the politics of the smaller European democracies',[33] I have tried to extend the model to account for variations in the entire process of mass mobilization: differences in the sequences and the timing of measures of democratization as well as differences in the aggregation of party fronts across historically given cleavage lines.

By contrast to Moore's schema, this model posits initial variations on both sides of the Parsonian diagram: the $G$ - $A$ - $L$ side as well as the $G$ - $I$ - $L$ side. The model proceeds in two steps: at the first step it maps variations in the *preconditions* for actual or potential nation-building in the period *before* the decisive thrusts towards mass mobilization in the wake of the French Revolution, at the second it traces options at a number of choice points in the early histories of mass politics in each country.

Again very schematically, the determining variable of the model can be set out as follows:

---

32    S. M. Lipset and S. Rokkan 'Cleavage Structures, Party Systems and Voter Alignments: an Introduction', in S. M. Lipset and S. Rokkan eds. *Party Systems and Voter Alignments* (New York: Free Press, 1967), pp. 1-64.

33    On this project see V. R. Lorwin 'Historians and other Social Scientists: the Comparative Study of Nation-Building in Western Societies', [*over*

| I. | Precondition variables | Location in diagram | Alternative states of system |
|---|---|---|---|
| 1 | Territorial | G—L | Timing of territorial consolidation secession:<br>—before 1648<br>—after Napoleonic wars |
| 2.1 | Cultural: *language* | L—I | Cultural dependence on outside metropolitan centre:<br>—high (same language)<br>—divided<br>—low |
| 2.2 | Cultural: *religion* | G—I | State-Church settlement:<br>—All Protestant<br>—Catholic minority<br>—Independent Catholic (France)<br>—Counter-Reformation State-Church alliance. |
| 3 | Economic | G—A | Centralization of urban network:<br>—monocephalic<br>—polycephalic |
| 4 | Political | G | Structure of central decision-making organs:<br>—continuous history of corporate participation, representation (city councils, estate assemblies)<br>—significant period of absolute monarchic rule |

*contd.*   in S. Rokkan *ed. Comparative Research Across Cultures and Nations, op. cit.* A first report on an attempt at a systematization of data on electoral arrangements and party systems in these eleven countries (the five Nordic countries, the three BE-NE-LUX ones, Ireland, Switzerland and Austria) will be found in S. Rokkan 'The Structuring of Mass Politics in the Smaller European Democracies', *Comp. Stud. Soc. Hist.* 10(2) 1968: 173–210. Cf. also *Citizens, Elections, Parties* (N.Y.: McKay, 1970).

| II. | System options | Location in diagram | Critical juncture | Alternatives |
|---|---|---|---|---|
| | 1 Cultural | L—I | 'Reformation': identification of culture and territory | —one standard national language, suppression of alternatives<br>—one or more minor (subject) languages tolerated<br>—two standard languages |
| | | G—I | National Revolution: control of educational agencies | —national Church allied to secular State<br>—supranational Church (Roman Catholic Church) allied to national State<br>—secular State opposed to supra-national Church |
| | 2 Economic | L—A | Industrial Revolution: agricultural versus commercial-industrial interests | —State allied to agricultural interests (high corn tariff)<br>—State allied to commercial-industrial interests (low tariff) |
| | | G—A | Industrial Revolution: owner versus worker interests | —protect rights of owners/employers<br><br>—protect rights of workers/propertyless |

These variations in nation-building history serve in the next round as parameters in propositions about steps in the democratization process and about the generation of party systems. The 'precondition' variables help to predict variations in the timing of decisions on democratization, the 'system option' variables to account for variations in party systems. In a fuller statement of the model the linkages between the early preconditions and the later system options will be spelt out in greater detail: in this context our primary concern is to bring out the similarities and the differences in structure between the Moore model for the eight world powers and this model for eleven smaller and five larger polities of Western Europe.

Moore's model focuses on the $L$-$A$ option but at a different stage in the development of each system: he seeks to characterize the conditions for alliances between rural and urban interests in the centuries before the National and the Industrial Revolutions and tries to generate propositions about the chances for competitive pluralist democracy or authoritarian monolithic rule given the variations in such initial conditions. In our model these early alliance conditions were not brought in to explain variations in the stages and the timing of the decisions on democratization: the $L$-$A$ alternatives were not included among the 'preconditions' variables, only at the level of elite options accounting for the structuring of the national party systems (II.2 above). This difference in the strategy of explanation has obvious consequences for the classification of empirical cases. Moore contrasts the English and the Prussian developments on the basis of the alliance choice of the landowners while our party systems model groups the two together because they constitute a configuration unlikely to lead to distinctive agrarian party formations.[34] All this finally comes down to a decision about the ranges of dependent variables to be accounted for in the model. Our eleven plus five country scheme restricts itself rigorously to the tasks of predicting variations in the steps taken towards full-suffrage democracy and in the character of the national party systems by the 1920s. Such a model does not necessarily generate propositions about the *stability* or the *vulnerability* of such full-

---

34        Lipset-Rokkan, *op. cit.*, pp. 44-46.

suffrage systems.[35] This is a different task: Moore has pointed to a possible scheme of explanation for the larger powers but has made no effort to account for variations among polities at varying levels of size and economic strength; in fact he rejects this task as unworthy of his intellectual efforts. To students of comparative nation-building this constitutes a real challenge: the small nations have developed their own distinctive strategies of consolidation and survival, they have accumulated a wealth of experiences of conflict resolution and institution-building, and there are enough of them to tempt the ingenuities of all manner of generalizers and model-builders.

We are, it is true, still far from any sort of general consensus on procedures in such comparative studies of nation-building. A number of enthusiasts have tried to develop schemes for world-wide comparisons of the nation-building process. Karl Deutsch's data bank was organized for this purpose; Arthur Banks and Robert Textor included all UN members in their *Cross-Polity Survey*;[36] Gabriel Almond, Lucian Pye and their colleagues have proposed paradigms for the comparison of nation-building processes wherever they might occur.[37] Our objectives in constructing a model for the eleven smaller and the five larger countries of Western Europe were much more restricted: our model is confined to the territories of Europe affected by the drive toward state-formation and the struggle with the supranational church in the 16th and the 17th centuries and serves to identify only the minimum of elements in the histories of these countries which help to predict the later variations in electoral arrangements and party systems. These are deliberate and programmatic restrictions: they serve to increase the possibilities of operationalization and empirical testing but for that very reason do not claim validity for polities developed from other initial conditions,

---

35     Cf. the discussion of the conditions for the breakdown of European multi-party systems in Lipset-Rokkan, *op. cit.*, pp. 50-56.

36     A. Banks and R. Textor, *A Cross-Polity Survey* (Cambridge: M.I.T. Press, 1963).

37     See the volumes listed in footnote 2 and especially Lucian Pye, *Aspects of Political Development* (Boston: Little & Brown, 1965) and 'Political Systems and Political Development' in S. Rokkan ed. *Comparative Research across Cultures and Nations* (Paris: Mouton, 1968), pp. 93-101.

or for other ranges of dependent variables. It is hoped, of course, that this is a case of *reculer pour mieux sauter*: similarly region-specific models are under construction for Latin America[38] and could certainly be developed for other parts of the world. Whether in the end it will be possible to validate universal, world-wide models of political development must still remain an open question: a great deal of hard work will have to be done, not only on the internal logic of each effort of model-building, but even more on the systematic coding of information country by country to test the alternative derivations of the models already advanced.

### Priority Variables for Comparative Developmental Research

However controversial the models, however imprecise the concepts, there is already a greal deal of implicit consensus on the ranges of data required for the testing of alternative derivations. There may be significant differences in the *strategy of data assembly and processing*: some of us find it easier to work with the extant series of bookkeeping data and simply want to transfer a maximum of the already coded information on to cards or tape for computer processing, while others among us are willing and anxious to take on the much more laborious, but possibly more rewarding, task of imposing their own classification schemes on the wealth of 'process produced' material they find at hand country by country, be they biographical records, legislative or ministerial documents, or literary products. Some division of labour is clearly essential: no single center can work on all countries and on all variables with any hope of intellectual payoff. But there *is* a need for cross-communication and a minimum of co-ordination. The 'archival revolution' will soon catch up with the vast masses of bookkeeping data for the 19th and early 20th centuries: these efforts will clearly help forward the work on each of the *national* sequences of development, but if they are also to advance *comparative* analysis, facilities will have to be set up for regular consultations on the definition of the variables, the coding schemes, data management, practices and analysis tools.

Gabriel Almond, Lucian Pye and their associates have suggested

---

38      Cf. O. Cornblit, T. DiTella & E. Gallo 'A Model for Political Change in Latin America'. *Soc. Sci. Info.* 7(2) 1968, 13-48.

a paradigm which may offer a convenient grid for the ordering of variables in such comparative research.

This paradigm is organized around six 'crises of development': these constitute challenges, issues, policy options, to be faced in the course of *any* process of nation-building.

Very schematically these six critical junctures can be described as follows:[39]

| Crises, challenges, problems | Institutional solutions: examples | Corresponding locations in A-G-I-L diagram[40] |
| --- | --- | --- |
| Penetration | Establishment of a rational field administration for resource mobilization (taxes, manpower), creation of public order, and the coordination of collective efforts (infrastructure development, emergency action, defense). | $G \rightarrow L$ (extension of centre control over periphery). |
| Integration | Establishment of allocation rules equalizing the shares of offices, benefits, resources among all culturally and/or politically distinct sectors of the national community. | $G \rightarrow I$ (sharing of control powers across elites, segments, strata). |
| Participation | Extension of suffrage to hitherto under-privileged strata of population. Protection of the rights of organized opposition. | $I \rightarrow L$ (equalisation of opportunities in mobilization markets). |

39 This schematic presentation reflects a reading of *early* drafts of chapters for the prospective volume on *Crises of Political Development*. These drafts were given restricted circulation by the Committee in 1967: James S. Coleman 'The Development Syndrome', draft Jan. 1965, 35 pp. Lucian Pye 'Identity and Legitimacy: Crises of the Political Culture', draft 1965, 96 pp. Myron Weiner 'Participation and Integration: Crises of the Political Process', draft 1965, 46 pp. Sidney Verba 'Crises, Capabilities and Sequences', draft June 1965, 60 pp.

40 These interpretations have not been checked with members of the SSRC Committee.

| Crises, challenges, problems | Institutional solutions: examples | Corresponding locations in A-G-I-L diagram[40] |
|---|---|---|
| Identity | Development of media and agencies for the socialization of future citizens into the national community: schools, literary media, institutionalized rituals and symbols (myths, flags, songs). | $L \rightarrow G$ (acceptance/support of territorial agencies). |
| Legitimacy | Any effort to create loyalty to and confidence in the established structure of political institutions in the given system and to ensure regular conformity to rules and regulations issued by the agencies authorized within the system. | $I \rightarrow G$ (acceptance/support of distribution of control powers). |
| Distribution | Establishment of social services and social security measures, income equalization through progressive taxation and transfer between poorer and richer localities. | $G \rightarrow A \rightarrow L$ (central control of labour-commodity markets). |

The sequences of such critical challenges will of course vary markedly from case to case. In the older European polities the challenges of state-building had to be faced long before the crises of identity and legitimacy triggered by the spread of the ideas of the French Revolution. In the later secession states and for the states emerging from the colonial empires in the 'third world' the time order of crises differed markedly from the earlier sequences and tended to cumulate one upon the other without much let-up. Lucian Pye's ordering and description of the six crises essentially fits the ideal-typical inchoate state emerging from colonial dependence:[41]

*The Identity Crisis.* The first and most fundamental crisis is that of achieving a common sense of identity. The people in a new state must come to recognize their national territory as being their true

---

41    L. W. Pye 'Political Systems and Political Development', *op. cit.*

homeland, and they must feel as individuals that their own personal identities are in part defined by their identification with their territorially delimited country. In most of the new states traditional forms of identity ranging from tribe or caste to ethnic and linguistic groups compete with the sense of larger national identity.

The identity crisis also involves the resolution of the problem of traditional heritage and modern practices, the dilemma of parochial sentiments and cosmopolitan practices. As long as people feel pulled between two worlds and without roots in any society they cannot have the firm sense of identity necessary for building a stable, modern nation-state.

*The Legitimacy Crisis.* Closely related to the identity crisis is the problem of achieving agreement about the legitimate nature of authority and the proper responsibilities of government. In many new states the crisis of legitimacy is a straightforward constitutional problem: what should be the relationship between central and local authorities? What are the proper limits of the bureaucracy, or of the army, in the nation's political life? Or possibly the conflict is over how much of the colonial structure of government should be preserved in an independent state.

In other new states the question of legitimacy is more diffuse, and it involves sentiments about what should be the underlying spirit of government and the primary goals of national effort. For example, in some Moslem lands there is a deep desire that the state should in some fashion reflect the spirit of Islam. In other societies the issue of legitimacy involves questions about how far the governmental authorities should directly push economic development as compared with other possible goals. Above all, in traditional societies there can be a deep crisis of authority because all attempts at ruling are challenged by different people for different reasons, and no leaders are able to gain a full command of legitimate authority.

*The Penetration Crisis.* The critical problems of administration in the new states give rise to the penetration crisis, which involves the problems of government in reaching down into the society and effecting basic policies. . . . In traditional societies government had limited demands to make on the society, and in most transitional systems the governments are far more ambitious. This is particularly true if the rulers seek to accelerate the pace of economic development and social change. To carry out significant developmental policies a government must be able to reach down to the village level and touch the daily lives of people.

Yet . . . a dominant characteristic of transitional societies is the gap between the world of the ruling elite and that of the masses of the people who are still oriented toward their parochial ways. The penetration problem is that of building up the effectiveness of the formal institutions of government and of establishing confidence and rapport between rulers and subjects. Initially governments often find it difficult to motivate the population or to change its values and habits in order to bring support to programs of national development. On the other hand, at times the effectiveness of the government in breaking down old patterns of control can unleash widespread demands for a greater influence on governmental policies. When this occurs the result is another crisis, that of participation.

*The Participation Crisis* . . . The participation crisis occurs when there is uncertainty over the appropriate rate of expansion and when the influx of new participants creates serious strains on the existing institutions. As new segments of the population are brought into the political process, new interests and new issues begin to arise so that the continuity of the old polity is broken and there is the need to re-establish the entire structure of political relations.

In a sense the participation crisis arises out of the emergence of interest groups and the formation of a party system. The question in many new states is whether the expansion in participation is likely to be effectively organized into specific interest groups or whether the pressures will lead only to mass demands and widespread feelings of anomie. It should also be noted that the appearance of a participation crisis does not necessarily signal pressures for democratic processes. The participation crisis can be organized as in totalitarian states to provide the basis for manipulated mass organizations and demonstrational politics.

*Integration Crisis.* This crisis covers the problems of relating popular politics to governmental performance and thus it repre-

sents the effective and compatible solution of both the penetration and the participation crisis. The problem of integration
therefore deals with the extent to which the entire polity is
organized as a system of interacting relationships, first among the
officers and agencies of government, and then among the various
groups and interests seeking to make demands upon the system,
and finally in the relationships between officials and articulating
citizens.

In many of the transitional systems there may be many different
groupings of interests, but they hardly interact with each other,
and at best each seeks to make its separate demands upon the
government. The government must seek to cope with all these
demands simultaneously. Yet at the same time the government
itself may not be well integrated. The result is a low level of
general performance throughout the political system.

*The Distribution Crisis.* The final crisis in the development process
involves questions about how governmental powers are to be used
to influence the distribution of goods, services, and values throughout the society. Who is to benefit from government, and what
should the government be doing to bring greater benefits to
different segments of the society?

Much of the stress on economic development and the popularity
of socialist slogans in the new states is a reflection of the basic
crisis. In some cases governments seek to meet the problem by
directly intervening in the distribution of wealth; in other cases
the approach is to strengthen the opportunities and potentialities
of the disadvantaged groups.

There are obvious difficulties of operationalization in this scheme:
what are the criteria for recognizing a particular set of differences
over strategy or policy as an element in a deeper crisis? What if there
are elements of two, three or all these challenges at a given critical
juncture? What indicators can be constructed for measuring (a)
the severity of the crisis on one or more of the six dimensions; (b) the
effects of the measures taken to solve it?

Very little work has as yet been done on the development of such
operational criteria or indices and very little has been done in the
way of systematic coding of extant cases of political change within
this framework. Sidney Verba has prepared a hardheaded analysis

of the problems of cumulation and compounding in the handling of critical challenges and has tried to work out criteria for the differentiation of long-run system management problems from short-run crises of imperative structural change:[42]

'A crisis of development may be defined as a short-run development cycle that involves

—a shift in the relationship between *environmental pressures* and *level of politicization* on the one hand, and *governmental output and institutionalizations* on the other,

—such that the *institutionalization of a new level of governmental output* is required,

—if the pressures resulting from the environment and/or the shift in politicization are to be prevented from leading to *the overthrow of the elite structure of the society* or to the changing of the societal boundaries.'

The obvious implication is that far from all such problems of system development need lead to threatening situations of 'either—or' option. Each of the six sets of challenges may be handled through long series of adjustments and need not increase in severity to the point where the choice is a brutal yes or no: quick changes in the output of commands and in the structure of institutions, or else revolution or invasion from outside. It is not difficult to identify for each of the six sets of challenges a set of crucial governmental decisions, but many if not most of these decisions are not taken in the face of severe internal or external threats but simply to gain strategic advantages in struggles between competing elites. In fact it would be possible to pinpoint, for any of the nation-states formed up to World War II or thereabouts (much more difficult for later states because of the compounding of challenges), the most significant legislative or ministerial decisions on each dimension of development and to classify each such decision on some index for the severity of the actually evidenced threat to the system:

—for the *'penetration'* challenge one would look for decisions on the reform of the administration (the equivalent of the Northcote-Trevelyan Act);

—for the *'integration'* challenge one would check decisions on

---

42     S. Verba, *op. cit.*, p. 30, our emphases and paragraph structure.

criteria of recruitment, the equalization of opportunities and obligations, etc.;

—for the *'identity'* challenge there would be decisions on language and religion in the schools, on the protection of national symbols, on the handling of minorities;

—for the *'legitimacy'* challenge one could count the number and the severity of the changes in the constitution, and check all decisions on the handling of anti-system movements, treasonable activities and subversion;

—for the *'participation'* challenge it is easy to list the laws on the extension and equalization of the suffrage and the protection of the rights of communication, assembly and association;

—and for the *'distribution'* challenge it is again easy to list the sequences of decisions on taxation, social services, pensions and other measures of income and opportunity equalization.

It is in fact tempting to go further in the reinterpretation of this paradigm: to treat it essentially as a series of *headings in a classification of time series data and composite indicators* of potential utility in comparative analysis of nation-building processes.

A first sketch of such a listing follows:

1. *Penetration*
   Time series data for *growth of public sector*:
   1.1  central personnel
   1.2  field personnel by region and type of locality
   1.3  recruitment criteria: family and localities vs. education, *cf.* 2.1 for recruitment by cultural /political *divisions*
   1.4  governmental share of GNP: central, intermediary and local
   1.5  bases of resource extraction: the change from external (customs duties) to internal control (property, income taxation)
   1.6  government investments in centre-forming infrastructure (build-up of capital, periphery to capital communications)
   1.7  levels of public debt and dependence on foreign finance
   1.8  levels of military preparedness and the extent of mobilization for armed service.

2. *Integration*
   Time series data for:

F

2.1   the recruitment of elite personnel (appointed officials, elected representatives, intellectual leaders) for each major regional cultural/political division of the country (*e.g.*, per cent Protestants/Catholics in bureaucracy, per cent from minority language groups, from peripheral provinces)

2.2   shares of infrastructure investments (roads, railways, schools, etc.) by region and distance from centre(s)

2.3   in religiously-mixed nations, government contributions per pupil for schooling

2.4   income differentials by region and type of locality (use of 'peripherality' scores).

3. *Identity*

Time series data for:

3.1   development of mass literacy by region and type of locality

3.2   development of secondary education: school places by region, type of locality, and affiliation of school

3.3   types of teacher education: numbers trained for each category of school (denominational vs. secular, elite vs. minority language)

3.4   religious affiliation and, for the years available, religious participation (no. of *messalisants*) by region and type of locality

3.5   linguistic divisions by region and type of locality.

4. *Legitimacy*

Time series data, if any, for:

4.1   numbers involved in strikes or lockouts, demonstrations, riots

4.2   votes for 'anti-system' parties in regular elections.

5. *Participation*

Time series data for:

5.1   per cent enfranchised by region and type of locality, whenever possible (Sweden) also by occupational stratum

5.2   per cent electoral turnout by region, by locality and for the two sexes

5.3   organizational participation: memberships in parties,

popular movements, unions and other interest associations

5.4 cultural participation: readership of newspapers, popular magazines, books, exposure to films, radio, TV.

6. *Distribution*

Time series data on:

6.1 shares of governmental revenue allocated for education, social services, pensions

6.2 categories, memberships and coverage of social services

6.3 central and local tax burdens by levels of income and, if possible, by major occupational groups (farmers, employers and employees).

Each of these variables bears in one way or another on governmental actions and will have to be studied against the background of a broader array of 'benchmark' data on demographic development, settlement structure and class divisions.

Karl Deutsch's ideal measure of mobilization cuts across the two fields of variations: some of the criteria refer to movements at a high level of independence from governmental actions, others reflect governmental interventions very directly.

In his *Nationalism*, Deutsch lists *fourteen* possible 'yardsticks of measurement'.[43] Nine of these are already covered in our list under Penetration, Identity, Participation or Distribution. The five others are:

—the proportion of the territorial population in *urban settlements*,

—the proportion in the *secondary and tertiary* sectors of the economy,

—the proportion *working for money wages in units of five or more employees*,

—the proportion *attending markets* regularly,

—the proportion *sending or receiving a letter* at least once a month.

Useful times series for *all* these variables are obviously very hard to come by even for a *single* country: there is no hope of acquiring such extensive batteries for *comparative* analysis. In fact in his four country analysis, Deutsch used only *one* criterion of mobilization

---

43 *Nationalism*, 2nd edition, p. 126, cf. the further discussion in 'Social Mobilization . . .' *op. cit.*

each time: urbanization in Finland and India, the proportion in the secondary or tertiary sectors in Czechoslovakia and Scotland. With the accumulation of time series data in computer archives it should clearly be possible to develop much more elaborate analyses of the relationships among the indicators and establish empirical typologies through such techniques as principal components analysis. An example of what can soon be done cross-nationally is Paavo Seppänen's analysis of overall social change in Finland from 1911 to 1961: this is based on over 100 time series variables and proceeds by factor analysis to establish basic dimensions as well as critical phases in the process of change.[44] Once the Yale Data Program[45] has been extended to cover time series country by country it should be possible to carry out comparative studies of rates and time phases of change for a broad range of countries, at least within Europe and the West. Wolfgang Zapf's work on comparative indicators of development shows how it is possible to proceed on the basis of careful library searches.[46] Once such analyses get under way there will clearly be pressures to go beyond the national aggregate to assemble data on the extent of variations among regions and provinces and between central and peripheral localities in each national territory. Ecological archives have by now been established for over a dozen countries and the time span of some of the variables, especially census and election data, will soon be stretched to cover most of the bookkeeping histories of each country.[47] The same goes for the developing archives of information from *elite biographies*: statistics of the background characteristics and careers of parliamentarians have been assembled for computer processing in a number of countries and will offer a basis for comparative studies of processes of

---

44    Paavo Seppänen 'Changing Society' (Finnish) *Sociologia* 2, 1965.
45    The second edition of the Russett *et al. World Handbook* will include a number of shorter, mainly post-1945, time series: this edition is due in 1969.
46    W. Zapf. *Materialien zur Theorie des sozialen Wandels*, 1968.
47    See S. Rokkan *ed. Data Archives* (Paris: Mouton, 1966) and M. Dogan and S. Rokkan *eds. Quantitative Ecological Analysis in the Social Sciences*. (Cambridge: M.I.T. Press, 1969).

social change.[48] The pioneering work of a group of Uppsala historians on the spread of *voluntary associations* throughout Sweden in the 19th century will no doubt lead to similar efforts in other countries.[49] The spread of computing facilities to more and more universities is bound to bring about a fundamental change in the conditions for comparative research within a foreseeable future: to forestall useless divergencies in the design of coding schemes and in data management procedures it will clearly be imperative to develop facilities for close cooperation among the active builders and users of such data archives.

The International Social Science Council has taken important steps in this direction through the establishment of a *Standing Committee on Social Science Data Archives*: this will help to spread technical and substantive information about archives at different stages of development and will facilitate exchanges of data for purposes of comparative analysis.[50] UNESCO has taken a further step in this direction through its plans to launch a series of computer-aided *data confrontation seminars*.

The idea of these seminars is deceptively simple but seems to hold great potentialities for the future of cross-national research: experts

---

48    Archives of biographical statistics for parliamentary personnel have been built up in Britain, Finland, France, Germany, Italy, Norway and Switzerland, and will be built up in the Netherlands, Sweden and several other countries in the near future. Among analytical publications based on such files these appear particularly important: W. L. Guttsman. *The British Political Elite* (London: McGibbon & Kee, 1963. G. Sartori, *ed. Il Parlamento Italiano* (Rome: Ed. Scientifiche Ital., 1963). W. Zapf. *Wandlungen der deutschen Elite* (Munich: Piper, 1965). E. Gruner & K. Frei. *Schweizerische Bundesversammlung, 1848-1920* vols. I-II (Bern: Francke, 1966). H. Valen. 'The Recruitment of Parliamentary Nominees in Norway' *Scand. Pol. Stud.* I, 1966, pp. 121-166. Mogens Pedersen 'Rekrutteringen av danske Folketingsmænd'. Paper, Nordic Conference on Political Science, Helsinki, Aug. 1968. Stein Rokkan and Kjell Salhus, "Changes in the Channels of Recruitment to Parliament: Specimen Tables for Three Countries". Paper, UNESCO Symposium, Gothenburg, 1968.

49    See report by Carl-Göran Andrae, UNESCO Symposium, Gothenburg, 1968.

50    See R. Bisco 'Social Science Data Archives: Progress and Prospects'. *Soc. Sci. Inf.* 6(1) 1967: 39-74.

on quantitative analysis from *n* countries are invited to join in a two-to-three week seminar of comparative analysis but are not asked to contribute papers in advance in the usual style of international scholarship; instead they are asked to send *data decks* covering an agreed set of units and an agreed range of variables to the seminar site for reformatting and advance analysis on the local computer; the task of the actual seminar is then to work out the details of the comparisons through joint interpretations of the initial output and through regular interaction with the computer through the introduction of further controls and through the testing of alternative analysis procedures.

This procedure seems to hold a great deal of promise in the analysis of data readily at hand in established archives, whether they are data from sample surveys or polls, data from ecological files for recent censuses, elections and other official statistics, or data from bibliographical files for given elite categories. Data such as these require very little recoding and can be prepared for uniform analysis without too great investments of time and personnel. The situation is quite different for longer-term developmental data of the type discussed in this paper: the planning of cross-national analysis seminars for 19th-century and early 20th-century materials will clearly require much more intensive interaction among the experts on each country's history and statistics and cannot be achieved in one single step. For such data the best procedure seems to be to persuade small groups of collaborating research centres to concentrate their efforts on the establishment of time series for their countries for some limited range of variables. This is in fact what has occurred, without much formal prodding, in the field of economic history and development economics. Similar working arrangements have been discussed for other sets of data:[51] there is a thriving international movement in demographic history,[52] and some initial spadework has been done to pre-

---

51    An important vehicle for communication on computerization projects in history is *Historical Methods Newsletter*, University of Pittsburg, Dept. of History: this was first issued in Dec. 1967.

52    See D. V. Glass and D. E. C. Eversley *eds*, *Population in History. Essays in Historical Demography* (London: Arnold 1965); E. A. Wrigley, *ed. An Introduction to English Historical Demography. From the Sixteenth to the Nineteenth Centuries* (London: Weidenfeld, 1966).

pare for international comparisons of data on political mobilization and the growth of mass organizations.[53] The international team currently at work on the politics of eleven smaller European democracies[54] have collected a considerable number of time series tables for indicators of political development and there is good hope that this work will be followed up in the future through further data collation and analysis. Within the four Scandinavian countries a collective study of differences and similarities in social structure is currently under discussion:[55] in this study it is hoped that it will be possible to enlist statistically-oriented historians for collaboration with sociologists and political scientists in comparative analysis of the initial conditions at some arbitrary 'year zero' (say, 1850) and of the subsequent variations in the rates of change.

For UNESCO such efforts of intensive comparative analysis of factors affecting the success or failure of nation-building would appear to be particularly fruitful. UNESCO has taken on important responsibilities for the advancement of literacy and culture in the

---

These works are heavily influenced by the French school of historical demography and suggest possibilities of comparative research on pre-censal populations on the basis of the Henry-Fleury method of family reconstitution from samples of parish registers. The rationale for work of the Cambridge Group for the History of Population and Sociology is set out with great enthusiasm in Peter Laslett, *The World We Have Lost* (London: Methuen, 1965), cf. the progress report on pre-censal ecology in 'Historical and Regional Variations in Great Britain', M. Dogan and S. Rokkan, *Quantitative Ecological Analysis in the Social Sciences* (Cambridge: M.I.T. Press, 1969).

53    See S. Rokkan 'The Comparative Study of Political Participation' in A. Ranney ed. *Essays on the Behavioral Study of Politics* (Urbana, Univ. of Illinois Press, 1962), pp. 45-90 and 'Electoral Mobilization, Party Competition and National Integration', *op. cit.* Also: S. M. Lipset & S. Rokkan eds. *Party Systems, op. cit.* and S. Rokkan and J. Meyriat eds. *International Guide to Electoral Statistics*. Vol. I (Paris: Mouton, 1969).

54    Cf. S. Rokkan 'The structuring of mass politics . . .', *op. cit.* and R. A. Dahl and E. R. Tufte 'Size and Democracy', manuscript, Stanford, Center for Advanced Study in the Behavioral Sciences, July 1967.

55    See Edmund Dahlström, 'The Project Scandinavian Social Structure'. Paper, UNESCO Symposium, Gothenburg. Aug. 1968.

developing world and is highly dependent on research on earlier experiences of mass education and cultural mobilization: this goes for the dominant countries and their histories of nation-building but it is of even greater importance to foster detailed comparative studies of *19th- and early 20th-century developments in the units most comparable to the new states of the 1950s and 1960s, the smaller and the more marginal of the European and the European-settled polities.* UNESCO has already taken steps to carry out comparative studies of the relationships between economic growth, mass education and the spread of the mass media,[56] but these have been limited to very short time series or very few countries and have not considered the broader context of nation-building. Within an expanded programme of comparative research on nation-building it should be possible both to extend the time series and to enrich the analysis through the addition of further contextual variables. It is not likely that this can be done for more than a few countries at a time but this may in itself be an advantage: 'third world' social scientists invited to attend seminars on such intensive comparative analysis may in fact carry home with them much more realistic notions of the strategies and costs of development and acquire deeper insight into the alternatives facing their own countries.

---

56      See UNESCO, *Freedom of Information: Development of Information in Under-Developed Countries* (Paris: UNESCO, 1961) and Wilbur Schramm, *Mass Media and National Development* (Stanford University Press, 1964). For similar work in another UN agency, see United Nations Research Institute for Social Development. *Research Notes*. No. 1. Geneva, UNRISD, June 1968, pp. 1-7.

W. G. Runciman

# Explaining Social Stratification

I

Despite (or perhaps because of) the amount that continues to be written about it, the prospect of some adequate general theory of stratification in human societies has appeared over the last few years to recede rather than to advance. The protracted quarrels between the partisans of a 'functional' approach on one side and a 'conflict' approach on the other have at last been recognised as very largely factitious; but this recognition has not yet led to the emergence of a satisfactory new framework in terms of which useful empirical hypotheses might be framed. The Marxist theory of classes (which can itself be interpreted as a fusion of the 'functional' and 'conflict' approaches) has in part, at least, passed into the common assumptions with which any investigator will approach the study of Western industrial society; but it cannot be claimed for it that it has been wholly vindicated even within societies of that one type, let alone furnishing a satisfactory theory of social stratification in general. In the same way, the ideas of Max Weber have exercised a strong and still growing influence on the subject; but Weber himself never offered a theory of stratification as such and it would be a fruitless exercise to try to derive one from his writings. Much progress has been made in the study of stratification in animal societies, including primates not too distantly related to man; but the dangers of extrapolating from these to a functional (or any other) theory of stratification in human societies are at least as clear as any possible benefits. The evidence from which one would hope a satisfactory theory might be constructed is being furnished in abundance by anthropologists, sociologists and historians; but in practice, this abundance serves more to undermine existing attempts to construct a theory of stratification than to vindicate them.

In this paper, I shall try to suggest that the situation is not quite as disheartening as my introductory paragraph implies. But before doing so, I had better make clear what I mean by a 'theory'. I do not mean either a mere analytical taxonomy (however useful) on one side or a mere idiographic explanation (however satisfying) on the other. What we are in the end looking for is a set of presumptively causal empirical generalisations about social stratification which can be vindicated by their derivation from a smaller number of more general laws which furnish them with their theoretical grounding. These generalisations—if they can be found—may need to be supplemented by any number of others drawn from adjacent fields of study if any particular case is to be satisfactorily accounted for in detail. But the sociologist, anthropologist or historian whose interest is in social stratification as such will be framing his conclusions in terms of a model, whether implicit or explicit, which describes systems of stratification in terms of a set of selected variables whose values are presumed to be susceptible to causal generalisation in terms of their relations either to each other or to designated independent variables which the model can be expanded to include.

Even this very general (and I would hope uncontroversial) account already raises two questions of definition which have provoked a fair amount of argument: first, should or should not 'stratification' be equated by definition with any system of institutionalised inequalities? Second, how should 'stratification', whether or not so equated, be distinguished from differentiation? But both can, I think, be fairly shortly dealt with.

The first question may be given a negative answer for one or other of three different reasons: first, because there are societies so near to perfect equality of condition among their adult members that they should be marked off from 'stratified' societies in kind and not merely in degree; second, because there are societies in which role- and status-sets cross-cut to such a degree that no 'strata' (i.e. clearly separate, externally visible, hierarchically ranked groups or categories of persons or families) can be distinguished; third, because there are societies, such as age-set societies, whose members are equal in the sense that they all move in sequence through the same series of (admittedly hierarchical) positions. All three of these reasons have been forcefully urged in a recent paper by M. G. Smith;[1]

---

1       M. G. Smith, 'Pre-industrial Stratification Systems', in N. J. Smelser and S. M. Lipset, eds., *Social Structure and Mobility in Economic Development* (London, 1966), pp. 141-176.

and unquestionably, different researchers are perfectly free to apply the term 'stratification' in different senses if they so choose. But what is gained by defining it in other terms than that of any and all institutionalised inequalities of access to valued resources? There is one exception which is I think universally agreed and that is the biologically grounded and thus insurmountable inequality between adults and small children. But once given that institutionalised inequalities among adults are universal, what reason is there not to regard the enormous variations in the form and degree of such inequalities as variations within a universal pattern? There are of course numerous differences in kind between the different forms which institutionalised inequalities can take; but why are the three we are considering here of such peculiar importance that they and only they should be marked off from all the rest?

This question is perhaps the more pertinent in view of Smith's justified objection to the assumption made by Kingsley Davis and others that stratification is universal *although* the unit of stratification is to be taken as the family. Since it is a matter of fact that intra-familial stratification (in the sense of institutionalised inequality) can be found where no supra-familial organisation exists, there is clearly a contradiction in Davis's claim. But this seems to me to be all the more reason for defining the whole subject in terms of institutionalised inequalities of access to valued resources between adults. 'Stratification' is then simply the most familiar and therefore useful term for this aspect of social organisation, and it is an empirical question how far distinct 'strata' are externally visible or how far inequalities of opportunity are systematically related to inequalities of position.

It might still be possible to claim that the most egalitarian hunting and gathering societies constitute a separate category: Smith cites the Pygmies and !Kung Bushmen, and there are of course other ethnographic favourites such as the Ammassalik Eskimoes of Greenland. But once given that there is *some* institutionalised inequality in these societies, however minimal, it is surely more natural to see them as lying as near the bottom of a hypothetical continuum of 'stratification' as is so far known to be possible than as constituting some 'unstratified' kind. Smith speaks of the Pygmies' lack of 'any discernible inequalities of rank or advantage', whether in ritual, hunting or kinship, and says of the !Kung that although each of their bands has a headman, 'headmen have no advantages that distinguish them from other !Kung'. But if we look in detail at the accounts given by Colin Turnbull of the Pygmies and Lorna Marshall of the !Kung, it becomes evident that institutionalised inequalities between adults, however minimal, do exist in both cases. Marshall, although saying of !Kung headmen that 'they have considerable responsibility without any specific reward', goes on to point out that a headman 'has the prerogative of choosing the best spot for his own fire and scherm', and explicitly asserts her belief that the authority of the headman derives 'from the concept of the father being the head of the extended family'.[2] Turnbull, although emphasising that leadership among the Pygmies is divided into different fields, so that almost (but not quite) every adult is accorded more of a hearing than others in at least one field, also points out that hunters and negotiators have higher status than others— although they must be careful to avoid boasting— and that 'older people always receive respect as such'.[3] In the same way, the Ammassalik Eskimoes, although they can be described in Smith's sort of terms as having 'no organised leadership, no social strati- fication'[4] do still accord differential privilege or prestige to par- ticularly skilful hunters, angakoks (shamans) and drum singers. All societies, in other words, are inegalitarian at least to some minimal degree, and it is the variations in both degree and kind in the institutionalised inequalities which can be universally observed that I take to be what those who choose 'social stratification' as their subject-matter are trying to explain.

The second definitional question is of a slightly different kind. Even if it is agreed that stratification in the sense of institutionalised inequalities between adults is universal, it may still be an open question whether a particular pattern of observed behaviour should

---

2       Lorna Marshall, '!Kung Bushmen Bands', *Africa* XXX (1960), pp. 351-2.

3       Colin M. Turnbull, 'The Mbuti Pygmies of the Congo', in James L. Gibbs, ed., *Peoples of Africa* (New York, 1965), p. 302.

4       Jeannette Mirsky, 'The Eskimo of Greenland' in Margaret Mead, ed., *Cooperation and Competition Among Primitive Peoples* (New York, 1937), p. 61.

be interpreted by the observer as stratification or merely as differentiation. For the observer to speak even of widely differentiated
roles or statuses as 'stratified' requires that the idea of a rank-
order have clear operational reference within the system described.
Burke says somewhere that 'in all societies, consisting of various
descriptions of men, some description must be uppermost'. But why
'must'? In what sense does there have to be the sort of consensus on
values that Burke held to sustain (and also to justify) social inequality? If the observer can distinguish the rulers from the ruled, or
even merely the rich from the poor, then he is presumably entitled
by definition to speak of a rank-order. But what does it mean to
attribute a 'system of stratification' to the society on the strength
of it? The sense in which the observer can, if he wishes, speak of
'stratification' in terms of common societal values is a trivial one.
It is true that if an economic or political system is operating at all,
this argues some minimal consensus on the part of the members:[5]
only when disaffection is taken to the point of rebellion will the
observer be forced to recognise that the system of stratification has
actually broken down. But what are we to say of those cases where
'values' in their more specific and concrete form are demonstrably
not held in common? In the ideal type of a homogeneous traditional
society the rank of each member is unanimously recognised and the
criteria by which access is given to privileged positions of wealth,
power and (whether or not some other value than these two is
relevant) prestige are universally agreed. But it is commonplace that
in actual societies, and not necessarily colonial or militarily occupied
societies, there may exist several distinctive sub-cultures or 'classes'
whose members hold quite incompatible standards by which the
rank of their fellow-citizens is to be assigned.

---

5    Thus e.g. Alain Touraine, *Sociologie de l'Action* (Paris, 1965), p. 157:
     'On pourrait en principe distinguer un grand nombre de principes de
     stratification, la profession, le revenu, l'éducation, le type de logement,
     etc. mais il est difficilement concevable que ces principes ne soient pas
     reliés les uns aux autres, car ceci supposerait que les valeurs institu-
     tionalisées d'une société ne sont pas cohérentes entre elles ce qui ne
     peut jamais être vrai que dans certains limites. Chacun de nous
     s'adapte à une certaine hiérarchie sociale, suffisamment au moins
     pour reconnaitre quand il s'élève ou quand il descend socialement'.

This, perhaps, is merely another way of saying that prestige is the 'subjective' dimension of stratification in contrast to the 'objective' dimension of power and wealth. It is not, of course, 'subjective' in the sense that a man's prestige is what *he* thinks it is, interesting though it may be to the sociological observer to discover what he does think it: it is 'objectively' a function of how he is regarded by other people. But even so, how is it to be assessed? It is customary among sociologists to analyse a hierarchy of prestige in terms of social exclusiveness, particularly as manifested by commensalism and endogamy, overt expressions of esteem or disesteem for other categories or groups, and differences in upbringing and life-style. But well-marked distinctions of this kind can exist without a coherent rank-order, and this not merely in cases of regional, racial or linguistic sub-cultures but even where one group is clearly the superior of the other in wealth and power. It may normally be the case that where this is so differentiation of life-styles is, or soon becomes, symbolic of a hierarchy of prestige. But this cannot be assumed; it has to be empirically shown. Differences of life-style and absence of social contact may be accompanied not merely by in-difference but even by reciprocal disesteem, and in this sense, there-fore, be symptomatic not of shared values at all, but of a lack of them. So when and on what grounds is the sociologist entitled to speak of such differentiated 'classes' as 'stratified'?

The answer, however, is that difficult though it may be it is still an empirical matter. The difficulty is not a sign of some fatal dis-order in the conceptual schema within which theories of stratification are to be formulated. It is a matter of fact that there is a general tendency in human groups and societies for distinguishable roles and/or statuses of various kinds to be differentially evaluated. It is similarly a matter of fact how much unanimity there is in any given group or society about the legitimacy of the evaluation (where wealth or power are unequally apportioned) or the criteria of evaluation (where the 'resource' in question is social esteem as such). In any large and complex society, it is inevitable that there will be discrepancies in the criteria of evaluation between one group or community and another if not actually within face-to-face groups or communities themselves; that even where there is agreement on criteria, individuals will differ from each other about actual rankings;

that social exclusiveness will sometimes be a sign not of differential esteem but merely of hostility; and that some differences of life-style will be irrelevant to social esteem and others deliberately assertive of a rival sub-culture to that of the ostensible elite. But it is up to the investigator to find these things out in the field. He is in no way committed in advance to finding 'stratification' where it doesn't exist simply because he has reason to believe that he will find some differential evaluation accorded to what S. N. Eisenstadt calls 'positions which are related to the central spheres and symbols of a society, and which represent the community'.[6] If it is the case that differentiation is never found without *some* degree of strati-fication, that there *are* discernible 'central spheres and symbols' in all societies, and that a rank-order, however imprecise, *is* generally recognised even by those who would like to see its criterion under-mined, these are all matters which the evidence could contradict. Indeed, it happens often enough that the basis of a stratification system *is* effectively undermined—which is merely a further empirical fact that a satisfactory theory of stratification must be able to account for.

Once, therefore, these verbal difficulties are out of the way, it becomes possible and indeed appropriate to ask what form a precise and testable theory of stratification might take. I have already remarked that the dispute between 'functional' and 'conflict' theorists has been recognised as factitious, even if no improved theory based on this recognition has yet been forthcoming. But before I enlarge on this, it is worth remarking that there does exist a satisfactory theory which does precisely this—the biological theory of stratification in animal societies. I am not suggesting that this theory can provide the explanations of stratification in human societies which we are lacking. But it would be equally mistaken for social scientists or historians to suppose that it is irrelevant to their concerns. Not only have human societies evolved (although we don't know quite how) from primate societies in historical fact, but there may also be a useful methodological lesson to be learnt from the success, within its proper limits, of the biological theory.

---

6    S. N. Eisenstadt, 'Prestige, Participation and Strata Formation', in J. A. Jackson, ed., *Social Stratification* (Cambridge, 1968), p. 64.

The biological theory of stratification is a functional theory in the sense of adaptation to the environment. But it is also a conflict theory, as the Darwinian notion of the competitive struggle for survival already implies. There appears to be some controversy among primatologists and others over the precise specification of the functions served by hierarchy in animal societies: defensive organisation and the inhibition of intra-specific aggression have obvious survival value, while intra-specific aggression itself has the function of reconciling the population of a species to its territorial resources. But it is perhaps less obvious whether the restriction of breeding by low-ranking males or, more generally, the mutual predictability of behaviour as such can be separately included in the list. It is also becoming clear that the idea of 'dominance' is altogether more complex than it at first seemed. Not only is it arguable that primate rank orders may derive as much from the deference of the low-ranking as from the aggression of the high-ranking,[7] but there has been shown to be very considerable variation in rank-orders resulting from different group memberships, different contexts of interaction, different social relations with other groups members, and different upbringings and therefore different chances of attaining high 'basic' rank.[8] But despite the unexpected complexities with which (as a result of the progress they have made) primatologists are increasingly having to deal, a biological theory of social rank can maintain scientific respectability for two reasons which cease to hold beyond the stage of evolution at which cultural speciation and information-transmission begins: first, the biological function—i.e. survival—can be adequately specified at the general level; second, the mechanism of evolution—i.e. genetics—is sufficiently well understood for the explanation in retrospect of particular evolutionary sequences to have adequate theoretical grounding.

Neither of these conditions holds for stratification in human societies. But once this is unequivocally recognised, a useful lesson can be drawn from it. A general 'functional' theory of stratification in

---

7    See M. R. A. Chance, 'Attention Structure as the Basis of Primate Rank Orders', Man n.s. II (1967), pp. 503-18.

8    See Masao Kawai, 'On the System of Social Ranks of a Troop of Japanese Monkeys: (I) Basic Rank and Dependent Rank', in Stuart A. Altmann, ed., Japanese Monkeys (Edmonton, 1965), pp. 66-86.

human societies is bound to be unsatisfying because without these conditions it is powerless to explain the enormous variation in systems of stratification which is the very puzzle that sociologists would like to be able to solve. It may be true for human societies that some degree of stratification is a necessary condition of social order. But to say this explains nothing by itself. Only when we can say both what specific 'adaptive' function is served by institutionalised inequality and also how it comes to be so served can we begin to offer a 'functional' theory which will tell us anything which is neither trivial nor false. And this can in fact be done, provided that we abandon the quest for a general functional theory of the form which is applicable only to pre-cultural species. It is true that the notion of adaptation for survival has little or no value in the study of stratification in human society. But suppose that, in the formulation of Marshall Sahlins, 'Stratification is viewed as an aspect of social structure functionally adjusted to the technological exploitation of the environment'.[9] It is a matter of fact about human society in general that its members, or at any rate enough of them, do share this common goal of technological exploitation of the environment. This, admittedly, has to be explained in its turn. But we do not need to be able to explain it in order to explain some variations in stratification systems by reference to the selection of mechanisms of social organisation and change which will in fact constitute an 'adaptive' response to the environment in these terms.

So delimited, one part of the argument of Davis and Moore[10] which has generated so much controversy is not only plausible but empirically testable. It might, of course, happen (although I doubt it) that advanced industrial societies will abandon the goal of productivity and embark on a deliberate policy of deindustrialisation. But once given that they haven't, the claim that they will all therefore maintain systems of differential rewards in order to attract and retain in certain occupations the ablest (in terms of the function of technological exploitation of the environment) of their members is testable by observation. In particular, it generates the

9    M. D. Sahlins, *Social Stratification in Polynesia* (Seattle, 1958), p. ix.
10   K. Davis and W. E. Moore, 'Some Principles of Stratification', *American Sociological Review* X (1945), pp. 242-249.

prediction that even in countries where the government is strongly committed to an egalitarian ideology, certain minimum differentials will be established, or re-established, between managerial and technical workers on one side and semi-skilled or unskilled workers on the other—a prediction which appears to be borne out by some of the evidence now becoming available from Eastern Europe.[11] It is still true that this apparent confirmation of the prediction could turn out to be misleading, that the hypothesis fails to specify with any precision the extent of differential which is 'functional', and that alternative motivations and rewards might under other conditions produce the same results. It is also true that many features of the stratification systems within which this may hold are not explicable in the same terms—notably the distribution of inherited wealth as opposed to that of earned income. But there is nothing wrong with looking for a 'functional' explanation of stratification in human society provided that (i) it is not presumed to be able to explain what a biological 'functional' theory can explain; (ii) a function of an adaptive kind can be plausibly specified; (iii) the mechanism by which the adaptation is effected can be identified and adequately described. Indeed the best example known to me of a good functional explanation of stratification is not the loose and abstract generalities of Davis and Moore, but Sahlins's study of Polynesia from which I borrowed the formulation quoted above.

Much the same thing can be said about the so-called 'conflict' theory of stratification which is (or used to be) the functionalists' presumptive rival. The propositions of the conflict theory, stated as they are, for example, by Dahrendorf[12] are of as limited value as those of Davis and Moore in explaining what sociologists want to explain. It may be true that since institutionalised inequality of power, or authority, is a universal feature of human societies, there is a perpetual conflict of interests between those who have more or less. But what does this explain about the enormous variations in

---

11     See Frank Parkin, 'Class Stratification in Socialist Societies', *British Journal of Sociology* XX (1969), pp. 355-374.

12     Ralf Dahrendorf, *Class and Class Conflict in Industrial Society* (Stanford, 1959), ch. 6; and 'On the Origin of Social Inequality', in P. Laslett and W. G. Runciman, eds., *Philosophy, Politics & Society*, Second Series (Oxford, 1962), pp. 88-109.

social and political systems? Even if, on the analogy with animal societies, we can specify the function of inhibiting intra-societal aggression and organising territorial defence, we cannot, as we can in the animal case, spell out the mechanism which relates a specific form of stratification to its (adaptive) origin. It is useful only when it is applied in a much less ambitious and more limited way. To explain, for example, the relative positions of Spartans and Helots requires the invocation of 'conflict theory' in the obvious sense that the question to be answered is how the Spartans, who had sub-jugated first the Laconian and subsequently the Messenian Helots by conquest, were able to keep them in subjection despite their numbers and the evident willingness of the Messenians, at least, to resist; and the answer lies in the celebrated and peculiar social organisation of the Spartans, with its rigorous military discipline and its deliberate and effective police-state methods. It is sometimes said of cases of this kind that they exemplify some general proposition to the effect that social conflict is ubiquitous and therefore stratification simply a function of the unequal distribution of power. But this, once again, is a statement which is trivial where it is not false; and it yields no ex-planation adequate to account for the wide variations in the degree to which different societies do distribute power unequally, however this power may or may not be used, and whatever the form it may take.

What is needed, therefore, is not a 'reconciliation' of the functional and conflict approaches, if by this is meant an attempt to formulate a general sociological explanation of stratification analogous to the biological. Sociological explanations of stratification must satisfy the condition which the biological explanation meets: which is to say, we must know both the history and the mechanism. But cultural, as opposed to biological, change being what it is, the two approaches cannot be fused into a single general theory of strati-fication which will provide a blanket answer.[13] It is true that, as in

---

13    As has been attempted by G. E. Lenski, *Power and Privilege: a Theory of Social Stratification* (New York, 1966). In practice, however, Lenski's thesis rests chiefly on the claim that the distribution of 'privilege' is a function of 'power'; and it is in any case so imprecisely set out as to be testable only to a very limited degree (cf. Figures 1 and 2 on pp. 437 and 438).

the biological theory, the two are complementary aspects of hier-archical social organisation: institutionalised inequality serves some 'adaptive' purpose, even if the purpose is not one to which every member of the society subscribes, and adaptation to the environment requires that institutionalised inequality should be sustained by some form of sanction even if, given sufficient agreement on values, these need never be invoked in an overtly coercive form. But these considerations cannot by themselves generate the sort of theory we are after; they are merely part of what a successful theory, if we ever have one, will have to include. As the successful biological theory demonstrates, and as the majority of sociologists who may incline to either the 'consensus' or 'conflict' party are increasingly willing to admit, there is no known society which does not, however minimally, display not only a functional and adaptive but a coercive and competitive aspect in its system of stratification. An ideal type in which there is a complete unanimity on means, ends and values and in which all institutionalised inequalities are seen to serve these agreed ends and to be justified accordingly may be logically conceivable; so may an ideal type in which every action of the subordinate strata is effectively commanded, or forbidden, by a dictator wielding a monopoly of physical sanction. But no such societies are to be found in fact, however wide the variations along the continuum. The sociologist's problem (as opposed to the political philosopher's) is to formulate generalisations which may enable him to explain which of these variations can be traced to what necessary and sufficient anterior conditions.

## II

But once again I am going too fast. For to describe and classify these variations which we wish to explain we need, as I pointed out at the beginning, to have decided on the dependent variables in terms of which stratification is to be operationally defined. Sur-prisingly enough, this task is nowhere (as far as I know) systematic-ally attempted in the academic literature. It is admittedly a very difficult task, and one which I have no intention of attempting here. There is not merely the risk, which is endemic to sociological gen-eralisation, of constructing a conceptual schema whose economy and scope, such as they may be, are bought at the cost of any explanatory potential it might have. There is also the further difficulty that the problems of cross-cultural comparison are at least as formidable on this topic as on, say, religion or politics (with both of which it may overlap); and in addition, there is the more strictly technical difficulty that even when sociologists of stratification know what variables they want to use in comparing one case with another, they are exceedingly hard put to it to find any satisfactory criteria of measurement for them. But the task will have to be undertaken sooner or later even if all that can be done in the present state of our knowledge is to suggest one or two possible tactics of approach.

The first move is to make the familiar distinction between 'economic', 'social' and 'political' inequalities, or 'class', 'status' and 'power'. It may be misleading to call these 'dimensions' of institutionalised inequality in any strict sense, and indeed it may even be better to talk about three different aspects of institutionalised 'power'. But if we imagine a hypothetical anthropologist (or sociologist or historian) approaching a society whose system of stratification is wholly unknown to him, it is difficult if not impossible to conceive of him as doing other than asking himself three separate kinds of question: first, who is more and who is less advantageously placed in the system of production, distribution and exchange? second, who is more and who is less highly regarded by the fellow-members of his society in terms of social prestige? third, who is and who isn't in a position to coerce or induce other members of his society into doing what they would not otherwise do even when they are averse to doing it?[14] The terminology in which these different questions and the more detailed enquiries deriving from them are framed is unimportant: however labelled, the dependent variables with which the sociologist (or anthropologist or historian) of stratification is concerned are of at any rate these three different kinds.

Within each kind, it is still more difficult to set out a complete and well-defined list. But as a rough classification, there are three categories of variables which for want of better terms I shall call the

---

14    The last time I saw Peter Nettl before his death he said that he was thinking of undertaking a study of the concept of power. It is much to be regretted that what might have been an important contribution on this topic is now lost.

objective-quantitative, the objective-qualitative and the subjective. By 'objective-quantitative' I mean, as the term no doubt suggests, all the formal properties of a rank-order which lend themselves to numerical measurement, both static and dynamic, such as the span (total distance from top to bottom), the spread (dispersion as measured by the Gini coefficient), the matrix of transition probabilities showing the chances of movement up or down from any given starting-point, and the rate and direction of change in any of these over time. By 'objective-qualitative' I mean such properties of a rank-order as the criteria by which rank is assigned, the nature of the sanctions upholding it or the visibility of the distinctions signifying it. By 'subjective' I mean such variables as the extent of unanimity on either the criteria or the rank assigned according to them, and the position of the members of the rank-order as perceived by themselves and its discrepancy from the observer's assessment.

If, therefore, there are three kinds of institutionalised inequality and three kinds of relevant variables which will feature in any generalisation which can be applied sufficiently precisely over a sufficient range of stratification systems to qualify for the status of a law, do we have any such laws? The answer must be no, even within carefully chosen cultural or historical limits. But it would be wrong to go so far as to say that either such broad but imprecise or such precise but limited generalisations as we do have are without value. I have already suggested that since it seems to be a well-founded empirical generalisation that societies seek to maximise technological exploitation of the environment, the further generalisation that the adaptive functions of stratification (if 'adaptive' is defined by reference to this end) will cause certain patterns of inequality of reward to be institutionalised and retained has some substantial measure of empirical support. Descending to the level of much more precise but much more limited generalisation, the distribution of pre-tax money wages or salaries of fully employed male adult workers in all industries but farming is sufficiently similar over a sufficiently wide range of industrial societies to suggest, even after full account is taken of uncertainties or deficiencies in the data, that some underlying regularity is present, whatever its causes may be.[15]

---

15    See Harold Lydall, *The Structure of Earnings* (Oxford, 1968), ch. 3.

(The 'functional' generalisation may furnish some of the answer, but certainly not the whole of it.) And at an intermediate level, the generalisation that degree of institutionalised inequality varies with size either of society or even merely of organisation is abundantly documented even if the definition of degree of inequality is discretionary within very broad, not to say ambiguous, limits.[16] Thus although it may be premature to talk about laws of stratification even in a loose sense, it would be hardly less misleading to suggest that the generalisations which we have are for some reason incapable of such elaboration and specification as might make the term law as appropriate here as in, say, learning theory in psychology or price theory in economics or some other relatively successful specialism among the sciences of man.

Whether such more respectable generalisations, if we ever have them, will fall neatly under the separate headings of the economic, social and political is something which only the future course of empirical research will settle. The overlap and the interdependence between the three are such that generalisation may well be most effectively pursued in terms of a typology of stratification systems which cut across their boundaries. But there will still remain three distinctive areas with their own distinctive variables. These may be classified as between my suggested categories of objective-quantitative, objective-qualitative and subjective. But they will not be the same variables. Social distance as a measure of status is something very different from the span and distribution of income and wealth as a measure of economic class; the ability of one member of a society to influence the decisions of the agents of government more effectively than another, or even directly to enforce coercive sanctions over another, as a measure of power is in turn very different from either income and wealth or social distance. It is true that for some purposes it may be useful to treat status as a commodity analogous to money, or to plot, say, voting rights in a legislative assembly along a Lorenz course in the same way as wealth.[17] But this does not, of

---

16    See K. Svalastoga, *Social Differentiation* (New York, 1965), p. 6 (Table 1).

17    See Hayward R. Alker Jr., *Mathematics and Politics* (New York, 1965), ch. 3.

course, make them equivalents; and given the nature of the differences between them it is not surprising that economic inequalities should be those most amenable to generalisation (as the example of the distribution of earned incomes serves to illustrate). Inequalities of status, by contrast, lend themselves to precise measurement only within rigid caste-like systems, and when it comes to inequalities of power the difficulties of definition and measurement are such that we do not (as far as I am aware) have anything approaching a lawlike generalisation even of the loosest and least precisely quantified kind.

But if there are at least some generalisations about stratification, however much they may stand in need of being supplemented and improved, what is their theoretical grounding? It would be foolish to hope that we shall ever find laws predictive of the future evolution of stratification systems as such, any more than that biologists will find laws from which they can directly predict the future evolution of species. The evolution of stratification systems and the cultures of which they are a part is as open-ended a history as that of kinds of biological organisms. But at the same time, any generalisation, however limited in terms of time or place, which can be formulated about stratification, whether in terms of objective-quantitative, objective-qualitative or subjective variables, can claim causal as opposed to merely descriptive status only if it could in principle be explained itself by reference to some broader underlying generalisation of a more lawlike kind, just as causal generalisation in biology ultimately rests on the laws of chemistry. What sort of laws there might be in the case of social stratification cannot be too confidently guessed. It may be that few sociologists, anthropologists or historians would nowadays accept that genetics is the science which stands to social stratification as pure to applied; but the progress of science is seldom as direct as it may appear in retrospect, and it might be foolhardy to dismiss out of hand, for example, the view recently argued by Professor C. D. Darlington (in the wake of Galton, Flinders Petrie and Fustel de Coulanges) that 'All governing classes, and all slave classes, evidently arose in the beginning from the coming together of different races to form stratified societies which always competed favourably with unstratified societies.[18]

18     C. D. Darlington, *The Evolution of Man & Society* (London, 1969), p. 675.

But biological explanation, to the extent that it may be empirically confirmed, does not rule out sociological; and it is still plausible to suppose that an effective theory of stratification would consist of a statement of underlying psychological laws such that given a conjunction of specified institutional and environmental conditions, the known predisposition of persons possessed of the set of attributes designated as relevant to respond to these conditions in specified ways would account for the attested generalisation about (or, for that matter, individual case of) stratification for which an explanation is being sought. This excessively abstract pro-forma is, of course, of no help whatever in suggesting what the substantive content of such laws might be. In fact, it may be worth my emphasising that to speak of them as 'psychological' carries no implication of an 'atomistic' or any other particular model of social structure: it means merely that laws of social behaviour of whatever kind are laws of the behaviour of individuals, however much influenced by institutional and cultural as opposed to 'endogenous' variables. The main use in trying to spell out the form which they would have to take is that it shows just how very much further we are in the social than in the biological sciences from adequate theoretical grounding.

On the other hand, it is no less important to realise that although any explanation presupposes a statement of laws and empirical conditions from which it could in principle be derived, it is still possible effectively to vindicate 'idiographic' explanation of a particular feature of a particular system of stratification without being able to state the laws on which it must somewhere rest. We do not know the conditions under which it could safely be predicted that a more powerful class will enslave a less powerful one or the introduction of a new technology will create a new economic elite or a traditional ideology of purity and pollution will retard occupational mobility. But we know that each of these things, and many others like them, *can* happen in, or to, systems of social stratification; and once we accept certain initial conditions as given in a particular case, we can often successfully vindicate a causal claim that in this case it did. Explanation is always a matter of context, and the degree to which you are satisfied by a validated statement of cause and effect will depend on the sort of causes you are interested in. But *ad hoc* explanations are still explanations, and sociologists, anthropologists or historians of stratification have produced a great many of them.

In practice, therefore, the generalisations which, if they can be vindicated, will be the most rewarding to look for in the present state of our knowledge will be of an intermediate kind. It is true that even the simplest-looking observational generalisations will already carry at least some theoretical content. But what I mean is rather generalisations in which one or more of the variables in terms of which a stratification system has been operationally defined is linked to one or more independent variables in a putatively causal relation deriving from the implicit appeal to underlying psychological laws. In terms of the analogy with biological explanations, we are looking for generalisations at a similar level to the generalisation linking, say, the observed patterns of 'linear dominance' in primate troops to inherited fighting ability in terms of the underlying mechanism of natural selection. In this example, just as in a sociological case, a *ceteris paribus* clause may need to be spelt out: thus, the rank of an individual troop member may be a function also of his proximity to its 'central hierarchy', as has now been shown by systematic observation in the field. But the organisation of the central hierarchy is itself explicable in terms of the same theoretical grounding furnished by our knowledge of natural selection, so that the two generalisations (in contrast to so many in the sciences of man) are not exclusive but complementary. Now since I have not, with the possible exception of a very provisional and limited 'functional' generalisation about adult male earnings in industrial society, been able to propose any actual sociological candidate, it may seem foolish to try to say anything more in the absence of further empirical research.[19] But it is perhaps still worth my citing

---

19    Not that every useful discovery about stratification need be empirical in the ordinary sense: for example, purely arithmetical demonstration of the constraints within which rates of intergenerational occupational mobility are limited has been most useful in the progressive attempt to specify the determinants of changes in such rates: see e.g. Saburo Yasuda, 'A Methodological Enquiry into Social Mobility', *American Sociological Review* XXIX (1964), pp. 16-23; or O. D. Duncan, 'Methodological Issues in the Analysis of Social Mobility', in Smelser and Lipset, *op. cit.*, pp. 51-97.

a few actual examples of plausible *ad hoc* explanations of stratification in human society in order to illustrate, in a very tentative way, the nature of the presumptive laws which must somewhere underlie them if they can indeed be legitimately claimed to be valid.

First, let me take a specific regional example from East Africa where the variable in question is objective-qualitative—the presence or absence of an age-set system of stratification. In a comparison drawn between the Tiriki, who borrowed age-set organisation from their neighbours, and the Gusii, who did not, it has been plausibly suggested that the reason lies in their different requirements for defence, and indeed survival, in the face of inter-tribal warfare. Not only were the Tiriki vulnerable because they were relatively small in number, but the Terik, who were the only tribe to make them an offer of alliance, made age-group formation a condition of it. In the authors' words, 'Given the general military prowess of the Nilo-Hamites and the ease with which age-group organisation can be borrowed, it seems likely that a Bantu group which did not have a clear advantage in terms of size, defensive capacity or strong allies lacking age-groups, would tend to imitate the successful Nilo-Hamitic military organisation and initiate far-reaching changes in their social structure'.[20] Now this is a very common-sense, not to say pedestrian, sort of explanation of the difference initially found puzzling. But there is no reason to doubt that it is an adequate one, once it is accepted that willingness to modify an existing form of social organisation in the interests of territorial defence is a motive which can, if the rulers' authority is internally stable, effect such a change and in this instance demonstrably did. We do not yet know why, or under what conditions, this motive will override others— which is once more to say that we have yet to discover the psycho-ethological laws governing territorial defence in human as opposed to animal society. Nor do we know how age-set organisation as such evolved in the first place (or when, or where). But these are not the questions directly at issue, and they do not need to be resolved in order to say why the Gusii did not borrow age-set organisation, while the Tiriki did. All we need is to be confident that they could in

---

20      R. A. Levine and W. H. Sangree, 'The Diffusion of Age-Group Organisation in East Africa: a Controlled Comparison', *Africa* XXXII (1962), p. 109.

principle be resolved and that the authors' suggested generalisation, rough-and-ready though it is, is good enough even as it stands in the absence of proper theoretical grounding to justify their explanation of the contrast.

Second, let me take an objective-quantitative variable which is not one of the most immediately obvious but which is of considerable importance in the pattern of institutionalised inequalities in modernising societies: the proportion of the agricultural labour force who are landless. This is the sort of variable which might well be observed to be consistently correlated with similar objective-quantitative variables of an economic or demographic kind. But any serious candidate for a causal generalisation from which landlessness of the agricultural labour force as the dependent variable could reliably be predicted would have to invoke a number of more fundamental propositions about social behaviour. Consider the case of Mexico,[21] where the proportion in 1960 was 53 per cent. Why? One answer might be to offer a generalisation (suitably hedged in with *ceteris paribus*) whereby it is shown to be a function of the area of cultivable land and the population increase which typically follows on industrialisation. But this is to assume that the figure should be explained in terms of why it is so high. Once recall that before the Mexican Revolution it was 89 per cent, and the question becomes not why it is high but why it is low: given the population increase, a drop of 36 per cent is after all considerable. Now here as always in sociological (or anthropological or historical) explanation, what actually counts as an explanation depends on what particular contrast has been held to call for it. But any plausible explanation of the 53 per cent figure for 1960 requires a fairly detailed account of the relevant aspects of the social and political history of Mexico during the previous decades, and in particular of the *ejido* system; and this account, to the extent that it explains the figure, will in turn rest on the implicit invocation of whatever underlying laws are presupposed by the assertion that the combination of social and

---

21    See Claudio Stern and Joseph A. Kahl, 'Stratification Since the Revolution', Rodolfo Stavenhagen, 'Classes, Colonialism and Acculturation' and Pablo Gonsales-Casanova, 'Dynamics of the Class Structure', in Joseph A. Kahl, ed., *Comparative Perspectives on Stratification* (Boston, 1968), Part I: Mexico, a Developing Society.

political influences cited did in fact have the effect of bringing this particular distribution about. The account will, incidentally, however uncertain and controversial in its details, contain both a number of features readily describable in terms of 'functional adaptation' and a number readily describable in terms of 'conflict'. But what is to the point here is simply that such an account could in principle be given, and that it would involve presuppositions at a more fundamental theoretical level than a purely demographic generalisation, however relevant the demographic constraints may also be shown to be.

Third, let me take a contrast in terms of a subjective variable—the contrast between the characteristic form of class consciousness observed in Australia and that observed in the United States.[22] As is well known, the American ideology of egalitarianism was the product of a 'middle class' of independent small producers owning their own means of livelihood. In Australia, on the other hand, the suitability of the land for grazing sheep and the consequent pattern of pastoral land tenure inhibited the emergence of any similar class of small producers: instead, there emerged at the same time a rural proletariat employed under conditions likely to promote strong feelings of collective solidarity and an urban proletariat under no illusions that there existed beyond the cities an open frontier where enterprising individualists might establish themselves as independent owners of property. In any history of this kind, however well documented, there are serious difficulties in assigning degrees of causal importance to one influence rather than another: the proportion of Irish immigrants, the need to centralise educational services if they were to be provided in the outlying areas at all, and the pattern of relations with the mother country during the early colonial period may all have been significant in forming the political and social outlook of the Australian working class. But it can safely be accepted that some such combination of environmental and social influences does account for the difference in question. Admittedly, a comparative history along these lines raises the further question of

---

22    See Kurt B. Mayer, 'Social Stratification in Two Equalitarian Societies: Australia and the United States', in R. Bendix and S. M. Lipset, eds., *Class, Status and Power* (2nd edition; London, 1967), pp. 149-161.

whether independent causal influence should be assigned to the ideology itself; but this question I shall certainly not go into here. For the purposes of this paper, the point is that an adequate explanation of the initial contrast is once again feasible, even if no precise assignment of causal weights will ever be possible; and it is once again an explanation which rests on the implicit invocation of such other lawlike regularities as are required to justify the claim that in this instance a sparsely populated territory suitable mainly for grazing could, and given the other specified influences did, produce an ideology quite different from that produced by the conditions of the American frontier.

Now at this point someone may want to object that despite my plea for generalisations with putatively causal content and therefore implicit theoretical grounding, my examples suggest that successful explanation in the field of social stratification is of an orthodox, historical, one-at-a-time sort of kind. But this simultaneous advocacy of *ad hoc* explanations such as we do have, causal generalisations such as we scarcely have, and underlying psycho-ethological laws such as we are nowhere near finding as yet rests precisely on the rejection of the supposed contrast between 'idiographic' and 'nomothetic' explanation. This is not the place to try to assess the damage which this distinction has done in the sciences of man.[23] But I can think of no better example to show it to be spurious in the field of social stratification than European feudalism itself. Unlike any of my previous examples, this is a system of stratification which is unique, so that generalisation about it is in this sense impossible by definition. But it is nonetheless explicable in terms of presumptive generalisations at a different level. Given its complexity and duration as a qualitatively distinct mode of stratification and the difficulties of any reliable objective-quantitative description of the inequalities generated and sustained by it, any illustration can be only of the most fragmentary kind. But let me take just one short passage from Bloch:[24] 'Consider, for example, the society of the Merovingian period. Neither the state nor the family any longer provided adequate protection. The village

---

23    I have however attempted a more general discussion of it in *Sociology in its Place and Other Essays* (Cambridge, 1970), ch. 1.

24    Marc Bloch, *Feudal Society* (tr. Manyon; London, 1962), p. 140.

community was barely strong enough to maintain order within its own boundaries; the urban community scarcely existed. Everywhere, the weak man felt the need to be sheltered by someone more powerful. The powerful man, in his turn, could not maintain his prestige or his fortune or even his own safety except by securing for himself, by persuasion or coercion, the support of subordinates bound to his service. On the one hand, there was the urgent quest for a protector; on the other, there were usurpations of authority, often by violent means. And as notions of weakness and strength are always relative, in many cases the same man occupied a dual role—as a dependent of a more powerful man and a protector of humbler ones. Thus there began to be built up a vast system of personal relationships whose intersecting threads ran from one level of the social structure to another'.

The precise relation between the presumptive psychological laws underlying the implication of cause and effect and the particular initial conditions which accordingly led to the emergence of feudal social relations is not spelled out by Bloch himself. But it is evident that his argument rests on unspoken assumptions about the generally predictable responses of individual persons or families to the social conditions which followed the dissolution of the *pax Romana*. We cannot state these assumptions in any form sufficiently precise as well as general to deserve the name of 'law'. But to accept Bloch's explanation as valid, as far as it goes, is to accept that the evolution of the 'feudal' system of stratification was not wholly random (even if at some points in the story random influences may need to be cited) and that our approximate knowledge of typical reactions to insecurity is sufficient, *post hoc*, to account for the emergence of intersecting relationships of dependence from the social conditions which on the evidence we have can be adequately specified. If, therefore, we ever do succeed in formulating an appropriate lawlike generalisation (which will not, of course, be about feudal relations as such but about some one or more variables of the kinds I have enumerated which are instantiated in the feudal, as in any other, system of stratification), it will not only furnish the necessary link between the initial social conditions and the aspect of feudal social relations in question but will also be much more closely grounded than our present broad assumptions in the laws by which individual responses to such conditions are governed. It will also, whatever form it takes, have both a 'functional' and a 'coercive' aspect, since whatever the theory of stratification of which it would form a part it would have to take account both of the survival function of the institution of personal subordination and also of the disparity of powers implicit in that relation (as is clearly brought out in Bloch's account). Now the prospect of a satisfactory set of such generalisations is not, for the time being, at all immediate, but it is not entirely visionary either; and if it is realised, this will depend as much on the *ad hoc* and, if you like, pedestrian explanations of particular aspects of particular systems of stratification as on the sweeping theoretical insights at the psychological or ethological level on which (despite successive disappointments) the social sciences must continue to rest their hopes.

Beyond this point, it does become progressively less interesting to protract a methodological discussion about what a theory of stratification might eventually look like. The one methodological task which could usefully be performed is the one which I said I had no intention of attempting, namely the specification of the variables in terms of which systems of social stratification of any kind could be operationally defined and thus described; and this already is closer to substantive research than anything I have put forward in this paper. But if I am right in what I have been saying, it may be appropriate to end the paper on a mildly polemical note. The likelihood of major advance in our understanding of social stratification may not, as I suggested at the outset, be quite as low as a review of the current social-scientific literature might make it seem. But it would none the less be higher than it is if those who have devoted themselves to the formulation of large-scale generalisations has paid a little more attention to rigorous measurement and historical detail, and if those who have devoted themselves to meticulous and well-documented case studies had paid a little more attention to issues of comparability and generalisation. The plea for hypotheses of the 'middle range' has become so familiar a catch-phrase that it ought not to need to be repeated in the area of social stratification any more than elsewhere in the social sciences. But unfortunately it does.

Hugh Freeman

# Mental Health and New Communities in Britain

Some of the material in this chapter originally appeared in the *British Journal of Hospital Medicine* (1970), *3*, 732.
Hugh Freeman, M.A., B.M., B.Ch., D.P.M., F.R.C.Psych.
Consultant Psychiatrist, Manchester Regional Hospital Board and City of Salford Health and Social Service Departments.
Chairman, Division of Psychiatry, Salford Hospitals Group.
Honorary Lecturer, University of Salford.
Editor of *Mental Health* and Honorary Medical Consultant, National Association for Mental Health.

Whatever the precise nature of sociological or political studies, it is inevitable that they will be concerned in certain dimensions with the functioning level of individuals. To express these in terms such as 'happiness', 'satisfaction', 'fulfilment' or even 'mental health' is very likely to involve value judgements which perhaps tell us more about the observer than those observed. Yet scientific medicine, at its present stage of development, can hardly neglect the exploration of any possible relationships of environment with health—in both physical and psychological aspects, and studies reviewed here show these two aspects to be closely inter-related. To some extent, this exploration must be done in the self-defence of scientific enquiry since the Western public is currently bombarded through the mass media with dogmatic pronouncements on the subject, which within themselves are often self-contradictory. For instance, psychiatric illness in general is at some times blamed on bad social conditions (poverty, overcrowding, high-level housing) and at others on greater affluence (excess leisure, lack of biologically useful stresses, boredom with conventional activities). In such statements about 'the conditions that caused the illness', certainty of conclusions tends to be in inverse proportion to scientific sophistication and the common level is

G

no more than anecdotal. The same fallacy underlies demands for 'preventive' or 'positive' activities in relation to psychiatric conditions whose fundamental causes remain unknown.

In this connection, the relationship between psychiatry and sociology has been surprisingly neglected, except by Elias (1969), who points out that though both disciplines are concerned with the study of human beings, we have at present no clear theoretical model to show how they relate to each other or to the other sciences of man. 'Faced with related problems, each offers its own type of explanation' and this tends to be followed by a competitive struggle in which both professions try to reduce the other's explanation to its own, as being the more 'fundamental'.[1] Elias goes on to criticise psychiatrists for vaguely conglomerating family, neighbourhood, community and other social configurations into a single factor of 'environment' or 'social background', whereas for the sociologist, each of these represents a separate highly structured element with dynamics of its own. (In much the same way, non-psychiatric physicians will dismiss the whole of an immensely complex psychopathological state as 'functional overlay'.) In Elias' view, psychiatric terminology and thinking imply a separation between a highly structured situation within the individual on the one hand and an apparently unstructured network of relations and communications in the background. Such differences in both basic concepts and in the evaluation of data that follow from them are likely to make collaborative efforts in the socio-psychiatric field extremely difficult. Elias finally makes the point that the psychiatric conception of the individual experiencing himself as the centre of the human universe, with all other individuals outside, is not a very old one. 'It is confined to a group of fairly advanced European and American societies during a limited period of their development, and even during that period, in all likelihood, mainly to the educated elites'.

These are important comments, which need to be kept in mind throughout the following discussion, since much 'social psychiatry' has certainly remained at a rather naive level in terms of sociological thought. However, Elias does seem to equate psychiatry to a large

---

1    Elias, N. (1969) in Foulkes, S. H. and Prince, G. S. (eds.), 'Psychiatry in a Changing Society', London: Tavistock.

extent with psychoanalytical theory and whilst this misconception is a fact of life in American writing, it is not strictly relevant to the situation in Britain. In itself, this does not much reduce the validity of the criticism that psychiatry (of any school) is too sharply focused on what is happening within individuals. There is also support in the results of existing studies for the view that the individual/outside world dichotomy is a phenomenon closely related to culture and social class.

On the other hand, Hare (1966) suggests that though much sociological work is based on the view that a person's social adjustment is considerably influenced by conditions of housing and neighbourhood and by such stress as a recent move to an unfamiliar district, we do not really know how far the sociological concept of adjustment is equivalent to the medical concept of health. He also suggests that sociologists may not always have pursued their investigations far enough, since people who are found to be socially maladjusted on a new housing estate may have been equally maladjusted before they moved there. In fact, there seems to be a need for greater sophistication by both disciplines when dealing with the other.

### New Communities

It should be appreciated from the outset of this discussion that searching for direct aetiological connections between specific forms of psychiatric illness and specific features of the social environment— whether in new communities or elsewhere—is a generally unrewarding task. As Carstairs and Brown have pointed out (1958) 'It is probable that when a person experiences a degree of stress sufficient to impair his health, the manner in which his ill-health is expressed—whether as a "physical" illness or a "mental" one— will often depend as much on his constitution as on the nature of the stress. Thus it is probably an over-simplification to suppose that unsatisfactory physical conditions impair physical health and that unsatisfactory psychological or social conditions impair mental health'.[2] In fact, from the point of view of scientific method, the

---

2      Carstairs, G. M. and Brown, G. W. (1958), J. Ment. Sci., *104*, 72.

whole subject-area is a veritable slough of despond, in which every step throws up further apparently unanswerable questions. As a result, reliable conclusions have so far been very few, but it is surely important for those working throughout the behavioural sciences to know what they are, if only because major decisions of public policy relating to these issues may be taken on the basis of mere hunches or of conventional myths. The purpose of this contribution is to summarise what is actually known about the relationship between levels of psychiatric health and a particular category of social environment. This category includes the three main forms of large new communities developed in Britain since World War Two—new towns, expanding towns and peripheral developments (HMSO, 1967).[3] I propose to accept this definition without further detailed discussion, which would be beyond the scope of my own discipline. From such a relatively small body of knowledge, some tentative conclusions can be drawn about the way in which mental health services (medical and social) should be provided for such populations and these conclusions in turn have wider implications.

The particular relevance of new communities to the more general problems of population morbidity and of delivery of medico-social care is that they can provide a fairly specific social situation, open to certain forms of manipulation. They also provide population laboratories which, in many practical ways, are more accessible to systematic research than older and larger areas of habitation. Sichel (1969) has suggested that while it is a difficult research problem in general to assess the efficiency with which medical services are provided, 'The new town situation may provide a suitable field for the development of its methodology'.[4] This is not to imply, though, that the opportunity has so far been taken in any significant way. Mullin's (1969) view in relation to British new towns is that '. . . we have failed to evaluate their achievements in the light of the assumptions on which their construction was based. Until recently we have refused to view the wealth of positive planning which has taken place in this country as a set of hypotheses which could and

---

3     H.M.S.O. (1967). 'The Needs of New Communities'. Ministry of Housing and Local Government. London.

4     Sichel, G. R. M. (1969), Health Trends, *1*, 18.

should be tested, or to bargain for their possible failure. Also, because we have largely failed to develop methods of inter-disciplinary study appropriate to such an environmental situation we have not been able to judge whether any successes we have achieved have been the result of conscious action or of entirely separate and perhaps fortuitous factors'.[5] Comparing the volume of public investment that has gone into the building of new communities with the puny efforts that have so far been made to study their human consequences, it is difficult to dispute this castigation, even though it is one which applies with at least as much force to many other areas of public policy.

Whilst the new towns are the 'newest' of these communities, in that they have been designed to be balanced and self-sufficient, with relatively small cores of pre-existing development, the peripheral housing estates of large towns have in fact accommodated a far greater total of people since 1945. Though the peripheral developments are so far more significant in terms of numbers, their form has been very conventional and the new towns have naturally attracted more interest. To a very varying extent, the actual new housing has been accompanied by other facilities which a modern population needs, such as employment, shops, places of entertainment, schools, public buildings, churches and medical and social services. But it is true almost everywhere that the provision of these facilities has lagged far behind that of housing—perhaps the most notorious examples being estates in Glasgow, such as Castlemilk. The short-fall of facilities has undoubtedly had unfavourable consequences for the populations concerned, even though these consequences have gone largely unmeasured so far.

*Mental Health*
The first and overwhelming question to be considered here is how the concept of 'mental health' is to be defined operationally. Hare and Shaw (1965)[6] follow the view of Eaton (1951)[7] that in practical terms, any such concept can only be distinguished through a variety

5      Mullin, S. (1969), *New Statesman*, 78, 818.
6      Hare & Shaw, G. K. (1965), 'Mental Health on a New Housing Estate'. London: Oxford University Press.
7      Eaton, J. W. (1951), Amer. J. Psychiat., 108, 81.

of criteria, rather than any single one. They emphasise that the more an operational definition is made simple and clear-cut for purposes of measurement, the greater is the danger that relevance will be sacrificed to clarity. Nevertheless, where two populations are being directly compared, any deficiencies of definition will presumably apply equally to both. In their own research study (to be referred to in more detail below) they followed Martin, Brotherston and Chave (1957) in using the three general criteria of cases treated by hospital, diagnosis by general practitioners, and symptoms or signs found in an interview survey of a population sample.[8] The third of these has been a subject of some controversy as a valid criterion of mental health, but Hare and Shaw clinch the argument by asking—'if by environmental changes we were able to reduce the number of persons in a population who admitted to symptoms of undue anxiety, depression, etc., in response to a questionary, should we have improved the mental health of the population?'.[9]

The answer to this must clearly be yes, but the situation remains highly complex because results can be strongly influenced by the design of the questionary itself, which may be based on a formulation of 'mental health' in ideal terms. This was seen particularly in the Midtown Manhattan Study of Srole et al (1962), where 75 per cent of a random sample of the population were found to show significant anxiety symptoms.[10] This means that the criteria of illness have been formulated so loosely that 'normality' has virtually ceased to exist or, as Taylor and Chave (op. cit.) suggest, the investigators 'may really have been measuring the amount of normal anxiety inherent in life in New York'.[11]

That three-quarters of the population of a Western metropolis are psychiatrically sick is a conclusion which would be neither surprising nor particularly unwelcome to those of certain philosophical or ideological standpoints. But in the very different conditions

8    Martin, F. M., Brotherston, J. H. F. and Chave, S. P. W. (1957). Brit J. prev. soc. Med., *11*, 196.

9    Hare & Shaw, *op. cit.*

10    Srole, S., Langner, T. S., Michael, S. T., Opler, M. K. and Rennie, T. A. C. (1962). 'Mental Health in the Metropolis'. New York.

11    Taylor, S. and Chave, S. P. W. (1964). 'Mental Health and Environment': London: Longmans.

of rural maritime Canada, 37 per cent of a surveyed population were also judged to be suffering from psychiatric illness (Leighton, 1957).[12] This suggests that it is in fact the measuring instruments which are at fault and that similarly alarming results might be obtained from almost any community, if approached in a similar way. This is confirmed by the fact that much more modest, and fairly consistent figures of morbidity have been obtained in Britain, both in new communities and in general practice surveys.

Any systematic attempt at measurement, therefore, must inevitably start from the negative, rather than the positive pole and examine as well as it can the extent of mental *ill*-health in any population. Here again, the situation is far from simple, since almost all reported figures are in fact measures of *treatment* given, rather than of distribution of illness (or total morbidity). Obviously, this quantity of treatment will be related more to a community's level of economic and social development than to its actual needs in terms of morbidity. The difficulty of measurement is further increased by the fact that the whole concept of 'illness' in psychiatry is much more influenced by social and cultural factors than is the case with somatic medicine. For instance, Carstairs (1969) has estimated that over the world as a whole, more cases of schizophrenia are under the care of witch-doctors than of psychiatrists trained in Western medicine.[13] However, in the present discussion, the treatment role can be simplified to some extent by keeping to Western developed societies, such as Britain. In these areas today, it can reasonably be assumed that most cases of severe disorder (psychosis or mental subnormality) will be known to the specialist psychiatric services. These disorders are generally held—except by schools such as that of R. D. Laing—to be biologically determined, with environmental factors being of secondary importance in aetiology. The research requirement then is to record the activities of these specialist services accurately in relation to defined communities, a task which might seem relatively simple, but which in fact is still in its beginnings through psychiatric case registers, such as those in Camber-

12    Leighton, A. H. (1959). 'My Name is Legion'. New York: Basic Books.
13    Carstairs, G. M. (1969) in Freeman, H. L. (ed.) 'Progress in Mental Health', London: Churchill.

well, Aberdeen and Salford (Fryers, Freeman and Mountney, 1970).[14]

On the other hand, most cases of the milder psychiatric disorders (neurosis and personality deviations) will probably *not* be known to the specialist services except under very atypical conditions, *e.g.* in the wealthiest communities of the United States. In this country, most such cases which come to medical attention are treated within general practice. For the epidemiologist, estimation of the extent of this second group is very much more difficult than that of the first (Shepherd *et al.*, 1966).[15] Nevertheless, much experience has been gained in recent years in the development of measurements of psychiatric disorder which could be used for whole communities. If we still lack this information on any large scale, it is mainly because the necessary resources have not yet been applied to obtaining it. Yet the subject is a most important one, since the only way in which medical services could be rationally planned would be on the basis of measured total community morbidity; in fact, very little is known about this in relation to any major form of illness. Even in most of the new communities, the enormous expenditure of the National Health Service mainly follows traditional, well-worn paths of delivering services, with some additions based largely on speculative hunches. Similarly, in the United States, the immense investment of the community mental health centres programme, following the Kennedy legislation of 1963, has been accompanied by little attempt to evaluate either the effectiveness of what is being done or the appropriateness of services offered to communities' needs.

In relation to new communities, there are two significant aspects of mental health. The first of these is the consequences of *moving* to such a community and the second is the effects of *living* there. However, as the second begins to overlap almost immediately with the first, it is obviously difficult to separate the two in practice to any extent and unless specifically designed otherwise, any investigations in this area are likely to measure only their combined effects. In

---

14    Fryers, T., Freeman, H. L. and Mountney, G. H. (1970), Soc. Psychiat., 5, 187.

15    Shepherd, M., Cooper, B., Brown, A. C. and Kalton, G. (1966). 'Psychiatric Illness in General Practice'. London: Oxford University Press.

general terms, moving to a new community is a form of social change and from surveying the effects of this, Murphy (1961) concluded that people undergoing rapid change of any kind tended to show more psychiatric pathology than others from the same background who were experiencing less change.[16] Therefore, a certain excess of psychiatric morbidity would be expected in the population of a new community, relative to more settled areas which were otherwise comparable. Some of this excess will result from quite mundane, practical problems; 'The wider family and the network of friends are left behind and new relationships have to be established. A new house has to be furnished. The children have to attend a new school—which may be organised on unfamiliar lines and may involve travelling. The husband may have a new job and workmates. The wife has to become acquainted with the local shops and tradesmen. Many adjustments have to be made' (HMSO, *op. cit.*).[17] Clearly, successful adjustment of this kind requires some degree of personality strength which will not always be present in residents coming to new communities. Evans *et. al.* (1969) reported that about 10 per cent of new families coming to the overspill development in Andover returned to London, often after only a few months. This was often through financial crises, resulting from higher rent or expensive central heating, hire purchase debts, lack of cheap street markets and the cutting of overtime, if not outright loss of a job. Though the borough councils from their original home areas tried to make sure that each family was free of debt before leaving, this did not exclude the arrival of many 'problem families'.

The social change will have maximum impact where there is a marked contrast between the family's previous social context and that it finds in a new community. This contrast is most likely to occur when the family comes from an old, stable working-class neighbourhood such as Bethnal Green (London), Ancoats (Manchester), Hunslet (Leeds) or 'Hanky Park' (Salford). Each of these was '. . . a closely-knit community, based on long residence and inter-marriage, with its own institutions and customary ways by which everyday life of the district was determined . . . social groups

---

16    Murphy, H. B. M. (1961), in 'Causes of Mental Disorders,' New York: Millbank Memorial Fund.

17    H.M.S.O. *op. cit.*

centred on the physical environment with its familiar streets, small shops and other informal meeting places. .... In the new setting, there are no longer commonly accepted standards. With the breaking of the kinship tie, there goes also the basis of community in the form in which it has been known and shared'. (Nicholson, 1960).[18] Although Britain has seen an enormous migration from these old communities, which were spawned by the Industrial Revolution, the only deep study of its emotional impact is American (Fried, 1963).[19]

Fried and his colleagues investigated the effects of enforced migration (or 'relocation' in their infelicitous phrase) on inhabitants of a former slum residential area of Boston. They found that among 250 women, 26 per cent reported that they still felt sad and depressed two years after moving and another 20 per cent reported having had these feelings for at least six months. Among 316 men, the percentage showing long-term grief reactions was only slightly smaller. These affective reactions showed most of the characteristics of grief and mourning for a lost person, but in addition, many other men and women indicated less severe depressive responses in their answers to questions. This study found that the two most important components of the grief reaction were fragmentation of the sense of spatial identity and dependence of the sense of group identity on stable social networks. These components, with their associated affective qualities, were critical foci for the sense of continuity, which in such a working class community is dependent on the external stability and familiarity of places and people. The implications of these findings are extremely important for social planning, which will be discussed later. They are fairly specific to the working class, but then most planned new communities are primarily for working class residents. However, Hall (1966) was less impressed by the significance of local migration in a study of 122 patients in Sheffield who attributed their symptoms to a move of house. A subgroup of 54 young women mostly had depressive or hysterical symptoms and their marital relations were uniformly poor, with

18      Nicholson, J. H. (1961), 'New Communities in Britain'. London: National Council of Social Service.

19      Fried, M. (1963) in Duhl, L. J. (ed.) 'The Urban Condition', New York: Basic Books.

often grossly neurotic attitudes to childbearing and children. Whilst the destination of the move appeared to have no specific effect on the clinical features, the origin of the move was often significant. Complaints about the new housing were numerous, usually vague and almost invariably a projection of other problems. A second subgroup of 16 male patients complained mainly of obsessional symptoms; their married life had been generally characterized by sexual inadequacy, hostility and a restless search for better things. A third group of 23 older women presented depressive symptoms and in 18 cases complaints about their new housing ceased when the depression had been treated. The fourth group consisted of small numbers suffering from schizophrenia and other conditions, but the actual conditions of the new housing did not seem to be aetiologically significant in any of them.

Hall suggests that a new housing environment forms a more suitable matrix for projection of personal difficulties by neurotic patients than a well-structured one. 'During psychotherapy, housing complaints were soon, in fact, spontaneously abandoned by patients. I have been unable to demonstrate the precipitation of illness by moving house in previously well adjusted personalities, neither does it seem to me that moves into municipal housing are more pathogenic than others. . . . Social planning of new neighbourhoods probably plays an important part in relieving a degree of unhappiness and isolation among certain tenants of new housing. From the point of view of the clinical psychiatrist, however, it may be desirable to try and identify such vulnerable individuals, and if possible to provide support and counselling at an early stage of their migration, preferably before this takes place'.

In Salford, my colleague Dr Donald Johnson has analysed applications for rehousing by the local authority on psychiatric grounds and followed up the individuals concerned (Johnson, 1971). As far as necessity for treatment was concerned, no difference was found between the group who were rehoused and those who were not; the same was found in respect of change in severity of symptoms. Irrespective of rehousing, the changes measured could be predicted from the usual clinical prognostic indications and psychiatric treatment appeared to be more important than this form of social manipulation.

*Population Character*

It has been a general feature of all new communities in Britain up to now that their population structures have been markedly different from those of established areas. These differences have resulted directly from public housing policy, though they have not always worked out entirely in the way that was intended. All new communities show a relative deficit of old people, which is particularly striking in contrast to the steadily increasing proportion of the aged in the general population. However, in the first group of new towns built after World War Two, the character of the incoming population was affected by the low birth rates of the early 1950s, whereas in the more recent new towns and town expansions, the age-distribution shows an even greater skew towards youthfulness. The consequences of such a maldistribution of age-groups will continue to develop: '. . . a high rate of natural increase for a number of years and considerable pressure on school accommodation may be expected. Moreover, since more children have already been born to incoming parents than was the case in the earlier new towns, the peak of school leavers will occur earlier and on a relatively larger scale. Similarly, second-generation family formation may be expected to occur a few years in advance of earlier new town experience'.[20] These simple facts of demography, with an initial bulge of young adults and young children, must profoundly affect the life of each community, as well as the demands which will be made in it for every kind of service. For instance, the time of young parenthood is generally felt to throw the greatest strain on both the personal and financial resources of married couples, compared with other periods of life.

Criticising this situation, Thomas (1969) states that the new towns have failed to become balanced communities of the kind that was originally planned and that this failure is mainly the result of the housing policy, whereby young married couples have special difficulties in getting accommodation anywhere else. '. . . this is an age-group with many of its members marrying and establishing new households. It is a fertile age-group whose housing requirements are changing with each new child. But adjustment to factors of this kind could have been accommodated by very local moves, if the con-

---

20     H.M.S.O. *op. cit.*

ditions of the housing market had been such as to make this possible'.[21] Not only that, but the new towns contain few middle-class people (since there is little private housing available) few of the lowest socio-economic groups (through lack of differential subsidies for rent rebates) and very little special housing for the elderly. Thomas also found that in the period 1961-66, in the second-generation new towns, the proportionate growth in the numbers of managers and professional workers was significantly higher than the overall increase in the economically active population, indicating a marked degree of upward social mobility. 'The new towns are manu-facturers of managers and producers of professionals'.[22] On the other hand, they have made little or no contribution to the housing needs of under-privileged groups, such as the poor and the aged, and seem to have suffered socially from having too high a population within a fairly narrow income range.

Contrasting the populations of peripheral developments with those of new towns, Clout (1962) states that in the former case '. . . the tenants came from housing lists, in order of priority. They included a high proportion of families who had been living in overcrowded conditions. Many members had tuberculosis, psychoneurotic disease or heart disease. In the new towns, on the other hand, the tenants came because they were employed in a factory that decided to move to the new industrial estate. As a result, they tended to be younger than the national average and to be healthy'.[23] This contrast, which refers mainly to Crawley new town, is probably something of an over-statement and would not apply, in any case, to people rehoused in peripheral estates through slum clearance. However, it does usefully draw attention to likely variations in morbidity, resulting from the way the populations of different new communities are selected. Lemkau (1969) emphasises that a significant number of mentally subnormal or otherwise handicapped children will in-evitably both arrive with incoming families and be born in the early years of a new community, whilst the parents are in an age-group

---

21    Thomas, R. (1969), 'Aycliffe to Cumbernauld,' London: P.E.P Economic Tract 516.
22    *Ibid.*
23    Clout, I. (1962). *Lancet*, i, 683.

with a relatively high risk of developing schizophrenia.[24] These phenomena are largely irrespective of environmental or stress factors which may, however, foster the emergence of some depressive or neurotic illnesses, though this is a more controversial suggestion, as will be seen later.

The distorted age-structure of new communities must represent a significant disruption of the networks of advice and assistance which exist among extended families in old-established areas and it is quite likely that the emotional development of the young will therefore tend to proceed less well than in a multi-generational setting. Under present conditions, there are also likely to be acute social problems when very large numbers reach adolescence or leave school within a short period of time. One particularly alarming aspect of this came to light in 1967 in Crawley, which then had 41 per cent of its population of 62,000 aged under twenty (comparable with an under-developed country). Surveying all cases of heroin abuse among young people there, d'Alarcon and Rathod (1968) found 92 cases or possible cases in the age-group fifteen to twenty.[25] Nine out of ten of these were males, representing 2.7 per cent of the entire male population in this age-group. Previous to this survey, only eight cases from the area had been known to the Home Office as addicts. This would seem to indicate that problems existing among young people in a community of average age-distribution may assume epidemic proportions when the population structure is so disproportionate, as in a new town.

*Psychiatric Surveys*
New communities, then, have a different population structure from the national average, and, at least in the case of working class families, will contain a certain proportion of adults likely to show grief reactions following their separation from the home area, in addition to the general effects of rapid social change. But what actual levels of psychiatric morbidity have been found in these communities?

---

24    Lemkau, P. V. (1969) in Shore, M. F. and Mannino, F. V. (eds.) 'Mental Health and the Community', New York: Behavioral Publications.

25    d'Alarcon, R. and Rathod, N. H. (1968), Brit. med. J., i, 549.

The first significant work on this question—though at a mainly anecdotal level—was Taylor's now classic paper on 'Suburban Neurosis' in 1938.[26] He recorded the stresses which commonly occurred after removal from a central city area to a peripheral housing estate (higher expenses, social isolation, distance from employment, loss of familiar surroundings, etc.) and noted that these seemed to result in a higher incidence of neurotic disturbances, particularly in women. During the war years, the whole question naturally lay dormant. I myself later found similar disturbances, though usually associated with more extreme forms of stress, among service wives living in barrack married quarters (Freeman, 1958).[27] Comparable reports also came from American suburban communities in New Jersey (Gordon and Gordon, 1961).[28] However, recent work really begins with the survey of Martin, Brotherston and Chave (1957), carried out in a housing estate about twelve miles from London—Oxley.[29] They found that the mental hospital admission rate there was higher than the national average at all ages, but particularly for females aged 45 and over; that consultation rates with general practitioners for neurosis and similar conditions greatly exceeded those found in a national sample and that the proportion of persons with nervous symptoms found in interviews with a sample of the estate population was nearly twice that found in a nation-wide survey. Taking into account other data, such as those for juvenile delinquency and the use of child guidance clinics, Martin et al. concluded that the rate of mental ill-health (particularly neurosis) in the estate population was higher than the national average. They suspected that this could be attributed partly to the shock of rehousing and partly to the poor social facilities, which led to a degree of loneliness and social isolation incompatible with good mental health. However, Hare and Shaw did not accept that these relatively high rates of illness were necessarily attributable to the social conditions peculiar to new housing estates.[30] For instance,

26    Taylor, S. (1938), Lancet, i, 759.
27    Freeman, H. L. (1958). J. of the R.A.M.C., 104, 31.
28    Gordon, R. E. and Gordon, K. K. (1961). 'The Split-Level Trap'. New York: Random House.
29    Martin, op. cit.
30    Hare & Shaw, op. cit.

general practitioner consultation rates for neurotic disorders are much higher in urban areas as a whole than in rural areas. Also, many studies have shown that people in good houses tend to have better physical health than those in bad ones, but this does not necessarily mean that the good housing is responsible for the better health. It might be due to one or more of any factors, such as differences in income, age or heredity, which tend to cluster in a positive or negative direction. Hare (1966) also suggests that the comparison of illness rates from the estate with national rates is not so sound a method as direct comparison with a nearby population in a comparable urban setting, made at the same time by the same study team, as in the Harlow and Croydon surveys.

Hare and Shaw's own study compared a new peripheral housing estate in Croydon with an older, central area of the town. Their positive findings were a marked association between mental ill-health and physical ill-health and a similar association between nervous disturbance and attitudes of general dissatisfaction with one's neighbourhood. Although more people in the new estate made complaints about lack of amenities than in the old area, attitudes of general dissatisfaction with the environment were no commoner. In the central area, in fact, over half the sample complained of the physical discomforts associated with industrialisation and old housing. Hare and Shaw concluded that every population contains a vulnerable group, who are more prone to the development of illness, both mental and physical. This group will tend to complain of their surroundings—wherever they are—probably because such complaints are mostly a projection of their poor health. They believed that the attention devoted to the health of new communities was mainly because of the interest of such areas to the news media at that time.

Here and elsewhere, Hare (1964) tends to a rather parsimonious view of the possible influence of social environment on mental health.[31] He points out that on the one hand, mental health might be expected to improve from moving, since the new houses are better designed and easier to run and the greater space and privacy should reduce fatigue, irritability and resentments within the family. On the

---

31    Hare, E. H. (1964). Ment. Hlth. (Lond.), 23, 58.

other hand, housewives who have grown up amongst a tradition of neighbourliness, with ready help and advice available from relatives, may be bewildered to find these missing in the artificially derived population of a new town or peripheral estate. On the whole, he believed that the conditions of new town life have no long-term influence on the mental health of adults who move there, though the process of moving (*i.e.* rapid cultural change) might cause a temporary exacerbation of symptoms in persons who were already neurotic. However, there was already evidence then that children in the new towns were showing improved physical health and this gave reason to hope that when they grew up, their mental health also might be better than that of their parents.

Hare's final conclusion (1966 *op. cit.*) is that the apparent precipitants of mental ill-health in new communities '. . . may be no more than small additional weights which tip the scales over to illness at a time when the really heavy weights in the scale-pans are equally balanced. Minor misfortunes are an inescapable part of the human lot and it would then be a vain hope to prevent neurosis by trying to exclude them'. Therefore, he suggests that the really weighty causal factors of neurosis must be looked for in the constitution, which is a compound of genetic endowment and the physical and psychological influences which have acted on this since conception. From this, it follows that the only feasible way of improving the constitution of future adults would be by reducing environmental factors that may damage the constitution in infancy. This view appears to be supported by evidence of association between complications of pregnancy and childbirth on the one hand and on the other hand, later ill-health or maladjustment; children with a congenitally impaired nervous system may be vulnerable not only to common ailments but also to the effects of a disturbed family life. The argument, however, is somewhat complicated by the fact that in respect of early life, 'constitution' and 'environment' are not clearly separated and unless they are rigorously defined, comparison with other statements becomes difficult.

These views of Hare appeared to have been supported by an earlier study in Baltimore by Wilner *et al.* (1962).[32] These workers measured

---

32    Wilner, R. P., Pinkerton, T. P. and Tayback, M. (1962). 'The Housing Environment and Family Life', Baltimore.

the health of 600 families who were poorly housed and half of whom were shortly to be rehoused on a new estate. The health of both groups was then observed for a follow-up period of two years. At the end of this time, the children who had moved showed less physical ill-health than those who had not; some benefit (though less) was seen in the case of young adults who had moved, but no difference was found in the physical health of those aged over 35. Adults in the new housing area were more ready to invite friends into their houses, were more interested in keeping their houses and gardens neat and tidy and were more optimistic in their outlook on life. On the other hand, there was no difference between the two groups in the amount of friction and quarrelling among family members or in the amount of irritability, nervousness and depression in individuals. Therefore, in terms of mental health, the effects of rehousing over this period of time were relatively unimpressive.

About the same time, Clout reported a comparison within his general practice of patients from the new town at Crawley with those from the older area of the district.[33] Whilst psychiatric illness was common in both groups, the total rate from the new town patients was only 4 per cent higher and this difference was accounted for entirely by women of reproductive age. He suggested that since the men had generally moved to the new town in working groups (which fostered factory-based social activities) their morale tended to remain high. On the other hand, many of the women had to face the problems of pregnancy and childbirth in a strange area, with very inadequate maternity services. Unfortunately, as Fox (1962) pointed out, this study was very unsatisfactory from the methodological point of view and it seemed quite possible that this particular general practice was unpresentative of the local population in its high rates of psychiatric illness.[34] The personal qualities of the particular doctors may have attracted a biased sample, the diagnostic criteria and validity are not entirely clear and the prevalence data are presented in such a way that they cannot be compared with other studies.

Rather different conclusions were reached by Taylor and Chave (1964), who had both been involved in previous studies—referred to

33    Clout, *op. cit.*
34    Fox, R. (1962), *Lancet*, i, 905.

above.[35] Collecting a remarkable amount of information with very limited resources, they compared measures of mental ill-health in Harlow new town with the peripheral estate studied in 1957 and also with an inner area of London from which many of the Harlow people had come. Like Hare and Shaw, they distinguished a constitutionally vulnerable group (described as having the 'sub-clinical neurosis syndrome'), which was found to be of about the same size in all three areas. However, in contrast to the housing estate, fewer people from Harlow than in the general population were under specialist psychiatric care. Taking general practice consultation rates for neurosis, Harlow gave a higher figure than the national average, as did the peripheral estate, but Taylor and Chave did not take this to show that neurotic illness was more common in the new town. In fact, Taylor frankly threw overboard his original conception of 'Suburban Neurosis'. Their explanation of this finding was that Harlow had an exceptionally good family doctor service, which people were more ready to consult than they would have been in their old city area. This view would seem to be supported by Butterfield's statement (1968) that though there has not been much medical planning for new towns in general, the two exceptions were Harlow in England and Livingston in Scotland.[36] However, this might correspondingly reduce the relevance of Taylor and Chave's findings to new towns as a whole.

Their other findings included the observation that neurotic illness did not become less with length of residence in Harlow and this was held to confirm the view that such illness is mainly of constitutional origin, rather than a product of the immediate environment. The neurotic group showed a greater tendency to be dissatisfied with their environment and to complain of loneliness; these features appeared to be results of their vulnerable personalities, rather than causes of neurotic reactions. As in Hare and Shaw's study, an association was found between physical and emotional ill-health. Finally, the rate of psychosis was found to be well below the national average (in contrast to the peripheral estate) and this was held to remain true even when corrections were made for the age and income structure of the

35    Taylor & Chave, op. cit.
36    Butterfield, W. J. H. (1968). 'Priorities in Medicine', London: Oxford University Press.

Harlow population and for a possible loss of schizophrenics in social class V, as a result of differential class migration to the new town.

In their conclusions, throwing epidemiological scruples to the winds, Taylor and Chave postulate that environment has a markedly determining effect on the manifestation and course of psychotic illness and that 'good social planning can reduce the incidence of psychosis'.[37] This optimistic view was strongly contested by Susser (1964), amongst others, who stated: '. . . the data cannot quite sustain the weight of interpretation the authors put upon it. Their analysis is weakened by the failure to consider the large disparity that is likely to exist, in long-term disorder, between the appearance of fresh cases in a population on the one hand and the total prevalence of cases on the other . . . (their) conclusion should be considered (only) as one of a number of possible hypotheses'.[38]

Taylor and Chave's work illustrates how easy it is to stumble into a methodological pitfall in this subject, through the inadequacies of survey measures. Their suggestion that psychosis is largely determined environmentally flies in the face of genetic evidence and of the remarkable constancy of schizophrenic prevalence rates at different times and places. The only support for such a view would seem to come (surprisingly enough) from existentialists such as R. D. Laing. On the other hand, Smith (1968) suggests that it is rather in the case of neurotic disorders where '. . . it seems likely that their causes will prove to lie in external factors involving the basic processes of social adaptation which are relatively recent in the evolutionary history of the human species and which are subject to continual change'.[39] In fact, we are very unlikely to secure the primary prevention of schizophrenia by building more new towns, however good they may be, though milder conditions (with a smaller degree of biological determination) may be rather more susceptible to the good effects of social planning.

Taylor and Chave were on firmer ground in pointing out that: 'The full measure of the success or failure of a new town will come only in the next generation, in the children who have been born and brought up in an environment which differs markedly from that

37    Taylor & Chave, *op. cit.*

38    Susser, M. W. (1964). Ment. Hlth. (Lond.) *23*, 68.

39    Smith, A. (1968). 'The Science of Social Medicine', London: Staples.

which their parents knew in childhood'.[40] In fact, not only has the time-scale so far been too short for striking changes to be expected, but our research instruments are still relatively crude. It may also be that the new communities so far well established have been too conventional in form for us to expect much firm evidence yet of influence on mental health, quite apart from the fact that they have generally failed to experiment boldly with medical, social or educational services. On the other hand, Cumbernauld, Milton Keynes, or Thamesmead may have more significant results to show in the course of time.

As far as neurotic disorders are concerned, the generally negative results of several careful surveys summarised here suggest that aetiological theories have been proposed and accepted in far too specious a manner. This is as much a criticism of Eysenck or Laing as of Freud and his successors and the new town studies indicate that the various relevant factors must be involved in far more subtle and complex ways than are usually acknowledged.

*Physical Structure*
Another general characteristic of new communities is their relatively low density of population, compared to older urban areas; this may be of significance in the development of neurotic disorders because of the greater amounts of open space and unfamiliar visual patterns. Ethological evidence on this point has been summarised by Marks (1969), who states that 'agoraphobic' behaviour in hamsters is mainly a response to illumination, above the level optimal for the animal, rather than a response to the openness of the situation.[41] Normally, excessively bright light causes avoidance responses, which are dissipated by searching behaviour, but if the latter is blocked, the animal shows evidence of increased stress. Similarly, human agoraphobics tend to feel easier in the dark and, if crossing an open space, feel less anxious if they can skirt the edge. Marks suggests that innate mechanisms probably do not produce phobias of themselves, but rather select as targets certain situations, which may then be affected by other conditions, *e.g.* space and light

40      Taylor & Chave, *op. cit.*
41      Marks, I. M. (1969), 'Fears and Phobias', London: Heinemann.

perception, through opto-kinetic reflexes. This is also seen in the fact that many people feel uncomfortable in high flats with exterior walls of glass. Whilst there is no firm evidence yet for direct connections between particular forms of urban development and the emergence of neurotic illnesses (such as phobic anxiety), these considerations suggest that there may be advantages in more traditional forms of living arrangement. The difference between the human scale of a terraced street and a tower block of flats in the middle of an empty space is only too obvious. Certain new towns (such as Cumbernauld) have tried to preserve these spatial advantages and it would be very valuable to have systematic evidence of the results—if any—in terms of psychiatric health. According to Gans (1967) the likelihood of social contacts was increased in the early years of the Levittown Community by physical factors such as spacing of homes, siting of doorways and kitchen windows and having communal recreation areas.[42] At this period, the development of friendships based on physical proximity was important. However, as the community matured, friendships were established through formal organisations, both within and outside it, occurring between people who were socially compatible, but not necessarily neighbours. This indicated that the effects of the physical environment on behaviour are often indirect and must be considered within a specific context. Since personal transport and mobility are generally less in Britain than in the USA, it is likely that the influence of proximity here would be greater and longer lasting, though it may also depend on the previous experience of those concerned. Other considerations about population density, on the basis of animal work, have been discussed by Leyhausen (1965), who believes that stable social institutions must rest on an innate biological basis. He states: '... the human species is adapted to social life in a small group, where each member knows each of the others personally, having a need for larger social gatherings from time to time, but not too often, feeling a need to be by himself quite often, and reacting to continued over-socialisation with all sorts of frustrations, repressions, aggressions and fears....'.[43] Here again, evidence is lacking in clinical

---

42      Gans, H. (1967), 'The Levittowners', New York: Pantheon.
43      Leyhausen, P. (1965). Discovery, 26, 27.

terms, and the whole question of 'territoriality' in humans has scarcely begun to be investigated, but on commonsense grounds, it would seem likely that certain features commonly found in new housing may have harmful effects on patterns of family and social relationships, believed to be related to psychiatric illness. For instance, informal contacts between neighbours are hampered both by the dispersed pattern of suburban housing and by the usual form of high flats. An investigation by Fanning (1967) compared the health of service families living in low-rise flats in Germany with similar families living in houses.[44] Measured by consultation rates, both with family doctors and specialists, flat-dwellers showed 57 per cent more morbidity than people in houses. The higher rates were most marked in the case of allergic, neurological, respiratory, psychiatric, genitourinary and skin conditions. The largest group of all was respiratory illness in the flat-dwellers, which might have been due to lack of open-air exercise or (perhaps more likely) to emotional stress. From the subjective standpoint, boredom, isolation and difficulty in coping with young children were certainly reported by those living in flats to a significant extent and it is quite likely that the 'surrender point' leading to medical consultation was lower in this group because their life was less satisfactory. However, as mentioned earlier, service families have particular problems of their own, so that these results may not necessarily be of general relevance.

Winkel (1970) suggests that people's feelings and decisions about the environment are often mediated by symbolic meanings which they attach to features of the physical world, though we know little so far about the way this process works or where it is especially relevant.[45] For instance, a particular form of housing which is the poorest in one community may symbolize what it means to be poor and dispossessed for the members of that community. Feelings of this kind which are held by different sections of society should certainly be important for social planning and should be susceptible to systematic investigation, similar to that of motivational research. So far, however, little information of value about them has emerged in any country; people who lack the financial resources to make a

44    Fanning, D. M. (1967). Brit. med. J., ii, 382.
45    Winkel, G. H. (1970). Psychology Today, 3, 31.

personal choice either get what it is easiest to produce, or else what some authority believes (often on quite irrational grounds) is good for them.

Planning of new towns in Britain has been strongly influenced by the concept of 'neighbourhoods' and according to Nicholson these '. . . have come nearest to success (where) they are either based on natural features, which would probably have created some degree of a sense of belonging anyhow, or are strongly reinforced by locally grouped services. If they are seen to have a meaning and a function, they can become a reality. . . . They must first satisfy felt needs— including the need to belong to some place which is recognisably different from the places where other men belong'.[46] In other words, while people still say 'I belong to Glasgow' (with all its faults), they will not say the same about a 'corridor of linear growth'. Silver (1968) challenges the whole fashionable viewpoint that because mechanical means of communication have been improved, urban growth must therefore be fragmented.[47] He suggests that this process is harmful in terms of cultural psychology, removing the diversity, choice and range of opportunities which are the main advantages of a great city; on the other hand, the conventional arguments against large cities could all be answered by the resources of modern technology, if rationally applied. Silver also believes that new towns will be unsatisfactory places to live in because '. . . there is no built-in steady state of change, just an all-at-once end state' and if the experience of inter-war dormitory suburbs is any guide, this may well be the case. 'Only when multiple changes begin to happen in them will new towns become towns *tout court*'.[48]

But in discussion of the physical structure of communities, one must return again to Fried's remarkable paper—'Grieving for a Lost Home'.[49] He points out that any severe loss disrupts the sense of continuity which is a framework for functioning in a universe with temporal, social and spatial dimensions. In traditional working class communities, the local area around the dwelling unit is seen as an

---

46    Nicholson, *op. cit.*
47    Silver, N. (1968), *New Statesman*, 149.
48    *Ibid.*
49    Fried, *op. cit.*

integral part of home and contains interlocking sets of social networks; this is in marked contrast to the typical orientation of the middle-class person, for whom the world is his oyster. Fried showed that following forced removal from the area, marked grief was the more likely, the more a person had been committed to that community in terms of liking it, feeling it had been his real home and having an extensive familiarity with it. He goes on to suggest that an integrated sense of spatial identity is fundamental to human functioning and that in the working class at least, this is tied to a *specific* place; '. . . largely because of the importance of external stability, dislocation from a familiar residential area has so great an effect on fragmenting the sense of spatial identity'.[50] Also, fragmentation of the external basis for interpersonal relationships and group networks destroys the sense of group identity of many individuals, causing a deep experience of loss. These phenomena, though, are not always harmful; a 'retreat to the home' has often been described following rehousing, whereby the marital and family unit becomes much more highly integrated, through a new-found independence from outside networks (though this independence may not serve it well in times of need). There may also be cases, *e.g.*, the religiously demarcated communities of Northern Ireland, where a break-up of established social patterns would be in the best interests of all concerned. But in general, it can only be concluded that these enormously important considerations for the health and happiness of the people involved have scarcely been considered by the authorities responsible for the creation of most new communities. In view of the scale of public rehousing in Britain, it is very surprising that no comparable study to Fried's has been attempted in this country up to now.

From a more aesthetic and subjective point of view, Chisholm (1968) attacks the way in which the industrial townscape of Lancashire is now being totally destroyed and believes that those responsible are 'blind to the accidental, but nevertheless important characteristics of what they are replacing . . . Streets, as such, no longer exist—merely amorphous spaces between the nondescript badly proportioned buildings'. Although the old houses and streets

---

50    *Ibid.*

were grossly deficient in essential services, 'traditional friendliness and continuous activity were always there'.[51] Now, '. . . women struggling with prams and their shopping up draughty staircases, children playing in special compounds and an overall illusion that the area has been depopulated are the first signs of trouble to come'. Chisholm believes that the human qualities of the people of Lancashire, admired for instance by George Orwell in *The Road to Wigan Pier*, '. . . will be seriously impaired by the new and impersonal environment being foisted on them'. The point cannot yet be proved scientifically, but to anyone like myself who is familiar with the area and people, it certainly has the ring of truth.

## Medical and Social Services

Every professional contribution on the subject of new communities pays at least lip-service to the need for special provision of medical and personal social services for the populations involved and most admit the general failure to do so, at least until very recently. On the contrary, most incoming residents have found such services to be less available than in the areas they come from; for instance, though the high birth-rate and absence of near relatives means an intense demand for home helps, there are simply not enough middle-aged women living locally to provide the service required. Whilst this represents an absolute lack of human resources of a particular kind, the failure to develop new, integrated patterns of medical care (with the two exceptions mentioned earlier) represents an absence of creative thought in the profession. The administrative framework of the National Health Service neither encouraged joint planning nor gave anyone the overall responsibility to co-ordinate services for each new community. As McQuillan (1968) remarks, '. . . "old" doctors with old ideas were established in the traditional pattern of medical care'.[52] However, there have been very profound changes recently, with great extension of group practice and the use of health centres, and it may well be that the advance planning done for the latest generation of new towns, including Milton Keynes, has helped this process along to a significant extent.

---

51    Chisholm, J. (1968) *Telegraph*, April 15th.
52    McQuillan, W. J. (1968). Roy. Soc. Hlth. J., 141.

Current plans are almost all based on health centres housing about twelve general practitioners and serving about 30,000 people (though Runcorn envisages much smaller groups). This population group would also be appropriate for a basic social work team, though not necessarily operating from the health centre, and for the education service. To make the maximum use of skilled manpower, doctors, nurses and other professional staff will be deployed throughout general practice, hospital work, school and public health and industrial medicine, without artificial barriers of demarcation. Having a large enough family health team will mean that every kind of professional worker can be attached to it, so that a genuine fusion of preventive and curative activities is possible. The Advisory Committee for health services in greater Northampton has recommended (1969) that the mental health of new residents might be fostered by four kinds of activity—play-groups, particularly for families in flats; ready access to a child-guidance clinic for disturbed children; encouraging social contacts, particularly amongst young mothers, and a comprehensive family planning service.[53] They also recommend that instead of traditional social welfare services, there should be '. . . experienced family case-workers who will . . . identify and give support to those families and individuals whose stability is threatened by separation from family ties and to those who find difficulty in facing the challenge of making new contacts and adjustments'. The Committee is certainly right in its aim and it is to be hoped that recruitment of staff of this calibre will prove to be possible. In a similar vein, the HMSO report on needs of new communities stated that 'proper social provision' for them consisted of: 'high quality physical planning, first-rate administration, an explicit . . . but flexible programme of social development and an adequate economic basis'.[54] We can all agree with these aims, in the same way that we are all opposed to sin, but the logistical problem of getting them carried out is a different matter.

Evans[55] and others have described their development in Andover

53    Northampton. Report of the Health Services Advisory Committee (1969).
54    H.M.S.O. *op. cit.*
55    Evans, J. W. Lovel, J. W. I. and Eaton, K. K. (1969), Brit. Med. J., i, 44.

of a group general practice which in addition to its traditional curative role, is fully involved with industrial medicine, family planning and infant welfare clinics, together with school medical examinations for nearly all the children in the practice. A health visitor, district midwife and district nurse are attached to the practice and hold sessions in its premises; this reduces their home-visiting and travelling times and greatly helps liaison with the doctors. Initially, most problems of social welfare and to some extent of mental health were referred to the health visitor, since the doctors saw her daily and could ask her for information about work done by other welfare workers. However, it soon appeared that an appropriate organisation was lacking for dealing adequately with the whole patient, fully related to his social, family and financial background. Therefore, weekly case conferences were arranged, attended also by the mental welfare and child care officers, two county welfare officers for the area and sometimes a psychiatric social worker. These doctors believe that the conferences have been of great value to all concerned—particularly in the circumstances of a new housing area—that they result in less duplication of work and that decisions are more purposeful. The content is '. . . the primary and often the long-term care of patients whose problems typically may have minimal medical content. Purely medical advice and treatment can do little more than scratch the itchy surface of their dis-ease'. The discussions have also made all the professional workers involved more aware of facilities which are underdeveloped in the area—nursery schools, play groups, registered child-minders, retraining for problem families and health education.

Before enthusiasm becomes too infectious about the provision of social services, it is worth noting the warning remarks of Parker (1970) that 'The personal social services are too frequently involved in dealing with problems which could, in all probability, have been checked or avoided altogether had other social policies been more successful or more energetically pursued. If there had been a sharper awareness of the ill-effects (the social costs) of particular social and economic policies the social services might less often be engaged with the consequences . . . Another (example) is our slow-dawning appreciation of the effect of the built environment upon personal relationships and mutual-aid systems. In judging the likely level of need which will face the personal social services of the future therefore, it is important to know just how fully and how keenly policies of social prevention and promotion will be pursued, not only in these services themselves but more widely throughout the whole range of social and economic planning'.[56]

One must add to these wise remarks that in spite of the rather varying research results reported above, it must be expected that a community with rising standards of living and education will make greater demands for socio-psychiatric care than have ever been known in the past. Furthermore, in recognising the influence of population structure and social changes in new communities, we will be unable to deal with mental health problems by a comprehensive approach unless we depart substantially from the conventional models of medicine and social work. The break-up of extended families and increasing social and cultural mobility result in demands for a much greater volume of support from the public services to make up for what has been lost through these changes. Many problems will need the efforts of a multi-disciplinary team, rather than merely the prescription of medication or even the admission of one person to hospital. More specifically in relation to psychiatric illness and subnormality, each new community will need an integrated and comprehensive service, accepting continuous responsibility and serving all age-groups and social classes (Freeman, 1968).[57] So far, pioneering efforts towards this goal have almost all occurred in older areas of population, but the new communities would seem to be natural foci for their further stages of development.

---

56    Parker, R. A. (1970) in Robson, W. A. and Crick, B. (eds.) 'The Future of the Social Services'. London: Penguin.

57    Freeman, H. L. (1968). Brit, J. Psychiat. *114*, 481.

Seymour Martin Lipset

# Academia and Politics in America

This article was originally prepared as a memorandum for the Special Committee on Campus Tensions of the American Council on Education. A condensed version was published in David C. Nichols, ed., *Perspectives on Campus Tensions: Papers Prepared for the Special Committee on Campus Tensions* (Washington, D.C.: American Council on Education, 1970). The concluding section of the paper, pages 265 ff has been used as the basis for chapter 6, 'Faculty and Students: Allied and In Conflict', in S. M. Lipset, *Rebellion in the University* (Boston: Little, Brown, London: Routledge, 1972), pp. 197–236. I would like to express thanks to the Carnegie Commission on Higher Education and its chairman, Clark Kerr, for support for research on faculty politics, of which this paper is one product.

The numerous attempts to understand the growth in politicalization in the American university have largely focused on student unrest. Clearly, student activism has been the most dramatic, the most visible form which politicization has taken. But it should be evident that increased concern with politics has also involved the faculty, both as initiator and as reactor.

Various critics of American faculty behavior have written harshly in moralistic terms concerning the causal role which faculty members have played in undermining the authority of the administration, in approving of the 'objectives if not the tactics' of the campus militants. John Roche, for example, points to ways in which faculties justify their refusal to support order on campus:[1]

Thus, if a faculty is reluctant to get into a fight it can find an infinite number of reasons why the present situation, however objectionable, is the inexorable consequence of the African slave trade, the Protestant Reformation, the treaty of Aix-la-Chapelle, or sexual deprivation in Western society. Obviously none of these factors can be altered in 1969, so the faculty retires from the field satisfied that since nothing can be done, it has properly done nothing. . . .

---

[1]   John P. Roche, 'Retreat of the Faculty', *The New Leader*, 52 (November 10, 1969), p. 15.

No university is pure, of course; therefore no university can act against disruption. (This is a variation on what I call the Kitty Genovese gambit: When asked why she did nothing to help Kitty, who was being publicly murdered in Queens and screamed for help, a neighbor said: 'Why should I help her? She had no morals'.)

The claim that faculty have been directly involved in stimulating or supporting campus unrest has been documented in an American Council on Education survey of 281 institutions of events which had occurred in 1967-68.[2] Most of these schools, 181, had demonstrations during that year. According to the reports received by the ACE, faculty were involved in the planning of over half of the protest, and in 11 per cent they were among the leaders.[3] In close to two-thirds of the demonstrations, the faculty passed resolutions approving of the protests.[4] Conversely, however, deans report that faculty gave the administration prior information about the protest in about a quarter of the situations. Faculty were most involved in protests defined as 'physical, but nonobstructive' or 'diplomatic'.[5]

Faculties, of course, have not been united on issues stemming from student unrest. Probably no other matter has so divided the university, has resulted in the severing of social and intellectual relations, as the internal faculty controversy over student protest on a given campus. The kind of research in depth which would enable us to understand such protest has not been made; little in fact has even begun. In this paper, I would like to bring together what we do know about the sources of faculty political involvement relevant to the current situation and to suggest various hypotheses most of which require further elaboration and research.

In the most general sense, I would argue the case that the major contribution of the faculty to student unrest in the post-1964 period has not been the various malefactions of which its critics accuse it, such as not teaching, ignoring students, spending time in extra-mural money making or status-enhancing tasks, but rather that a significant section of the faculty in the institutions which have been the largest centers of student radicalism have encouraged the

---

2        Robert F. Boruch, 'The Faculty Role in Campus Unrest', *ACE Research Reports*, 4 No. 5 (1969).
3        *Ibid.*, p. 50.
4        *Ibid.*, p. 21.
5        *Ibid.*, p. 24.

political values underlying such protest. In this, they closely resemble the parents of the student activists. The many surveys of the social characteristics of student activists agree on the whole with Kenneth Keniston's description of them as 'red diaper' babies. In the United States they tend to come from relatively privileged families who formed a liberal to left political commitment as a reaction to the depression of the 1930s, the anti-fascist war, the (Joe) McCarthy period, or aspects in their own family cultural background. The children of this large minority of the middle class spent their formative years hearing about the reactionary, racist, undemocratic character of the United States. Beginning in the late 1950s, as they came of age, and in response to various events which encouraged moral protest (first the revived civil rights concerns following the failure to implement the desegregation decision of 1954, and subsequently the visible disaster in Vietnam, together with the break-up of the image of a monolithic expansionist Communism as a result of deStalinization), the scions of the liberal segment of the privileged increasingly turned to protest politics. Studies of parental reactions indicate that such behavior won their approval, or at least their tacit acceptance; rarely did it result in familial opposition. The parents approved of the goals of their activist children; their primary concern was that they might get jailed or hurt in their activity. (Parenthetically, it may be noted that in a number of European countries, left-disposed students tend to come from the less-privileged segment of the undergraduates. The differences reflect the fact that in the United States the greatest source of the ideologically left is among the 'intelligentsia' and the Jews, while, in Europe, to be of working-class origin more often means a leftist family background.)

On the campuses to which they went, which were the better schools of America in terms of wealth, facilities, faculty scholarship, entrance requirements, and the like, these students found many professors who shared their parents' social and political values. The liberal-left students tended to take courses in the liberal arts, particularly and increasingly in the politically relevant social sciences where the assumptions of their professors again coincided with their own, but some of them found to their increased dismay that their professors not only resembled their parents in social values, but also fostered a polite gradualist version of reform

H

politics. That is, both their affluent parents living in lily-white suburbs and going to business or to their professional office every day and their prestigious liberal professors appeared to do little to change America, to get rid of the evils they talked about. Thus, the student activists hurled the charge of 'hypocrisy' against both their parents and the university. The very charge testifies to an agreement in values. One does not attack as hypocrites those with whom one is in disagreement. The liberal students found kindred spirits among their fellows, and found encouragement for their moral concerns among the faculty. Ultimately when they turned to using the tactic of civil disobedience against the university, they discovered that the university, unlike the southern states or the public authorities elsewhere, was unable to defend itself, that the faculty and even occasionally the administration acting *in locus parentis* could not endorse the use of force against their own students, acting for moral ends with which they agreed. And once the activist students discovered this in Berkeley in the fall of 1964, the wave of comparable disturbances across the nation and even the world was inevitable.[6]

It is true, of course, that in a number of cases university administrations or the public authorities have resorted to calling in the police against student protestors who have violated the law, particularly through sit-ins in university buildings. But at Berkeley in 1964, Columbia in 1968, and Harvard in 1969, the faculty as a body refused to support the action. In each case, they called on the university to request the public authorities to drop the charges against the arrested students. In each case, also, large segments, perhaps the majority, of the faculty turned against the university administration, equating, in effect if not in form, as immoral the initial law violation by the student demonstrators and the sending in of the police to remove the protestors. In other universities, faculty groups played a major role in pressing the administration not to call in the police.

The sources of opposition to police on campus have deep roots in

---

6        See S. M. Lipset and Paul Seabury, 'The Lessons of Berkeley', in S. M. Lipset and S. Wolin, eds., *The Berkeley Student Revolt* (Garden City: Doubleday-Anchor, 1965), pp. 340-49, for an analysis of the prospective consequences of this discovery.

the university world. In a number of countries, including even Czarist Russia at various times and parts of Latin America, the norm of autonomy has been institutionalized. Yet in the contemporary United States, it seemingly rests in the strong feelings of faculty members concerning the validity of the norm. No public authority has ever granted the university autonomy. To a considerable extent, one of the major reasons that students have been able to be the potent anti-establishment force that they have been in various countries is the existence of norms that insist on autonomy from outside police interference, and which restrict efforts to punish students for behavior which would frequently result in severe penalties being levied against non-students engaged in similar actions. Daniel Cohn-Bendit, the leader of the 1968 French student upheaval, argued that students are obligated to be politically active, precisely because they are protected against the much more severe sanctions which would be meted out to other groups for doing what they do. 'The student, at least, in the modern system of higher education, still preserves a considerable degree of personal freedom, if he chooses to exercise it. . . . He can, if he so chooses, take extreme political positions without any personal danger; in general, he is not subjected to formal sanctions or even reprimands'.[7]

More important in general consequences for the politics of universities has been the predominant sympathy of intellectuals as a whole, and the academics among them in particular, for liberal-left political causes and ideologies. Such sympathies both stimulate their antagonism to sanctions against activist students and lead them to welcome actions ostensibly designed to implement comparable political sentiments by a section of the student body. The leftist students, as a youthful group without the responsibilities inherent in career and family, uninured to the pressures for compromise and without experience concerning the complexities and unanticipated consequences stemming from rapid and major change, press through the implications of the ideological positions which they share with much of the faculty in a more absolute and total fashion. The faculty liberal-left will on the whole disown and oppose

---

7    Daniel and Gabriel Cohn-Bendit, *Obsolete Communism: The Left-Wing Alternative* (New York: McGraw-Hill, 1968), p. 47.

the drastic tactics and/or more extreme objectives of the student activists, but such opposition will be voiced from an ideological stance which is generally sympathetic to these objectives.

The commitment of academic intellectuals to an anti-establishment position has been deduced by many writers from aspects inherent in the very definition of the concept of the intellectual and scholar. Intellectuals, as distinct from professionals, are concerned with the *creation* of knowledge, art, or literature. In awarding status within the occupation, the emphasis is on creation, innovation, *avant gardeness*. Professionals are the *users* of knowledge. And many writers have pointed out that inherent in the obligation to create, to innovate, has been the tendency to reject the *status quo*, to oppose the existing or the old as philistine. Intellectuals are also more likely than those in other occupations to be partisans of the ideal, of the theoretical, and thus to criticize reality from this standpoint. The need to express the inner logic of their discipline, of their art form, also presses them to oppose the powers, the patrons, who seemingly are philistines, who prefer continuity rather than change.

The pressure to reject the *status quo* is, of course, compatible with a conservative or right-wing position as well as with a liberal or left-wing radical one. In the nineteenth century when one found in the United States the two often antagonistic emphases on populist egalitarianism and on business growth, the intellectual elite, linked to the declining values of New England and southern aristocracy, tended to be opposed to both. In an early comparative discussion of American and European universities, C. A. Bristed, a Yale graduate of the late 1830s who then studied at the University of Cambridge and visited continental schools, generalized that university students 'under any government are opposed to the spirit in which that government is administered. Hasty and imperfect as the conclusion is, it certainly holds good of many countries. . . .'.[8] To justify his case, he argued that American students of his day were opposed to the dominant ethos of the American polity, *i.e.*, they were conservative opponents of mass electoral democracy, while German students ruled by an authoritarian oligarchy were

---

8    C. A. Bristed, *Five Years in an English University* (New York: G. P. Putnam and Sons, 1874), p. 61.

radical democrats. The same thesis concerning the political role of scholars was presented almost 100 years ago in talks at various colleges by Whitelaw Reid, the new young editor of the New York *Tribune*. He saw then an inherent tension between academe and the rest of the elite, whom he identified as 'the established':[9]

Exceptional influences eliminated, the scholar is pretty sure to be opposed to the established. The universities of Germany contain the deadliest foes to the absolute authority of the Kaiser. The scholars of France prepared the way for the first Revolution, and were the most dangerous enemies of the imperial adventurer who betrayed the second. . . . While the prevailing parties in our country were progressive and radical, the temper of our college was to the last degree conservative. As our politics settled into the conservative tack, a fresh wind began to blow about the college seats, and literary men, at last, furnished inspiration for the splendid movement that swept slavery from the statute book. . . . Wise unrest will always be their [the scholars] chief trait. We may set down . . . the very foremost function of the scholar in politics, *To oppose the established*.

. . . As for the scholar, the laws of his intellectual development may be trusted to fix his place. Free thought is necessarily aggressive and critical. The scholar, like the healthy redblooded young man, is an inherent, an organic, an inevitable radical. . . . And so we may set down, as a second function of the American scholar in politics, *An intellectual leadership of the radicals*.

In some European countries, intellectual opposition to the *statu quo* often took the form of right-wing extremist critiques of democracy for creating a mass society in which the vulgar taste of the populace destroyed creative culture, or in which populist demogogues undermined national values. Such positions were found particularly among Catholic intellectuals, and in significant sections of the German academic world. They helped to undermine support

---

9    'The Scholar in Politics' (a Commencement Address delivered at Dartmouth and Amherst Colleges, and before the alumni of Miami University), *Scribner's Monthly*, 6 (1873), pp. 613-614. (Emphasis in Original.) Twenty-eight years later speaking at Stanford in 1901, an older Reid saw the same behavior by American academics as bad. 'It is a misfortune for the colleges, and no less for the country, when the trusted instructors are out of sympathy with its history, with its development, and with the men who made the one and are guiding the other'. Whitelaw Reid, *American and English Studies*, Vol. 1 (New York: Scribner's, 1913), pp. 241-242.

for democracy in a number of countries:[10] 'In Germany . . . where the university professor has always had exceptional standing . . . it was from the universities that most of the other intellectuals drew the disintegrating poison that they then distributed. . . . Naturally the faculties of social science provided a special opportunity for practicing intellectual treachery and preparing the way for Nazism. . . . [I]t is mainly the names of jurists and philosophers that could here be given'.

The lead given by German professors was followed by their students. The Nazi student movement captured most of the universities by 1931, winning control of the national student organization and dominating student council elections, before the Nazis won over any other segment of German life. By so doing they were following the lead set earlier by Italian students, who also constituted one of the earliest major sources of fascist strength there before Mussolini won absolute power.[11]

Although important segments of right-wing intellectual criticism remain, it is clear that since the 1920s, in the United States and increasingly in other western countries as well, intellectual politics have become left-wing politics. The American value system with its stress on egalitarianism and populism fosters criticism from the left which challenges the system for not fulfilling the ideals inherent in the American creed.

Most recently, three of the most prominent economists in America have publicly stressed the inherent innovative and critical role built into the university and intellectual role. Milton Friedman, the doyen of conservative economists, approvingly quoted an unpublished manuscript of his colleague, George Stigler, to this effect:[12] 'The

---

10     Wilhelm Ropke, 'National Socialism and Intellectuals', in George B. deHuszar, ed., *The Intellectuals* (New York: The Free Press of Glencoe, 1960), pp. 346-348.

11     Guido Martinotti, 'The Positive Marginality: Notes on Italian Students in Periods of Political Mobilization', in S. M. Lipset and P. Altbach, eds., *Students in Revolt* (Boston: Houghton Mifflin, 1969), pp. 173-174.

12     George Stigler, unpublished memorandum, as quoted in Milton Friedman, 'The Ivory Tower', *Newsweek*, 74 (November 10, 1969), p. 92.

university is by design and effect the institution in society which creates discontent with existing moral, social and political institutions and proposes new institutions to replace them. The university is, from this viewpoint, a group of philosophically imaginative men freed of any pressures except to please their fellow faculty, and told to follow their inquiries wherever they might lead. Invited to be learned in the institutions of other times and places, incited to new understanding of the social and physical world, the university faculty is inherently a disruptive force'.

A leading liberal economist, Paul Samuelson, wrote to the same effect two weeks earlier:[13] 'Intellectuals, the world over, are the despair of their well-to-do uncles. . . . He must forever be examining things—and talking about them'.

Similar comments and analyses have been suggested over the years by men as diverse as Joseph Schumpeter, Robert Michels, Reinhold Niebuhr, Crane Brinton, Carl Becker, Sidney Hook, Edward Shils, and Lewis Coser in their efforts to account for the 'critical attitude' of intellectuals, both academic and non-academic. From a similar perspective Arinori Mori, the first Minister of Education in Meiji, Japan, recognized the dangers presented by the universities to a rapidly modernizing authoritarian system. He attempted to establish a first-rate educational system in which one part of that system, going from elementary school up to and including teachers' colleges, could be expected to do its job of education while also inculcating uncritical loyalty to the Emperor and the social system. The universities, however, could not be required to indoctrinate loyalty if they were to be first-rate. To accomplish their task of research and educating leaders for a modern society, universities must be allowed freedom. This freedom of inquiry would inevitably produce dangerous thoughts and results. Hence, 'he was convinced that what was taught in Tokyo University should not be conveyed to the masses. . . . [U]niversity graduates should not influence the masses directly'.[14]

---

13   'The Economics of Class', *Newsweek*, 74 (October 27, 1969), p. 105.
14   Michio Nagai, 'The Development of Intellectuals in the Meiji and Taisho Periods', *Journal of Social and Political Ideas in Japan*, 2 (April, 1964), p. 29.

This stress on the critical anti-establishment role of the intellectuals would seemingly imply much more support for student activism and protest among the faculty than in fact exists. Most descriptions of faculty reactions on specific campuses characterized by student activism have properly pointed to the tremendous divisions among the faculty, to the fact that only a part of the faculty appeared sympathetic to the student demands, or sought to protect them from civil or university sanctions. A comprehensive discussion of the role of the Berkeley faculty during the first four years of campus turmoil on that campus (1964-68) emphasized this division:[15]

The faculty, during all this, has been rather sharply split along a number of lines. Some have quite consistently supported student demands and positions, some have done so with qualifications, others have supported the administration, while the great majority have tried to get on with their own work, returning to the political arena only at moments of great crisis, when ordinary work on campus was clearly disrupted; and when they did so, they tended to search for some reasonable compromise, some kind of broad consensus that would resolve the immediate conflict, allow the campus to 'return to normal' and themselves to return to their unfinished manuscripts and experiments.

. . . the faculty has uneasily and without enthusiasm continued from time to time to intervene in student affairs, while at the same time refusing to take a major role in day-to-day administration. It has thus allowed the students to see it as a part-time (and not wholly trustworthy) ally against the administration, encouraging actions designed to strengthen the alliance forged and reforged in moments of crisis.

But while the faculty as a whole has by no means been hostile to the administration during this period, its support has been qualified and erratic. It has thus eroded the authority of the administration, whom it has in a sense been able to heckle and second guess between votes of confidence, even while it has disappointed the hopes of the activist students.

On almost every campus which has faced a major crisis, the faculty has split, sometimes formally, into two or three major factions or faculty political parties. These groups have usually operated with elected executive committees, have prepared strategies for dealing with faculty committees, and the like. The parties have

---

15     Martin Trow, 'Conceptions of the University: The Case of Berkeley', *The American Behavioral Scientist*, 11 (May-June, 1968), p. 15.

been described as right, center, and left—hard, compromise-y, and soft—hawks, temporizers, and doves. In many schools, although three basic positions may be perceived, a two-party system emerged with the leadership of each party tending to be chosen from the more moderate members, thus facilitating compromise and cooperation. Although the groups have differed sharply in their estimate of responsibility for the campus crisis (the hards blames the student activists, the softs hold responsible the uncompromising stance of the administration), both groups as a whole seek a return to campus peace. Thus, the hards tend to become a vehicle of faculty communication and pressure on the administration and trustees, the softs tend to act as an intermediary with the radical students. From time to time, therefore, these roles lead critics to see the other party as a tool or stimulator of radical student or administration policies.

One report on the conflict at Cornell during 1968-69 described the different ways on which the two main groupings of faculty saw that situation:[16]

The Concerned Faculty ('liberal leanings') are more likely to:
justify more disruptive forms of protest,
be more approving of the Black Studies Program, and to believe in more autonomy for it
stress more the importance of social reform in education (while also insisting strongly on intellectual experience)
de-emphasize faculty rights in reference to academic freedom,
and stress more a revision of the judicial system (including a multiple judicial procedure, which recognizes the special nature of dissent problems)
On the other hand, the 'conservative' groupings . . . characteristically hold attitudes which:
stress a lesser degree of autonomy in the Black Studies Program
stress the importance of career skills in education (while also insisting strongly on intellectual experience, as do the *Concerned Faculty*)
are more convinced that academic freedom is actually being threatened
are more disapproving of the Constituent Assembly [i.e. student participation in university governance]
are more strongly against change in the judicial system [except

16    'Cornell University Survey conducted for Special Trustee Committee' (New York: Douglas Williams Associates, October 1969), p. 43.

that the Administration should take a stronger hand]; and insist more strongly on a single judicial system, be the problem one of individual misbehavior or politically initiated group dissent.

The general pattern has been described by John Spiegel, whose Lemberg Center for the Study of Violence has been engaged in analyses of various specific situations. He describes the three faculty positions as follows:[17]

(1) a desire to support the goals of the aggrieved students while minimizing any loss of face to the institution for what may be interpreted as surrender. This position is usually called the 'soft line' advocated by the 'doves'; (2) a desire to defeat and punish the students while minimizing any loss of face to the institution for what may be interpreted as callousness or cruelty. This policy is the 'hard line' pursued by the 'hawks'; (3) a middle ground, or temporizing position, which attempts to placate both the 'hawks' and the 'doves', in part, while also partially satisfying the demands of the students—a balancing act which requires great skill, diplomacy, flexibility and inventiveness, plus some Machiavellian sleights of hand.

. . . The 'hawks' can scarcely conceal their contempt for the 'doves'—those 'bleeding hearts', those 'masochists' who, perhaps unconsciously, are out to wreck the university. On their side, the 'doves' show a mild but persistent abhorrence of the wrath, and in their eyes, 'sadism' of the 'hawks'. Privately, they tend to believe, for the moment at least, that most of the 'hawks' are paranoid personalities.

. . . The 'temporizers' had been impressed by the amount of movement shown by the school prior to the initial disorder. They had shared, vicariously or actually, the 'liberalization' of American life in recent decades. . . . Accordingly, they feel offended by the ingratitude of the aggrieved students, who, in their perception, are 'biting the hand that feeds them'.

These descriptions of division among the faculties clearly raise the question as to why this should occur, why the supposedly critical, liberal, and anti-establishment professoriate divides up when faced by a challenge from the student left which seeks to use the university to implement liberal-left objectives. A large part of the answer, of course, lies in the fact that American academics vary considerably in their commitment to intellectual and hence 'critical'

---

17     John P. Spiegel, 'The Group Psychology of Campus Disorders— A Transactional Approach' (mimeographed paper, Lemberg Center for the Study of Violence, Brandeis University, Waltham, Mass.), pp. 13, 17.

functions. Most of them are, in fact, primarily teachers, not scholars, and hence dedicated to the passing on of the existing tradition, not the enlargement or critical rejection of it. Many of them are involved in teaching or doing research relevant to narrowly professional and vocational fields, not to the basic core of ideas centered in the so-called liberal arts faculties. But beyond these variations linked to the dimension of intellectuality, professors, like others, vary considerably in social outlook, differences which obviously stem from the host of experiences which they have had from birth to the present moment. These other factors or experiences impel them in different political directions, so that while predominantly liberal, they include among themselves almost every possible political position.

While a general analysis of the political outlook of American academia is clearly relevant to any concern with student activism and political protest, there is clear evidence that the sources of variation in political orientations along liberal-conservative, radical left to reactionary right dimensions also go very far to account for differences within the academic community on ways to treat the issues stemming from student protest. Wilson and Gaff's study of faculty opinion in six diverse colleges and universities reported that their respondents divided sharply as to whether students had the right to participate in decisions concerning social and academic matters, and if so to what degree. Attitudes on these issues were strongly associated with general political orientation:[18] '78 per cent of the *Equal vote* group checked the terms "liberal", "very liberal", or "radical" to describe their political position. . . . Only 12 per cent of the *No voice* group chose any of these three terms'.

A study of the Columbia University faculty's attitudes towards the sit-in and student strike in April 1968 also pointed to the strength of the relationship between general political ideology and reaction to campus issues;[19] and comparable results are indicated

---

18    Robert C. Wilson and Jerry G. Gaff, 'Student Voice—Faculty Response', *The Research Reporter* (The Center for Research and Development in Higher Education, University of California, Berkeley), 4, No. 2 (1969), p. 3.

19    Stephen Cole and Hannelore Adamsons, 'The Student Demonstrations at Columbia University: Determinants of Faculty Support'

by the data from the massive (60,000) national sample of American faculty gathered for the Carnegie Commission on Higher Education a portion of which Everett Ladd and I are currently beginning to analyze.[20] Clearly then, much, though of course far from all, of the explanation of current divisions among faculty must be traced to their previous political outlooks.

The evidence that the dominant mood on the campus is liberal and hence predisposed to favor student politics dedicated to equalitarian social changes is clear and decisive, even though the first detailed national survey of faculty political opinion in all disciplines did not occur until 1966, an interesting fact in itself. A National Opinion Research Center (NORC) survey found that 61 per cent of the respondents described themselves as 'liberals', as contrasted with 28 per cent 'conservative' with 11 per cent neither.[21]

---

*Cont'd*   (mimeographed, Bureau of Applied Social Research, Columbia University, 1969), p. 3.

20      In 1969 the Carnegie Commission on Higher Education initiated several large-scale national surveys of students, faculty, and administrators. These studies were administered by the Survey Research Center of the University of California, Berkeley, with advice and technical assistance from the Office of Research of the American Council on Education. Financial support was provided by the Carnegie Commission and the United States Office of Education, Department of Health, Education and Welfare. A disproportionate random sampling procedure was used to select colleges and universities, to obtain adequate numbers of institutions of various types and characteristics. The 303 schools thus chosen included 57 junior colleges, 168 four-year colleges, and 78 universities. Next, a six-in-seven random sample of faculty was drawn from the rosters of the included institutions, yielding a sample of 100,315. A very high return of 60,028 completed questionnaires (60 per cent) was achieved. The returned questionnaires, finally, were differentially weighted, adjusting the data for the disproportionate sampling of institutions and the unequal rates of response. Tabulations from the weighted data of this survey, then, may be taken as reasonably representative of the entire population of teaching faculty at colleges and universities in the United States.

21      C. Edward Noll and Peter H. Rossi, *General Social and Economic Attitudes of College and University Faculty Members* (private report, Chicago: National Opinion Research Center, University of Chicago, November 1966), p. 17.

The most recent evidence is the data collected in the Spring of 1969 for the Carnegie Commission study. These findings, together with the results of similar studies of American students, the US public, and British academics, are presented in Table I below. Both faculty and American students gave comparable distributions of responses. They were each much more liberal-left than the US public as a whole.

TABLE I

*Political Ideology of Undergraduates, Graduate Students, and Faculty in All Institutions, and of United States Public*

|  | | Campus | |
| --- | --- | --- | --- |
| *Political ideology** | *Under-graduates* | *Graduate students* | *Faculty* |
| Left | 5% | 5% | 5% |
| Liberal | 38 | 36 | 39 |
| Middle-of-the-road | 35 | 27 | 26 |
| Moderately conservative | 16 | 26 | 24 |
| Strongly conservative | 2 | 4 | 3 |
| Don't know or no answer | 4 | 2 | 3 |
| *Total* | 100% | 100% | 100% |

|  | Public |
| --- | --- |
| *Political ideology†* | *U.S. Public* |
| Very liberal | 5% |
| Fairly liberal | 16 |
| Middle-of-the-road | 36 |
| Fairly conservative | 30 |
| Very conservative | 9 |
| Don't know or no answer | 4 |
| *Total* | 100% |

* Response to the question 'How would you characterize yourself politically at the present time (left, liberal, middle-of-the-road, moderately conservative, or strongly conservative)?'

† Response to the question 'How would you describe yourself (very liberal, fairly liberal, middle-of-the-road, fairly conservative, or very conservative)?'

(1) *Campus opinion*: Carnegie Commission survey of undergraduates, graduate students, and faculty in 1969-1970. (2) *Public opinion*: Gallup poll from November 1970.

Source: *Dissent and Disruption*. A Report and Recommendations by the Carnegie Commission on Higher Education (New York: McGraw-Hill, 1971), pp. 24-25.

TABLE I (CONTINUED)

*Political Ideology Responses of National Sample*
*of British Faculty—1966 (Per cent)*

| | |
|---|---|
| Far Left | 5 |
| Moderate Left | 48 |
| Total Left | 53 |
| | |
| Center | 28 |
| | |
| Moderate Right | 18 |
| Far Right | 1 |
| Total Right | 19 |

Source: A. H. Halsey and Martin Trow, *The British Academics* (London: Faber 1971), p.403.

Other data dealing with party and candidates choice over a long time span decisively confirm the relative liberalism of college faculty as compared with other segments of the middle class, and often even as compared with manual workers and low income groups generally.[22]

For example, Lazarsfeld and Thielens show that in 1948, 63 per cent of a sample of social scientists voted for Harry Truman, eight per cent for Henry Wallace or Norman Thomas, and only 28 per cent for Thomas Dewey. Four years later, Adlai Stevenson took 65 per cent of their vote, as contrasted with 34 per cent for Dwight Eisenhower.[23]

The Carnegie Commission's massive national survey inquired as to voting choices in 1964 and 1968. In the former year, 80 per cent of the faculty respondents report having opted for Johnson over Goldwater. In 1968, 58 per cent of those who voted cast their ballot for Humphrey, 38 per cent were for Nixon, close to three per cent

---

22     Arthur Kornhauser, 'Attitudes of Economic Groups', *Public Opinion Quarterly*, 2 (1938), p. 264. This same study indicated pro-New Deal attitudes among manual workers (56 per cent), lawyers, physicians, and dentists (16 per cent), and engineers (13 per cent). For references to other studies see also S. M. Lipset, *Political Man* (Garden City: Doubleday, 1960), pp. 315-16. Lawrence C. Howard, 'The Academic and the Ballot', *School and Society*, 86 (November 22, 1958), p. 416.

23     Paul F. Lazarsfeld and Wagner Thielens, Jr., *The Academic Mind* (Glencoe: The Free Press, 1958), p. 402.

supported leftist candidates, and less than one per cent chose Wallace.[24]

Similar findings are reported in a national sample of British faculty, which found the Labour party in the lead among them. In Britain 'university teachers look very much more like the working class in their political affiliations than like the upper middle class to which they belong in respect to their incomes, status, education, styles of life and other objective indicators of social class'.[25]

Most faculty surveys, with the exception of the Lazarsfeld-Thielens one, deal with the whole of academia, *i.e.*, they include those in liberal arts departments as well as faculty in professional and vocational education. They cover institutions ranging from the major graduate training and research centers of America to small church-controlled colleges. In a real sense, as noted earlier, a very large proportion, if not the great majority on whom these studies report, have not been 'intellectuals', 'scientists', or 'scholars', if these terms are arbitrarily limited to those involved in *creative* scholarly and artistic endeavors. The hypothesis that intellectual scholarly pursuits predispose their incumbents to a left or liberal critical position in America would imply that such an orientation should be found most heavily among those in the more 'intellectual' disciplines, *i.e.*, the liberal arts.

---

24    A number of papers have been completed by Everett Ladd and Lipset reporting on the political aspects of the Carnegie Commission data. These include: '. . . And What Professors Think', *Psychology Today*, 4 (November 1970), pp 49–51; 'The Politics of American Political Scientists', *PS*, 4 (Spring 1971), pp. 135–149; 'The Divided Professoriate', *Change*, 3 (May-June, 1971), pp 54–60; 'American Social Scientists and the Growth of Campus Political Activism in the 1960s', *Social Science Information*, 10 (April 1971), pp. 105–120; 'Jewish Academics in the United States: Their Achievements, Culture and Politics', *The American Jewish Year Book 1971*, vol. 72 (New York: The American Jewish Committee, 1971) pp. 89–128; 'The Politics of American Sociologists', *The American J. Sociol.* (in press); 'The Politics of Academic Natural Scientists in the United States', *Science* (in press).

25    A. H. Halsey and Martin Trow, *The British Academics* (London: Faber, 1971), p.401.

The assumption that these fields attract the more intellectually inclined has been borne out by a large number of studies of students comparing the characteristics of these majoring in different subjects or varying in their career choices. The following table from a national survey of undergraduates which classified a variety of responses in an index of 'intellectual disposition' illustrates the point that those in the liberal arts are in fact more 'intellectual'.

TABLE II

*Percentage of Students in a National Sample in Various Curricula at Each Level of Intellectual Disposition*

| Level of Intellectual Disposition | Major Subject | | |
|---|---|---|---|
| | Liberal Arts | Education | Technology and Business |
| High | 28 | 11 | 7 |
| Middle | 37 | 34 | 25 |
| Low | 35 | 55 | 68 |
| N | (1096) | (572) | (899) |

Source: James W. Trent and Judith L. Craise, 'Commitment and Conformity in the American College', *Journal of Social Issues*, 23, No. 3 (1967), p. 42.

This study also reports that the students in the non-liberal arts fields 'were, and very significantly so, the least interested in education for the sake of knowledge, ideas and creative development; the least interested in such cultural activities as the theatre, book-browsing and artistic activities; and the least concerned about human relations and justice'.[26] The Carnegie Commission data indicate that a similar relationship exists among faculty, whether differentiated by subject field or by other indicators of intellectual involvement such as scholarly activity, and also institutions, with the higher calibre ones as judged by scholarly resources, calibre of faculty, graduate programs, and student entrance requirements, containing a much higher proportion of faculty liberals and leftists, much as the student studies indicate that in such schools are found a disproportionate number of student activists and radicals. Within the liberal arts, innovative orientations are more likely to take a political (left)

---

26     James W. Trent and Judith L. Craise, 'Commitment and Conformity in the American College', *Journal of Social Issues*, 23, No. 3 (1967), p. 42.

form among social scientists, next among humanists, who though less political are involved in the world of politically relevant intellectual ideas, and least among the natural scientists.

Similar sets of differences in faculty political orientation have been suggested by Frank Pinner in his distinction between 'consensual' and 'dissensual' disciplines. Consensual fields are those 'with respect to which the public at large tends to have no reservations, either as to the competence of the scholars and the truth of their findings or as to the values which inform their work'. The dissensual ones are those 'whose value or procedures are widely questioned among the public, either explicitly or implicitly'.[27] Mathematics, the natural sciences, and such applied sciences as engineering or veterinary medicine are typically consensual disciplines. Philosophy, the social sciences, music, literature, and the fine arts are dissensual. The public easily discounts the teachings and even the data of dissensual disciplines either by directly opposing or by conveniently forgetting and ignoring them.

Many currently consensual subjects once were in the dissensual category. Some dissensual disciplines include consensual sub-fields. What distinguishes them is not content or methods, but the public image. And Pinner suggests that dissensual subjects tend to attract individuals who hold deviant views. They are less likely 'to compromise with community sentiments. They hold values and are led to findings which typically are not shared by the community'. They are more prone to question 'conventional wisdom'. Thus faculty in the dissensual fields should be more likely to favor liberal-left views than those in the consensual ones. And the more distinguished men in these fields, those most committed to its scholarly values, should be most disposed to such outlooks. This result Pinner sees as inherent in the separation of these fields from community values:[28] 'To divorce oneself from conventional beliefs requires intelligence and courage. . . . It is for this reason that the best minds in each of the dissensual disciplines, the most intelligent and the most courageous, are most likely to believe in unaccepted truths'.

27    Frank Pinner, 'The Crisis of the State Universities: Analysis and Remedies', in Nevitt Sanford, ed., *The American College* (New York: John Wiley, 1962), p. 943.

28    *Ibid.*, p. 947.

As indicated in various publications, cited above, the Carnegie Commission study supports Pinner's assumptions as do a variety of earlier investigations. A national sample which inquired as to presidential choices in 1948, 1952, and 1956 reported that the social scientists and humanists were preponderantly and increasingly Democratic, while the natural scientists, education and business professors 'presented a Republican Party return for all three elections'.[29] The survey of 1,500 University of Washington faculty in 1960 comments decisively:[30] 'Of departments generally described as arts and sciences, all but two voted for Kennedy, many of them heavily; five were unanimous, many ten to one or thereabouts; two split votes evenly. The situation was quite different in most of the professional or vocational departments, although Nixon carried none unanimously; and on the whole, the margin of Nixon votes here was less than the Kennedy margins in the arts and sciences'.

A 1961 study of actual party registrations among University of Arizona faculty yielded similar results.[31] A 1962 national survey of 979 academics which inquired into party affiliation found that 70 per cent of the 'behavioral scientists' favored the Democrats, while the physical scientists and those in the fine arts divided equally between the two major parties.[32]

The 1966 NORC national survey differentiated by major groups of disciplines with respect to opinions concerning the social worth of government control of business and labor. The social scientists were most favorable to increased control over business (68 per cent) and least supportive for such policies with respect to labor (35 per cent). Humanists were second in giving this type of response. Those in the 'hard sciences' were third in approving of greater controls over business (58 per cent), but were first in approving of greater controls

29    Howard, *op. cit.*, p. 418.
30    Gottfried, 'Political Attitudes & Behavior of a University Faculty', *Western Political Quarterly*, 16 (1961) p. 44.
31    Conrad Joyner, 'Political Party Affiliation of University Administrative and Teaching Personnel', *Southwestern Social Science Quarterly*, 43 (March 1963), p. 354.
32    D. Stanley Eitzen and Gary M. Maranell, 'The Political Party Affiliations of College Professors', *Social Forces*, 47 (December 1968), p. 148.

over labor as well (58 per cent). Respondents in the more vocationally-oriented schools of education, business, and engineering were more disposed to favor greater increases in control over labor than over business.[33] In effect, the rank order going from left to right based on responses to these two questions was social science, humanities, natural science, education, and business and engineering. The much larger sample gathered by the Carnegie Commission in 1969 found an identical rank order among the discipline groups as indicated in Table III below.

TABLE III

*Political Self-Appraisal of the Faculty and 1968 Support for Nixon, by Field of Study (per cent)*

| Field of study | Left or Liberal | Conservative | Nixon Support |
|---|---|---|---|
| social sciences | | | |
| (n = 6,845) | 71 | 11 | 19 |
| humanities | | | |
| (n = 9,546) | 62 | 17 | 23 |
| fine arts | | | |
| (n = 3,732) | 52 | 22 | 36 |
| education | | | |
| (n = 3,277) | 41 | 27 | 40 |
| physical sciences | | | |
| (n = 7,599) | 44 | 26 | 38 |
| biological sciences | | | |
| (n = 4,403) | 44 | 27 | 40 |
| business | | | |
| (n = 2,080) | 33 | 36 | 53 |
| engineering | | | |
| (n = 4,165) | 29 | 41 | 60 |
| agriculture | | | |
| (n = 1,348) | 18 | 50 | 61 |

Similar results were obtained in Britain as well. The per cent voting Labor was 66 among social scientists, 47 in the arts, 36 in natural science, 32 in technology and 26 among medical school faculty.[34] The rank order was similar with respect to the replies to the ideological identification question (far left to far right).

Special studies of sociologists, political scientists, psychologists, and social scientists as a group reinforce the conclusion that these

33    Noll and Rossi, *op. cit.*, p. 89.
34    Halsey and Trow, *op. cit.*, p. 430.

fields tend to be among the most liberal in the American university. The findings of the Lazarsfeld-Thielens 1955 survey of social scientists with respect to voting in 1948 and 1952 were noted earlier.[35] A group of sociologists at the University of California have been conducting a series of studies, first of various social science disciplines individually, and most recently of a number of humanities and natural science fields, through sending questionnaires dealing with political issues, including presidential voting back to the 1920s for those old enough, to national samples of those academically active in the different professions. Over three-quarters (78 per cent) of the sociologists were Democrats, as compared with but 10 per cent Republican. When asked for past votes, it was clear that those who were old enough have voted heavily for Roosevelt, Truman, Stevenson, and Kennedy by four to one or more. Third-party left-wing candidates also did relatively well among them.[36]

The political scientists as a group appeared to be only slightly though consistently less liberal Democratic than the sociologists, with a history of voting Democratic by large majorities going back to 1932 among the older ones. A secondary analysis of the Lazarsfeld-Thielens study revealed that political scientists were more Democratic in 1948 and 1952 than other social scientists with the exception of the sociologists.[37] This pattern has held up as we shall see with respect to attitudes toward the Vietnam war.

The third group studied intensively, the psychologists, also had a history of voting overwhelmingly for the Democrats going back to Franklin Roosevelt's first election in 1932. A comparison of party affiliations indicated that 'proportionately more sociologists (77.9 per cent) identify with the Democratic Party than political scientists (73.9 per cent), and than psychologists (70.2 per cent)'.[38]

---

35    Lazarsfeld and Thielens, op. cit., p. 401; Henry A. Turner, et al, 'Political Orientations of Academically Affiliated Sociologists', Sociology and Social Research, 47 (April, 1963), p. 276.

36    Ibid., p. 275.

37    Henry A. Turner, et al, 'The Political Party Affiliation of American Political Scientists', Western Political Quarterly, 16 (September, 1963), pp. 652-53.

38    Charles G. McClintock, Charles B. Spaulding and Henry A. Turner, 'Political Orientations of Academically Affiliated Psychologists', American Psychologist, 20 (1965), pp. 218-19.

Spaulding and Turner used the technique of 'test factor standard-ization' to find out whether the differences between groups of disciplines are primarily inherent in characteristics of the fields, rather than in background factors (*e.g.*, family, community, or party origins) or environmental conditions (*e.g.*, quality of school, rank, income) disproportionately distributed among the subject areas. Their analysis concluded that, if anything 'some of the small differences tended to mask the actual association between academic professional and political orientation'.[39] And they interpret their results as showing that the 'fundamental explanations' of the differences in political behavior 'lie in the [varying] perspectives of the professional groups. The findings also appear to be consistent with the idea that important elements in these perspectives are the degrees to which the various professional groups are oriented to-ward the role of social criticism. . . .'[40]

The concern among academics over the Vietnam war has resulted in recent years in a number of studies of faculty attitudes and behaviour toward that conflict. As might be expected, the massive Carnegie Commission study suggests that opposition to continuation of the war has been associated with general liberal political values. This and earlier studies indicate that the factors differentiating those supporting or opposing the war within the university are comparable to those separating liberals from conservatives and Democrats from Republicans.

A survey of attitudes toward the Vietnam war among a random sample of 152 academics in the Boston area conducted in April-May 1966 showed a relatively even distribution between those who thought the United States had no choice except to continue the war and those opposed to these policies. Among the liberal arts fields, the humanists and social scientists were more likely to oppose the war than the natural scientists.[41] A second study based on a questionnaire survey sent to 300 University of Michigan faculty early in 1967 of whom 242 replied also indicated that liberal arts

---

39    Charles B. Spaulding and Henry A. Turner, 'Political Orientation and Field of Specialization Among College Professors', *Sociology of Education*, 41 (1968), p. 261.         40        *Ibid.*, p. 262.

41    David Armor, *et al*, 'Professors' Attitudes toward the Vietnam War', *Public Opinion Quarterly*, 31 (Summer, 1967), pp. 162–70.

faculty members were more likely to favor an end to the bombing of North Vietnam than those in other more professional schools.[42]

Finally, we have Everett Ladd's analysis of the characteristics, and later of the attitudes, of academics who signed eight anti-Vietnam war statements which were published as advertisements in the Sunday *New York Times* between October 1964 and June 1968.[43] Ladd computed a Profession Representation Index by dividing the number of full-time faculty in the category by the percentage of all faculty signers in that category. A score of more than 100 means that a category is over-represented among the signers. The results by academic categories and disciplines are reported in Table IV below. Once again the liberal arts faculty were more likely to actively oppose the war than those in other schools, and within the liberal arts the social scientists were more involved than the humanists, who in turn rank higher in these terms than the natural scientists.

TABLE IV

*Distribution of Faculty Signers among Academic Fields and Selected Subjects*

| Field and Subject | Number of Signers (3,037) | Percentage of all Faculty Signers | Profession Representation Index |
|---|---|---|---|
| *Social Sciences* | *747* | *24·6* | *251* |
| Sociology and anthropology | 171 | 5·9 | 304 |
| Political science | 146 | 5·0 | 284 |
| Psychology | 213 | 7·3 | 281 |
| Economics | 110 | 3·8 | 211 |
| *Humanities* | *844* | *27·8* | *132* |
| Philosophy | 124 | 4·3 | 287 |
| History | 184 | 6·3 | 166 |
| English | 264 | 9·1 | 110 |
| Languages | 138 | 4·8 | 89 |

42    Howard Schuman and Edward O. Laumann, 'Do Most Professors Support the War?' *Trans-action*, 5 (November, 1967), p. 34.
43    Everett C. Ladd, Jr., 'Professors and Political Petitions', *Science*, 163 (March 28, 1969), pp. 1425-30.

| Field and Subject | Number of Signers (3.037) | Percentage of all Faculty Signers | Profession Representation Index |
|---|---|---|---|
| Physical Sciences | 489 | 16·1 | 122 |
| Physics | 231 | 7·6 | 253 |
| Mathematics | 185 | 6·1 | 127 |
| Chemistry | 61 | 2·0 | 54 |
| Life Sciences | 556 | 18·3 | 117 |
| Health fields | 337 | 11·1 | 137 |
| Biology | 207 | 6·8 | 85 |
| Fine Arts | 149 | 4·9 | 60 |
| Engineering | 140 | 4·6 | 60 |
| Education | 94 | 3·1 | 18 |
| Business | 12 | 0·4 | 10 |
| Agriculture | 6 | 0·2 | 6 |

Source: Everett C. Ladd, Jr., 'American University Teachers and Opposition to the Vietnam War', *Minerva*, 8 (Oct. 1970).

In a follow-up study, Ladd produced some interesting variations between sociologists and political scientists who had signed public anti-war statements which point to possible consequences of the approach of different academic fields. The sociology anti-war group differed from the political scientists in being much more pro-McCarthy rather than Kennedy in the 1968 pre-convention campaign, in being much more likely to voice their opposition in 'moralist' (*i.e.*, US is aggressor, imperialist, etc.) rather than 'realist' (US made mistakes, it pursued wrong policies) terms, and in voicing support for campus demonstrations. On all of these items, these two fields stood at polar opposites among the social sciences. Psychology appeared to fall closer to the 'moralist' approach of sociology, while economics produced more 'realists' among the anti-war group. Sociology was the only field in which supporters of student demonstrations outnumbered opponents, while the other fields reacted to this issue in the same order as on the moralist-realist dimension. Anti-war political scientists were least enthralled with student sit-ins. Ladd sought to account for the differences between the two polar disciplines:[44] 'It seems that political science has emphasized a "hard-headed", "realistic" approach to power and its uses, in contrast to an old tradition in sociology—now resurgent—oriented to social reform and social action'.

There have been various earlier efforts to account for the greater emphasis in sociology on support of reformist tendencies in the body politic. The discipline was founded by reformers and continues to deal with topics which inherently remain a focus for discontent, *e.g.*, race, urbanism, stratification, poverty, power, crime, delinquency, etc. Studies of prospective sociology concentrators, both entering freshmen and beginning graduate students during the 1950s, found a high proportion of them oriented to social reform.[45] As Charles Page pointed out, the view of sociology as 'an ameliorative enterprise . . . fairly widespread in academic faculties and among college students, draws many of the latter to classes in sociology. . . .'[46]

In addition to the manifest concerns with reform, strains inherent in the supposedly 'marginal' position of the field, uneasily located on the border between humanism and science, between qualitative and normative concerns and a desire to be perceived as a science which involves a high degree of quantitative rigor and formal theory, may make the sociologists feel more like 'outsiders', possessors of a low level of 'legitimacy', of low prestige within academia generally.[47]

---

44    Everett C. Ladd, Jr., 'American University Teachers and Opposition to the Vietnam War', *Minerva*, 8 (Oct., 1970), pp. 553-55. The percentage supporting demonstrations at Columbia, Cornell, etc. were sociologists, 39; psychologists, 27; economists, 10; and political scientists, 8.

45    Hanan C. Selvin and Warren O. Hagstrom, 'Determinants of Support for Civil Liberties', in S. M. Lipset and Sheldon Wolin, eds., *The Berkeley Student Revolt* (Garden City: Doubleday-Anchor Books, 1965), pp. 512-13.

46    Charles H. Page, 'Sociology as a Teaching Enterprise', in Robert K. Merton, *et al*, eds., *Sociology Today* (New York: Basic Books, 1959), p. 586. See also Robert H. Bohlke, 'The Activist, Value-Committed Sociologist: An Emerging Role' (paper presented at the 38th Annual Meeting of the Eastern Sociological Society, April 6, 1968, Boston, Mass.), p. 3.

47    Page, *op. cit.*, pp. 587-90; Donald G. MacRae, 'The Crisis of Sociology', in J. H. Plumb, ed., *Crisis in the Humanities* (London: Penguin Books, 1964), pp. 128-31; for a detailed discussion see Lipset and Ladd, 'The Politics of American Sociologists', *op. cit.*

In discussing this thesis, Robert Bohlke argues that marginality in terms of the scientific establishment presses sociologists towards a set of political actions which increase their marginality:[48] 'They have turned their back on the status of humanist or social philosopher, but they are still not fully accepted within the scientific fraternity. Thus, we are suggesting that their recent deviant behavior is a function of increased marginality. If this analysis has any validity the response to marginality—that is, an increased activist orientation as sociologists—will, if anything, increase, or reinforce, their marginal position'.

Daniel Cohn-Bendit, himself a student in sociology at Nanterre, the only French university with a full-blown sociology department then, has discussed in some detail the role of sociology students.[49] The explanation offered for their involvement is that sociology has adjusted its theory, concepts, methods, and problems of research to facilitate the growth of a stable capitalist system. It serves the need of the system more directly than any other discipline, and seeks to account for basic social problems such as racism, unemployment, delinquency, and slums as if they were isolated phenomena, not inherent in the nature of capitalism. And by adapting to the ideological and practical needs of capitalism, first in America and then in other industrialized countries, sociology has forced its students to oppose the university. Its very claim to be a 'leftist' field, while depreciating political action, fosters political protest:[50] 'The two great "hopes" of French sociology are the jargon of Parsons (author of "The place of ultimate values in sociological theory") and the cult of statistics (at least a bit of real science, this); these are the keys to every problem. In short, sociologists by a *tour*

---

48   Bohlke, *op. cit.*, p. 4.
49   D. and G. Cohn-Bendit, *op. cit.*, pp. 35-36.
50   *Ibid.*, p. 39. David Riesman has noted the same fact about sociology. 'The field is becoming so politicized it's hard to bring sober people into it. Sociology is the soft underbelly of the soft underbelly of society. It is interesting that all over the world student revolutionists have been led by sociologists; from Tokyo to the Free University of Berlin, sociologists have been the vanguard.' See 'The Young Are Captives of Each Other: A Conversation with David Riesman and T. George Harris', *Psychology Today*, 3 (October, 1969), p. 63.

*de force* have succeeded in taking out the political sting from their doctrines, which is equivalent to sanctifying the *status quo*. Sociology professors like to pass for Leftists, in contrast to the heads of other departments who apparently still hanker after the good old times. While the latter try to cling to their crumbling ivory tower, sociologists welcome "modernization": *planning, rationalization and production of consumer goods in accordance with the economic needs of organized capitalism'*.

Many hypotheses have been suggested to account for the relatively greater leftist sentiments among sociologists as compared to other social scientists generally, who in turn must be differentiated from the natural scientists and the humanists, and from members of various other professions. But, given the abundant evidence of the consistency of this pattern, Lazarsfeld and Thielens have suggested that if we assume the preponderance of left-liberal opinion in a field like sociology then its continuation and even growth may occur out of the results of 'mutual interaction':[51] '[T]wo factors crystallize and reinforce the nonconservative component. For one, young teachers see that professional success is attained more often by [liberal] seniors. Furthermore, once [left-oriented] colleagues are in the majority, even a slight numerical differential may build up to a considerable effect on the uncommitted man. By mere chance he is likely to find friendships among the less conservative; the result will be a slow atrophy of conservative potentialities unless they were very strong to begin with'.

But these clearly do not explain the beginning of the cycle, as Lazarsfeld and Thielens well recognized. They went on to suggest that the relative leftness of American professors generally, and of social scientists in particular, is derivative from or sustained by (if they bring such an orientation with them, as they assume many do) the relatively low income and social prestige of their occupation, as compared to other elite positions. 'Small economic return, little prestige on the outside, and scarce means of mutual prestige reinforcement—little wonder that the very position of the professor in the American social structure is not likely to make him approve of it

---

51    Lazarsfeld and Thielens, *op. cit.*, p. 150.

unequivocally'.[52] I have questioned some of the factual assumptions about the income and status of professors in *Political Man*, but I will not repeat them here, particularly since I agree that the data of Lazarsfeld and Thielens and others demonstrate that American intellectuals *believe* that they are underprivileged, in part because they, like Lazarsfeld and Thielens, take the deference given to academics (and all other elite members) in the more explicitly elitist European society as a reference point from which to judge the status of American intellectuals.[53]

The Columbia scholars presented an alternative hypothesis to account for the liberalism of social scientists which makes them a more extreme case of the general thesis advanced earlier that a critical anti-establishment stance is inherent in intellectual activities:[54] 'The social scientist faces an additional situation deriving from the nature of his work, which is likely to strengthen a basically permissive (liberal) attitude. The intellectual task involved in these and many similar endeavors of the social scientist are contingent on his ability to visualize a state of human affairs radically different from that of today . . . for ultimate scholarly accomplishment must depend upon a kind of imagination which has initially to be akin to criticism and is not, therefore, consonant with the intellectual mood of the conservative'.

A somewhat similar interpretation has been suggested more recently by Eitzen and Maranell. 'The behavioral sciences demand intellectual inquiry into areas of traditional belief. This inquiry in turn demands some objectivity regarding tradition and this in turn tends to weaken the tradition'[55].

---

52     *Ibid.*, p. 149.
53     See *Political Man, op. cit.*, pp. 323-30. American intellectuals, in effect, are objecting to the consequences of American egalitarianism which denies the marks of status to the elite, even though analyses of the status of professors indicate that they rank close to the top of the occupational status ladder. See Robert W. Hodge, Paul M. Siegel and Peter H. Rossi, 'Occupational Prestige in the United States', in R. Bendix and S. M. Lipset, eds., *Class, Status and Power* (New York: The Free Press, 1966), pp. 324-25.
54     Lazarsfeld and Thielens, *op. cit.*, p. 149.
55     Eitzen and Maranell, *op. cit.*, p. 152.

A number of German scholars, however, including Helmut Plessner, Karl Mannheim, and Robert Michels, have argued that fields concerned with the past and tradition press their practitioners towards conservative beliefs.[56] American data do not sustain this thesis, except that history does appear to be a more conservative field than the social sciences.

Among other disciplines, there is some indication that the more theoretical, abstract fields tend to have higher proportions of left-wing supporters, or as in the case of political theory, an over-representation of the ideological extremes at both ends of the spectrum. It has been suggested that theoretical physicists are much more liberal or left than experimental ones. The well-known conservative leanings of chemists has been accounted for by their supposed closer connections to industry. Helmut Plessner has posited 'a general connection between the exact sciences, and a leaning towards left-wing ideas. . . . For those engaged in the exact sciences, where ideas are mainly framed in a mathematical form, and where the progress of knowledge is based on controlled experiments and on the different applications of theoretical results to objective experience, there is a strong attraction in the doctrines of enlightened positivism.'[57]

Although these various comments and interpretations point to elements in the intellectual orientation of the various disciplines which press men in diverse political directions, studies of student politics, some dating back a number of decades, and dealing with entering freshmen who knew what they wanted to major in before they had taken any courses, indicate that the major source of political differentiation may be, as Ladd notes 'the fact of selective recruitment'. Morris Rosenberg found a strong relationship between prospective major subject and political orientation among freshmen and sophomores. In a follow-up study two years later, Rosenberg

---

56    Helmut Plessner, 'Ideological Tendencies Among Academic Thinkers', Congress for Cultural Freedom, *Science and Freedom* (London: Secker and Warburg, 1955), p. 155; Karl Mannheim, *Ideology and Utopia* (New York: Harcourt, Brace, 1936), pp. 119-22; Robert Michels, *Political Parties* (New York: Hearst's International Library, 1915), pp. 256-57.

57    Plessner, *op. cit.*, p. 178.

reported that political attitudes were associated with changes in career plans or subject major. Conservative students who had chosen liberal (in political terms) fields tended to change to subjects whose student concentrators were more conservative, and conversely, the minority of liberals who had planned to major in conservative subjects also tended to shift their field to one more compatible with their political beliefs.[58] Selvin and Hagstrom in a survey of the attitudes of entering freshmen at Berkeley in 1959 also found correlations between prospective major and political opinions, relationships comparable to those found among students in their latter years in college.[59]

These data obviously argue for the thesis that selective recruitment plays a major role in determining the predominant political orientation of different disciplines. As yet, however, we know little concerning the images of different fields among students and the general public which produces such selectivity.[60] In general, the student surveys do indicate, that those from more lowly backgrounds, i.e., in terms of parents' occupation, income, and education, are much more disposed to see higher education as a means of securing the credentials and skills necessary for a 'good job', while the more abstract, intellectual, less vocationally specific subjects, i.e., often the liberal arts, gain their students from those reared in more affluent, better educated, more intellectually involved (occupationally or book-oriented) and (in the United States at least) more politically liberal environments. They do not see college as a means to economic success, but rather as a way of gaining knowledge, or finding way to do good. The parents of the first group encourage their children to work hard to get ahead; those of the second tend to want their children to develop intellectually, assuming that their occupational careers will work out well.

A study of a sample of Berkeley undergraduates in 1959-61, analyzed the characteristics of those who 'realistically considered'

---

58    Morris Rosenberg, *Occupations and Values* (Glencoe: The Free Press, 1957), pp. 19-22; see also James A. Davis, *Undergraduate Career Decisions* (Chicago: Aldine, 1965), pp. 52-53.

59    Selvin and Hagstrom, *op. cit.*, pp. 513.

60    For a discussion of some evidence, see Spaulding and Turner, *op. cit.*, p. 249.

becoming a college professor. Many of the findings are congruent with the analysis presented thus far. Not surprisingly, 'intellectualism is indeed important in determining whether the student will or will not consider college teaching'. More significant, however, is the finding that interest in college teaching is closely related to political self-identification, going from left to right. Those describing themselves as 'socialists' were most inclined to become professors (62 per cent), followed by liberal Democrats (34), liberal Republicans (20), conservative Democrats (14), and conservative Republicans (15)[61]. Studies of student images of the characteristics of professors as compared to other occupations give them 'a high score on radicalism', and on 'power in public affairs'.[62]

It is difficult to establish precise links between the political attitudes and behavior of professors and those of student roles which lead into different academic fields. The data do, of course, suggest a close correlation between the two.[63] This does not demonstrate the causal effect of student political beliefs on the discipline variations among the professoriate, since much of this association appears to be a function of the recruitment process. The interplay between structural attributes and self-selection is one that we need to learn much more about before reaching any definitive conclusions about the politics of students or professors.

Presumably, although early social and political values may play a considerable role in dictating fields of study, they should not have a comparable effect in determining who among prospective scholars

---

61    Ian D. Currie, *et al*, 'Images of the Professor and Interest in the Academic Profession', in Ronald M. Pavalko, ed., *Sociology of Education* (Itasca, Ill.: Peacock, 1968), pp. 540-41, 549-50; see also Martin Trow, 'Recruitment to College Teaching', in A. H. Halsey, *et al*, eds., *Education, Economy and Society* (New York: The Free Press, 1961), pp. 609-17.

62    David C. Beardslee and Donald D. O'Dowd, 'Students and the Occupational World', in Nevitt Sanford, ed., *The American College* (New York: John Wiley, 1962), p. 615; and Robert H. Knapp, 'Changing Functions of the College Professor', in *Ibid.*, pp. 301-03.

63    Glaucio Soares, 'Ideological Identity and Political Ideology among University Students', in S. M. Lipset and Aldo Solari, eds., *Elites in Latin America* (New York: Oxford University Press, 1967), pp. 445-50.

and intellectuals will be most successful in the role. Yet the thesis that a commitment to 'intellectuality' predisposes men to a critical political stance should mean that those most involved in creative activities will be more liberal or left in the American political context. The data bearing on this proposition tend to sustain it.

The earliest studies of faculty attitudes, analyses of variation in religious belief of various groups of Americans conducted by James Leuba, a psychologist, in 1913-14 and again in 1933, indicated that academics and writers were much less religious than businessmen, bankers, lawyers, and the public at large, facts which reinforce the latter findings that these intellectual groups are among the most liberal or left-wing. More relevant to the immediate thesis, however, was his finding for both periods that the more distinguished professors were much more irreligious than their less eminent colleagues.[64]

Using scholarly productivity as an indicator of academic achievement or in our terms of intellectual or scholarly creativity, the 1969 Carnegie Commission study found within different age groupings a clear relationship between productivity and propensity to take liberal to left-wing positions.[65] The earlier Lazarsfeld-Thielens survey of social science opinion also reported that 'the proportion of productive scholars rises as we move from the very conservative to the very permissive [liberal] respondents'.[66] The study of social science signers of anti-Vietnam war statements also indicated a relationship between scholarly achievement and liberal political beliefs and action.[67] Another indicator of the relationship between 'intellectuality' and political orientation is the predominant political outlook at institutions which emphasize scholarship.[68] In the 1955 national survey Lazarsfeld and Thielens found a strong correlation between

---

64    James H. Leuba, *The Belief in God and Immortality* (Chicago: The Open Court Publishing Co., 1921), pp. 219-87; and *The Reformation of the Churches* (Boston: The Beacon Press, 1950), pp. 50-54. I have also discussed these materials previously in *Political Man*, op. cit., pp. 313-14.

65    See papers cited in footnote 24.

66    Lazarsfeld and Thielens, *op. cit.*, pp. 144-46.

67    Ladd, 'American University Teachers and Opposition ...' *op. cit.*

68    Paul Lazarsfeld and Wagner Thielens, Jr., *op. cit.*, pp. 132, 162.

the academic quality of institutions and the willingness of social science faculty to be 'permissive' with respect to various forms of political and personal non-conformity and dissent. The NORC and Carnegie surveys taken more than a decade later reported comparable findings in their more general samples.[69] Similar findings are indicated in a number of the other studies dealt with here.[70]

The special studies of samples of the American Sociological and Political Science Associations indicate that both sociologists and political scientists are more likely to be Democrats if they teach in universities with well-developed graduate schools, while the small minority of Republicans among them tend to be located in relatively small colleges with few, if any, graduate programs.[71]

The one exception to the relationship of high academic prestige or scholarly emphasis to liberal-left opinion may be found in Armor's study of Boston faculty opinion towards the Vietnam war. But his sample for the various groups of colleges is quite small, however, and no reliable conclusions may be drawn from it.[72]

The greater liberalism of the faculty at the high quality schools has been explained by the authors of the two earlier national surveys in terms congruent with the assumption that an emphasis on intellectuality, on scholarly creativity, is linked to such values. Lazarsfeld and Thielens point out that such institutions 'attract more distinguished social scientists':[73] 'The original and creative minority among them will often have analytical minds which do not automatically accept current beliefs, minds willing to entertain unorthodox ideas as to how a modern society can best function'. Noll and Rossi point out that faculty have a 'greater likelihood of being involved in the "world of ideas" in high quality schools and

---

69    Noll and Rossi, *op. cit.*, p. 21. The same relationship occurred for party identification. Republicans were strongest in low quality schools, Democrats in high quality ones (p. 16).

70    Eitzen and Maranell, *op. cit.*, p. 150. Ladd, 'Social Scientists and Opposition . . .' *op. cit.*

71    Turner, *et al*, 'The Political Party Affiliation of American Political Scientists', *op. cit.*, p. 660; Turner, *et al*, 'Political Orientations of Academically Affiliated Sociologists', *op. cit.*, p. 287.

72    See Armor, *et al*, *op. cit.*, pp. 169-70, 175.

73    Lazarsfeld and Thielens, *op. cit.*, pp. 161-63.

much greater likelihood of being vocationally and pragmatically oriented at lower quality schools'.[74] These differences in life style show up clearly in the fact that more of those at the high quality institutions than at the lower quality ones show a preference for research as compared to teaching.

Factors of income, rank, and age are major determinants of variations in political orientations in the community at large. Within academia, they are intercorrelated with each other and are also affected by type of institution in which men are located and their relative scholarly productivity. The better institutions, which are also centers of greater liberalism, pay much higher salaries on the average than the less prestigious, more conservative schools. Hence, income as such does not appear as a major source of ideology in any of the extant surveys. The data available on the political correlates of rank and age indicate that younger and lower statused faculty are more liberal and Democratic. Lazarsfeld and Thielens found that the older and higher statused were more conservative regardless of quality of school.[75] The differences were least in the high quality institutions where senior men were among the most liberal in academia, a finding reiterated in the Carnegie Commission data. This means that the most visible and distinguished men in the academe, who presumably constitute important reference individuals are among the most liberal or left and that this orientation is often tied up with the image of professional success.

The 1966 NORC national survey of academics found that more of the younger scholars tended to favor increased government controls over business while showing more opposition to controls over labor; older faculty as a group tended to have the opposite pattern of response.[76] The surveys of sociologists and political scientists reported large age differences between the Democrats and Republicans among them. 'Only seven of the Republicans (or 20 per cent) were

---

74    Noll and Rossi, *op. cit.*, pp. 33-34; see also on these different styles, David Riesman and Joseph Gusfield, 'Styles of Teaching in Two New Public Colleges', in Robert Morrison, ed., *The Contemporary University: U.S.A.* (Boston: Houghton Mifflin, 1966), pp. 242-65.

75    Lazarsfeld and Thielens, *op. cit.*, pp. 249-50.

76    Noll and Rossi, *op. cit.*, p. 88.

I

under 40 years of age; but 73 of the Democrats (or more than 46 per cent) were in that age group. Forty-three per cent of the Republicans were over fifty years old, while only 25 per cent of the Democrats had reached that age'.[77] In comparing the academic ranks of major party supporters in 1962, Eitzen and Maranell found a difference between those in the north and the south. In the former, non-tenure faculty were more Democratic than those in the higher ranks; in the south, the lower-statused ones were more Republican.[78] This variation may be a reaction to the party most identified with the *status quo* in the different sections. It may be that identifying with the Republicans for southern academics in 1962 meant choosing the party in their state or section which was viewed as more likely to contribute to breaking up the racial *status quo*.

The studies of reactions to the Vietnam war, however, present a dilemma. Both Ladd and Armor find older professors more hostile to the war than younger ones.[79] The more recent Carnegie Commission data, however, reaffirm the more commonly reported finding; the younger are more opposed to the war, at least as of 1969.

The Halsey-Trow British survey reported that younger and lower statused academics were more likely to vote Labour and identify with the left, but the differences were not very large with 45 per cent Labour among the lower ranks and 36 per cent for the full professors.[80]

Most of the studies of the opinions and behavior of academics agree that religious orientation and background make a considerable difference in political choice. There is some indication from the special surveys of political scientists, sociologists, and psychologists discussed earlier that Republican social scientists tend to come from small town and rural Protestant backgrounds and to continue to be more involved in religious activities than Democrats who are much

---

77    Turner, *et al*, 'The Political Party Affiliation of American Political Scientists', *op. cit.*, p. 660; Turner, *et al*, 'Political Orientations of Academically Affiliated Sociologists', *op. cit.*, p. 280.

78    Eitzen and Maranell, *op. cit.*, p. 151.

79    Ladd, 'Professors and Political Petitions', *op. cit.*, pp. 1427-28. Armor, *et al*, *op. cit.*, pp. 169-70. Schumann and Laumann, *op. cit.*, pp. 34-35.

80    Halsey and Trow, p. 437.

less Protestant, less religious and more metropolitan in their community background. These variations tie into differences in the
types of institutions in which the different groups are employed.
Religious Protestants and those from small community origins are
more likely to be found in less prestigious smaller schools which are
away from metropolitan centers. Non-Protestants, particularly Jews
and the irreligious, tend to be located in schools with the opposite
characteristics. A large segment of the Catholic scholars, of course,
is located in Catholic, usually less scholarly eminent institutions.

The contribution of faculty of Jewish background to liberal
political groupings has been stressed in a number of surveys. Although Jews are only 3 per cent of the national population, those of
Jewish origins were nine per cent of academia in 1969 according to the
Carnegie Commission sample.[81] And, they constitute much larger
proportions of various disciplines and types of institutions, since
they are concentrated in a few professional schools, the liberal arts
faculties, and at the more prestigious or higher quality universities.

All of the studies which deal with religious background indicate
that close to 90 per cent of the Jewish academics are Democrats.
They also have contributed highly to the backing of leftist third
parties. Thus in 1948 30 per cent of the Jewish professors were for
Henry Wallace, the Progressive party nominee, while another 12 per
cent voted Socialist.[82] Catholics, who according to the Carnegie
Commission constitute only 19 per cent of academia, have tended to
be largely Democratic in party affiliation and normal voting preferences. The survey of Boston academic area opinion on the
Vietnam war indicated that religious background was the most
crucial factor. Among Jews, 73 per cent were anti-war; the 'none'
group, some of whom were undoubtedly of Jewish background, were
62 per cent opposed; among Protestants, only 28 per cent were anti-
war; while the war opponents were only 13 per cent of the Catholics.[83]
Since Jews constituted full 38 per cent of this random sample of
Boston professors, it is clear that the special political values of this
group contributes greatly to the results for the total population of

---

81    Lipset and Ladd, 'Jewish Academics in the United States . . .', *op. cit.*;
      see also Spaulding and Turner, *op. cit.*, p. 253.
82    Howard, *op. cit.*, p. 418.
83    Armor, *et al*, p. 170.

scholars, particularly in metropolitan centers with a concentration of graduate and research-oriented universities. Similar results are indicated in studies which report on the relationship between general ideological identification and religious background and practice.[84]

Analyses of the Carnegie Commission's national sample yield the same strong relationship. The Jews and the large 'no religion' group (about one quarter of whom are of Jewish origin) and the 'other' religion category (6 per cent of sample) tend to be much more liberal or radical on all questions than the currently identified Protestants (46 per cent) or Catholics (12 per cent). For example, those who described their own politics as 'left' or 'liberal' constituted 73 per cent of the no religion group, 69 per cent of the Jews, 58 per cent of 'others', 39 per cent of the Catholics and 34 per cent of the Protestants. Conversely, those who considered themselves 'conservatives' included 38 per cent of the Protestants, 24 per cent of the Catholics, 18 per cent of the 'others', 9 per cent of the Jews, and 9 per cent of the 'no religion' group.

In Britain also, religion proved to be a major differentiating factor in affecting party vote and ideological identification. 'The Church of Scotland [proved] to be the most conservative group. The Church of England is fairly near the average, and then follow the Roman Catholics and the nonconformists close together, with the children of agnostics and, finally, Jews, the most Left-wing of all. . . . Religious upbringing is a powerful determinant of political-ideology and disposition'.[85]

These extreme differences in political philosophies among academics of different religious and cultural backgrounds suggest that efforts to account for the greater liberality of American professors by attributes inherent in the nature of intellectual life, of academia, of or specific institutions or disciplines may be in error. The differences may rest in the differential participation of the diverse cultural-religious groups in different occupations. Academia may have become more left-wing because it has admitted or become more attractive to a changing clientele, one which derives its

---

84    Cole and Adamsons, *op. cit.*, p. 3.
85    Halsey and Trow, p. 415.

political orientation from its pre-academic social background, not the intellectual enterprise itself.

At the moment, there is no way to deal conclusively with the complex methodological issue posed by this question by reference to the literature. The question has been almost entirely ignored, even by those studies which do report on religious variations, and a number did not even do that.

It should be made clear that the issue of the causal weight of intellectual orientations on other aspects of belief systems is not eliminated by the finding that those who hold the hypothesized set of values come from specific, highly delimited backgrounds. We should expect a high degree of congruence between the personal values present disproportionately in various social milieus (class, religious, regional, ethnic, etc.), and the over- or under-representation of persons from such backgrounds in given types of jobs. The research on occupational choice or job placement indicates logical relationships between the values and special abilities of individuals and the jobs they prepare for and take. Those sub-groups in American life which value intellectuality more highly than others should, all other things being equal, contribute in heavily disproportionate numbers to the intellectual occupations. Conversely, those milieus which are anti-intellectual or which believe that other forms of human activity are worth more will contribute less. Further, it should follow that those individuals socialized in a highly intellectualized family and cultural environment should do better in intellectual jobs than those who enter such pursuits without the advantage of a strong family and cultural encouragement and early experience. The children of intellectuals, for example, regardless of religious background, should do better in intellectual pursuits and should possess more of the core values of intellectualdom than those of other backgrounds.

Some time ago, a young conservative writing in a Stanford conservative magazine complained that adult conservatives in the business or political world did not encourage student conservatives to become academics. He stated that whenever he mentioned his desire to become a professor among older non-academic conservatives he immediately met with arguments about his wasting his talents if he did so. His understandable challenge to those who held this view was how did they expect to find any support in the academic world if they regarded academia as unfit for anyone they knew. Thus we see the makings of a self-sustaining or even self-escalating cycle. Intellectualdom recruits from groups who value intellectuality. And to value intellectuality is associated with a preference for the ideal, for a rejection of the world of money-making and formal power. The studies of occupational choice indicate that those who prefer intellectual occupations tend to come from relatively privileged, well-educated, and politically liberal backgrounds, regardless of religion or ethnicity. Those of more lowly origins tend to see education as a means of getting ahead vocationally. They tend to be found disproportionately in pre-professional courses. Those of this group who do decide on academic careers presumably would do so more for vocational and status reasons than because of a commitment to intellectuality. One would expect them to be both more conservative politically and less successful occupationally than those who came to academia or other intellectual pursuits with a desire to be creative.

These assumptions are congruent with the findings of an earlier study which also involved the interviewing in depth of a small sample (45) of assistant professors in the humanities and social sciences in a large midwestern university. The purpose of the study was to analyze the nature of feelings of self-hatred or disesteem among American intellectuals about their own roles, that is, the extent to which they accepted as valid negative valuations. Those interviewed were differentiated into two groups, high and low, with respect to responding similarly to an ethnic minority to their sense of occupational inferiority. Others in the same fields were asked 'to judge the professional creativity of those interviewed'. Those who took a positive view towards intellectual activities on each of three qualitative criteria, acceptance of negative stereotypes, approval of efforts to conform to gain acceptance by non-intellectuals, and denial of membership in the intellectual group, had a consistently higher creativity score.[86]

The findings of these two studies may be linked to the report of Lazarsfeld and Thielens that 'professors from high socio-economic

86    Melvin Seeman, 'The Intellectual and the Language of Minorities', *American Journal of Sociology*, 64 (July, 1958), pp. 33-34.

backgrounds are more likely to be highly productive . . . [within] each age group'.[87] The more productive tended also to be the most liberal in this study, suggesting anew that a higher status background, presumably from more intellectually-oriented families, is more conducive to such liberal views within academia than a deprived, typically less intellectual one.

The fact that the more successful within academia, also the most liberal, are more likely to see academia as a place in which intellectual and non-conformist styles of life may be best fulfilled may be seen in some results from the NORC national survey. Noll and Rossi asked their respondents to compare academic and non-academic jobs with respect to which they thought was better on a number of job characteristics. A consistent set of differences emerged with respect to the answers by faculty at low quality as contrasted with those at high quality schools. Those at low quality schools were more likely to say that academic jobs were superior to non-academic ones on opportunity 'to work with people', 'to be helpful to others', 'to be helpful to society', and 'to exercise leadership'. Those at high quality schools were more prone to stress the desirability of academic jobs with respect to the opportunity 'to be creative and original', 'to achieve recognition in own field', and to have the 'freedom not to conform in personal life'.[88] Noll and Rossi correctly conclude that their findings reinforce the Riesman-Gusfield thesis of two academic worlds, 'one linked to the world of ideas, the second to a helpful or vocational and pragmatic orientation'.[89] There is no way of telling, of course, to what extent faculty at different types of schools developed such varying orientations as a reaction to their experiences in the differing academic worlds or whether they brought much of these values with them, that their personal orientations helped to determine what part of academia they would inhabit.

The values of the cosmopolitan liberal scholars continue to dominate academia since new recruits to the profession are socialized in the graduate schools. Those who most resemble their professors are most likely to be recommended for the best jobs, to be defined as the most promising. It is clear that graduate students see their professors

---

87    Lazarsfeld and Thielens, *op. cit.*, p. 10.
88    Noll and Rossi, *op. cit.*, pp. 44-45.
89    *Ibid.*, p. 45.

as valuing creative scholarship above all other things. A national survey of graduate students asked respondents to choose among a number of behavioral items those 'which gave a student high prestige with the faculty'. The item which was chosen by 96 per cent and ranked way ahead of all the others was 'demonstrating research or scholarly capacity'. The second most popular choice (76 per cent) was 'being original and creative'. Less than half the students thought that evidence of 'teaching ability' yielded them any prestige with their graduate professors.[90] These values, of course, are in conflict with those now espoused by the activist students.

*Student Orientations*

Perhaps the most impressive conclusion to be drawn from the results of the studies of faculty opinion is the high congruence between the correlates of liberal-left points of view among faculty and among students. Both are concentrated among the more highly intellectually committed disciplines and institutions. Both come from social backgrounds conducive to intellectualism and liberalism. And consequently, the activist-inclined student finds support both at home and in his university. The generational struggle is not a gap: it is a matter of pace, temperament, and willingness to risk careers and institutions that separates the student activist from his parents or the faculty in his subject at school. Some comments by recent analysts of student protest may illustrate this point. Thus Richard Flacks, SDS founder and serious scholarly student of activist protest, reported on his research in the following terms:[91]

'In sum, our data suggest that, at least at major Northern colleges, students involved in protest activity are characteristically from families, which are urban, highly educated, Jewish or irreligious, professional and affluent. It is perhaps particularly interesting that many of their mothers are uniquely well-educated and involved in careers, and that high status and education has characterized these families over at least two generations.

---

90    David Gottlieb, 'Processes of Socialization in American Graduate Schools', in Ronald M. Pavalko, ed., *Sociology of Education* (Itaska, Ill.: Peacock, 1968), p. 263.

91    Richard Flacks, 'The Liberated Generation: An Explanation of the Roots of Student Protest', *Journal of Social Issues*, 23, No. 3 (1967), pp. 66, 68 (emphases in original).

*'Activists are more "radical" than their parents; but activists' parents
are decidedly more liberal than others of their status. . . .* Our data
clearly demonstrate that the fathers of activists are disproportionately liberal. . . .

'It seems fair to conclude then, that most students who are involved in the movement . . . are involved in neither "conversion"
from nor "rebellion" against the political perspectives of their
fathers. A more supportable view suggests that the great majority
of these students are attempting to fulfil and renew the political
traditions of their families. . . .

*'Activism is related to a complex of values, not ostensibly political,
shared by both the students and their parents. . . .* Our findings and
impressions on this point may be briefly summarized by saying that,
whereas nonactivists and their parents tend to express conventional
orientations toward achievement, material success, sexual morality
and religion, the activists and their parents tend to place greater
stress on involvement in intellectual and esthetic pursuits, humani-
tarian concerns, opportunity for self-expression, and tend to de-
emphasize or positively disvalue personal achievement, conventional
morality and conventional religiosity'.

Flacks also found that the activists score very high as a group on a
scale of 'Intellectualism' derived from answers to ten questions. This
variable is described as 'Concern with ideas—desire to realize intellectual capacities—high valuation of intellectual creativities—
appreciation of theory and knowledge—participation in intellectual
activity (*e.g.*, reading, studying, teaching, writing)—broad intellectual concerns'. They also score high on scales purporting to
estimate 'Romanticism: Esthetic and Emotional Sensitivity',
'Humanitarianism', and 'Moralism and Self-Control'. These values
appeared to be highly intercorrelated, and 'most importantly, parent
and student scores on these variables are strongly correlated'.[92]

A variety of other student surveys, some limited to specific
schools, Berkeley more than any other one, some based on national
samples, completed by scholars from a variety of disciplines or by
commercial market research agencies and using a number of different
methods, have generally come up with conclusions concerning family
backgrounds and personal values which are highly comparable, if not
identical, to those reported by Flacks, and agree with the findings

---

92    *Ibid.*, pp. 69-70.

reported here concerning the correlates of faculty liberalism.[93]

It should be noted, however, that efforts to compare left activists with others active in conservative or even non-political activities indicate little difference among them in actual grades received. There are many personality qualities which activists share, regardless of ideology.[94]

The relative lack of tension between students and their parents and teachers as compared to other groups comes through in various national opinion surveys, in spite of the fact that most students will also talk of the great 'generation gap'. Thus a national Gallup survey conducted in November 1969 of 1,092 students on 57 campuses reports that the two institutions which received the highest ratings (excellent or good) were universities (68 per cent positive) and the family (58 per cent).[95] Jeffrey Hadden put the situation well in discussing the results of a national poll which he supervised in the Spring of 1969:[96] 'Even the contempt for the older generation operates on an abstract level, not much on the specific and personal. There's no general alienation from parents. . . .'

'The irony of the students is not their rebellion but their docile

---

93  Kenneth A. Feldman and Theodore M. Newcomb, *The Impact of College on Students*, Vol. I (San Francisco: Jossey-Bass, 1969), p. 161. Richard G. Braungart, 'Family Status, Socialization and Student Politics: A Multivariate Analysis' (Ph.D. Thesis: Department of Sociology, Pennsylvania State University, 1969), p. 61. Kenneth Keniston, 'Notes on Young Radicals', *Change*, 1 (November-December, 1969), p. 29. Roger Kahn, 'The Rank and File Student Activist: A Contextual Analysis of Three Hypotheses' (unpublished mimeographed paper, Department of Sociology, S.U.N.Y., Stony Brook), pp. 8-9.

94  For a detailed presentation and discussion of the background factors which differentiate various types of activists, see S. M. Lipset 'Who are the Activists?' in Lipset, *Rebellion in the University, op. cit.*, pp. 80-123.

95  'The New Mood on Campus', *Newsweek*, 74 (December 29, 1969), p. 43. The other institutions rated, each on an absolute basis, were Business, Congress, Courts, Police, High Schools, Organized Religion and Political Parties.

96  Jeffrey K. Hadden, 'The Private Generation', *Psychology Today*, 3 (October, 1969), p, 69.

conformity to the stated ideals, if not the example, of their parents and teachers. . . .'

The congruence in values between liberal-left faculty and students, the strong relationship between a critical anti-establishment ideology and a commitment to intellectual values has obvious implications for the political future of academia. It is quite likely that the activist students of today will be the faculty of tomorrow. Clearly, many of the younger academics today are alumni of the student 'movement'. They may be found in the ranks of assistant professors, instructors, and graduate students. Many of the more senior faculty on the left tend to abstain from public support of activist organisations because of opposition to the confrontation tactics which some of these groups employ, or because they object to explicit politicization, to the insistence by many of these radical academics that the ideal of 'objective scholarship' is reactionary, that all research and teaching should be openly partisan.

A preliminary report on a study involving responses from samples of 1,600 faculty and 3,500 doctoral students in the ten leading graduate universities in the country reinforces the earlier indications that academia is attracting a disproportionate share of the most militant students, because they are also the most oriented toward intellectual careers. The analysis, however, also suggests that in moving through to the status of doctoral students, the prospective faculty members while retaining much of their critical outlook with respect to the university will seek to effect changes within academia through established channels. The only statistical data reported indicate, however, that although presumably more liberal or critical of the university than the faculty, the doctoral students also remain a divided group. 'Forty-eight per cent of the 3,500 respondents . . . said they would join a teaching assistants' union if a chapter were available on their campuses'.[97] It will be interesting to learn how this more politicized group of prospective faculty react to the teaching-research dilemma.

*Political Ideology and Campus Response*
This discussion of the sources of faculty political orientations,

97     Ann M. Heiss, 'Today's Graduate Student—Tomorrow's Faculty Members', *The Research Reporter*, 4, No. 2 (1969), p. 6.

voting, and party preferences has been premised on the assumption that the ideological predispositions which faculty bring to campus political crises have been major determinants of the way they have responded to the campus issues. It is obvious, of course, that no one factor can explain a given type of behavior, and consequently a considerable amount of deviation is to be expected from a statistical point of view. Secondly, on an impressionistic basis, it is again clear to all participants in internecine campus conflicts that the division has not been that simple. In almost every well-known conflict prominent liberals and even radicals have strongly opposed confrontationist tactics as destructive of the basic conditions for scholarship or as politicizing, and hence reducing the academic freedom present within the university. Conversely, some men of conservative values have sharply opposed the policies of the administration in using force against student demonstrators on the grounds, among others, that the administration and faculty, as the adult members of the university, have a greater moral obligation than students to restrain their use of sheer power; that in the given situation, they should have negotiated much longer than they did or been willing to change outmoded policies, even under duress.

Although the survey of British faculty opinion was conducted before the current wave of student unrest and hence did not inquire into it, it is interesting to note that a major correlate of attitudes toward department and university governance was political position. The further left a British academic's general political views, the more likely he was to favor 'democratization' of university administration.[98] When left-right orientation was combined with cosmopolitanism-localism, they predicted much of the attitudes: 'Three times as many Left-wing cosmopolitans as Right-wing locals are [campus] "democrats". These two factors taken together have a substantial degree of predictive power and show that views on the structure of power in universities . . . are strongly influenced by the attitudes and orientations that academic men hold toward more general issues than the specific matters about [university and department governance] which respondents were being asked'.[99]

---

98      Halsey and Trow, *op. cit.*, pp. 386-87.
99      *Ibid.*, p. 397.

Halsey and Trow conclude that a 'recurrent if largely unanticipated theme in [their study] ... has been the extraordinarily large bearing that university teachers' political positions and loyalties have on their more narrowly academic attitudes and behaviour'.[100]

The 'non-political' factor which impressionistically has had the most impact in differentiating faculty groups in America is age and / or rank. At most schools, the more left caucus is invariably reported to be heavily composed of younger and non-tenure faculty, the more conservative one of senior tenured professors. While such differences may largely reflect variations in general political ideology linked to age, it is also possible that they are related to clear-cut interest differences, as well as to a variation in the degree of involvement in and commitment to the institution. To the junior faculty, the administration and the university are often a 'they', an employer who may require them to move on. To senior men who have spent the bulk of their lives at the university, the university is 'home', but perhaps more relevant the administrators who are under fire are men they have known for many years, who, they feel, deserve the benefit of the doubt, and may even be excused blunders.

Studies of the attitudes of faculty toward university governance suggest that rank and age are important sources of difference. An early empirical study completed in the late 1950s before the current wave of protest by interviews with faculty at six diverse institutions indicated sharp rank and age differences in attitudes toward administrative prerogatives and university government.[101]

Two studies of the correlates of faculty opinion in institutions which have had major internal battles, Columbia University and the University of Connecticut, permit some test of the assumptions concerning the bases of faculty diversity developed in this paper. The study at Connecticut is a very limited one since it is based on an analysis of the signed ballots cast in a mail referendum on two questions which concerned the issue of allowing outside recruiters on campus following a major campus conflict over Dow Chemical recruiters. On the whole, the factors associated with opposition to

---

100    *Ibid.*, p. 398.
101    K. W. Leffland, *The College Administration and Faculty: A Study of Administrative Functions and Roles* (D.P.A. Thesis: School of Public Administration: University of Southern California, 1959), pp. 315-16.

recruiting coincide with those reported earlier as characteristics of liberal sentiment or opposition to the Vietnam war. Specifically, the disciplines differentiated left to right from the social sciences (64 per cent) through the humanities (56 per cent) to the physical sciences (42 per cent).[102] By rank, the lower the status, the more left the faculty vote. Thus, 82 per cent of instructors took the left position, as contrasted with 40 per cent of full professors. Longevity at the institution, however, turned out to be more important then rank. Among those at the school for a decade or more, less than one third (31 per cent) took the anti-recruiting position, as compared with 71 per cent among those new to the institution (three years or less). When rank was controlled for longevity, the authors found that full professors new to the institution turned out to be more likely to be opposed to recruiting than assistant or associate professors who had longer experience at Connecticut. The authors conclude that 'there is no conflict of generations in this academy. But there is a conflict of the newly-arrived faculty of all ranks against the locals of all ranks'.[103]

It is, of course, difficult to tell what the source of the differences between the 'locals' and the 'newly arrived' is. It may reflect the fact that the latter, being more mobile, are more oriented to the larger values associated with intellectualdom and scholarship in academia discussed earlier. It may also result from the lesser ties of the 'newly arrived' to the university administration and existing faculty leadership implied in the discussion of attitudes toward university governance. In any case, this study suggests that universities which emphasize turnover through stringent requirements for tenure, seeking to build a high calibre 'cosmopolitan' and scholarly faculty, may by so doing increase the sources of opposition to the administration in intra-mural disputes, a conclusion which has been implicit in many of the previously reported findings.

---

102    Rosalio Wences and Harold J. Abramson, 'Faculty Opinions About University Functions and Autonomy' (unpublished paper, Department of Sociology, University of Connecticut, October, 1969), p. 13. The percentages refer to the proportion who gave a 'left' answer to both resolutions.

103    *Ibid.*, p. 9.

Fortunately, this effort to specify the determinants of faculty diversity in the current campus crisis may conclude its report on the assorted empirical studies with the methodologically most rigorous and sophisticated effort to tease out the causal significance of the variables treated in many of these surveys. Stephen Cole and Hannelore Adamsons of the Bureau of Applied Social Research of Columbia University conducted a survey of the Columbia faculty shortly after the police expelled the student protestors from the buildings they held during April 1968. Slightly more than 50 per cent of the faculty, 1,061, returned completed questionnaires which elicited their opinions on administration policy, the justification of the sit-in, the goals of the demonstration, and the general strike called after the police action, as well as their general political philosophy, attitudes toward scholarship and teaching, and academic scholarly record, and assorted background factors. Specifically, political identification (radical to conservative), religion (none, Jewish, Catholic, Protestant), party affiliation (other, Democratic, Independent, Republican), father's occupation (professional), age (youth to older), and sex (female-male), were related in the order given to support of the demonstration.[104] The initial uncontrolled differences were quite large on some, e.g., 21 per cent of the conservatives were high on support as compared with 88 per cent of those who described themselves as 'strongly liberal' or radical. Fifty-nine per cent of the Democrats were high as compared with only 18 per cent among the Republicans. Jews were 52 per cent high as contrasted with 30 per cent among the Protestants. But unlike most of the other studies discussed here, Cole and Adamsons sought to separate out the independent weight of the different interrelated variables using the technique of test factor standardization, which gave them 'results equivalent to those obtained from three and four variable tables'.[105] The analysis indicates that when political identification (conservative to liberal) is standardized the effect of the other independent variables is considerably reduced though still present. They conclude, for example, that much of the effect of religion is in early political socialization setting an intial frame of reference; it is much less potent distinguishing within established

---

104    Cole and Adamsons, *op. cit.*, p. 3.
105    *Ibid.*, p. 4.

categories of liberals and conservatives. The effect of party affiliation also was reduced within the ideological categories.

Standardization, however, did not reduce the relationship between age and support for the demonstration. That is, older liberals or radicals were much more opposed to the demonstration than younger ones who identified with the same ideology. This is, perhaps, the most interesting finding yet located since it suggests the basis for a genuine division within ideological groupings. The authors' effort to interpret this result makes good sense. They argue:[106] '. . . it was perhaps attitudes towards political tactics rather than goals which differentiated the young from the old. Older radicals may have been less likely to support civil disobedience as a tactic than young radicals. The one question which came closest to measuring attitudes toward civil disobedience is whether or not the faculty member supported the Poor People's March on Washington; 43 per cent of the youngest and 22 per cent of the oldest said they supported the March. . . . [W]hen attitudes towards the March were held constant, the effect of age on support of the demonstration was cut in half. . . . This demonstrates the validity of Herbert Hyman's suggestion . . . that the meaning of terms such as liberal and conservative change with history. Older faculty members who called themselves strongly liberal or radical probably imputed different meaning to these categories than their younger colleagues'.

Looking at factors internal to the university, Cole and Adamsons conclude that differences linked to rank and academic tenure can largely be eliminated when the two important external factors, age and political identification, are controlled. Salary, however, continues to differentiate supporters from opponents even when the two external variables are standardized. Curiously, discipline group had little independent effect after standardization; and orientation toward research or teaching had no effect.[107]

Although Cole and Adamsons point out the way in which a variety of university-linked experiences, including friendship patterns and opinion in one's department or school, may deflect faculty members from acting on the political predispositions which they brought to

---

106    *Ibid.*, p. 6.
107    *Ibid.*, p. 10. As the authors suggest this may reflect cross pressures in the student ideology.

the conflict from their non-teaching statuses and experience, they conclude that 'non-teaching statuses provided the professors with a political orientation which guided the development of their opinion as the crisis progressed. Non-professional statuses tend to be very important in influencing behavior on professional issues for which there is little precedence'.[108] They also found that those who had succeeded most in academic life are less dissatisfied and more committed to the university system which has been the source of their reward, and presumably, therefore, 'less likely to support demonstrations'.[109] This latter conclusion, however, awaits further specification of the effect of intellectuality on success and campus attitudes.

Clearly, more studies of specific campus reactions such as the Columbia study are needed if we are to understand the complexities of faculty reactions to campus political crises. Findings from the Carnegie Commission's national sample concerning reactions to student demonstrations also indicate that age has much more effect on this set of matters than on other ideologically-linked issues. Older academics who tend to the left on assorted civic concerns are much more conservative on campus related problems than younger faculty who share their general ideology.

The extant studies, of course, are unable to specify the dynamics of faculty opinion and roles during intra-mural crises. Every participant and observer of a major campus confrontation has noted two types of changes among both faculty and students: initial radicalization, particularly after the police were called in, and a subsequent much slower process of growing disillusionment with the activists. This involves increased support for effective administrative measures to restore a normal state of teaching and research to a campus bedeviled by recurrent radical demands, confrontations, heated controversies, and frequent faculty meetings.[110]

At the beginning of campus protest, many non-political and even conservative faculty may join in the various meetings of *ad hoc* groups called to mediate the situation and prevent the police from

---

108     *Ibid.*, p. 17.
109     *Ibid.*, p. 18.
110     Nathan Glazer, 'Student Politics and the University', *The Atlantic*, 224 (July, 1969), p. 50.

being called in. Many faculty and non-activist students are initially inclined to consider the demands of the activists at their face value. That is, many not involved in the protest assume quite naturally that the only matter at issue is the one raised by the demonstrators. And the liberals among the university population will more often than not conclude that the protestors have a good point, that the policy they are objecting to is wrong or that the reform they demand would probably be a good thing. Consequently, they agree that the university ought to negotiate, compromise if possible, give in if necessary. Since their major objection is to the tactics, not seemingly to the demands, they find it difficult to uphold strong action against the demonstrators. Others object to repressive tactics, even against law violators, because they perceive the conflict as one between (weak and politically inexperienced) students and (powerful and politically sophisticated) administrators. They, too, see the situation as calling for compromise on the part of the university. Hence when the university or public authority sends in the police, much of the community is morally outraged. Many are 'radicalized' in the sense of now accepting the view of the situation of the more radical students, that they are the victims of the university's collaboration with reactionary social forces.

In this first stage, the left faction among the faculty gains heavily. Many join it who might be expected to take a more conservative stance. Those who feel that the protestors represent a dangerous politically astute radical grouping, who have been able to out-manoeuver the politically unsophisticated administration which has had no experience in dealing with revolutionists, find it difficult to endorse the tactics of the administration. They, too, include faculty who feel that the administration by its mishandling of the situation has lost its legitimacy, that part of its claim to authority which rests on the prestige, the personal reputation for competence, of the particular president, chancellor, provost, or dean. (As should be obvious, administrators in schools with distinguished faculties have relatively little power which derives from their formal office. They are in the position of political leaders of unorganized collectives; their power is to a large extent personal rather than institutional.) As a result, even many sharply critical of the activists will not seek to defend the particular incumbents, or if they do because of personal loyalty or a desire to uphold authority, they will not do it enthusiastically or effectively. The upshot of such a series of events has often been the overthrow of the administration through the 'resignation' of its most prominent officers.

The next stage often witnesses a revival of conservative or moderate strength, including the involvement in the more conservative groupings of faculty, usually older ones, who have been quite liberal or radical in their general societal politics. This change occurs, in part, as a reaction to a continued state of disorder on campus. The student radicals have been both greatly strengthened or exhilarated by a sense of power and influence as a result of the after effects of the first major demonstrations. Many of them seek new issues around which they can organize new protest demands. These can take a variety of forms, including efforts to reorganize the internal operation of the school. And some of the more extreme elements among the students initiate what appear to be provocative and disruptive activities, *e.g.*, filthy speech campaigns, disruption of classes, raids on the library or faculty club, and the like. As a result, many faculty who thought the settlement of the initial major confrontation, often by agreeing almost totally to the demonstrators' demands, would end the period of disorder, now shift to support more conservative policies, turn against the student movement and the faculty left.

Obviously, changes of the magnitude suggested by these events cannot be explained by any simple cross-sectional analysis of the sources of diversity in faculty opinion such as has been presented in the results of the various surveys. Such a static analysis is only the beginning of the effort to interpret the role of the faculty in campus political controversy. Specific events, the tactics followed by administrators or activist demonstrators, the sophistication of the faculty leadership who rise to the forefront of the different groupings will produce sharply different results. The 'Chicago plan'—not calling the police, wearing out the demonstrators, and then enforcing university sanctions after order is restored—has been effective twice—in 1966 and again in 1969—in preventing the undermining of administrative authority and community radicalization. Most recently, however, radicalization appears to be occurring among segments of the Chicago faculty who object to the expulsion and suspension of many students as unduly harsh. At San Francisco State and Cornell, John Summerskill and James Perkins, liberal presidents who sought to handle the crises by constantly negotiating, by repeatedly compromising with activist demands, found their campus support declining because these tactics did not prevent increased activist demands and recurrent crises. At Cornell, very liberal administrative policies eventually resulted in a more 'conservatized' faculty who felt that academic freedom was being undermined by concessions to student agitators.

The opportunities to study the changes in faculty mood and behavior over time have been increased by the creation in many universities of campus-wide senates with elected representatives from different constituencies of students, junior faculty, senior faculty, administrators, and staff. In general, the constitutions of such senates give large majorities to the faculty. Almost all of them initially and currently have been chosen among ideological groupings, and the student and junior faculty members tend to be sympathetic to the more left positions. Given differential political interest (the more left, the more interested and active generally), and available time (the younger have more), the campus left is in a position to use many of these senates to press a variety of issues, both extra-mural and intra-mural. Such elected senates have helped to institutionalize left-right related political controversy on campus, and also provide a basis through annual elections for changes in reaction to be registered and analyzed.

Clearly more studies in depth which combine sophisticated investigations of the behavior of the different actors in the campus controversies are needed if we are to understand the complexities of faculty reactions to political crises. Yet we obviously know enough both from the historical record and from the large number of faculty and student surveys referred to here to conclude that one of the major reasons that the university has been a center of unrest during this period in which the legitimacy of authority has been undermined generally is the outcome of the incentives in intellectual values and occupational role requirements to take a critical anti-establishment stance. The university is inherently egalitarian and meritocratic in its self-conception. It views discrimination against the talented because of background factors as destructive to its own purposes.

It recruits from those who are critical of the Establishment. One may wonder that the university has so often been a center of conventional politics, not that it has supported unrest.

It remains true, of course, that relatively few university faculty are political activists in normal times. It is also true that the bulk of the faculty, even when sympathetic to the goals of student protest, dislike seeing the campus used for political purposes. The majority of the social scientists who signed advertisements against the Vietnam war indicated their opposition to student demonstrations. Thus, the faculty seems to justify the charge levied by many activists that they are hypocrites, that they do not act in ways congruent to their beliefs.

It becomes necessary for the liberal faculty to explain themselves to their students. The conservatives will obviously oppose the politicization of the campus from the left, but theirs is not a relevant objection to leftist students. There are important reasons why scholars have opposed politicization, regardless of their political ideology, which derive from the very nature of scholarship. And just as it is possible to argue that a critical anti-establishment stance is inherent in the functions of the intellectual and the university, it is also possible to urge that the university cannot accomplish its task if it becomes a center of political advocacy. This is a view not easily or normally understood by morally concerned, politically dedicated students.

Politics and scholarship are highly different types of human activities even though many scholars are also political actors and some men shift from a political to an academic career or vice versa. Both activities also involve the same types of actions, namely writing and lecturing. Many academics, of course, are experts in policy relevant fields and may be called upon to advise policy-makers. Yet, in spite of the considerable overlap in activity and concern, the difference between the roles are greater than the similarities.

The political activist, whether a member of SDS or a leader of the Republican party, is expected to be an advocate. One of his major tasks is to mobilize support behind his group or party. To do this, he presents a point of view which emphasizes all the arguments in its favor, which ignores or consciously represses contradictory materials. In a real sense, the political activist is like a lawyer, whose obligation is to make the best case possible for his client. Inherent in the effort to gain a following and to win power is the need to simplify, to insist that the policies fostered by the group can eliminate evil, can gain the goals of the group, whether these be the ending of a war, the elimination of corruption, the end to depression or inflation, law and order in the cities, the end of poverty, the elimination of ethnic-racial discrimination, social equality, religious morality, mass participation, and so forth. The political leader who points out that life is complicated, that he is uncertain about the way to end practices which his group regards as evil, will not last very long in the role. Political leadership calls for decisiveness, for the ability to make decisions which may have beneficent or disastrous consequences quickly on the basis of limited knowledge, with the awareness that there is a good possibility that the action will be wrong.

Scholarship, clearly, emphasizes the opposite characteristics. A scholar should consider all existing points of view and all available evidence before reaching a conclusion. He is expected to take as long as necessary to come to a definitive conclusion before publishing his findings as knowledge. One of the worst things that can be said about an academic is that he publishes too quickly, that he rushes into print before he has exhausted the possible areas of inquiry. A scholar is normatively required to present contradictory evidence, to point to any methodological weaknesses in his materials. In attacking a research problem, he is initially required to complicate the issue, to introduce as many factors as appear at all relevant. Thus scholars writing on issues of race relations, equality, poverty, inflation, foreign policy, war, etc., tend to emphasize the indeterminate character of knowledge in these fields, the fact that the evidence rarely justifies any simple cause and effect relationship.

The dialogue between the scholar and the activist must inevitably be one in which the former undercuts the will of the latter to act, if he remains in the academic world. Or conversely, if the scholar takes to the hustings, he must cease being a scholar. There are, of course, considerable areas of overlapping usefulness. Any good political leader will want to have as much information as possible about a given topic before he makes a decision. He may call upon the scholar for policy-relevant research, which he wants to be cautious, to err, if at all, on the side of complexity and conservatism. The politician will often still have to make a decision, which assumes an ability to predict consequences with great probability, even when the extant knowledge implies a very low order of predictability about outcomes of different policies. Ironically, in his use of the scientific policy-advisor, the politician, therefore, is not looking for originality, but for 'safety'. He calls upon the scholar in much the same way as he might ask an engineer to plan a new bridge. The latter will always put in a great safety factor to make sure the bridge will not fall down. For this reason, the most brilliant and prestigious scholars may not make the best policy-advisors.

The scholar, even when concerned with applied politically relevant problems, is committed to the notion that visible forms of behavior which can be described in common sense terms can be better understood as the product of a complex set of underlying relationships which must be treated analytically in an effort to synthesize such linkages. A variety of seemingly disparate behaviors can only be identified as having common causal elements through use of abstract theoretical models.

The scholar involved in basic research will often deliberately separate himself from any substantive (policy relevant) problem so as to be free to look for more abstract levels of generalization.[111]

The differences between scholarship and politics are particularly significant for the social sciences, and to a lesser extent for the humanities, since matters of academic concern in these disciplines are often also political policy issues. As has been noted, many students who take social science courses or decide to major or do graduate work in these fields often do so because of the subject matter, because they see ways of enhancing their political objectives. Hence the interest of many students in these disciplines is not that of the scholar but of the politician, of the political activist. Such an interest is clearly a valid one, much as is the interest of the pre-engineering student in physics, or the pre-medical candidate in biology. But the activist-oriented social science student often wants his professor to join him in his efforts to gain social change by immediate political activities. When he asks for 'relevant' courses,

---

111    Christopher Lasch, *The Agony of the American Left* (New York: Knopf, 1969), p. 21.

he is asking for courses which involve advocacy, or which see the faculty members acting as policy advisors. Efforts by faculty to be 'objective' in courses which bear on politics are often regarded as forms of escaping from an obligation to fight evil, or even of supporting the system. And the committed activist, regardless of ideological stance, regards any claim to objectivity as pretence, as an effort to conceal the ideological commitments, the value preferences, and the biases which all men have.

Many social scientists, on the other hand, will argue that precisely because their fields touch so directly on politics, are involved with subjects about which they, like all aware men, have strong feelings, that it is important to try to separate their values from their research *as much as possible*. The effort to engage in objective scholarship is clearly much more difficult in the social sciences and humanities than it is in the natural sciences. The gap between the interests of the students and those of the faculty in their conceptions of the discipline, of the appropriate content of courses, of the topics which should be investigated, is much smaller in natural sciences than in the other fields.

This stress on the problems of scholarship in the social sciences and humanities does not mean that any such thing as objective or value-free scholarship occurs in any pure or absolute sense. Practically every major writer on these methodological problems has recognized that personal values, variations in life experiences, differences in education and in theoretical orientation strongly affect the kind of work which men do and their results. Such differences enter first into the choice of problems, then they affect the variables dealt with, the rigor with which they explore alternative explanations for given phenomena, and the like. Max Weber, who is frequently credited with being the major exponent of value-free, politically neutral scholarship in the social sciences, clearly enunciated the impossibility of such work. He argued, in fact, that the concept of ethical neutrality was spurious, and that those who maintained this 'spuriously "ethical neutral"' approach were precisely the ones who manifested 'obstinate and deliberate partisanship'.[112] He stated

---

112     Max Weber, *The Methodology of the Social Sciences* (Glencoe: The Free Press, 1949), p. 6.

unequivocally that all 'knowledge of cultural reality, as may be seen, is always knowledge from particular points of view'.[113] He pointed out that the 'significance of cultural events presupposes a value-orientation toward these events. The concept of culture is a value-concept. Empirical reality becomes "culture" to us because and insofar as we relate it to value ideas'.[114]

Weber was a highly political individual. He stressed that every professor had a personal 'party-line'. Because of this, and even with his general recognition of the role of personal values in affecting what we see as problems and facts and his deep political involvements, he insisted that teachers and scholars were all the more obligated to try to be as objective as possible in their teaching and scholarship. As a teacher, he must set 'as his unconditional duty, in every single case, even to the point where it involves the danger of making his lectures less lively or attractive, to make relentlessly clear to his audience, and especially to himself, which of his statements are statements of logically deduced or empirically observed facts and which are statements of practical evaluation'.[115]

As a methodological precept, Weber suggested that scholars should be more disposed to accept as valid, findings which challenged their values and preconceptions than those which agreed with them. Clearly, he assumed that scholars, regardless of their efforts at objectivity, will be prone to recognize results and deductions which indicate they are right rather than the opposite. Hence, if science is to progress, particularly the strongly value-laden social sciences, great care must be exerted to reduce the impact of personal preferences on research results. The ultimate test, however, of scientific validity is the exposure of research results to the community at large. Any given scholar may come up with erroneous results stemming, in part, from the way in which his values have affected his work. But the commitment of scientists to objective *methods* of inquiry, the competition of ideas and concepts, will heighten the possibility of finding analytic laws which hold up regardless of who does the investigation. 'For scientific truth is precisely what is valid for all who seek the truth'.[116]

---

113    *Ibid.*, p. 81.
114    *Ibid.*, p. 76.
115    *Ibid.*, p. 55.
116    *Ibid.*, p. 84.

These are complicated methodological issues which have concerned scholars for many decades. They are not issues which should be of any great interest to the politically involved, students or others. Yet the politically concerned students live in the university. It is their home, their political base, and they, not unnaturally, want others in the institution to join them as allies in their morally justified political efforts to eliminate evil. Faculty who seek to deal with politically relevant matters in any 'objective' fashion, who refuse to engage in advocacy, who point up the complexities involved in any causal treatment of the subject, necessarily become enemies, are seen as partisans of the *status quo* who, if listened to, reduce the commitment to moral action.

The argument against overt political involvement by the university or the faculty as a body must also be dealt with. This issue is linked to the historic struggles of universities to free themselves from clerical and state control. In demanding and securing freedom from such controls, the university argued that its members as individuals must be free to come to any conclusion about topics relevant to religion or politics. In turn, it implicitly committed itself to ignore *officially* religious or political commitments in making appointments to its faculty, or in its formal policies. This meant that a university could appoint men who agreed with one political or religious point of view, who were liberals, atheists, radicals, or conservatives, as long as they never spoke out as a corporate body on such issues. In the United States, conservatives like William Buckley, Ronald Reagan, and others have argued the need for political balance, that is, for more conservative professors to reduce the predominant liberal-left dominance within liberal arts faculties in major universities. Others denounce the university faculty for being disproportionately composed of agnostics and atheists. And today, they are joined by student radicals who argue that more radicals should be named to academic appointments.

The university can only fight off such renewed demands by political and religious groups by insisting that the only formal criteria for appointment be scholarly, and that even if this results in a faculty weighted toward any given side in extra-mural conflicts, the university and its faculty do not use their corporate prestige as a weapon in such extra-mural conflicts. Of course, such a formal position does not mean unpoliticized or neutral universities. That is impossible. But as Robert Wolff, the Columbia philosopher who co-authored *A Critique of Pure Tolerance* with Herbert Marcuse and Barrington Moore, points out, the myth of the apolitical university, though a myth, serves to protect unpopular minorities, that is, radicals. To insist that the university make manifest its politics would 'have reactionary rather than progressive consequences. . .'.[117]

It is important to recognize that many of the faculty, administrators and trustees who now would emphasize the inherent need for university autonomy against pressures from leftists to manifestly combine politics and scholarship have contributed to the current situation. Since the 1930s, the American university has increasingly become a major center of political involvement. Many faculty have engaged in applied, policy-oriented research, and have not taken care to separate their academic from their policy advisor role. Professors and institutions have lent their prestige to 'establishment' as well as other causes. Universities through their choice of politically involved men to receive honorary degrees and other indicators of esteem have implicitly endorsed the value of the work which these men have done. And if the name of the university is used in ways which have clear political consequences, it is difficult to argue now that leftist efforts to use the university should be ruled out, even though they may involve more overt forms of politicization. The argument that the defenders of the *status quo* can be more subtle in their politically relevant endeavors clearly has merit. Now that the issue of politicization and university autonomy has been joined again, there is a clear need to think through the rationale behind the involvement of academia as such in non-academic concerns. Again, it may be appropriate to quote from Max Weber precisely because he was a student of politics, the son of a politician, and a political activist himself. A friend has described his care in this area in the following description of one occasion when Weber was discussing politics with two friends:[118] 'The door opened and two new guests, who happened to be students, came in and sat down with us. After

117    Robert Paul Wolff, *The Ideal of the University* (Boston: The Beacon Press, 1969), p. 75.
118    Paul Honigsheim, *On Max Weber* (New York: The Free Press, 1968), p. 8.

an informal greeting, Gundolf said to Weber, "You were interrupted, and were saying . . ." whereupon the master answered, "I must stop; there are students here now, and naturally I don't have the right to talk politics in front of them; it might influence them". So great was his respect for the sanctity of autonomous decision and so great his sensitivity'.

The issues of university governance, as far as they involve student participation, relate in part to the same set of concerns about politics and scholarship. Since the students in the social sciences and to a lesser extent the humanities are the most radical, the demands for student participation have generally been raised most in these fields. These areas, however, are not only the most politically relevant, they also differ from the natural sciences in that judgments concerning methodological issues and research competence remain highly subjective. There is almost no recognized piece of research, or scholar, in these disciplines whose distinction is not controversial. With few exceptions, it is quite possible to argue that any given work is either methodologically inadequate, that it is following a sterile approach, and/or that its weaknesses stem from biases which have led the researcher to ignore important factors and to come to erroneous conclusions.

In these less precise fields of scholarship, the more committed individuals are to a political role, as distinct from a scholarly one, the more likely they are to judge scholarly work by its presumed political consequences. Obviously, such factors and other sources of personal values as well affect the way in which academics evaluate each other, regardless of age or institutional status. But in a politicized era, those who have not been fully socialized to the norms of the academy, who are more wont, as students, to feel the primacy of politics, will look for political allies among their professors. Not accepting the worth of the particular discipline in the same terms as its professional practitioners, being less disposed to believe that most scholars try to be objective, students will be more prone to want the university to act in directly political terms than will professors. In dealing with curricular matters, they will be less likely to respect the need for abstract theoretical, methodological, or 'basic' fields which do not deal directly with social problems than their elders. An increase in 'student power' in matters of faculty appointments or curriculum, therefore, almost inevitably means greater politicization in the methodologically soft disciplines.

Another source of controversy within the faculty and between faculty and students involves the relative role of teaching and research. This is not a new issue. There is a considerable literature analyzing and debating the matter in American journals dating from the late nineteenth century. Curiously, that period, which was also characterized by considerable student unrest, found men writing that more concern with research and less with their students would be a good way of reducing student resentments. The argument, then, was that the non-research faculty concerned themselves too much with the activities of their students, that the students resented being observed and closely supervised by a faculty who had nothing to do but control the student body. If American professors turned to research on the model of the German universities, the argument ran, students would be happier because they would be let alone and the country would benefit from the scholarly output of its academics. And ever since that time, those concerned with the optimum college or university have argued the relative advantages for teaching and intellectual life of varying emphases and encouragement to research or teaching. The thesis that research interferes with teaching, that undergraduates are being short-changed as a result, was present by the beginning of this century. Suggestions that universities establish teaching doctorates which do not require a dissertation as a means of upgrading undergraduate teaching also date back to that period. The 'neglected' undergraduate has been a favourite article topic for well over half a century. And such writings have pointed to the pressures on professors to engage in extra-mural activities for almost as long. Thus the eminent professors of earlier decades were accused of neglecting their university duties for the lecture circuit and for writing financially lucrative textbooks or articles for magazines or the popular press.

The issue of teaching versus research, however, did not take on a political character until recently. In fact, if any deduction concerning the ideological correlates of those on different sides of the question may be identified, it is that the conservatives have favored more teaching. The data presented earlier concerning the links between intellectuality and political liberalism clearly point in this direction. Conservatives have defended the teaching function of the university seeking to preserve the classical ideal, to stress the need to absorb the wisdom of the past, the 'great books', not the creation of new knowledge. The pressure to make the university a center of research and innovation has more frequently come from those imbued with the idea of progress, of social change.

Student movements, however, insofar as they represent the 'class' sentiments of students have perceived professors primarily, if not solely, in their role as teachers. They want more time from them. And they have seen grades as mechanisms of social control, as means of getting them to conform to the authority or whims of the teacher. The leftist students have added to this criticism the idea that grades help maintain the 'capitalist' emphasis on competition, on the 'rat race', on the struggle for success, rather than on learning for its own sake.

The faculty, of course, also divides on these issues. Many younger professors in recent years have accepted the doctrine that research is often self-serving careerism. Some resolve to devote their careers to teaching, to working with students. Those who disagree with this position argue that an emphasis on teaching can be a way of escaping from being judged in the necessarily highly competitive intellectual world. It has also been suggested that a stress on teaching as the primary function of the academic job makes the task of 'succeeding' easier. There is less strain in devoting oneself to lectures and discussions with students than in seeking to produce research which is regarded as first-rate.

There would appear to be an 'interest' factor in this discussion which is partially generational. The older more 'successful' faculty, who have acquired academic distinction through their research, have an obvious reason for defending the existing system, including the ways in which support has been distributed. Those who have 'failed', or are too young to have succeeded, are more prone to stress the virtues of teaching. Yet the inherent requirements of an intellectual career will press many younger faculty to seek jobs which facilitate their concentrating on research and writing. Presumably, it will be precisely those who are high in intellectuality, in scholarly competence, and hence also in political liberalism who will want this. As a group, at the moment, they are clearly in a cross-pressure situation. They, in effect, are the one group in academia who are pressed to resolve the dilemma between degree of emphasis on teaching or research in their own behavior.

Thus far, there is little evidence that the increased concern for undergraduate education which is manifest in the myriad of articles, books, national commissions, and local campus surveys has, in fact, changed the dominant practice of the American academy. Some years ago, the Israeli sociologist, Joseph Ben David, suggested as a general proposition concerning American academia that any event which reduces the attractiveness of a given university to retain or attract faculty would necessarily result in an increase in the bargaining power of faculty *vis-à-vis* the administration. A major crisis, a change in the ecological environment of a campus, meant that the university had to pay more to gain or maintain a high level faculty. His first example was Berkeley after the loyalty oath crisis of 1949-50. He suggested that the cut in the pre-oath teaching load, three courses a semester, six a year, to a four or five course a year load, together with a rapid increase in upper-range salaries, which occurred soon after the oath fight, reflected the need of the university to improve faculty working conditions and income, to make up for the negative image. A similar sharp drop in teaching load and increased salaries which occurred at the University of Chicago in the late fifties and early sixties seemed linked to the decline in the attractiveness of the neighborhood surrounding that school. And Ben David, who happened to be a visiting professor at Berkeley during 1964-65, the year of the Berkeley Revolt, predicted similar results from that event. History has seemingly validated his prediction. The teaching load at Berkeley which is under the control of departments has been sharply reduced since 1965.

Few observers of the Berkeley scene who have commented in detail on the various experimental programs designed to improve the quality of undergraduate education there have noted that the biggest change in faculty-student relations is less faculty classroom contact with students than before. Crisis, as Ben David suggested, means greater bargaining power for faculty, and faculty use such power to reduce their teaching obligations. A similar set of events followed on the Columbia sit-in and student general strike in the Spring of 1968. The reasons are obvious, and no amount of moral advocacy that is not accompanied by a change in the reward structure will affect practice. As Jencks and Riesman put it:[119] 'There is no guild within which successful teaching leads to greater prestige and influence than mediocre teaching. . . . No doubt most professors prefer it when their courses are popular, their lectures applauded, and their former students appreciative. But since such successes are of no help in getting a salary increase, moving to a more prestigious campus, or winning their colleagues' admiration, they are unlikely to struggle as hard to create them as to do other things'.

It is important to recognize that the teaching issue is one in which the student activists can expect more support from administrators, trustees, alumni representatives, and politicians than from the faculty of major universities. The former are much more disposed to view the university as a school, are more concerned with the way it treats the students than are the professors. The highly competitive nationally-oriented research faculty are seen by the administrative classes of the university in much the same way as the radical students see them, that is, as self-centered, self-serving individuals, who are using the university to benefit themselves, and who give as little as possible to more campus-centered activities, what Clark Kerr once called 'the faculty *in absentia*'.[120]

The same criticism has been made by Governor Reagan himself:[121] 'Young men and women go to college to find themselves as individuals', the Governor declared in the speech that has become a kind of educational testament. 'They see the names of distinguished scholars in the catalogue and sign up for courses with the belief that they will learn and grow and be stimulated by contact with these

---

119     Christopher Jencks and David Riesman, *The Academic Revolution* (Garden City: Doubleday, 1968), p. 531.

120     For an analysis and description of faculty activities along these lines, see Clark Kerr, *The Uses of the University* (Cambridge: Harvard University Press, 1963). One of the key documents of the Berkeley Revolt which outlined student grievances drew heavily on Kerr's analyses of faculty behavior. See Bradford Cleaveland, 'A Letter to Undergraduates', in Lipset and Wolin, eds., *op. cit.*, pp. 66-81.

121     A. H. Raskin, 'Where it all began—Berkeley, 5 years later, is Radicalised, Reaganised, Mesmerised', *New York Times Magazine*, January 11, 1970, p. 85

men. All too often they are herded into gigantic classes taught by teaching assistants hardly older than themselves'.

A similar political line-up on issues such as these occurs among the faculty. As has been noted, the less research-oriented faculty tend to be more politically conservative and locally oriented in terms of campus affairs, and more concerned with teaching as an institutional function. They, too, deprecate what they consider to be the exaggerated emphasis and rewards given for research. They are the people who staff the committee system, who assist the deans, who keep the place going in normal times. Hence when student groups raise the teaching-research issue, they are likely to confound the basis for faculty political cleavage. The 'conservatives' and the Establishment agree with them while the more research-oriented 'liberals' and 'leftists' will, if they honestly speak their minds, disagree.

The same apparent 'contradiction' exists with respect to outside involvements as consultants for government agencies or business firms. The radical students assume that both sets of institutions are reactionary, and presumably those faculty who are involved with them have 'sold out' and should be among the more conservative members of the faculty. But in fact the 1966 NORC national survey indicates that professors who had *never* worked for extra-mural organizations, whether business or government, were most disposed to *back* government policy on Vietnam. Those who had served government were most opposed to the policy.[122] An even stronger relationship between having been called in as a consultant to business and political liberalism was indicated in the study of social scientists' reaction to (Joe) McCarthyism. Holding age constant, those who strongly favored academic and civil liberties for Communists and other unpopular minority dissidents were most likely to have been consultants for business. At every age level, the 'clearly conservative' had the lowest level of involvement with business.[123] Most recently, the Carnegie Commission materials have iterated a similar pattern. The 'missing' intervening variable in these sets of findings presumably is that the most successful scholars are the ones called on to consult, and as indicated by many surveys, academic

---

122  Noll and Rossi, *op. cit.*, p. 58.
123  Lazarsfeld and Thielens, *op. cit.*, p. 443.

K

success regardless of how measured is correlated with degree of leftism in political attitudes.

These differences between the student activists and many of the faculty who stand relatively close to them in general political philosophy or ideology can be conceptualized in another way. Students, including, or especially, the radicals among them, want the university to retain the characteristics of a school and the faculty to behave like teachers in lower levels of education. Many students seek teachers who will tell them what they think about life generally. They will see in professorial claims to seek objectivity by introducing contradictory material an evasion of their responsibility to take a stand. The faculty, particularly at universities which are major centers of research, who are themselves committed to a life of productive scholarship, see higher education and the role of the professor as highly differentiated, in which teaching is only one of the activities.[124] Florian Znaniecki, in his analysis of the role of the intellectual, pointed up the distinctively different functions of the university and the school:[125] '. . . [T]he school of higher learning performs the specifically social function of an educational institution only because its main activities are not social but scientific, do not aim to contribute to the maintenance of the social order but to the maintenance of knowledge as a supersocial domain of culture supremely valuable in itself. . . . The school of general education, on the contrary, as an institution of the modern society serves directly the maintenance of social order—whether it be a traditionally static order or a more or less dynamic new order'.

It is important to note in Znaniecki's distinction that he describes the institution which advocates radical change and the one which supports the *status quo* as both being primarily schools rather than scientific organizations. As Michio Nagai points out, 'the roles of the school teacher are expected to be like those of a parent-substitute, a community leader, a statesman, a guide in life, and even . . . a pro-

---

124     In the following discussion, I am highly indebted to the brilliant analysis of Michio Nagai, *The Problem of Indoctrination: As Viewed from Sociological and Philosophical Bases* (Department of Sociology: Ohio State University, 1952).

125     Florian Znaniecki, *The Social Role of the Man of Knowledge* (New York: Columbia University Press, 1940), p. 155.

pagandist. . . . The "parent-substitute" often develops particularism in place of universalism'.[126]

The teacher in non-university education is expected to consider all aspects of the child's life. He should emphasize the 'whole child' and his requirements:[127] 'The reason why it is difficult to establish professional standards for teachers may be found in the diffuseness of the function of the teacher. . . .' One expects a high degree of affectivity in the teacher-pupil relationship. Although the pupil 'becomes more and more independent as he grows up, a large element of helplessness is still present during his school age. Thus children in school like to love teachers as they like to be loved by them'.[128]

The school is characterized particularly by the content and method of instruction in it as distinct from the university:[129] 'The content of school education is above all diffused. . . . Children are educated in schools not only to be future university students, but also to be members of a family, community, and the world. . . .

'Consequently, the content of instruction in school cannot be restricted alone to empirically verified and logically consistent knowledge. It also contains family norms, national ideals, customary belief, and etiquette'. Given the assumption that teachers have diffuse authority over pupils and that they have a particularistic relationship with them, it follows that the method of teaching, the very role of the teacher in the classroom and in personal discussions must be different because the school teacher has authority over children in many aspects of their lives.

It may be argued that when the activists criticize the educational system today, they seek to retain the status of pupil and to have teachers rather than to be students of university professors. Although their demand is now couched in terms of the faculty taking an activist position in support of radical social change, it is a demand that their professors act like their school teachers, that they take part in 'bull sessions' in which they discuss the totality of human experience not simply their subject matter. When the students

---

126    Nagai, *op. cit.*, pp. 20-21.
127    *Ibid.*, p. 45.
128    *Ibid.*, p. 48.
129    *Ibid.*, pp. 51-52.

oppose grades, they are demanding the restoration of a particularistic relationship with their teachers, one in which they are not judged objectively according to highly specialized criteria, but rather continue to be treated as total human beings. The available evidence with respect to school teachers in the lower schools indicates that such forms of particularistic treatment in the schools facilitates discrimination in favor of those from more privileged backgrounds who conform to middle-class morality.

The argument concerning grades also cuts across the usual left-right dimensions, although in recent years, it has been raised largely by student activists.[130] Radicals see in the power to grade an instrument of coercion which prevents the free interchange of ideas and opinions between faculty and students. The fact that a meritocratic grading system once was seen as an instrument of freedom by those from under-privileged backgrounds is foreign to them. Felix Frankfurter, who came to Harvard Law School as an immigrant Jewish youth before World War I, never got over his awe at the democratic implications of the rigorous grading system:[131] 'What mattered was excellence in your profession to which your father or your face was equally irrelevant. And so rich man, poor man were just irrelevant titles to the equation of human relations. The thing that mattered was what you did professionally. . . . [T]he very good men were defined by the fact that they got on the *Harvard Law Review*. And so I say . . . the *Harvard Law Review* in particular and the Harvard Law School in general are to me the most complete practices in democracy that I have ever known anything about'.

The general issue is how much and under what conditions institutions of higher learning should reflect in their internal structure the different norms and orientations of the worlds of the school and scholarship. In this respect, we meet again a congruence between the left and the right. The leftist students agree with many conservative critics of the university. Both want the university to be a school. The left, however, wants a school which will favor radical social change while the conservative politicians and alumni want a school

130    Robert S. Powell, Jr., 'Participation is Learning', *Saturday Review*, 53 (January 10, 1970), p. 58.
131    Felix Frankfurter, *Felix Frankfurter Reminisces* (Garden City: Doubleday-Anchor Books, 1962), p. 43.

which will defend the *status quo*. Neither wants an institution which is dedicated to subject all simple propositions, all explanations, all reforms, to the test of scientific validity. For in essence the university is the enemy of simplification. The norms which must govern a university make of it a qualitatively different environment than a high school. In shifting from the status of high school pupil to university student, youth must adjust to a world which is highly specialized and segmented in which they are no longer spoon-fed by their instructors, in which their professors will be men for whom undergraduate teaching is necessarily only one of a number of functions, and not even the most important one in the better institutions.

It is essential that those concerned with university life recognize that universities are not schools, that the norms which govern scientific activities are quite different from those which characterize schools. The approach of science and of the university has been analysed in formal analytical terms by Talcott Parsons and Robert K. Merton. Both have pointed to criteria for scientific behavior, including university teaching, which are basically in variation with the involvement in indoctrination, in preparation for life, and with total personality and character of the school.

Merton sought to specify the 'cultural values and mores governing the activities termed scientific'.[132] These include a number of imperatives which he calls universalism, communism, disinterestedness, and organized scepticism. Parsons has posited a similar set of elements in 'the role structure of the scientist—functional specificity, universalism, achievement orientation, collectivity orientation, and affective neutrality'.[133] And he points out that the ethos of science has 'above all become embodied in the university as its principal institutionalized frame'.[134]

In Parsons' language, a key requirement of the academic role in a university, that is, a center of scientific scholarship rather than a

132    Robert K. Merton, *Social Theory and Social Structure* (Glencoe: The Free Press, 1949), p. 308.
133    Nagai, *op. cit.*, p. 19.
134    Talcott Parsons, *The Social System* (Glencoe: The Free Press, 1951), p. 342.

school, is *functional specificity*.[135] This means that it is 'only in matter touching his academic specialty that the professor is superior by virtue of his status, to his student'. This condition not only implies that professors have no general claim to superior knowledge in public matters or concerning the sex life of their students, but it also means that non-scientists, non-professionals, whether politicians, the clergy, businessmen, or students, may not interfere with science. It asserts that a necessary condition for the free development of a field is its autonomy from outside control or pressure. Judgments about scientific findings or the competence of scholars should be made solely on scientific grounds. But the requirement of functional specificity works both ways. Scientists may not lay a diffuse claim to be wise men.

*Organized scepticism* involves 'the suspension of judgment until "the facts are at hand" and the detached scrutiny of beliefs in terms of empirical and logical criteria'.[136] This norm calls for the scholar to question all judgments and values, to doubt the conventional verities.

*Universalism*, a condition stressed by both Merton and Parsons, is expressed 'in the canon that truth claims, whatever their source, are to be subjected to preestablished impersonal criteria: consonant with observation and with previously confirmed knowledge'.[137] Essentially, this means that the *validity* of scientific statements should be evaluated without reference to the political beliefs or any other attribute of the person asserting them. This norm is also expressed by Parsons in his insistence that science must emphasize the *achievement orientation*, that it must be rigidly meritocratic, in its treatment of prospective recruits (students) as well as members.[138]

*Communism* in scholarship involves a recognition that findings 'are a product of social collaboration and are assigned to the community'.[139] All findings are to be made public and to be available to all other scientists to build on. Secrecy, efforts to retain discoveries

---

135    Talcott Parsons, *Essays in Sociological Theory Pure and Applied* (Glencoe: The Free Press, 1949), p. 189.
136    Merton, *op. cit.*, p. 315.
137    Merton, *op. cit.*, p. 309.
138    Parsons, *The Social System, op. cit.*, p. 434.
139    Merton, *op. cit.*, p. 312.

for the use of limited groups, is to be condemned. Parsons' insistence on the need for a *collectivity orientation* in science, that scientists should be more concerned for the advancement of the field than their own narrow interests, also indicates that knowledge should be publicly available.[140]

*Disinterestedness*, a term used by Merton, does not refer to altruism but rather to a 'wide range of motives which characterizes behavior of scientists'.[141] Its implications are close to those of Parsons' collectivity orientation—the scientists should try to act as much as possible as if they were essentially concerned with the advancement of science rather than their own prestige or a gain for a group with which they are associated.

*Affective neutrality*, another condition stressed by Parsons, essentially calls for the scholar to repress his emotional or subjective feelings in evaluating scientific matters, including his judgment of students. It is obviously also linked to the concept of disinterestedness.

These value orientations which are inherent in the scientific ethos contain liberal-left political implications and call for emphasizing the role of the student as apprentice scholar, not as the pupil of a Mr. Chips-type teacher, whether radical or conservative. The values of science emphasize the need for a free society operating under the rule of law. State interference to guarantee that science adheres to a party, national, or religious line, that scientists are not free to criticize each other, makes for bad science. There is considerable evidence to indicate that the scientists of the communist countries recognize this, and that they are a continuing force pressing for an end to authoritarianism and arbitrary power. The stress on universalism, on functional specificity, on achievement orientation, implies opposition to those aspects of stratified societies which limit equality of opportunity. For science, trained intelligence, not family background, race, or wealth, must be the primary quality associated with status and social rewards.

Hence, one would anticipate that the more committed an academic is to scientific research, the more likely he will be to oppose those aspects of the social system which appear to perpetuate inequality of opportunity.

---

140    Parsons, *op. cit.*, p. 344.
141    Merton, *op. cit.*, pp. 313-14.

Some of the same elements of the scientific ethos which press men in a liberal and left direction politically also, of course, include the action imperative to treat students in a highly specific, meritocratic manner. To advance scientific knowledge means that all qualified youth must be encouraged and rewarded, but that little reward (or attention) should be given to the unqualified or to the less able. Science is inherently concerned with locating and rewarding the aristocracy of talent. Anyone familiar with the norms of major centers of graduate study in the liberal arts fields knows that this is the way they operate.

The differences between graduate school university faculty and those at four-year colleges are also to be found among the colleges. Jencks and Riesman have detailed the way in which the ethos of graduate education has affected the entire character of American academia.[142] In an earlier study, Riesman and Gusfield have shown how undergraduate schools vary in faculty and student orientation with respect to the different concept of the college they sustain. Much of the consequences of the distinction attempted here between the school and research institute graduate-training role of the university, and between the pupil and student roles open to undergraduates, were developed by Riesman and Gusfield in their analysis of the differences in the activities of undergraduate institutions. They distinguish between the 'adult-forming' and 'youth-prolonging' aspects of higher education:[143] 'To the extent that colleges have become the great sorters, selectors, and gate-keepers for the academically talented, they may be thought to serve an "adult-forming" function, weeding out both the childish and the childlike and judging the young by adult standards of competent performance. In this aspect of the college's functions, the professors act not only as gate-keepers but also as models, however limited, of at least one possible adult role. . . . But there is also an aspect of college which may be called "youth-prolonging". Ordinarily, we think of this aspect as extra-curricular and existing in opposition to faculty and adult demands. But an instructor who sees himself rather less as a specialist and more as a member of an intellectual subculture may

---

142    Christopher Jencks and David Riesman, *The Academic Revolution*, *op. cit.*

143    Riesman and Gusfield, *op. cit.*, pp. 257-58.

value in his students precisely their youthfulness and seek to protect them against what he may regard as premature and dehydrating adult demands'.

Riesman and Gusfield were able to point up some of the implications of this analytic distinction by an empirical comparison of the activities of two new undergraduate publicly-supported colleges with comparable student bodies and with aspirations to give a first-class elite education. 'Elmwood' established a conventional department structure with a system of rigorous examinations. 'Hawthorne' opposed departmentalization, 'proto-graduate' education, and the segmentalization of the roles of faculty members. Elmwood's faculty 'asked of the students a more rapid "putting-away" of childish things'. And they found that 'a certain dehydration' occurred among them, an 'excessive task-orientation'.[144] Hawthorne, by contrast, 'found itself beset with problems of a somewhat different order'. At the start of the 1960s, before the emergence of a national movement of cultural and political protest, some of Hawthorne's students showed 'a willingness to try out behavior which later adult life might not permit. Some became politically active on behalf of peace or civil rights. . . . [A] small number of students found it easy to move into flats near the campus . . . making it possible . . . to take part in nonacademic activities, in politics, the arts, and personal exploration'.[145]

It may be argued that the traits of science enunciated by Parsons and Merton and of 'adult-forming' educational functions specified by Riesman and Gusfield are relevant to scientific research and the work of research institutes but not to colleges and universities. The latter are primarily educational not research organizations. Hence the application of scientific traits to the college proper has made for student dissatisfaction and unrest. This argument, made by both students and politicians in authority over universities, clearly is quite valid. Much of what is done in the American system of higher education is closer in function to the work of high schools than it is to graduate centers of education and research. The courses usually taught in lower division, in the freshmen and sophomore years, in

---

144    *Ibid.*, pp. 259, 260.
145    *Ibid.*, p. 260.

most colleges and universities are extensions of high school work, if they are not in fact courses identical to those given in many high schools. Elementary work in languages, in mathematics, in English, in a variety of other subjects, is not on the level of university courses in the sense in which the university has developed in Oxford and Cambridge, in Germany, and elsewhere. The university in much of Europe has ideally at least been closer in requirements to the American graduate school than to the undergraduate college. The *gymnasium*, lycée, grammar or public schools in Europe cover many of the courses which in the United States are included in colleges or universities. A university degree in Europe is a specialized degree, often in one subject, requiring a thesis. The doctorate is the only degree given in Germany, northern Europe, and many Latin countries and is more akin to the American Master's degree than the Ph.D.

American institutions of higher education today are torn between being schools and graduate research centers. Although in fact relatively few institutions are in the latter category, probably the majority of students attending four year degree-granting colleges are in institutions in which the faculty is held to the requirement that they engage in productive scholarship, that they be judged for salary, rank, and local prestige by their presumed research rather than teaching merits.

Students and faculty are properly in a confused state with respect to their respective roles. As the importance of the research function for the larger society increased, the more prestigious professors in the centers of graduate training and research took on a variety of activities in addition to research and teaching. A relatively small segment of the American professoriate has been asked to serve as consultants for government, industry, political parties, and international agencies. The same men are in demand for extra-mural lectures, articles, books, editorial consultation. They are invited to participate in the increasing number of international conferences made possible by the jet plane and foundation funds, which are often genuinely necessary to facilitate rapid communication of research results and new ideas. While few schools have separated the graduate from the undergraduate faculty, the number of graduate students increases rapidly. Research in many disciplines now involves the administration of substantial funds and the coordination of the work of various colleagues and assistants. All of these tasks have been added to the work of undergraduate teaching which was the primary, usually the exclusive, task of professors in the major institutions in the nineteenth century.

To put the whole matter another way, the leading universities and professors have been accumulating more tasks, while they continue to do their old one, undergraduate teaching, as well. These institutions and faculty are judged for eminence and the rewards which go with high status by their research output. This increased pressure on faculty at such institutions for differentiated involvements and the lesser time given to undergraduate education should make the university world an increasingly less happy place for both faculty and undergraduates.

And as we have seen, both the leading faculty and the students at institutions with the highest admission standards tend to be among the most rebellious politically. The political rebellion stems from factors other than the tensions inherent in institutional and faculty role conflict, but a liberal-radical political ideology and 'job dissatisfaction' should reinforce one another. As we have noted, the upshot of many politically-motivated campus disturbances has been an attack on the governance or other aspects of the university as a place in which to work or learn.

The emphasis on the internal governance of the university to which many faculty and student activists have turned as a 'solution' to the problems of higher education seems to me to be misplaced. More faculty work, more committees, only makes the situation worse. In previous crises, efforts to democratize university government resulted in involvement in 'busy' work (committees) of the less research involved, also more conservative faculty, once the original crisis which activated the concerns of the younger and more liberal-left faculty ended. The increased 'democratization' (more elected faculty committees) thereafter increases the importance of the role of the more conservative and scholarly less prestigious 'committeemen' since they can claim to be the elected 'representatives' of the faculty rather than the appointed consultants of the administration. In effect, faculty elections often serve to give populist legitimacy to locally-oriented relatively conservative professional faculty politicians, who rise to the 'top' because the 'cosmopolitan' more research-involved liberal faculty see campus politics as a waste of time in normal periods. In a period of renewed crisis, the elected spokesmen of the faculty, chosen before the troubles, usually differ greatly in their political orientations from the dominant faculty mood. The general situation has been well described by William Roth, a leader of the liberal minority on the Board of Regents of the University of California:[146] 'The rhetoric of faculty governance, however, betrays the usual cultural lag. . . . It maintains the pretense of a self-governing community of scholars. The inaccurate word is "community", for its members are more concerned with doing their own thing than with the general welfare of the particular society which nourishes them. Traditionally, the professor does not want to be bothered by problems of governance. When there is a dramatic, albeit often symbolic, issue to be confronted, the faculty turns out *en masse*. But the day-to-day business of university government that must be carried on is left to a small minority. . . .' Student participation on a representative basis, as a minority of a campus-wide faculty-student senate, is not likely to give the bulk of the student body any sense of increased participation or involvement. All that they get out of such reforms is the opportunity to vote once a year.

There does seem to be a set of problems calling for reform stemming from the multiplication of tasks handled by faculty as individuals and by universities as institutions. Differentiation, separation of functions, has been the pattern of response in all institutional life as tasks have multiplied. In the Soviet Union and other communist countries, the research institute-graduate training set of activities is conducted separately from that of undergraduate teaching. Japan is planning to separate graduate work from other forms of higher education. These alternative systems clearly have liabilities of their own. But if the current wave of politically-induced discontent within the American university is to have any useful function for the life of the university itself, there is a clear and present need to examine the need for, and the possibilities of, a restructuring of the system into a variety of component parts.

---

146    William M. Roth, 'The Dilemmas of Leadership', *Saturday Review*, 53 (January 10, 1970), p. 68.

This counsel does not imply the necessity to separate research and teaching It does suggest, however, the need to recognize and not be afraid to state that a genuine university should not have the attributes of a school in the sense used earlier in this paper. If a university is to educate for adulthood, it cannot be concerned with continuing to be a *gemeinschaft*, a community which resembles an extended family. Students must learn that intellectual life is complicated and difficult, that professors are also scholars who cannot have the time to hold their hands or spoon-feed them with intellectual nourishment. The scholar must share with the student the tentativity of knowledge, his uncertainties about his conclusions, his self-doubts, and his triumphs. The student must be prepared to challenge the findings of his professors, after he has learned the methodology of the field, as another searcher for truth. To communicate the complexities of knowledge to sharp questioning minds is essential to the process of intellectual clarification. Scholarship, particularly in what Pinner calls the dissensual disciplines, requires dialogue, controversy, not only among established men in the same field, but with students as well. Those who would turn universities into schools or into research institutes are both seeking to escape the intra-mural conflict by an easy capitulation. The primary function of the university is scholarship, which includes rigorous education, not politics or therapy. This means, of course, that there can only be a relatively small number of universities which have severe standards for faculty and students, although there will be thousands of accredited institutions of higher education.

Richard Rose

# The Variability of Party Government:
# A Theoretical and Empirical Critique

Reprinted from *Political Studies*, vol. xvii, No. 4 (1969), pp. 413-445.
Earlier drafts of this paper, then entitled 'Party Government vs. Administrative Government', were presented to conferences of the Committee on
Political Sociology of the I.S.A., at the Free University of Berlin, January
1968, and of the Political Studies Association, York, April 1969. In making
revisions, I have benefited specially from criticisms by Raymond Aron, David
Coombes, Juan Linz and Peter Self.

The author is also indebted to various British and American daily and weekly
papers for providing financial assistance for the participant-observation
research upon which the article is based.

'Parties live in a house of power', Weber wrote in one of his most
gnomic sentences. While emphasizing the proximity of political
parties to power, the quotation leaves unclear whether parties reside
in a house of power as masters, prisoners, courtesans or eunuchs.[1]
The purpose of this article is to consider under what circumstances
and to what extent a party *may* translate possession of the highest
formal offices of a regime into operational control of government.
The conditional verb is important. Discussions of parties often
assume rather than demonstrate that occupancy of office is proof of
partisan control.

From the time of Ostrogorski and Michels up to the contemporary
work of McKenzie and Eldersveld, political scientists have devoted
much attention to the question: Who—if anyone—controls political
parties? Such research is always interesting, because parties seem to
violate so many criteria of organizations.[2] Yet such findings are only

---

1      H. H. Gerth and C. Wright Mills (eds.), *From Max Weber* (London:
Routledge, 1948), p. 194.

2      cf. S. J. Eldersveld, *Political Parties: a Behavioral Analysis* (Chicago:
Rand, McNally, 1964), Chap. 1; and Richard Rose, *Influencing Voters:
A Study of Campaign Rationality* (London: Faber, 1967), Chap. 10.

significant to political scientists if parties, in turn, control government. Since political parties claim to control the civil, police and military personnel of many different types of regimes, party government is potentially central in many different types of political systems: a single-party state in Eastern Europe or Africa, a decentralized federal government in North America, or a parliamentary democracy.

Making explicit all that is involved in taking control of government is no easy task. Parties are only one among a number of political institutions seeking to influence government. The more-or-less permanent administrators and the institutions of a regime have very considerable inertia. Sometimes it is momentum for change along pre-determined routes and sometimes, resistance to change. Extra-governmental influences, whether organized as specific pressure groups or as diffuse as the market behaviour of consumers, affect actions of government too. Only in a totalitarian society would one expect party government to reign absolutely. Therefore, one should conceive of the importance of party in government as a continuous variable, rather than as an all-pervasive force; one can have more or one can have less of party government. When party government is diminished, other institutions may replace parties as policy-makers. But it is also possible that when this occurs, no other institution can adequately perform the functions attributed to parties in the government of modern states.

The governing party is unique in its claim to have the right to choose what solutions shall be binding upon the whole of a society. This legitimacy usually carries with it the corollary expectation that it will wish to affect the content of government decisions, by adding something to that which is already present in the policy process. Otherwise, a change of party is of little more significance than the change of a king in a constitutional monarchy. The importance of parties and elections in one-party as well as in competitive party systems suggests that they constitute part of the legitimate or dignified aspect of government.[3] It is less certain what their efficient contribution is to policy-making. The waning of totalitarian and ideological parties in the Western world since 1945 gives some

---

3    cf. Richard Rose and Harve Mossawir, 'Voting and Elections: a Functional Analysis', *Political Studies*, Vol. XV, No. 2 (1967), pp. 175 ff.

grounds for believing that parties are no longer 'decisive', *i.e.*, concerned with making governmental decisions that advance toward or achieve partisan goals. The rise of programmatic ideological parties and party-sponsored regimes in the non-Western world points in the opposite direction.[4]

The purpose of this article is to examine rigorously the extent to which and the conditions under which party government is likely to be realized. The first part sets out a general paradigm of conditions implied by the doctrine of party government. The second tests the importance of party by analysing in terms of the paradigm the actions of British government since Labour took office in October, 1964. To consider whether these findings are peculiar to Britain or widespread, the paradigm is applied in part three to government in the Soviet Union and the United States. The concluding section considers the implications of these findings for the operation of government in societies where parties contribute little to directing the activities of a regime.

I

Whatever expectations one has of the role that party ought to play in government, there can be little doubt that making decisions about the allocation of material goods and symbolic values is an important activity of government.[5] In theory, the ideal way to study the importance of parties in government would be to examine the things that governments do and the processes by which they reach their decisions to find where, if at all, parties fit into a very complex process. Generically, one can identify at least six different steps in the process of making government policy—publicizing a problem, initiating a search for a solution, evaluating alternative solutions, choosing a solution or a combination of solutions, implementing the

---

4    See *e.g.*, the importance attributed to parties by Samuel P. Huntington in *Political Order in Changing Societies* (New Haven: Yale, 1968), especially Chap. 7.

5    The chief difficulty with the placeman's theory of the function of parties—that they exist to hold office and nothing else—is that it proposes to settle by *a priori* stipulation what ought to be decided by empirical investigation.

measures decided upon, and finally, evaluating the consequences of a measure. The burden of studying all that is involved here is great, since there are good grounds to assume that the process varies from issue-area to issue-area. The workings of government and, potentially, the contribution of parties, may not be a constant, as one moves from a consideration of nationalization legislation to foreign policy or from race relations to economic policy or regional devolution.[6] Since parties would appear only intermittently in such a grand decision-making scheme, the approach would be very uneconomical in terms of the use of resources, as well as impossibly lavish in the amounts of data required.

Pending the solution of some very complex conceptual and methodological problems involved in decision-making studies of government,[7] there is much to be said for concentrating attention upon parties in relation to the structure of government. As Michels and Ostrogoski long ago demonstrated, even if this type of analysis cannot lead us to a single source of sovereignty, at least it can make clear who does *not* govern. It may also give pointers about the nature of the groups, if any, that can fill the vacuum resulting from an absence of party direction.

If a party is to have a large amount of influence upon government, then the following political conditions must be met before it enters office or at the time of its accession to office:

(1) At least one party must exist and, after some form of contest, become dominant in a regime. This condition is necessary but non-restrictive. Banks and Textor report that in the 96 countries for which unambiguous information is available, 91 have at least one party. The condition is primarily important for the fact that it does not make a competitive party system a necessity for party government.[8] Elections are not the only way in which a party can gain

---

6     See the discussion in Richard Rose, *Politics in England* (London: Faber, 1965), pp. 207 ff.; and in Richard Rose (ed.), *Policy-Making in Britain* (London: Macmillan, 1969), especially 'Introduction'.

7     For a discussion of the problems of generalizing from a few cases which have no claim to representativeness, see Richard Rose, *People in Politics* (London: Faber, 1970), Chaps. 6-7.

8     cf. Arthur Banks and Robert Textor, *The Cross-Polity Survey* (Cambridge, Massachusetts: MIT Press, 1963), pp. 86 and 97-98, and variable 44.

office. One might even hypothesize that a party is more likely to control government if it gains power by a civil war or insurrection against a foreign or Imperial power. Such a victory is a greater test of effectiveness than electoral success, and a better indicator of widespread popular commitment to the party.

(2) Nominees of the party then occupy important positions in a regime. These nominees constitute the party *qua* government or, in American terms, the Administration. They are the only resource that the party adds to the continuing personnel and institutions of government. The particular titles given to important positions will vary from regime to regime, and, presumptively, will include those positions which are formally described as the highest political offices. One might also expect partisan nominees to hold *ad hoc* or extra-constitutional posts of considerable significance, by virtue of party patronage.

(3) The number of partisans nominated for office is large enough to permit partisans to participate in the making of a wide range of policies. As Lenin said, 'What is the good of having a party if it can't appoint the people in the management?'[9] While the number of persons appointed by a party need not equal the total number of public employees, taking office should involve much more than the change of one titular leader, if partisans are to be part of the efficient machinery of government. When a government has hundreds of thousands of employees, the 'few' who constitute the oligarchy are more likely to be a few hundred or a few thousand than a handful.

(4) The partisans given office must have the skills necessary to control large bureaucratic organizations. This condition does not stipulate that all appointees have the same kind of education and experience or even a common high level of intelligence. The work of government is sufficiently varied to give scope to men with differing talents. To accept variety is not, however, to assume that all conceivable skills and experiences are equally suited to the work of governing. The particular skills needed in countries where competitive elections lead to frequent rotation in office are, as V. O. Key noted, those that will enable men 'to manage and control the

9  Quoted in Ghita Ionescu, *The Politics of the European Communist States* (London: Weidenfeld and Nicolson, 1967), p. 117.

bureaucracy from their posts as the transient but responsible heads of departments and agencies'.[10]

(5) Partisans must formulate policy intentions for enactment once in office. Policy intentions are statements that specify what a party-in-office will do in a form capable of empirical *post hoc* assessment. It may be argued that this is not a necessary condition of party government: a party in office may do no more than react 'empirically' to problems as they are reckoned to arise. As Michael Oakeshott, no particular friend of ideology, has demonstrated: 'purely empirical politics are not something difficult to achieve or proper to be avoided, they are merely impossible'.[11]

(6) Policy intentions must be stated in a 'not unworkable' form. This condition does not require that every detail of a policy must be spelled out. It notes only that a policy intention with no reference to means of execution cannot be carried out as it stands. A pledge of 'peace and prosperity' is not a statement of policies to be carried out, but a hope of what might happen, whether by intention or by accident. A statement of general principles is also insufficient as a basis for party government. Partisans may still disagree about the relevance or applicability of general principles to particular conditions, as in the case of Socialist principles of foreign policy.[12] A party which takes office committed to unworkable policies or to very general principles cannot direct government, but only react to circumstances with which it is confronted.

Once in office, the following conditions must also be met if party government is to result:

(7) Partisans in office must give high priority to carrying out

---

10    *Politics, Parties and Pressure Groups* (New York: Crowell, 4th ed., 1958), p. 764. At the end of the paragraph, the last in the book, Key adds: 'It is through such persons who owe their posts to the victorious party that popular control over government is maintained'.

11    *Political Education* (Cambridge: Bowes & Bowes, 1951), p. 11.

12    See C. R. Rose, 'The Relation of Socialist Principles to British Labour Foreign Policy, 1945-51' (Oxford: D.Phil. thesis, 1960). There is no stipulation that the policies are, or must be, different in content, direction or timing from those of an Opposition party if it were to have held office. Such a statement, by its nature, is incapable of direct empirical test, though it is of considerable practical as well as conjectural importance.

party policies. Unforeseen circumstances and changing environmental conditions will inevitably lead a party to do things that it did not propose before taking office. However, the more its leaders plead circumstances as a justification of actions, then the more they are diminishing the contribution they themselves make, beyond that of bowing to the inevitable. Another obstacle to the implementation of party policies comes from partisans themselves; they may already have or develop in office other loyalties, *e.g.* deference to advisers or personal ambition.

(8) The party policies that are promulgated must be put into practice by the personnel of the regime. No distinction is intended here between administration by partisans or administration by career civil servants. Partisans may make more enthusiastic administrators of programmes, but civil servants may make more competent administrators, Civil service norms assert that such men are ready— some might argue, only too ready—to serve whatever orders are given them. Instead of assuming partiality among civil servants, this condition requires that the men who nominally form the government be astute enough politically to secure compliance to their own directives from a massive but passive bureaucracy.

(If one rejected the assumption that parties can or should influence policy, but that individual politicians can affect government by their relative style or competence, the foregoing paradigm could still be adapted to use by eliminating conditions 5 and 6 and modifying condition 7 so that partisans would only be expected to give priority to policy-making. The paradigm then becomes a description of conditions under which the competence or incompetence of partisans is likely to affect government.)

The conditions stipulated for party government in the above outline may seem onerous: this is because they are onerous. The conditions make explicit what is often left implicit. Assuming direction of a very large bureaucratic organization on short notice is not to be done easily, nor to be taken for granted. There is, after all, no necessary reason why parties should govern. A variety of ideal-type alternatives can be considered. There is government by charismatic leadership. In traditional government, a change of leadership makes no difference, since men in office are not expected to make decisions, but only to proceed in customary ways. In military government, soldiers occupy the position here assigned to partisans, as well as providing manpower to enforce orders. In Western societies, one obvious alternative to party government is administrative government, in which civil servants not only maintain routine services of government, but also try to formulate new policies. Empirically, the political system of a country may embody elements of several ideal-types. It is also possible that no group of men consciously make policies in the name of the regime and that government is run by inertia.

## II

In the world today, one can expect an extremely wide range of variations in the role of party in government, ranging from the Ethiopian 'no-party' state to Communist countries, where party is sometimes said to make the state.[13] Britain might be thought to be in between these two extremes. The importance of party as a necessary link between Parliament and Cabinet has time and again been asserted by contemporary writers on British government. While there is widespread criticism of the civil service, Parliament and party politicians as a class, there has yet to emerge a broad and serious attack upon the mechanics of the party system that has prevailed in Britain since 1945.[14] The period since the entry of Labour into office in 1964 provides a particularly good study in party government. The Conservatives, after 13 years in office, had become widely discredited as a governing group. The leadership and policies of Labour in opposition were regarded as unusually credible as an alternative government. The long decline of the Conservatives, moreover, gave the Labour Party several years time to prepare for the task of governing.

---

13    On Communist countries, see Section III. On Ethiopia, see Robert L. Hess and Gerhard Loewenberg, 'The Ethiopian No-Party State', *American Political Science Review*, Vol. LVIII, No. 4 (1964).

14    The reception of Samuel Brittan's critique, *Left or Right: the Bogus Dilemma* (London: Secker & Warburg, 1968), indicates that the intellectual climate is not yet ripe for attacks on the British party system.

(1) The Labour Party took office on 16th October 1964 as a majority Government, with full powers to make all the appointments it wished to Government posts and with a very small but clear majority in the House of Commons. Any inhibitions arising from the size of that majority were washed away by the scale of its victory at the 1966 general election 18 months later. The relatively steady course that the Government has pursued since October 1964 suggests that the size of its first majority was not a major determinant of what Labour has done in the 4½-year-period under review here. (This paper was completed in Spring 1969. The actions of the Labour Government in its last year in office do not significantly affect the analysis.)

(2) The nominees of the Labour Prime Minister filled all the posts conventionally considered important in British government. The Prime Minister's prior experience as a civil servant as well as in Cabinet suggests that he was more likely to be aware of the workings of the Whitehall machine than an average leader. Moreover, his actions in office have demonstrated that patronage is not the least of subjects to which he devotes attention. The only step that Harold Wilson did not take—at least to the extent that had been anticipated —was the development of a much enlarged Cabinet Office, providing the Prime Minister with a partisan staff comparable to that available to a President.[15]

The great majority of partisans were placed in departmental posts at the apex of formidable hierarchies. In order to evaluate the importance of the jobs held by partisans, one must therefore consider the importance of the Minister and junior ministers in departmental terms. The first point to note is that the political nominees are confined to the top-most level of the department; their eminence thus places them at a considerable distance—measured in terms of hierarchical layers or horizontal and vertical movement in an organization chart—from the great majority of officials in their

---

15    cf. Wilson's own remarks in Norman Hunt (ed.), *Whitehall and Beyond* (London: B.B.C., 1964), Richard Neustadt in conversation with Henry Brandon, '10 Downing Street: Is it Out of Date?', *Sunday Times*, 8 November 1964, and, latterly, Ian Trethowan, 'A look at Mr. Wilson's 'Power House' ', *The Times*, 6 June 1968.

department.[16] The isolation from the continuing work of a department is reinforced by the fact that the Minister and the civil servants who most immediately surround him are expected to take advisory roles, acting as ultimate court of appeals for briefs that have travelled up from low down in the hierarchy and to initiate policies without becoming deeply involved in all that follows. The divorce of advisers, *i.e.* very senior civil servants and political ministers, from management is peculiar to British government. In many foreign countries, persons with considerable management responsibility are in direct contact with ministers and *vice versa*.[17] Contact between the Minister and departmental officials operating policies is further inhibited by the funnelling of advice to the Minister through the Permanent Under-Secretary. The practice may be criticized, as in the Fulton Report, as administratively undesirable because it places too many burdens on the P.U.S. and leaves no time to think of long-term problems. It can also be criticized as undesirable on political grounds, because it allows non-partisans to limit a politician's options.[18]

Because of the degree to which Ministers are remote from the workings of their department, they cannot be responsible in fact as well as constitutional theory for all that is done in their name. Conditions have changed greatly in this respect since the first half of the nineteenth century.[19] However, the convention of responsibility requires that ministers must still devote a substantial amount of time to defending what they are responsible for in name if not in fact. The way in which parliamentary questions are answered

---

16    cf. the remarks of Anthony Wedgwood Benn, Peter Shore and Dame Evelyn Sharp, quoted in Lewis A. Gunn, 'Ministers and Civil Servants: Changes in Whitehall', *Public Administration* (Australia), Vol. XXVI, No. 1 (1967), p. 85.

17    See F. F. Ridley (ed.), *Specialists and Generalists* (London: Allen & Unwin, 1968).

18    cf. *The Civil Service: Vol. 1* (London: H.M.S.O., Cmnd. 3638) para. 172 ff.; and Richard Neustadt, *Presidential Power* (New York: Wiley, 1960).

19    cf. Henry Parris, 'The Origins of the Permanent Civil Service, 1780-1830', *Public Administration*, Vol. LXXXVI, No. 2 (1968), pp. 155 ff.; S. E. Finer, 'The Individual Responsibility of Ministers', *Public Administration*, Vol. XXXIV, No. 4 (1956); and G. Marshall and G. Moodie, *Some Problems of the Constitution* (London: Hutchinson, 2nd ed., 1961), pp. 67 ff.

suggests that most answers encourage, if only defensively, the minister's identification with what the department has been doing, rather than stimulating him to take new initiatives.[20] In positive terms, a minister's responsibility to fight at Cabinet level for the department against other departments in claims for limited national resources and his responsibility for public relations activities from which civil servants are debarred mean that he spends a very substantial amount of time projecting, defending or 'selling' what the department is already doing.[21] A minister's career not only depends upon his ability to get a department to follow party or personal policy preferences, but also upon his ability to convince people outside his department that the things for which he is technically responsible are good things.

(3) The number of partisan nominees—in a single department or collectively—is an important limitation upon the amount of influence that partisans can bring to bear, whatever their position in a governmental organization chart. At the commencement of his administration, Harold Wilson appointed a ministry of 87, plus whips and law officers; it has not altered much in size since. In addition, an uncounted number of Labour sympathizers—usually journalists or academic economists—were given 'irregular' jobs outside the civil service hierarchy with direct access to ministers, though without formal authority to command. At any one time the total is likely to be less than that of ministers; their partisan significance is downgraded by the variability of the roles that these men actually undertook. By 1968, Lewis Gunn could suggest that the most important feature of their career in Whitehall has been the 'retreat of the irregulars'.[22]

There is no basis for assuming that the present number of partisan officials in Whitehall is optimum, in terms of any particular ob-

---

20 The inference is drawn from D. N. Chester and Nona Bowring, *Questions in Parliament* (Oxford: Clarendon Press, 1962), pp. 236 ff.

21 It may be, of course, that the speeches the Minister makes, rather than defending the department, have little reference to its work at all. Cf. Sam Brittan, 'The Irregulars', in Richard Rose (ed.), *Policy-Making in Britain*, pp. 335-36.

22 cf. Lewis A. Gunn, 'The Fulton Report on the Civil Service: Part I' (Mimeograph: University of Glasgow, 1968), p. 4; and Sam Brittan, 'The Irregulars'.

jective. The numbers are justified by tradition and by the constitutional fiction that one man directs everything in a department. Because of the convention that ministers should normally come from the House of Commons, there is also resistance to increasing the strength of the payroll vote *vis-à-vis* backbenchers in Parliament, without regard for the constraints this places upon the party's executive strength.[23]

The number of partisans in ministerial posts is discounted by allowances that must be made for other claims upon their time. Ministers perform many roles in British politics: such things as attendance at the House of Commons for non-departmental business and constituency affairs can take up substantial amounts of a man's time. Ernest Marples, one of the most cost-conscious of ministers, reckoned that he could devote only about one-quarter of a 13-hour day to paper work concerned with his department, and another quarter to meetings and discussions concerning departmental matters directly. Marples is likely to have been above average in the ability to allocate his time.[24] One might therefore conclude that the complement of 86 ministers working half-time on departmental affairs should be regarded as the equivalent of 43 full-time executives. The manpower strength of ministers must further be discounted by the inefficiencies arising from frequent movement from office to office, without any special provision made for breaking in a man new to his department.[25] At the end of a month, a new minister might be able to master departmental briefs with sufficient skill to put its view to those outside the department. It would almost certainly take longer to master the department's affairs so that he was putting his

---

23    For trends since 1900, see D. E. Butler and Jennie Freeman, *British Political Facts, 1900-1967* (London: Macmillan, 1968), p. 57; and for comments, D. N. Chester, 'The British Parliament, 1939-1966', *Parliamentary Affairs*, Vol. XIX, No. 4 (1966).

24    See Ernest Marples 'A Dog's Life in the Ministry' and essays by Patrick Gordon Walker and Lord Strang, all reprinted in *Policy-Making in Britain*. Note also, for example, Julian Holland, 'Do We Make our Top Men Waste too much Time?', *Daily Mail*, 4 August 1966.

25    See confidential remarks of Labour Ministers, recorded by diarists in *The Guardian*, 6 April 1968, and the *New Statesman*, 10 May, 1968.

and his party's views to the department.[26] In the first four years of
the Labour Government, ten major departments of state had an
average of 2·6 changes of minister, giving each man a term of 18
months in office. This rate of turnover means that in an average
month, 4 or 5 men would be changing jobs, and thus not even
effective as half-time departmental ministers. It is worth noting that
the practice of frequent rotation from department to department is
not followed by other major Western governments, or by the civil
service in the appointment of Permanent Under-Secretaries.[27]

The number of men required to control British government is
rarely discussed—at least in public. Here, one can only point out considerations that any assessment would have to allow for. The first is
that departments vary considerably in size, the dispersion of responsibilities, the intrinsic complexity of their work, the political
importance of tasks and, more arguably, the degree to which work is
routinized. (Today's routine may, of course, be tomorrow's 'shocking'
example of the dire need for reform.) Whatever their differences,
all established departments have a very considerable amount
of inertia. For party politicians to initiate policies—or at least,
to participate sufficiently in preliminary stages of discussion to
make sure that *they* control their own options—is likely to require
considerable effort, whether measured in terms of intelligence,
political perseverance, or manpower. There are also threshold problems of critical size. A group of 80 partisans in a single department
may be much outnumbered by their civil servants, but they form a
large phalanx. Typically, ministers average about four per government department, few enough to make one wonder how far down into
a department their views can trickle before they are diluted or
evaporate.

The exercise of influence is not only a function of hierarchical

---

26    cf. the remarks of Robert Lovett, former U.S. Secretary of Defence,
      that it takes two years for a political appointee to learn the substance
      of problems in that department, quoted at p. 80 of Henry M. Jackson
      (ed.), *The National Security Council* (New York: Praeger, 1965).

27    cf. Anthony King, 'Too Many Reshuffles', *Spectator*, 12 April, 1968;
      'Britain's Ministerial Turnover', *New Society*, 14 August 1966; and
      John S. Harris and Thomas V. Garcia, 'The Permanent Secretaries:
      Britain's Top Administrators', *Public Administration Review*,
      Vol. XXVI, No. 1 (1966), pp. 36 ff.

distance, but also of the fact that many major departments, such as the Home Office or Education and Science, are divided up into a dozen or two dozen operating units, headed by officials at the rank of an assistant secretary or above. It is unreasonable to imagine that one man could be *au courant* with the latent problems as well as the pressing emergencies of all or even most of these units. Perhaps the simplest index of the volume of important work in central government departments might be given by the number of senior civil servants employed, *i.e.* men at the rank of assistant secretary or above. In the DES, there are approximately 76 such officials, excluding regional staff concerned with inspecting schools and such autonomous units as the University Grants Committee. The department has five ministers, plus one part-time research consultant with partisan leanings, A. H. Halsey. Reckoning that each partisan nominee devotes about half his (or her) time to departmental matters, one has a staffing ratio of about 25 to 1.[28] If one ignores departmental lines and looks at the ratio of partisan appointees to senior civil servants, then the contribution of the partisans is likely to be reduced further. The number of partisans is limited, as well as part-time. The number of civil servants who might be reckoned important can be extended almost indefinitely as one starts to make allowance for professional, scientific and technical men as well as for administrative class officials. A minimum calculation of senior grade officials at something comparable to the assistant secretary level indicates that the half-time partisan nominees are effectively outnumbered by a ratio of about 50 to 1.[29] Whatever calculation is accepted, it is clear that partisans cannot make their influence felt in British government by weight of numbers.

(4) The skills most appropriate for a partisan official have not been assessed—in Britain or elsewhere—with any precision. In a political system in which members of a government were recruited

---

28     For another calculation, see F. M. G. Willson, 'Policy-Making and the Policy-Makers., first published in *Policy-Making in Britain*, at pp. 360-61.

29     Calculated from figures on senior staff given in *The Civil Service: Vol. 4*, pp. 184-91. The figures exclude the Foreign Office staff and ministers. Civil servants at assistant secretary level or above in the administrative class number 1,129, by far the largest category in the 1,895 identified as very senior for this reckoning.

for specific skills, then it would be very important to define them with considerable precision. In Britain, the academic's problem is greatly simplified because of the highly restrictive criteria concerning eligibility for office. The principal criterion for appointment to a partisan post in a British government is membership in the House of Commons, or for a handful, membership in the House of Lords. When a new government is elected, prior membership is usually a *sine qua non* for office. Seniority is specially important at higher reaches of government. Of the 23 people whom Harold Wilson appointed to his first Cabinet in 1964, 19 had originally entered the Commons no later than 1945. Long service in the legislature as a prerequisite for executive office is a feature of British government which distinguishes it from many others—including, it should be noted, Canada and Australia.[30] Since MPs enter Parliament in Britain at a relatively young age and since the median Cabinet minister is likely to have entered the Commons in his 30s to devote his energies fulltime to political life, Parliament is not only a chamber for electing governments and debating their activities, but also a school for ministers.

What qualifications and training do MPs have for the job of a Minister? In terms of formal education, MPs and ministers are increasingly likely to be university graduates, an indication of a reasonable level of general intelligence. There is, however, no necessity that an MP meet a particular level of examination standard as, for example, is the case of the civil servants whom he must direct. The initial occupations characterizing Labour MPs are ones in which skill in handling words and people is particularly important—teacher, lawyer, journalist, or trade union official. The competitive character of the contemporary business world makes it increasingly difficult to combine a management post with the political activities of a parliamentary aspirant.[31] As Edinger and Searing have shown, social

---

30    See Richard Rose, 'The Pathway to Power at Westminster', *The Times*, 6 December 1966; and for comparative data, Joseph Schlesinger, 'Political Careers and Party Leadership', in Lewis J. Edinger (ed.), *Political Leadership in Industrialized Societies* (New York: Wiley, 1967), pp. 285 ff.

31    See *e.g.*, Adrian Norman, 'Candidates from Industry', in *Crossbow*, Vol. XII, No. 45 (1968).

background characteristics are unlikely to determine current attitudes and policies.[32] But they can condition the way in which a man goes about his work. The verbalist's skills are useful for the Commons, for much work there involves dealing with people in small groups or discussion, where skill in self-expression is specially valuable. Last and not least, such skills are also of value in securing promotion to the front bench, for promotion is an act of co-option. An individual does not earn his place by demonstrating that he can perform certain objectively measurable tasks. Instead, he is invited to join the ranks of junior ministers by virtue of the opinion he has led others to form of him. The course of promotion up the ladder of the ministerial hierarchy also involves a very considerable element of co-option.[33]

The work of the Commons does not lead naturally to the work of a departmental minister, as prep school leads to public school. A minister's job differs in important respects from that of an MP. In addition to dealing with people, he must deal with mountains of paperwork. Instead of dealing on a face-to-face basis with people he knows intimately, he must delegate many tasks to civil servants whom he hardly knows, without losing all chance of influence. It would seem that the skills necessary for managing a large government department might be better learned in a large organization—whether profitmaking or non-profitmaking—or at a lower tier of government, as in a federal system, where a learner can do less damage. In recent years, the expansion of the committee work of the House of Commons has given MPs increased opportunity to meet civil servants, and to see how government departments work, even if only in pathological instances. While some insights are acquired into government departments in this way, it seems the work is of limited

---

32    For British data, see D. E. Butler and Anthony King, *The British General Election of 1964* (London: Macmillan, 1965), pp. 234 ff.; and, more generally, Lewis J. Edinger and Donald Searing, 'Social Background in Elite Analysis', *American Political Science Review*, Vol. LXI. No. 2 (1967).

33    See Richard Rose, 'The Emergence of Leaders', *New Society*. 17 October 1963; and, more generally, Ralph Turner, 'Sponsored and Contest Mobility and the School System', *American Sociological Review*, Vol. XXV, No. 6 (1960).

value in preparing MPs to become ministers.[34] It is also noteworthy that the development of specialist committees has been strongly opposed by frontbenchers.

The inability of an MP to acquire administrative expertise simultaneously with acquiring eligibility for office means that the chief skill he might hope to bring to a department is subject-matter expertise. Unfortunately, membership in the House of Commons does only a little to develop subject-matter competence. Specialized expertise must be acquired prior to entering the House, or simultaneously with pursuing an active parliamentary career. As constituency welfare officer or intermittently employed professional, an MP has opportunities to note symptoms of difficulties that government ought to try to solve. He is not so well placed as a civil servant to learn the causes of difficulties. Yet even civil servants, notwithstanding their fulltime engagement with problems of managing society in one small sector, are also coming under intense official criticism for not knowing enough about the problems that they and their ministerial overlords are supposed to solve.[35]

Given the large number of jobs that must be filled in relation to the number of partisans eligible for appointment, it might be more appropriate to speak of a Prime Minister filling up the ranks of his government rather than selecting it. In 1964, the Prime Minister had only 229 MPs in the Commons with prior parliamentary experience. The number of appointments—including ceremonial posts and jobs as parliamentary private secretaries—meant that about half of his experienced MPs had to take something, if the Queen's Government was to be carried on. Studies of MPs over lengthy periods of time indicate that a very large proportion eventually receive some office. Sainsbury calculated that 45 per cent of Conservative MPs elected

---

34    cf., *e.g.*, R. Kimber and J. Richardson, 'Specialization and Parliamentary Standing Committees', *Political Studies*, Vol. XVI, No. 1 (1968); N. Johnson, *Parliament and Administration: the Estimates Committee 1945-1965* (London: Allen & Unwin, 1967); and David L. Coombes, *The Member of Parliament and Administration* (London: Allen & Unwin, 1966).

35    See the discussion of 'professionalism' in *The Civil Service*, Vol. 1, paras. 32 ff.

in 1951 got some appointment in the subsequent 13 years.[36] In filling up his Cabinet, as in appointing junior ministers, there is no obligation for a Prime Minister to make skill in performing official duties a primary or necessary qualification for appointment. Conventions of party politics create a presumption that some kinds of people will be named to certain offices, whether or not they are qualified to undertake the duties involved. The Prime Minister's necessary concern with using patronage powers to protect an institutionally insecure position ensures that the purely political qualifications are not overlooked.[37] In twentieth-century Britain, giving patronage on grounds irrelevant to performance is increasingly dangerous, for the number of sinecure posts or 'non-jobs' is continuously shrinking as the responsibilities of government expand. It is noteworthy that in America, this change in government work has meant that candidates for senior executive appointments are now usually meant to have performance qualifications in addition to party backing.[38]

Whatever their general preparation, once in office ministers vary considerably in their ability to give direction to their part of the Whitehall machine. Differences in ability are recognized by the fact that only a fraction of those who at sometime are a parliamentary secretary eventually gain a seat in the Cabinet. In the 1951-64 period, 40 of 123 persons appointed to some job eventually gained a seat in the Cabinet.[39] If one posits that ministerial appointees divide into good, bad and indifferent and that the numbers in each category are about even, then two-thirds are of at least passing competence. This means that the Labour Government of Harold Wilson was attempting to carry out its ambitious programme with a staff of approximately 50 to 55 men working half-time, plus about 25 half-

---

36    See Keith Sainsbury, 'Patronage, Honours and Parliament', *Parliamentary Affairs*, Vol. XIX, No. 3 (1966), p. 348; more generally, note P. W. Buck, *Amateurs and Professionals in British Politics, 1918-59* (Chicago: University Press 1963), pp. 47 ff.

37    For a comparative discussion of this point, see Kenneth N. Waltz, *Foreign Policy and Democratic Politics* (Boston: Little, Brown, 1967), pp. 55 ff.

38    cf. Dean E. Mann with Jameson W. Doig, *The Assistant Secretaries* (Washington: The Brookings Institution, 1965), Chaps. 3-4.

39    K. Sainsbury, *op. cit.*, p. 348.

timers of limited ability, and another five trying to learn quickly the ropes of a new department.

(5) Prior to the entry of Labour to office in 1964, there was a widespread belief, within and without the Party, that Labour had a programme for government. The programme was invoked in general terms more than it was specified in detail. Learning from the bitter policy disputes of Hugh Gaitskell's years as leader, Harold Wilson avoided precise commitments. The general purport was perhaps best summed up in the Party's campaign slogan, 'Let's Go With Labour—and we'll get things done'.[40] The direction in which the Party was to go was left unspecified, but few in the Party seemed to doubt that the general tendency would be 'progressive' or 'radical'. In retrospect, it is now clear that the statements of intention by Labour in opposition were primarily rhetorical. Lack of preparation should not be blamed on a few individuals. The important point is that the institutions of British politics do not encourage a party in Opposition to develop clearcut policies. Some politicians, such as Harold Macmillan, have even argued that an Opposition should avoid such commitments.[41]

In the course of a lengthy pre-election campaign, there is no need for an Opposition party to produce policies. The one thing that is certain in this period is the record of the governing party. A reasonable strategy for an 'out' party is to attempt to maximize dissatisfaction with an existing government's shortcomings. Instead of committing itself to positions on issues, a party can campaign on the grounds of its style or leadership competence, as Labour increasingly did before the 1964 election. Yet the origins of the Labour Party as a movement with ideological aspirations makes it readier than the Conservatives to try to formulate policy goals in opposition. Labour's commitment to programmatic politics is underscored by the fact that many who have become disillusioned with the Wilson Government do not seem to doubt that there was a programme to be carried out.[42]

---

40     For a description of Labour's move away from programmatic details to a concern with generalized values and the personality of Harold Wilson, see Richard Rose, *Influencing Voters*, Chap. 3.

41     See D. E. Butler and Richard Rose, *The British General Election of 1959* (London: Macmillan, 1960), pp. 32-33.

42     See *e.g.*, Dudley Seers, 'The Structure of Power', in Hugh Thomas (ed.), *Crisis in the Civil Service* (London: Blond, 1968).

L

(6) Since the actions of the Labour Government have deviated in a number of instances from opposition intentions, it is not possible to offer conclusive empirical proof of a negative proposition: the party had few workable plans to carry out its pre-election promises. The burden of evidence and analysis, supplemented by personal knowledge, supports the most parsimonious explanation: many were the intentions, but few were the plans. Re-reading statements of what Labour would do in office, e.g. the speeches of Harold Wilson, the essays of Anthony Crosland, or two frequently invoked Party pamphlets, *Labour in the Sixties* (1960) and *Signposts for the Sixties* (1961) one sees a deterministic note. Labour believes in things that will happen anyway, such as the technological revolution; *ergo*, Labour can govern because its principles are in accord with the *zeitgeist*.

The paucity of Labour's pre-election plans has been testified to by none other than Peter Shore, head of the Research Department at Transport House during the opposition period, 1959-1964. Writing in 1966, he noted:[43] 'Ministers may bring with them broad ideas of how future policy should develop. But in the transformation of policy goals into realistic plans, in the execution of those plans and, still more, in policy responses to new and unexpected developments, Ministers are largely, if not wholly, dependent on their official advisers'. The lack is not the fault of the under-staffed Research Department. If it is anyone's fault, it is that of the party leaders who countenanced inadequate facilities. In party headquarters, 'research' tends to mean the preparation of materials for next week's committee meeting, tomorrow's debate, or tonight's press release. In both major parties, staffs are small and much burdened with work that has nothing to do with the preparation of detailed policies. At Transport House prior to the 1964 General Election, the Research Department had a staff of only about 12 recent graduates or their equivalents.[44] Labour was able to draw upon outside experts to

---

43    Peter Shore, *Entitled to Know* (London: MacGibbon & Kee, 1966), p. 153.

44    The position worsened after the 1964 general election. Cf. Richard Rose, 'The Professionals of Politics', *New Society*, 8 August 1963; and 'Doubts Over Role of Transport House', *The Times*, 6 March 1965. The Conservatives also have problems in Opposition. See Paul Dean, 'A Look at the Conservative Research Department', *Crossbow*, Vol. XI, No. 41 (1967).

serve on a variety of research committees,[45] but these reported to the Party's National Executive Committee, hardly a forum for thoughtful discussion of the contents of a draft policy statement. A few individuals maintained contact with outside research institutions, but the informal oral exchange of ideas over dinner or at a weekend gathering need not go beneath the surface. Moreover, as Sam Brittan has pointed out, the best ideas, without reinforcement at opportune moments by strategically placed persons on the inside of government, are likely to have no follow through.[46]

Shadow ministers suffer from the same disabilities as backbench MPs when it comes to preparing workable policies. They also suffer from an additional disability: their prominence and 'shadow' responsibility for specific departments makes it incumbent on them to appear to know better than the government of the day what should be done at almost every juncture. This follows from the adversary and partisan nature of parliamentary debate, and from the career importance of demonstrating superiority, in debating terms at least. The poor performance of the Conservatives in the early 1960s undoubtedly encouraged the feeling among Labour MPs that they could easily do better than *that* lot. A measure of indolence, plus outside engagements, arising from the low salaries then prevailing, plus some uncertainty about *which* department he would inherit, were further incentives for a shadow minister not to trouble himself about the details of what to do when at last in government.

The procedure by which an Opposition becomes a government gives partisans little time to prepare workable plans. Until election day, Opposition politicians concentrate efforts upon securing election. The future can be reckoned to look after itself.[47] Once elected, politicians have no time to make the transition to office. They must take office on 24 hours notice and attempt to introduce distinctive changes while simultaneously superintending and defending all that the department is already doing. In the United States, there is a period of approximately 11 weeks between election

---

45    See *e.g.*, the report of the Research Department in *Annual Conference Report* (London: Labour Party, 1964), pp. 38-40.

46    'The Irregulars', p. 333.

47    cf. Richard Pryke, *Though Cowards Flinch* (London: MacGibbon & Kee, 1967), p. 10.

and installation in office. The period is, in the words of one American expert 'scarcely long enough' to prepare for governing.[48]

If ministers or their staffs have not formulated ideas prior to entering office, they are unlikely to have time to do so in office, as things now stand. The Fulton Report has given official recognition to what many have long hinted at: the difficulty that senior civil servants and ministers have in giving attention to anything beyond 'urgent deadlines'. Characteristically, the Fulton Report recommended that a Planning Unit with a civil service head be established to prepare long-term policy planning. Such a reform, it is argued, would 'increase the control of ministers over the formulation of policy in their departments'. It would also obviate the need for a partisan-oriented departmental *cabinet* on the French model. In other words, the capacity of a government department to prepare policies should be increased, but participation by partisans in departmental policy should not be increased.[49]

(7) In office, Labour ministers have given low priority to party policies. For example, Anthony King, in a review of the first four years of Wilson's Government, reckoned that the Party had unequivocally carried out only four of 16 major pledges—nationalizing steel, abolishing selective state secondary education, extending rent controls, and altering the tax system. Similar estimates have been given by others sympathetic to the government, but outside office.[50] Of all the policies that the government failed to carry out, the most important was that favouring economic growth. Since the growth policy was technically possible and strongly supported in Whitehall as well as among partisans, it is particularly significant that the opposite policy has been followed. In the event, the policy was followed without any Labour minister putting his commitment to previous party policy ahead of his commitment to office, and re-

---

48    cf. Herman M. Somers, 'The Federal Bureaucracy and the Change of Administration', *American Political Science Review*, Vol. XLVIII, No. 1 (1954), pp. 132 ff.; and David Stanley, *Changing Administrations* (Washington: Brookings, 1965), pp. 135-136.

49    cf. *The Civil Service*, Vol. 1, paras. 172 ff. and 285.

50    See Anthony King, 'The Party's Over Now', *Spectator*, 20 September 1968; and Tyrrell Burgess (ed.), *Matters of Principle* (Harmondsworth: Penguin, 1968).

signing. In the crisis of July 1966, for instance, only Richard Pryke, a part-time assistant at the Cabinet office, among the lowest ranking of the *ad hoc* partisan recruits, resigned. A pessimist might argue that the Wilson Government's *bouleversement* was nothing new in Labour history.[51]

Explanation of this limited commitment to party policy can be pursued on two levels. At the personal level, it would be reasonable to infer that individual Labour politicians did not particularly value the achievement of ideological goals, nor had they strongly identified with particular policies. Survey studies of local politicians in Britain suggest that whatever the motivations that bring people into politics, ideological or policy goals are not today the chief satisfactions that they gain through continued political participation.[52] Institutionally, one can note that the role-relationships into which a minister enters are firstly with civil servants, and secondly with MPs *from the vantage point of departmental spokesman*. In view of the multiplicity of roles, the shortage of time, and, not least, withdrawal from many party activities because of office-holding, it is hardly surprising that tho party goalo booomo looo oaliont to individual miniotoro.[53]

(8) There is no substantial evidence to suggest that the partisan failures of the Labour Government have been the result of efforts by civil servants to frustrate ministerial policy directives. In fact, there is evidence to suggest that a plurality of administrative class civil servants actively preferred a Labour to a Conservative Government.[54] The role socialization of a civil servant emphasizes the norm that he ought to give loyalty as well as form to the vague commitments of a changing series of partisan ministers. But there are many difficulties in realizing this. Nearly all senior civil servants are completely removed from party politics outside Westminster. In trying to serve

---

51   cf. Ralph Miliband, *Parliamentary Socialism* (London: Allen & Unwin, 1961).

52   On local politicians, see John M. Bochel, 'Activists in the Conservative and Labour Parties' (Manchester: M.A. thesis, 1965), and unpublished reports by Dr. J. A. Brand, Politics Department, University of Strathclyde.

53   See Richard Rose, *People in Politics*, Chap. 4, 'The Roles of Politicians'.

54   See Richard Chapman, 'Profile of a Profession', in *The Civil Service:* Vol. 3:2, p. 9, for a statistical indication of this.

his minister, he may under *or* over-estimate the partisan significance of various points on which he is meant to give advice. Put conversely, it would be extraordinary if he could understand an institution as complex as a party without any close or continuous involvement in its activities. A civil servant's most marked characteristics are shared by his minister, instead of compensating for the latter's 'generalist' background, remoteness from experts, lack of experience in management work, and constant shifts in his career.[55] This tends to make civil servants and ministers qualified or disqualified for the same sorts of tasks. Given the very considerable advantages that senior civil servants have in terms of experience, departmental expertise, etc., it would be most surprising if often they did not succeed in leading rather than following 'their' minister. There is only one field in which a minister can claim special expertise— awareness of public opinion. Knowing what the public wants or won't stand for is not, however, a guarantee that what is desired will be deemed administratively practicable.

In practical as well as constitutional terms, civil servants cannot be blamed for the actions of partisan ministers, for the latter have the power to alter things—if they will. It is the responsibility of the minister to ensure that civil servants attempting to read the minister's mind will not draw a blank. Even Labour critics of the civil service have admitted this. Dudley Seers writes:[56] 'Civil servants often in fact wish politicians would give them clearer directives. A Permanent Secretary sometimes tries quite genuinely to formulate what his minister would want, if the latter had the time and capacity to decide himself. The majority at least believe that they are doing this. If they do not succeed, the fault may well be the minister's. Few have political views worked out in sufficient depth or expressed clearly enough for a civil servant to be able to interpret them at all precisely'.

The events following the accession of the Labour Party to office in 1964 hardly meet the conditions specified in the paradigm of party government. The one condition met equivocally—the first—is also the least restrictive. It is particularly important to note that the

---

55    These are, of course, five of the six major criticisms of the *Fulton Report*, Vol. 1, para. 15 ff.

56    *op. cit.*, p. 91.

chief obstacles to the creation of party government were not the failings of a few individuals, but rather, institutional, sociological and political conditions that have long been an integral part of British government. In short, although the foregoing evidence comes from only one case, the conclusions reached are likely to be of recurring significance in British government.[57]

Before proceeding further, it is well to consider at least four other possible explanations of the preceding facts. The first is that the presence of Labour politicians in office altered government decisions, because of the added weight given Labour or socialist values in the general climate of opinion, or the special weight it gave the interests of working-class and trade union groups. Such interpretations reject the assumption that government decision-making combines ideological *and* technical considerations. The instances where Labour's 1964 victory most clearly seem to have affected the climate of opinion are libertarian measures, where few or no technical problems are involved, *e.g.* the abolition of capital punishment, reform of homosexuality and abortion laws and legislation involving divorce and censorship practices. It is also noteworthy that these are decisions in which backbenchers, rather than ministers, took the initiative. It is easier to conceive of governments favouring interests, *e.g.*, *at the margin* making economic or social policies bear more heavily upon their implacable opponents than upon their friends. The Wilson Government has not produced a shoal of welfare measures comparable to those enacted by the 1945-51 Labour Government. Moreover, in housing, trade union legislation, and in such symbolic measures as charges for prescriptions on the health service, the Government has frequently increased burdens upon interested supporters. Whether this is explained in terms of necessity or by some elaborate calculus intended to reward floating voters at the expense of unwavering supporters is beside the point. The fall in Labour's vote at the 1970 election suggests that some in the coalition

---

57    Unfortunately, the one study of the Conservatives in Opposition, while generally emphasizing the limitations of Opposition, does not address itself specifically to this problem. See J. D. Hoffman, *The Conservative Party in Opposition, 1945-51* (London: MacGibbon & Kee, 1964). Cf. Anthony King, 'Oppositions: Illusions and Realities', *Spectator*, 14 October 1966.

that put Labour in office did not feel rewarded by what the Wilson Government did.

Another possible objection to the thesis of this article is that the Labour Government has done the only things possible to do, given the exigencies of the contemporary world. Party policies were abandoned because they were 'impossible' to realize. It was, presumably, impossible to do anything other than defend the £ against devaluation up to November, 1967, and then to do anything other than devalue it the week in which the Government did this. To suggest that only one policy is possible at a given time implies some very curious beliefs. It suggests that not only can situational and environmental circumstances veto some courses of action but, much more narrowly, that they can dictate that one and only one course of action *is* possible. A negative inhibition is not equal to a precise, positive compulsion. To argue this is to advocate either a very gross sociological determinism, or a naive and long discredited form of behaviourism which assumes that the character of a stimulus invariably determines the response, without allowing for the intervening influence of individuals or institutions. Moreover, the intentions of parties that are never carried out cannot be dismissed as 'impossible': such policies can only be labelled unpalatable, ill-considered, impracticable, risky, or likely to have undesirable side-effects. Empirically, a policy might be considered impossible only as and when a government tried and failed to carry it through. (Ironically, the adjective 'impossible' could be applied to many things that the Wilson Government in fact attempted, *e.g.*, maintaining the value of the £ at $2.80.) For party policies to be abandoned untested not only leaves ministers open to charges of deceiving the electorate, but also to the most grievous charge of all: self-deception.

Another view is that the policies involved so little that was distinctively Labour because the 'median' opinion registered by the electorate would be adopted by leaders in both parties, acting like two firms in duopolistic competition. Downs has presented the argument for this interpretation with considerable elegance, though no empirical data. Here, it suffices to point out that if this be true—and criticisms can certainly be advanced—then it means that non-median voters will never have a chance to put their preferred party in office by conventional electoral means, and that intense minorities, (or even intense majorities if distributions of opinion be U-shaped), will tend to be disfranchised. The actions of temporarily unrepresented minorities, such as the opponents of coloured immigration, and student and anti-Viet Nam rebels, have shown that these groups are not trivial politically. The existence of measurable differences of opinion on almost every major problem facing the government is massive evidence against the hypothesis that there is a consensus representing what 'everyone' wants.[58] The agreement on fundamentals that Balfour described is properly interpreted as an agreement about regime procedures, and not about decisions at the level of party government.[59]

If parties do not have the function of giving direction to British government, then what are the political consequences of their activity? British parties continue to have a constituent function; they are necessary for the formation and maintenance of a government, *i.e.*, a Cabinet in the Commons, even if they do not give much direction to the government once formed.[60] Parties are also important in mobilizing voters into relatively stable groupings that persist through time, thus reducing the volatility of the electorate and the uncertainties that frequent elections might otherwise induce.

---

58    The variable nature of opinion distributions in the period can most readily be ascertained from the Gallup Poll *Monthly Political Index*, and the monthly reports of National Opinion Polls. For background, cf. Anthony Downs, *An Economic Theory of Democracy* (New York: Harpers, 1957); V. O. Key, *Public Opinion and American Democracy* (New York: Knopf, 1957); and Robert Dahl, *A Preface to Democratic Theory* (Chicago: University Press, 1956).

59    cf. Earl Balfour, 'Introduction', pp. xxiv, of Walter Bagehot, *The English Constitution* (London: World's Classics, 1955 ed.); and G. A. Almond and S. Verba, *The Civic Culture* (Princeton: University Press, 1963), with monthly opinion poll surveys in the period. To note that often differences within a party are greater than those between parties is not to deny that differences on issues exist. Cf. Samuel Brittan, *Left or Right*.

60    For a discussion of this function in the American context, see Theodore J. Lowi, 'Party, Policy and Constitution in America', in W. N. Chambers and W. Dean Burnham, *The American Party Systems* (New York: Oxford, 1967). Lowi, it should be noted, has a different view than argued here about the relative policy significance of American and British parties.

In Britain, groups are mobilized on lines which do not threaten the maintenance of the regime. This need not necessarily be the case, as the experience of Northern Ireland demonstrates. By nominating candidates with readily discernible social characteristics, parties provide expressive representation for societal groups, whether the persons nominated are typical of sections of voters, as in the case of an ethnic ticket or a trade union MP, or whether they typify the idealized norms of governors.

It is also noteworthy that in a number of crises of modern British history, from the Repeal of the Corn Laws up to the threat of invasion in 1940, when hard decisions were required of men in office, parties have failed to provide clearcut choices. Crisis decisions have led to party splits, government coalitions, or both. Since the advent of a Labour Government in 1964, calls for coalition government have been heard and popular support for the major parties appears relatively low. [61] One interpretation of this evidence is that parties serving simply as agencies to distribute public office can be popular with Members of Parliament, but unpopular with a substantial proportion of the electorate who may wish parties to do something more than this.

### III

An evaluation of the importance of party in other countries can put findings from British research in perspective, as well as test their generality. It may be that party government is nowhere possible, or that there is more evidence of party government in Britain than in other countries. The paradigm of party government is intended to fit a very wide range of countries. Because of limitations of space, only two countries—Russia and America—will be considered here. In the Soviet Union one might expect party to be much more important than in Britain. In the United States, the low cohesion and non-ideological character of parties would imply that party government would be less important.

---

61    For a historical discussion, see R. O. Bassett, *The Essentials of Parliamentary Democracy* (London: Macmillan, 1935). For evidence giving some indication of a decline in support for the two major parties, see Richard Rose, 'Voters Show their Scepticism of Politicians', *The Times*, 9 April 1968.

The Soviet Union meets most of the criteria for party government. (1) The Communist Party of the Soviet Union has been dominant in the regime for two generations, without competition from other parties. (2) Party nominees occupy the most important posts in Soviet government. At all levels of government, party activity or membership is likely to be a significant criterion in the appointment of officials. In addition, the scale of party organization and authority *vis-à-vis* thes tate gives party office a significance rarely found in the Western world, except perhaps in the boss system of a few American cities. (3) The number of partisans nominated to office is sufficient to permit party members to participate in making policies at all levels. All experts on Soviet government agree on the substantial size of the *nomenklatura*. Stalin himself reckoned that the party had about 3,000 to 4,000 first-rank leaders as its 'corps of generals'.[62] (4) The partisans given office have skills appropriate to their tasks. The formal training given party cadres and potential leaders stresses both party doctrines and substantive problems of government. Career lines reinforce this training, for individuals tend to be moved back and forth between work which is primarily party-oriented to that which is primarily concerned with using the state apparatus to achieve policy targets laid down by the leaders of the party-state. The emphasis upon meeting performance criteria and selection by a process of survival of the fittest in a very wide field of competition means that aspirants to high political office are likely to have proven skills. In the words of Brzezinski and Huntington, the Soviet party *apparatchik* is both 'a politician and a bureaucrat'.[63]

(5) In the period up to the Soviet Revolution, partisans had ample opportunity to prepare policy intentions. The *raison d'être* of the revolutionary effort was to achieve material changes in society, and not to gain office for its own sake. Even after decades in office, the party's ideological character continues to be evidenced in the extent to which governmental decrees are goal-oriented, and government action is concerned with mobilizing the resources of Russian society

---

62    See John Armstrong, *The Soviet Bureaucratic Elite* (New York, Praeger, 1959), p. 1 ff., and G. Ionescu, *op. cit*, pp. 60 ff.

63    Z. Brzezinski and S. P. Huntington, *Political Power: USA/USSR* (New York: Viking Press, 1964), p. 170; see also, Frederick Barghoorn, *Politics in the USSR* (Boston: Little, Brown, 1966), Chaps. 2-6.

to achieve specified goals—whatever the costs—rather than reconciling differences between competing groups.[64] (6) The extent
to which the policies of the Communist Party have been made to
work is a reminder that many things initially dismissed in the West
as impossible can be done—if a party is determined and willing to
pay almost any costs. In Britain, policies are typically dismissed as
unworkable when resistance to them is reckoned to be substantial, or
administration is thought inconvenient. In the Soviet Union indoctrination and socialization experiences produce a different outlook. In the words of Brzezinski and Huntington, 'Political experience
and engineering background combine to give Soviet leaders a highly
focused, direct, down-to-earth problem-solving approach, without
concern for legal niceties and with little tendency toward compromise solutions'.[65] (7) The high priority given party directives in
the Soviet Union is expressed by the emphasis upon *partiinost*, a
phrase for which there is no comparable term in the Anglo-American
political vocabulary.[66] The concept expresses a demand for ultimate
loyalty to the party and its decrees, a loyalty which old Bolsheviks
were willing to give, even though it meant admitting crimes they had
not committed, and ultimately, their own degradation and death.
(8) The readiness of state officials to put party decrees into practice is
seen not only in the success of certain Soviet policies, but also in the
willingness of officials to persist in policies that meet very great
popular resistance or appear to be unsuccessful, as in the field of
agriculture.

Soviet politics illustrates both the extent to which party government can go and the obstacles to party government inherent in
every political system. Ideologically, the party has succeeded in
legitimizing its claim for authority. Institutionally, it has created a
parallel apparatus in which party surveillance of state activities is

64     For the distinction between reconciliation and mobilization systems,
       one very relevant to British government, see David E. Apter, *The
       Politics of Modernization* (Chicago: University Press, 1965), Chap. 1.
65     *op. cit.*, p. 146.
66     On the concept generally, see Merle Fainsod, *How Russia is Ruled*
       (Cambridge, Massachusetts: Harvard, 1963 edition), p. 116 *et passim*.
       For a classic illustration of the importance of party, even to those who
       have been deprived of its patronage, see Arthur Koestler, *Darkness
       at Noon* (London: Cape, 1940).

very great, and party control of nominees to office is also great. Yet, as Fainsod succinctly notes, 'Monolithic unity is only imperfectly realized'.[67] There remain functional and structural barriers against party domination. As Communist societies become more complex, the state increasingly becomes dependent upon persons with relatively scarce technical skills, and it must give prestige to those with technical competence, whether space physicists, agronomists or military officers. Formally, the claims of party and of professional criteria can be met by ensuring that every member of a technical intelligentsia is also required to hold a party card. Possession of dual organizational affiliations symbolizes the potential for role conflicts within an individual. Professional norms and *partiinost* may sometimes point in the same direction, but, as the literature on Soviet government continually demonstrates, they are frequently sources of conflict. Insofar as conflict is contained within individuals, the resolution of cross-pressures is likely to lead to unstable behaviour; outcomes depend upon the primacy of pressures at a given moment. The necessary differentiation of personnel into many specialized industrial, administrative, and cultural groups, some with regional centres of influence more or less remote from Moscow, gives stability to this conflict, by creating interest groups that can engage in conflicts not unlike those known in Western societies.[68] Ionescu has outlined in very substantial detail the range and character of institutions that can act as 'the plural checks' upon the party government in a Communist society. In Eastern European societies outside Russia, these checks are likely to be relatively strong, because of the opposition of nationalist loyalties to party directives imposed by external powers.[69] One can therefore conclude that the Communist Party of the Soviet Union is not totally in control of government:

---

67    *op. cit.*, p. 387. See parts III and IV for illustrations.
68    See H. Gordon Skilling, 'Interest Groups and Communist Politics', *World Politics*, Vol. XVIII, No. 3 (1966). The theme is pervasive in the literature of Russian politics. See *e.g.*, Barghoorn, *op. cit.*, Chaps. 6-7.
69    *op. cit.*, Part II. See also, Carl Beck, 'Bureaucracy and Political Development in Eastern Europe', in Joseph LaPalombara (ed.), *Bureaucracy and Political Development* (Princeton: University Press, 1963) especially pp. 291 ff.; and Jerzy J. Wiatr, 'One Party Systems' in E. Allardt and Y. Littunen (eds.), *Cleavages, Ideologies and Party Systems* (Helsinki: Academic Bookstore, 1964).

its main achievement has been to demonstrate the extent to which party influence can reach. This extent can vary from period to period and situation to situation; on average, it appears to be much more substantial than the influence of party in Britain.

In the United States, though parties are very differently organized than in Britain, the party—or at least, its Presidential wing—appears stronger in government. (1) On the basis of a party election, a single individual gains an unqualified hold on the Presidency. The existence of separate legislative elections may create conflicts reducing the powers of a President, but this makes the art of party (or bi-partisan) management more important. Legislative majorities cannot be taken for granted, as in Britain. (2) Nominees of the President occupy important posts in government without objection, for the traditions of the long ballot and of patronage, plus the antiquity of party politics in America, create presumptions in favour of partisans in government. (3) The number of jobs to which partisan appointees are named when the Presidency changes hands is about two thousand at a minimum, including substantial numbers of administrative or management posts that in Britain would be held by career civil servants.[70]

(4) The recruitment of men for partisan appointments in America emphasizes skills relevant to a particular job. This, incidentally, is also found in recruitment for the federal civil service.[71] The specialization of political life in America has meant that experts in legislation or electioneering tend to be excluded from appointments to posts in the new Administration, since they lack executive expertise. John F. Kennedy, for example, is said to have felt that the experience of constructing a Cabinet made him feel that he didn't know the 'right people', *i.e.*, the right people for administrative posts.[72] The authoritative study of the recruitment of Assistant Secretaries for government departments—jobs held by civil servants in Britain—emphasizes the importance that recruiters have given to *relevant* skills. A man is not evaluated as a potential minister *in vacuo*, but

---

70      See *e.g.*, David Stanley, *op. cit.*, pp. 131-38; and Herman M. Somers, *op. cit.*, pp. 142 ff.

71      See Richard Pear, 'United States', in F. F. Ridley (ed.), *op. cit.*

72      cf. the first-hand account by Arthur M. Schlesinger, Jr., *A Thousand Days* (London: Deutsch, 1965), Chaps. 5-6.

rather, as a secretary of a particular type of department. This is possible because the field for recruits is vast in size. Moreover, the annoyance of dislocating a career to transfer to Washington at a salary less than normally earned outside government means that claimants for office are not so intense as in Westminster, where the needs of an MP for office are much greater.[73] In America, as in the Soviet Union, a substantial proportion of appointees to government posts are men with both political and bureaucratic experience, the 'in-and-outers' of Neustadt's description; 85 per cent of executives studied by the Brookings group had had at least some prior experience in federal government.[74]

(5) The weakness of central party headquarters in America means that these institutions can play no part in formulating policies in Opposition. By contrast with Britain, however, individual candidates build up research staffs of a size and calibre that British party officials would often envy, and research institutes proliferate inside and outside universities. In seeking nomination for the Presidency, an individual may stress positions on issues or a personal style. In view of the tendency of political scientists to deride party platforms in America, it is noteworthy that Gerald Pomper, in a review of what happened to platform pledges after an election, has found that a substantial proportion were carried into law by the newly elected President.[75] On balance, one might conclude that the degree of concern with policy intentions in America is a reflection of the character of individual Presidential candidates, rather than of the parties *per se* and thus subject to considerable variability. In Congressional voting, party is an important and persisting influence. (6) Once elected, a President has a period of $2\frac{1}{2}$ months in which to appraise, with substantial staff assistance, the workability of his policy intentions, or to formulate intentions for areas of government neglected

---

73  See Mann and Doig, *op. cit.*, Chaps. 2-4.

74  David Stanley, Dean E. Mann and Jameson Doig, *Men Who Govern* (Washington: Brookings, 1967) pp. 41-42; and more discursively, but with important British comparisons, Richard Neustadt, 'White House and Whitehall', *The Public Interest II* (1966), reprinted in *Policy-Making in Britain*.

75  Gerald Pomper, *Elections in America* (New York: Dodd, Mead, 1968), pp. 149 ff.

prior to election. Kennedy, for example, had 26 task forces containing men with considerable prior experience as political executives working for him on a variety of problems between election and inauguration. Schlesinger is undoubtedly right that the documents they produced varied 'in length and quality'.[76] No doubt the same can be said of memoranda that British civil servants give incoming ministers to digest upon entering office. The key point is that the American memoranda are prepared by partisan nominees, and not by career administrators.

(7) The freedom given to the President to select men for office means that men can be chosen on more than one criterion. According to one Brookings study: 'There was generally an implicit assumption that only the candidacies of those who had a policy orientation similar to the President's were ever seriously considered'.[77] Commitment to the President's programme can be maintained by the right of the President to ask for a resignation, or alternatively, by the ease with which persons disenchanted with what they are doing can resign from public life at no loss to their alternative career prospects. In Britain, by contrast, the fulltime professional MP cannot resign from a ministerial post without risking his future and sacrificing his past career. Comparative reviews by both British and American observers have specially emphasized the much greater degree of programme commitment by partisan appointees in Washington than in Westminster. This is understandable, inasmuch as an American minister will expect to succeed within his department; in Britain, success means spiraling into another department.[78] The incentive for the civil service in Washington to take on the coloration of their much more numerous partisan overlords appears as great as it is in Whitehall for a partisan to take on the appearance of a Permanent Under-Secretary. The Fulton Report notes without comment that many American senior civil servants are prepared to move 'at their

---

76     op. cit., p. 145. Cf. Laurin Henry, 'The Transition: the New Adminis-
       tration', in Paul T. David (ed.), The Presidential Election and
       Transition, 1960-61 (Washington: Brookings, 1961).
77     Mann and Doig, op. cit., p. 92.
78     See Richard Neustadt, 'White House and Whitehall'; and, for a
       British view, James Douglas, 'The Nixon Changeover', New Society,
       6 February, 1969.

peril' into Schedule C posts 'which called for public advocacy of controversial programmes'.[79] Pear adds, 'neutrality of commitment to a programme' is 'not acceptable'.[80] The only danger of inculcating programme loyalty and partisan styles of activity in civil servants is that they can then block a Presidential programme conceived as detrimental to their own department. In the one case where obstruction was most anticipated—the transition to a Republican Administration in 1953—examination of results indicates that obstruction did not occur.[81]

Among the three countries reviewed here, Russia is pre-eminent in meeting the conditions of party government. This is a reminder that parties are ethically neutral institutions: the maximization of their power may not be a supreme good, or even a good in itself. What is particularly noteworthy is that the United States meets most of the conditions of party government. The chief limitation is the difficulty in identifying a President's programme with a party programme, because of the conglomerate nature of Presidential measures and the fragmented (but not necessarily un-programmatic) character of American parties. In Britain, long regarded as a stronghold of party, the analysis shows that only one condition—clearcut electoral victory—is fully met. The result is a form of government in which the tensions that characterize party-state relationships in Russia are absent, as is the passionate energy with which programmes are advanced in America.

## IV

When parties fail to provide the expected sense of direction for government policies, this function can be undertaken by other institutions. The extent to which other institutions can properly substitute for parties will vary considerably from society to society, according to its other institutional resources and political problems. In view of the attention lavished upon parties by students of politics, it would be surprising if the failure of parties to direct policies made no difference to the operations of government.

---

79    *The Civil Service* Vol. 1, Appendix C, para. 20
80    *op. cit.*, p. 184.
81    See Herman Somers, *op. cit.*

In most Western countries, parties are intended to be only inter-mittently involved in a lengthy and complex process of making policies. In general terms, parties are crucial in giving force to what W. J. M. Mackenzie has described as 'the active power' model of government, *i.e.*, government as something more than the preserve of a social or technocratic elite, or as something more than the resultant of the demands of ungovernable interests.[82] Parties and partisans are particularly important in early stages of policy for-mation, agitating for solutions to social problems and creating a sense of urgency in the search for solution or amelioration. Once alternative courses of action have been identified, the party in government is expected to choose the most suitable policy, by reference to pre-existing criteria that owe something to the particular principles or sub-cultural values of the party. In one-party states as in competitive party systems, parties have a distinctive role to play in implementing policies. By virtue of election, in a psephological or Calvinist sense, a party can claim that its decisions are binding upon society because they are legitimate. Through propaganda activities, partisans seek to win acceptance for the measures necessary to put a policy into effect. While partisans may little concern themselves with detailed administration, they affect administration by the work they do in selling a policy and in interposing themselves defensively between critics and civil service administrators. The less popular the policy, the greater the significance of partisan efforts to mobilize consent.[83]

In default of parties, a variety of institutions may substitute as sources of policy directives. The most obvious inheritors are civil administrators. The structural advantages of the personnel of the permanent state are many; moreover, collectively and as individuals, they usually continue to operate efficiently from behind a dignified screen of partisan politicians, nominally acting as the government.

---

82   See 'Models of English Politics' in, Richard Rose (ed.), *Studies in British Politics* (London, Macmillan, 2nd ed., 1969).

83   For a discussion in a British context, see Samuel H. Beer 'The British Legislature and the Problem of Mobilizing Consent', in Elke Frank (ed.), *Lawmakers in a Changing World* (Englewood Cliffs, N.J.: Prentice-Hall, 1966); more generally, see J. P. Nettl, *Political Mobilization* (London: Faber, 1967).

Military personnel provide a second alternative. It is noteworthy that studies of military regimes stress the difficulties that exist when a government has 'only' coercive force to rely upon.[84] The literature of group theory, and latterly, of market decisions made by collective partisan mutual adjustment, suggests that there need not be a central co-ordinating agency in politics. Undoubtedly, there is something to the argument that the whole is but the sum of its diverse and fragmented parts, and that many disjunctions exist in government.[85] Yet systems theorists have forcefully reasserted an old idea in new terminology. Because the parts of a political system are interdependent, and government is the most nearly central institution in a network that is only imperfectly disjunctive, it is possible for its partial influence to be felt, directly and indirectly, through many ramifications.

In default of party government, who, if anyone, governs Britain? The most obvious candidates—in the sense of proximity to ministerial authority—are civil servants. Whether or not the departmental minister or the Cabinet has a mind on a subject, civil servants must see that the Queen's government is carried on. The obligation is practical as well as normative. Failure to take some decisions on their own initiative would soon produce widespread social and political disorganization in a mixed economy welfare state. The Fulton Report has given the official seal of approval to what many people have recently been noting: civil servants, especially very senior men, tend to be shaped and driven by the system of which they are a part. They are recruited and trained as specialists in negotiation and conciliation. Their lack of training in a specific discipline as well as lack of identification with the programme of a single department provide practical reinforcements for the conventional norm that civil servants should not care much about the content of the policies which they are supposed to carry through.[86] Apart from the pro-

---

84      cf. S. E. Finer, *The Man on Horseback* (London: Pall Mall, 1962) and Dankwart A. Rustow, *A World of Nations* (Washington: Brookings, 1967) Chap. 6.

85      See particularly, C. E. Lindblom, *The Intelligence of Democracy* (New York: Free Press, 1965).

86      cf. American data in David T. Stanley, *The Higher Civil Service* (Washington: Brookings, 1964) pp. 25, 29 and 33; and arguments in Richard E. Neustadt, 'White House and Whitehall'.

cedural norms generic to the civil service, plus the conventional wisdom that sanctifies much of existing departmental policy, civil servants are, as a collective entity, directionless. An intensive study of principals recruited in 1956 found that the motives leading men into the service were unrelated to programme achievements.[87] The three most frequently named—being at the centre of things, belief in the public service, and work with congenial colleagues—undoubtedly have been important for generations. In short, civil servants require external direction, not only as a 'cover' legitimizing their actions, but also, in practical terms, as cues to which they can then respond. In the absence of a forceful partisan initiative, providing both protection and direction, the simplest course of action is for administrators to seek out the lowest common denominator of opinions among affected interests. The negotiating machinery of Whitehall makes this readily possible, and the social status of civil servants is itself of some use in negotiation with outside interests.[88] Normatively, the argument that a policy is what 'everyone' is most willing to accept is a justification with at least as much *prima facie* appeal as justification by the endorsement of the majority party.

If one had to pick a label for this type of politics, a suitable phrase might be 'government by directionless consensus'.[89] The process of building consensus becomes the end toward which government works. In the language of David Apter, one might regard Britain as engaged in the politics of reconciliation rather than that of mobilization.[90] Keeping harmony between disparate group interests in society is valued much more highly than advancing toward the goals of any particular group or party. This system of government is by no means immobile. The consensus of opinion can change and, as the measures of elite opinion are unreliable and uncertain, it can change

---

87    Richard Chapman, 'Profile of a Profession', in *The Civil Service*, Vol. 3 (2), p. 12.

88    cf. J. P. Nettl, 'Consensus or Elite Domination: the Case of Business', *Political Studies*, Vol. XIII, No. 1 (1965).

89    In previous drafts, the British alternative was described as 'administrative government.' The change in the argument here owes much to rethinking stimulated by forceful comments from David Coombes and Peter Self.

90    *The Politics of Modernization* (Chicago: University Press, 1965).

very rapidly.[91] One might even argue that the characteristic course of policy-making in such a system is the occasional and rapid lurch first to one side, and then to another. It is perhaps specially symbolic that the most important Whitehall policy commitment in the post-war period had the maintenance of an equilibrium as its goal: keeping the value of the £ at $2.80. It involved a long series of abrupt shifts between inflation and deflation, with every change justified as representing the consensus of the best economic opinions.

The consequences of government by directionless consensus are multiple: a number might briefly be suggested here. First, routine administration should be handled well. This has long been true in Britain. Secondly, strategies appropriate to administration by civil servants should be strongly favoured. In Britain, one can note particularly the attention given to conciliating pressure groups, notwithstanding the formal power of the government of the day to impose a pattern of party policy upon recalcitrant groups, at the price of temporary administrative inconvenience. One can also note the extraordinary emphasis upon secrecy and anonymity for civil servants, practices omitted in the Fulton Report's criticism of so much of the conventional wisdom of the civil service. Thirdly, the bias toward routine administration and defence of the *status quo* is likely to make government ill-suited to prompt solutions of major substantive problems and demands to adapt rapidly. In both the First and Second World Wars, ministers and senior administrators were both recruited from outside the conventional pools of eligibility in Whitehall and Westminster.[92] In peacetime, existing governmental departments have been supplemented by efforts to establish new departments too. The history of British economic policy since the First World War illustrates how numerous are efforts to adapt machinery, with substantive and procedural solutions still not yet in sight. In some instances, a solution has been to sub-contract the work of government to agencies outside the conventional departmental structure, to boards of nationalized industries, or, in the case of *ad hoc* problems, government committees or Royal Commissions.

---

91    See e.g., articles by W. J. M. Mackenzie, L. W. Martin and D. N. Chester, reprinted in Richard Rose (ed.), *Policy-Making in Britain*.

92    See F. M. G. Willson, 'The Routes of Entry of New Members of the British Cabinet, 1868-1958', *Political Studies*, Vol. VII, No. 3 (1959).

Finally, one might expect that a system which was ill-suited to adaption would come under criticism in a period in which environmental pressures and popular demands have created a situation in which innovation was required. This last expectation has certainly been realized in Britain today.

The limited role of party government in Britain is particularly striking, inasmuch as parties, in some form or another, became important in British government long before a non-partisan civil service was established. In a comparative discussion of the sequence of party and political developments in Western Europe, Hans Daalder has emphasized the importance of the time at which representative parties appeared, as conditioning later developments in a political system.[93] Following Daalder (who does not apply his analysis intensively to public administration), parties should be important in Britain, because they antedated the modern civil service, just as one would expect parties to be less important, say, in Prussia, where they were formed relatively late. Studies of mid-nineteenth-century Britain, moreover, indicate that partisanship and policy-orientated patronage were significant in politics then.[94] Subsequent changes may well have involved alterations in parties, the civil service and, most importantly, in the complexity of political decisions. It is striking to note that in African societies, where parties have usually antedated a native civil service, the trend is also said to be away from party domination of government. In the judgement of Immanuel Wallerstein, 'If an individual has a key position in both the party and the government hierarchy, he tends to operate in terms of the priorities, exigencies and pressures of the governmental structure'.[95]

---

93    See Hans Daalder, 'Parties, Elites and Political Developments in Western Europe', in J. LaPalombara and M. Weiner (eds.), *Political Parties and Political Development* (Princeton: University Press, 1966).

94    cf. Henry Parris, 'The Origins of the Permanent Civil Service, 1780-1830', *Public Administration*, Vol. XXXVI, No. 2 (1968); and G. Kitson Clark, 'Statesmen in Disguise', *The Historical Journal*, Vol. II, No. 1 (1959).

95    'The Decline of the Party in Single-Party African States', in J. LaPalombara and M. Weiner (eds.), *op. cit.*, p. 214. See also the similar analysis by Aristide Zolberg, *Creating Political Order* (Chicago: Rand McNally, 1966).

The difficulty that British civil servants have in substituting for parties might be viewed as a consequence of peculiar local circumstances. Where administrators are specialists, trained and committed to particular fields of activity, their active powers might be much greater than in Britain. This would especially seem likely in Continental countries where theories of the state anticipate that governments will intervene much more in society than is the case here. France is usually cited as the Western nation where administrators have best substituted for party leaders, because of positive characteristics of the administrators as well as because of party weaknesses. Conclusions from a careful review of the civil service in the Fourth and Fifth Republics by Alfred Diamant are therefore particularly significant and worth citing at length:[96] 'The French experience would indicate that, in fact, during periods of political indecision the *grands corps* do not really govern the country, they simply continue routine operations, maintain the status quo and protect their own interests. It would seem, particularly from the experience of the Fourth Republic, that under then prevailing conditions the administration could carry on from day to day, but it could not carry through radical innovations. There was no lack of ideas, plans, proposals, but in the absence of a determined political will these plans remained dormant'.

Administrators of the Commission of the European Communities are another group frequently credited with independent powers of political initiative. Here too one finds, according to a recent study by David L. Coombes, that civil servants are no substitutes for partisan type ministers. Coombes concludes that lacking both the impetus and the defensive assurance that comes from politicians taking initiatives and providing normative justification for policies, the so-called Eurocrats increasingly emphasize details of policies and mediation between interests groups, *i.e.* maintaining a consensus.[97]

---

96  'Tradition and Innovation in French Administration', *Comparative Political Studies*, Vol. I, No. 2 (1968), p. 255; Michel Crozier's *The Bureaucratic Phenomenon* (Chicago: University Press, 1964 ed.) provides additional arguments that these things are not always well ordered in France.

97  See David L. Coombes, 'The Bureaucracy as Political Leader' (Mimeograph paper, Political Studies Association, York, 1969).

It would be premature to offer a detailed explanation of the factors that account for variations in the importance of party government from political system to political system. A considerable amount of research is still necessary to determine how much and what kinds of variations occur among Western nations and in non-Western nations. It is possible to suggest hypotheses that might explain at least part of the variations observed above. (The initial number corresponds to the reference in the model outlined above.)

2.1 The more managerial positions that partisan nominees hold, the greater the tendency toward party government.
3.1 The more numerous the jobs open to partisan nominees, the greater the tendency toward party government.
4.1 The more prior experience partisan nominees have in administrative as well as political work, the greater the tendency toward party government.
4.2 The less restrictive the criteria of eligibility for office, the greater the tendency toward party government.
5.1 The more radical the substantive ideology of a party, the greater the tendency toward party government.
6.1 The more that partisans are familiar with the machinery of executive government, the greater the tendency toward 'workable' policies for party government.
7.1 The greater the involvement of partisan nominees in party life, the greater the tendency toward party government.
8.1 The more 'ends' oriented the party in office is, the greater the tendency toward party government.

The hypotheses suggested here are *not* necessarily prescriptive. Hypothesis 5.1 implies that party government has the greatest attraction for extreme and probably small groups. Given the entrenched strength of administrators, however, it is unlikely that many countries will suffer from 'too much' party government, however this is defined. The hypotheses, like the comparative analysis, demonstrate that it is possible to increase the degree of party government in a society—if politicians have the desire and will to do so.

George Steiner

# Israel: A View from Without

Only those closest to Peter Nettl, and perhaps not even they, are in a position
to give a full account of his involvement with Jewish and Israeli concerns.
One day the story may be told. In the meanwhile, it suffices to say that Peter
Nettl was profoundly Jewish in his culture, humour, commitments and habits
of thought. His great intelligence and the acute moral discriminations that
characterize his work as historian and sociologist, are everywhere marked by
the genius of the Diaspora. We talked very often of Israel and of the uneasy
relations between Zionism and other aspects of the Judaic tradition. He saw
an early draft of the following essay, which I delivered as a lecture at the
Weizmann Institute in July 1968. Some of it struck him as unrealistic. Other
points he agreed with. Without Peter, it has become even a little more difficult
to think, to feel clearly about these complex issues.

One possible definition of a Jew is to say that he is a man who,
when he speaks of his condition, will in some measure speak for all
other Jews but in great measure for none. When a Jew speaks to
other Jews there will be immediacies of recognition, a quickness of
understanding that lies deeper than speech. But what he says will
also rouse in every other Jew a sense of singular being. Each listener
will experience, like a subtle ancient hurt, the conviction: 'this man
assuredly speaks to me, and indeed he speaks of me, but not for me'.
Whoever has not understood this will flinch—as each of us has on
occasion—from the bitterness, from the salt-sharp intimacy of
Jewish controversy, from the ability of Jews to hurt one another in
debate. To speak to Jews on Jewish affairs is to court offense and
rebuke; it is, almost inevitably, to provoke misunderstanding. But
not to do so is to betray our common need.

My own disqualifications go beyond the general case. They are
three-fold. I was not in Israel in 1948 when Israel became again
Israel, at high cost and by dint of fierce courage and intelligence. I
was not there in June of 1967 when Israel faced annihilation and

entirely alone won a military—though indeed it was, at the source, even more a social and psychological—victory that has already passed into legend. What is gravest: I am not in Israel now. Not as someone who has come to Israel with his wife and two young children to live, to take root, to do what work would be most fruitful toward the survival of this community. I am here as a guest, with the irresponsibility of a guest—although to be a Jew visiting Israel is to be a guest in a very special way. Why do I not emigrate, while fully recognizing the validity of the question, its 'right of pressure' on all Jews who could freely come and choose not to? The answer ought, of course, to be a private one, of no interest or concern to anyone outside my family or close personal friends. Yet in the nature of the case it cannot be, not wholly. Any Jew who merely visits Israel, any Jew who speaks of Jewish problems while visiting, is in a deep sense accountable to his hosts. Unavoidably my reasons, private, muddled, perhaps ill-conceived as they are, will be a part of anything I say in this 'Dialogue'. In some degree they will be misconstrued as I myself, perhaps, misconstrue them. But we are not, I think a people of dialogue. We overhear each others' millennial monologues, understanding and not understanding but glorying in the fact that our tongues are still alive and able to interrupt.

Looking back on the development of one's thoughts and feelings about Israel, on the alternance of exultancy and stress which the existence of Israel has brought and brings now to every Jew in the Diaspora I am struck by an impression of naiveté. Did anyone of us really believe that matters would go smoothly, that Jewry would find a lasting haven, that a significant part of the Jewish people would pass out of destiny into mere history (history being the condition of the ordinary nation-state)? If we did believe so, we were being foolish; and we are foolish still if we consider the precarious material position of Israel or the dilemmas of mind and conscience its existence poses as an accident or unfairness. Surely it is the opposite that would have been a paradox; the notion that Jewry could have returned to Israel, that it could have become a nation among nations without taxing the mind with a radical mystery of injustice, without being, as has been so much of the core of Jewish history, a 'scandal'.

Let me try and explain what I mean. The links between nineteenth-century Jewry and the territory of Palestine were a radiant fiction, not a legal or political reality. Were the ethnic groups of the earth to seek returns to their locale of origin—so far as such a locale can be determined, so far as genetic continuity has any demonstrable meaning—the map would be chaos. Other minorities had been harried, splintered, driven over frontiers, even annihilated. Yet only Zionism demanded as a right this marvellous leap against time, this fantastic translation of a dream into daylight. All this is obvious and a platitude. But one worth remembering accurately and worth repeating to oneself in the hour of fear and exasperation.

The existence of Israel is not founded on logic; it has no ordinary legitimacy; there is neither in its establishment nor present scope any evident justice—though there may be an utter need and wondrous fulfilment. There are men, women and children in refugee camps and shanty towns not very far from here whose families have, for documented generations, inhabited Jerusalem. There are Israelis who themselves grew up in Vilna or Hamburg or Manchester. In what way is this their lawful home? How are those who have been driven out not to nurse hatred? How can they be men and not seek to return to the places of their birth, neglected, economically or socially wasted as these may have been? Each time we ask such questions something, as it were, bleeds in our mouths. But we must ask. We cannot accept the ready answers of legalistic myth or political necessity—or if we must accept them let it never be with ease of heart. Very possibly this is our job in the Diaspora; to insist that if there is, if there must be, for many Jews and, it may well be, for all our children a new homeland here in Israel, there is also an ancient homeland especially entrusted to us, that of truth. And to say, as if it was a secular prayer, that justice matters most, is most intimately our concern, where it is least comfortable, where it is a thorn to the skin.

The foundation of the State of Israel, the brilliant economic achievements of that State, its military triumph a year ago, have added to the stature of every individual Jew wherever he may live. But with every year it becomes plainer that the existence of Israel also poses exacting problems to all Jews elsewhere, that their own identity and context are altering. Even as no Jew has failed to benefit, be it only in the inward of his pride, from the survival of

Israel, so there is none whom the mystery and moral or philosophic 'scandal' of that survival leaves untouched. The very term Diaspora is one of relation, between this piece of earth and the sum of our other habitations. Each time this parcel of harsh, beautiful ground changes, each time it is threatened or exultant, the Diaspora changes with it. It is some aspects of that change that I want to discuss.

Post exilic Jews have always been suspect to their hosts. The Kafkaesque mechanism is all too familiar: the Jew has been excluded and then accused of being exclusive, of refusing assimilation. Through this sinister and mendacious dialectic the Jew was made and kept a stranger among others; but he was also made, in rather complex ways, a 'stranger' to himself—especially if he was not or no longer fully a religious, a practising member of his community. It is precisely in a limbo of identity, in an extra-territorial zone between gentile acceptance and the 'transcendental separateness' of religious faith and practice, that there occurs the explosion, the quantum jump of Jewish artistic, scientific and philosophical genius that has marked western civilisation from Spinoza to Noam Chomsky. Concomitant with the exclusion of the Jew, with his reduction to the ghetto, the venom of anti-semitism spread. In all its recurrent manifestations, the pogrom, be it medieval-apocalyptic or petit-bourgeois-racist, represents a spasm against 'alienness', an attempt to extirpate from physical neighbourhood a *Fremdkörper*, a somewhat mysterious foreign body suspected of occult malignities. By his very presence, abject and scorned as that presence was, the Jew seemed to infirm the time scale, ritual conventions and consensus-mythologies of the gentile body politic. In fourteenth-century France he did so by poisoning wells (itself a fiercely suggestive image of infection); in late nineteenth-century France he did so by 'committing treason'. This link between Jewishness and alleged treason is an ugly but important matter.

With the development of modern nationalism treason became the arch-sin; losing nothing of its almost occult horror, military or political treason, usually in the guise of espionage, took on in a secular form the symbolic values of the crime of Judas. It may well be that the ready proximity of Jewishness and treason in the gentile mind is rooted, ultimately, in the Iscariot-myth. Being a late, marginally placed member of the gentile nation-state, being a person whose stake in that nation-state is somehow artificial and technical rather than hereditary, the Jew is a natural courier, intelligencer, sapper for the enemy. His genius at monetary exchange, his notorious facility in foreign tongues, his demonstrable kinship with Jews across the frontier—all these make him 'the natural traitor'. From Dreyfus to the Rosenbergs, the intimation or explicit indictment has always linked the Jew and the traitor. And there is no use in obscuring the facts. Far more Jews have been totally innocent of any breath of treason than have been guilty; far more have been innocently hounded to disgrace than have ever been justly convicted. Nevertheless, the incidence of Jewish men and women in modern espionage, particularly scientific, is higher than random. Jews can understand why this should be so, what condescensions and oppressions can make a man seek vengeance on his hosts; each of us in the Diaspora knows that we are guests on sufferance and that any sense of condition can cut a man loose from any sense of community. But in some measure the facts do exist: they affirm that the relationship of the Jew to his nationhood is a vulnerable one.

This vulnerability has been tremendously heightened by the coming into being of Israel. Since 1948 the Jew in the Diaspora appears to have what his gentile neighbours have always accused him of having, a 'home elsewhere', a focus of loyalties far removed geographically, spiritually, at times politically, from that of the nation whose passport he carries and whose flag he may, with fervour, salute. The schizophrenic nature of a Jew's loyalties comes to the surface whenever Israel is in crisis. He may have lived in Paris, New York or Alexandria for generations; let Israel be menaced or triumphant and he will be transmuted, like a strayed animal scenting the herd. Anyone who saw New York during the June war will carry with him the impression of a city metamorphosed, of a vast American community whose entire intellectual and emotional focus lay thousands of miles away, whose very sense of continued life seemed concentrated on a situation in which the United States has, at best, a marginal and ambivalent stake. But not only New York; exactly the same impression of instantaneous 'inner displacement' could be had in Stepney, among the the Jews of Marseilles or in Prague. For six days their world had become Jerusalem and Gaza, Sinai and Hebron.

The practical and psychological consequences of this division of loyalties, of the fact that the Jew wherever he may make his home, however little else he knows of practices of Judaism, feels the presence of Israel in his marrow, are serious. That risible and uncomely phenomenon, Jewish anti-Zionism, particularly in its American guise, or Jewish pro-Nasserism as shown by the 'Jewish loft' in England, stems directly from a bitter fear of ambiguity. Like the Jewish war veterans who hastened to assure Hitler of their complete loyalty when he became Chancellor in 1933, the anti-Israel Jew seeks desperately to prove to his gentile hosts, but even more desperately to himself, that he is a normal, loyal citizen; that he is merely a neighbour among gentile neighbours to whom the fate of Israel is a matter of indifference, of lofty displeasure. But the bewildered compulsion is understandable. How is a Jew in the *galut* to scour himself clean of the suspicion that he is a traitor, a parasite or gipsy who will strike no roots? How, save by berating Israel, can he satisfy those who say that that is where he belongs, that his heart and purse are there already? And who continue to say so however many sons he loses at Verdun, however many medals he brings back from Khe-San? In eastern Europe and Russia the old suspicions and the persecutions they engender are again rife. No Jew from East Berlin to Birobijan who did not walk a touch more erect in June 1967, in whom the ex-Gestapo men of Pankow or the police of Leningrad did not see the maddening reflection of a distant glory. When the Russian bureaucrat says that no Jew will ever think of Russia as his true home, when the Polish politbureau, in terms nauseatingly reminiscent of those used by the Nazis, denounces Polish Jews as 'inevitable subversives' and 'foreigners in our midst', how is the Jew to answer?

One answer is straightforward: the Jew says to his seeming fellow-citizen, 'You are right. You have never wanted me but I have never wanted you. I have dwelt among you as in a station waiting-room. I belong in Israel. Let me go in peace. If you prevent me by force, may my "treasons" be on your stupid, accursed head'.

There is another answer but it is, very obviously, an entirely personal one.

Nationalism and tribalism—its atavistic spectre—are the nightmare of our age. In their hollow name human beings have visited, and are visiting, lunatic ruin on one another. In the wake of a coloured piece of cloth nailed to a stick, over the matter of fifty miles of stony ground, men otherwise rational are prepared to perpetrate any measure of violence. The reasons for this lunatic parochialism, for this recrudescence of tribal savageries which the eighteenth century had in significant measure overcome, are difficult to make out. The passionate desire of men to be only with their own kind even where such localism is economically suicidal (in Belgium, in the Alto Adige, in Nigeria) may embody a desperate reaction to the splintered, intellectually fluid character of modern technological civilization. Unable to cope with the world we cling to our village.

But whatever the deep causes the consequences are getting plainer and plainer: armed with modern weapons of mass destruction and manipulated by the 'neo-primitivism' of electronic hysteria, national-ism may bring on final wars, wars with no calculable aftermath. This crisis, this 'barbarism of blind loyalties' must lead one to re-think this whole matter of 'belonging' and 'treason'. There may be a sense in which the act of treason is a premature but prophetic image of sanity. It may well be that we shall not survive unless a number of men and women—few at first, more by force of example—free themselves from the myths of nationalism and proclaim that whereas trees do indeed have roots, human beings have legs with which to move freely. It may be that our only way out of the present tunnel of mutual hatreds is to assert that passports are bi-lateral contracts covering certain obligations and safeguards, not mystical instruments binding a man to some legacy of collective clichés. Perhaps the darkest commission of treason is to yield one's in-telligence, one's moral uncertainties, one's instincts into the hands of the nation-state. In political treason, where it is not merely a matter of financial corruption or pathological rancour, there is an element, though admittedly a parodistic element, of radical Socratic irony. The *polis* has claims on our allegiance only so long as its ideals and actions are, in broad measure, consonant with our self-respect, with our sense of potential humanity. Where they are not, we do best to leave and, quite conceivably, to tear open something of the spiked gates as we pass through. Or to put it more modestly: it may be that the right course is for all of us to learn that we are guests of each other as we are demonstrably, guests in the bio-chemical and inorganic totality of creation. And if it be true that to be a guest is a marginal condition under pressure of psychological and social stress, it is no less true that such a condition can be richly creative.

Far from resenting his guest-status in the gentile communities or, more accurately, armed camps of Diaspora, the Jew ought to welcome it. What he may have inherited of nomadic centuries, the remarkable antennae he has grown for linguistic adaptations, his skills as an *agent de change*—of currencies, of styles, of life, of ideas— his fascinating ability to live in time where others tend to live in concrete space, these equip the Jew to exist and flourish, as it were, 'in transit'. To those who accuse us of harbouring divided loyalties, we answer that our loyalties are as divided as are the possibilities of right action, that they cannot be fixed because they are at all times subject to moral re-examination. To those who denounce us because we have never fully accepted the hopes or purposes of the nation-state in which we are citizens, we say that no nation-state so far established by men has produced hopes or purposes fully acceptable. When mocked for imperfection of native speech, for our failure to achieve some final, somnambular at-homeness in the idiom of our community, we plead guilty, and say that with Heine and Kafka we seek to look at reality not through the slit of one language but through the windows of several. To those who vaunt their ancestral graves, we confess that it is not the most ignoble of fortunes to die in exile, that Marx lies in Highgate and Freud in Golders Green and that Einstein's ashes were scattered off New Jersey. Do you have a homeland such as we do, a *patrimoine*, an antique acre of *Blut und Boden*? No, you have never allowed me that. So I have learnt to feel at home wherever I can do my job and count the stars. Because you would not let me take root in your sense, in old earth, I have had to develop unusual powers of abstraction; I have been compelled to find moorings in the symbolic rather than the concrete. Hence my mastery of the esperantos of our civilization, of those modes of discourse that are truly universal: music, mathematics, the symbolic languages of logic and the exact sciences. Where you have sought to exclude me from your jargon I have invented new grammars: the transcendental numbers of Cantor, the twelve-tone rows of Schoenberg, the analytics of Wittgenstein. Yes, I am a wanderer, a *Luftmensch*: 'unto the elements be free'. But I have made of my harrying, and of the ironies, stress, sophistication such harrying provokes in the Jewish sensibility, a creative impulse so strong that it has recast much of the politics, art and intellectual constructs of the age. I am whatever the modesty of my personal station, a fellow-citizen of Trotsky and of Freud; a *Landsmann* of Kafka and Roman Jakobson; I need the same visa as Lévi-Strauss.

The condition of the Jew in the Diaspora predisposes him toward internationalism, towards a refusal of patriotic idols to whom he has never, in fact, been granted complete access. But there is a far more ancient motive for Jews, or a certain number among them, to lead the marginal, unstable life of a guest.

The question of the historical sources of nationalism and racism is a vexed one. Clearly, the Attic view of the 'barbarians' was not gracious and the Chinese sense of superior destiny, of the unique stature of the Middle Kingdom among lesser and tainted breeds, does go back thousands of years. Nevertheless, Judaism played its part. Whatever modern apologists may argue, the thrust of ethnic arrogance, the dramatic concept of a nation chosen among all others for revelation and a unique kinship with the Deity, the notion of history as singular, destined unfolding—these are unmistakable in the Books of Moses, in *Joshua* and in *Judges*. As God proclaims in *Exodus* 23, the Amorites, Hittites and Canaanites shall be broken before Israel and their rites utterly overthrown; the marvels promised in *Exodus* 34 are such 'as have not been done in all the earth, nor in any nation'. Time and again the promise and precept ring like a hammer: 'But ye shall destroy their altars, break their images, and cut down their groves'. There is a fearful prescience in *Deuteronomy* 12: 'When the Lord thy God shall cut off the nations from before thee, whither thou goest to possess them, and thou succeedest them, and dwellest in their land. . . .' And can we, in that disturbing ninth chapter of *Joshua*, fault the Gibeonites when they seek to justify their vain resistance? 'Because it was certainly told thy servants, how that the Lord thy God commanded his servant Moses to give you all the land, and to destroy all the inhabitants of the land from before you, therefore were we sore afraid of our lives because of you'. Antique texts, to be sure, formulaic as are the blood-lists and triumphal dicta of Assur-ba-Nipal. Texts that have scarcely any bearing on the ethics of Judaism and the subsequent fate of

M

the Jewish people. But they exist nevertheless and their influence
has been great. Wherever a nation has thought itself exalted over
others by fiat of God or history, whenever conquest or enslave-
ment have been sugared over with the rhetoric of pre-eminent
destiny, the phrases of the Old Testament have rung out. We hear
them today in the mouth of *apartheid*. Nor are these images of a
chosen people, of a seed covenanted as no other, wholly, irrelevant to
the hatred of the Nazi for the Jew. A parody of Mosaic and Davidic
terms is visible in the nauseating Nazi doctrines, in their fictions of
Aryan purity, in their vision of promised lands from which inferior
tribes were to be scoured or sent forth as 'hewers of wood and
drawers of water . . . in the place which he should choose'. Worse
than a parody; a satanic travesty, yet related if not to what Judaism
itself has made of these Biblical passages, then assuredly to what
others have made of them.

Thus it may be that the Jew bears some part of the historical
responsibility for the crime against man that is tribalism, chauvinism,
the myth of racial election. That crime almost annihilated the Jewish
people in this century, coming like a boomerang out of a travesty of
the remote Judaic past. Now it may be our task to undo, by the mere,
banal example of our uprooted personal lives, something of the
lunacy. To be wanderers and scattered among nations may, for some
of us, be a moral necessity.

How does such a stance (what I would like to call 'the ideal of
Socratic or ironic subversion') accord with the claims and needs of the
State of Israel? Obviously, the relation is not an easy one. The
coincidence between certain aspects of Zionism and the upsurge of
European nationalism, between the very idiom of Herzel's *Judenstaat*
and the Bismarckian programme, is evident and perfectly natural.
Within the Jewish sensibility at the turn of the century both a
nationalist and internationalist current were powerfully at work:
say Herzel against Trotsky or Rosa Luxemburg. Since 1948 Israel
has survived through a constant miracle of cohesion, of compacted
national consciousness. In Israel extreme patriotism (dare one say,
chauvinism?) has not been a vanity, but an indispensable mechanism of continued national existence. No nation today, unless it be

North Vietnam, is more tightly knit, more conscious of the enemy outside the walls. *Which is as it must be.* Yet there is here a divergence, if not an outright clash, of ideals. The case is, I think, comparable to that of the rigorously orthodox Jew to whom the State of Israel presents the image of a false or premature Messianic fulfilment; the Jerusalem of his parables is built in time rather than in bricks and space. Internationalism too has its Messianic strain. If one considers what the Jewish genius achieved in the European Diaspora, what it is achieving in America now; if one deeply believes that the nation-state is an obsolescent model for economic, political and moral association—then the State of Israel looks like a solution which is, in part at least, irrelevant or even inimical to the criteria, to the obligations of Judaic humanism. What have the kindred of Spinoza and Heine to do with flags or oaths of national fidelity?

But even as one asks such a question, the answer or, rather, counter-questions come through with urgent plainness. Where else should the hounded remnants of European, East European and Middle Eastern Jewry have gone? Where but in Israel will my children find refuge when next the pogroms start in, say, Rabat or Argentina or, perhaps, Mississippi? I speak of internationalism, of being a guest in diverse languages and cultures. For how many outside an intellectual or artistic *métier* is such a formula anything but a fantasy? And could my self-respect, my sense of spiritual identity really endure if the State of Israel was to be destroyed? To which, quite simply, the answer is, No.

Here again, as in the matter of Israel's taking over of Palestine, there is no way out of the 'scandal', of the simultaneous pressures of contrasting hopes, of conflicting yet essential forms of morality. For myself I see no way except the awkward if bracing stance of the equilibrist. Though 'stance' is wrong; one must keep moving. In other words: someone like myself must do what he can, financially, by means of information and argument abroad, to support the State of Israel—knowing full well how *little* he contributes so long as he does not settle in Israel with his children. But at the same time he must work toward the evolution of political concepts, of habits of personal and social feeling, which will subvert tribalism and the nationalist mystique. He must simultaneously labour for Israel and against it—or, more exactly, against all those forms of power relation and nationalist sentiment which compel Israel to be an armed state, just another nation among nations. For I am arrogant and dreamer enough to believe that we Jews were meant for something even more unusual.

To recapitulate: for those Jews in the Diaspora (the very great majority, the great bulk of the American community) who have sought full acceptance in the gentile nation-state, the existence and dramatic fortunes of Israel pose a more or less acute problem. Israel quickens in the gentile milieu and in the Jew himself the suspicion of divided loyalties. In the United States or Great Britain this problem has, until now, been kept at a level of intellectual debate and occasional emotional *malaise*. In Eastern Europe, the Soviet Union and the Arab countries it crowds on Jews with ugly menace. For those Jews (obviously few) who feel that the just condition of Jewry is one of creative exile, of provocation through radical irony and a refusal to 'belong', the State of Israel poses a subtler but no less penetrating problem. To the wanderer it offers the temptation of a natural goal; to the pessimist who believes, as I do, that no gentile nation-state will ever fully accept its Jews or keep its bargains of safeguard with them in times of political or economic crisis, Israel offers the deep, emotionally-charged temptation of returning to one's own. Both of these temptations ought to be resisted, at least by a few, at least for a while longer, because there are in Judaism other perceptions, other politics outside this *polis*.

Compared to these problems that of the 'Levantinization of Israel and its effects upon Western Jewry' as frequently posed does seem to me a special case, if it is a case at all. Montesquieu teaches us that a society necessarily mirrors the terrain it exploits, the landscape it moves in, the graphs of temperature, rainfall and wind. The white light in Rehovoth, the ink-pools of shadow, are like those in Amman or Cairo or Tunis; the air in Tel Aviv is not that of Hampstead, the Bronx or Mödling. What does it mean to speak of Israel 'taking its place in the Middle East?' It is in the Middle East, ineluctably. The impress of this geographical-climatic fact on its manners of dress, dietary habits, uses of leisure are already patent. How could it be otherwise? Evidently something deeper, more internal is meant by 'Levantinization'. But it is not altogether clear what the term covers. The notion of the *Levant* has a distinctly nineteenth-century

flavour. Implicit in its vague contours is the image of a faintly
sinister, faintly comical Ottoman empire. The 'wily Levantine',
grease in his hair and rings on his hashish-stained fingers, stems from
the powerful mythology of Victorian condescension as it extends
from Gilbert and Sullivan to Kipling and John Buchan. Somewhat
earlier, in the late eighteenth century, the name had acquired an
anti-semitic aura, dimly coloured by feelings against Venice and the
northern European fear of sharp commercial, fiscal practices in the
eastern Mediterranean. In short it is neither comely nor pertinent.

Something else is meant: a re-orientation (no apologies for the
pun) of Israel, a gradual change in the habits of emotion, social
flavour and spiritual cast of Israeli life. Culpably indistinct as the
notion is 'Levantinization' points to the possibility or, indeed, likelihood that a Jewish community whose character has until now been
strikingly western will become a Middle Eastern society. Such an
evolution—some would say regression—could create considerable
psychological and strategic vexations, making it difficult for the
American Jewish community to give active, personally committed
support to the new nation. That support has, in vital measure, sprung
from the readiness with which an American Jew can identify and
empathize with his Israeli counterpart. However distant geographically, here is a fellow-westerner, an individual whose parentage
is often the same as that of his American underwriter and whose
codes of conduct and political argument have remained squarely
in the western or Anglo-American framework. Would this identification, with all its implications of financial and diplomatic backing,
weaken if Israel was to become an essentially Middle Eastern, or to
put it more exactly, semitic society? Would a more or less orientalized
Israel come to seem as remote, as abstractly alien to the New York
or Chicago Jew as the Jewish communities of, say, Baghdad or
Tunis seem to him today?

Surely there are too many unknowns for the question even to be
put intelligibly. Which is more rapid and penetrating, the drift of
Israel toward regional modes of existence or the almost universal
advance (if that be the right word) of underdeveloped and ex-
colonial societies toward a standardized consumer-technocracy? In
other words, could Israel become anything like its Arab neighbours
before the latter become, admittedly in a shoddy variant, like all

other emergent nations, a kind of pseudo-technology? The forces of uniformity, of centripetal *mimesis* are stronger today than any genuine cultural autonomy. Whether we will or not much of the world, and particularly of the world that is trying to catch up on history, will come to look like Detroit or Birmingham or Yokohama. The very concept of 'Levantinization' may be a piece of nostalgic myth. Moreover, what of Russian Jewry, of that great community of silence and waiting? In its intellectual and moral potential, in its continued exposure to persecution and the threat of dissolution, a number of Jewish thinkers see embodied the very mystery of Judaism, its messianic unknown. What if that community or some significant fraction of it was allowed to settle in Israel? The problem —and how providential a problem it would be!—would then seem not one of 'Levantinization' but of 'Slavicization'.

But let us allow the hypothesis that the State of Israel will 'go Middle Eastern'. Let us assume that the grandchildren of those who came from Europe will be completely housed in the deeply semitic, orientalizing genius of Hebrew, that they will share fewer and fewer memories, fewer and fewer intellectual reflexes with their Jewish guests from America, that we will have less of a 'Dialogue' and more of an exercise in translation. Would this necessarily be a bad thing?

At present it is difficult to imagine how Israel could survive without massive material aid from American Jewry, but can this dependence continue for ever? Ought it? Again, I allude to platitudes when I recall the tensions that have developed between Israel and the World Zionist movement, between Israel's natural insistence on running its own affairs and devising its own foreign policy, and the hopes, no less natural, of those who have so long and generously supported it from abroad that their wishes be reckoned with. Nothing emerged more graphically from the Six-Day War than Israel's realization that today a sovereign power can count only on its enemies, never on its friends. Sooner or later the State of Israel— precisely because it has opted for the formula of the post-Bismarckian, post-Wilsonian nation-state—will have to be autonomous financially and psychologically as it already is politically and militarily. Israel will only have 'taken its place in the Middle East' when American Jews will feel as familiar and unfamiliar here as American Catholics do when they visit Rome (the analogy is overstated because it leaves out racial affinity but is, I think, roughly indicative).

Nor should we ever overlook the degree to which Israel's links with decaying English colonialism until 1948 and with American expansionism since has complicated its moral and strategic position. That inheritance, so tangibly dramatized by American financial aid, has made plausible the Arab contention that Zionism is a veiled form of neo-colonialism, that Israel is a characteristic western, caucasian enclave in the underdeveloped *tertium mundum*. To many Arabs and western radicals, Israel's presence has no more validity than the presence of the United States in the Caribbean or South-East Asia. In both instances technological superiority, a superiority based on the availability of outside capital, has been made an excuse for social and territorial usurpation. Whatever the inferiority complexes, the *mauvaise foi*, the rancour over charities received at work in this proposition, the proposition itself is true: the United States of America is today, and may be for some time to come, the most resented, the most widely feared of world powers. On realities or fictions of American life much of underprivileged and evolving humanity right now focuses its hatreds, its will, often ludicrously unrealistic, to be independent. Inevitably, Israel is tarred with something of the same brush (though it has succeeded brilliantly in dissociating its own image from that of ex- and neo-colonialism in certain parts of Africa). It should also be kept in mind that a 'distancing' between Israel and American Jewry may be a reciprocal dynamism. If we anticipate 'Levantinization' here we ought at the same time to anticipate the possibility of deepening isolationism in America, of an isolationism born of disillusions in a world complex, ungrateful and intractable to what Americans regard as common sense or altruism. Numerous signs of such a 'new isolationism' are already notable. As the American Jewish community continues to assimilate—at least in its political and psychological attitudes—it will, by natural processes, become more remote from Israel's immediate interests and, most strikingly, from those traditions of socialism which are so proud a part of the history of Zionism and of the life of Israel from Aharon David Gordon to Ben-Gurion. Analyses of voting patterns among American middle-class Jews or of the ambivalent posture of American Jewry toward Vietnam, suggest that the radical, utopian-socialist strain in modern Judaism will hardly find its natural base in the United States of the 1970s and 1980s.

To summarize: any 'distancing' between Israel and the Jews of Diaspora, particularly the Jews of America, whether or not that distancing is caused by 'Levantinization', will have serious consequences. It will affect both parties: the position of the Jew in the *galut* will become more artificial and more vulnerable to assimilation. The Israeli will become more parochial, more estranged from the great middle-period of his own past (that estrangement can already be felt among younger Israelis today). But there will also be favourable consequences, especially in regard to Israel's independence from less acceptable elements of American life and foreign policy. Detailed predictions would be foolish, but one central fact is obvious: no solution of the Israel-Arab conflict is even conceivable outside a Middle Eastern context. Here is Israel; here it must live. And by 'context' I mean a totality of psychological commitments, an internal recognition on both sides, Arab and Israeli, that for good or bad Israel is here to stay. Such commitments are enormously difficult to formulate and realise (the United Kingdom's bewildered ambiguity over any genuine entrance into Europe is a parallel case). If 'Levantinization' be a step toward Israel's acceptance of itself as a Middle Eastern community, let us have more of it! Only if one's own identity is explicit can one seek acceptance by others.

Can a guest, an 'outsider' however concerned, say more? The problem of Israel's relations with the Arabs, internally and externally, underlies every word spoken in this conference. It is the drastic simplifier as well as the unknown in every equation.

The Six-Day War has *de facto* reunited the two halves of Palestine; here as in the crises of 1921, 1929, 1936 and 1948 superiority in educational background and technology, superiority in intellectual and moral cohesion, have overcome prior but long inarticulate claims and indigenous rights. But the high Arab birth-rate and the increasing role of the oriental Jew in Israel itself mean that the problem of Israel's future is going to be, more and more, a Palestinian problem, a matter of co-existence at the most intimate level.

Just now in Israel one often hears the quip: victory has brought far more problems than we ever had before. Yes, but they are

radically creative problems, problems that have in them the forms—
violent and demanding as they may be—of their own necessary
solution. A united Palestine is, by definition, a land of Jewish Arabic
congruence, a semitic community among other semitic communities.
Pointing to the hysteria of Arab hate-slogans, to the terrible gift
of the Arab temper for self-intoxicating myths, Walter Laqueur has
rightly stressed that the Jewish problem is, not a jot less, an Arab
problem. He has added :'On the present basis it is illusory to hope
for a meeting of minds between Arab and Israel'. Who would
contradict? But there are preliminaries to a 'meeting of minds',
preliminaries that engender their own habits of tolerance, their own
routines of mutual understanding. Daily life is a master contriver
of 'impossible possibilities'. In Jerusalem and throughout the West
Bank, indeed across the Jordan, contacts are multiplying. Jew and
Arab move together through narrow streets; there are bonds of taste
and inner rhythm between the oriental Jew and his new Arab
neighbour—bonds that long predate the establishment of modern
Israel. There was a time when the close co-existence of Muslim and
Christian seemed an outrageous fantasy; in Lebanon it became
routine. In Israel a co-existence no less fantastic must one day
become banal fact. The alternative is everlasting civil war, open or
clandestine. In short: I believe that what the Six-Day War has
gained in compelled violence must be preserved; for only a united
Palestine will force Arab and Jew to resolve, first separately, then
together, the equation of life on this spot of earth.

One's other thoughts are of symbolic acts. Of the possibility that
the university on Mount Scopus be assigned to Islamic-Hellenistic-
Hebraic studies, that it be made a focus, comparable to that in Cairo,
for the study of Islamic history and culture and of the vital inter-
actions of that culture with the Hellenistic and Judaic current in
western civilisation. Already now, when no one will come forward to
claim them, scholarships and fellowships should be advertised and set
aside for students from the Arab world; already today, when none
will step forward to receive them, doctorates *honoris causa* should be
conferred on ranking scholars from Beirut, Damascus or Alexandria.
One reflects on Jerusalem as a city set apart, as an international
centre for the arts, scholarship and political argument (how much
apter would a United Nations be in Jerusalem than it is in

Manhattan). The place that Jerusalem holds in three major religions and their numerous splinters has long made it a city like no other. It may well be that these religions are a decaying force, a set of mythological structures now passing into metaphor and conventional after-life. There is no more dignity or humane vitality in the squabbles between orthodox and reformed Jews over access to the Wall than thore is in the wrangles between Uniates and Nestorians over whose incense shall waft where in the Church of the Nativity. These things may soon be of the past. But even then Jerusalem would have a unique, privileged situation; even then it would be a meeting place of common remembrance and archive of men's dreams. This singularity ought to be made manifest, now and henceforth. Israel must say to all who would listen, and more loudly to all who won't: 'join us here; bring your academies and centres of study; this city is ours as it always has been; it is also yours; even if it is no longer or only to a diminishing number a city of God, help us make it a city for man'.

Two pictures bewilder my mind. The first of a procession of old Arab men and young Arab boys seeking to mourn the anniversary of their defeat and being broken up by Israeli police because 'they had not applied for or received official permission for such a ceremony'. The second of a scene outside the Sorbonne on the night of May 22nd, 1968, when, after an address by Daniel Cohn-Bendit, a group of Arab students rushed forward shouting 'we are all German Jews now'. Is there much doubt which picture is truer to the genius of Judaism—a genius deeply implicated in the State of Israel, but also at work beyond it?

A. Kriegel

# Communism in France

This article has been kindly translated from French by Mr. D. Shaw of the Department of French, the University of Leeds.

For six years, from 1962 to 1968, the best informed observers of French political life all agreed week after week that the Communist Party 'was changing'—for the better, naturally, and, it was implied, in the direction of an increasingly 'democratic' party, a 'party like the others'.

They did not convince general opinion. Firstly, because they too often tended to present the event as if it had already happened. It is true that on such a question the role of observers is a delicate one: they can either exaggerate a vaguely perceived tendency and so run the risk, if it should come to nothing, of seeming either in sympathy or naïve; or they can minimize it and not encourage its first faltering steps, thus running the opposite risk of contributing to its failure. But above all it was the *Party* itself which was changing: and as one can well imagine, at the very brink, having realised just where it was being pushed on a particular issue, it rebelled lustily against whoever was trying to make it change unwittingly and against its will.

However, the observers were not wrong: something was indeed happening, but only at the very top—inside the very head in fact of the Secretary General of the time.

Now that the chapter is closed, one is better able to see beyond Waldeck Rochet's muddled, devious method and to understand how, whether knowingly or in the semi-darkness of this political animal's deep-rooted instinct, he had had a great ambition: to lead the PCF (French Communist Party) away from Stalinism.

In actual fact, one might even wonder whether Maurice Thorez had not chosen him with this precise end in view: for nothing else, it would seem, required Thorez to name as his successor an old colleague who was not his closest ally and who had the reputation and manner, if not of a freethinker, of at least an eccentric—or of an outcast.

Moreover, the choice had at the time caused some surprise. Had Thorez felt that, six to eight years after the 20th Congress and as soon as the worst of the backlash from de Stalinisation had been absorbed, the moment had come for him to step down and—why not?—to return to those two preoccupations which he had formerly denied almost before he had given them expression: the 'French Front' in 1937, the 'French way towards Socialism' in 1946.

Whatever the case may be, Waldeck Rochet, during the four or five years that he held office, took a series of timely and wide-ranging decisions which, placed side by side, reveal, a three-pronged plan.

An international prong: the French position in the international Communist movement was to deviate and to approach that of the Italians so that, without provoking idle comment or creating suspicion, it might present itself as a political negotiating force with ready access to all the partners of which none, not even the Soviet Communist Party—which had relinquished, in theory as in practice, its former rôle of 'guiding party'—would be singled out or privileged.

A national prong: the PCF was to venture resolutely into virgin territory in order to work out a doctrine on how to reply to those who, within its own ranks and outside, were worrying about the possible recurrence of a Stalin-type 'proletarian dictatorship' in the event of socialist forces taking over our country. Hence the hypothesis of a pluralist democracy *after* as well as *during* the setting up of a socialist regime. This was considered by the National Conference of February, 1963, the central committee in May and October of the same year and the 17th Congress the following year. As Waldeck Rochet was to stress, it was during these debates that 'two decisions of fundamental ideological importance were solemnly taken': that of 'rejecting the idea, long held by Stalin, that the existence of a single party would be an obligatory condition for the passage from capitalism to socialism' and that of proposing an attempt at reaching a lasting understanding between Communists and Socialists, 'not just for today but for tomorrow as well in the struggle for the realisation of socialism'. At the St. Ouen central committee meeting on 5th January, 1966, he even added: 'that the recognition of the existence of more than one democratic party and of the necessity for lasting collaboration between the Communist Party and the Socialist Party presupposes a political regime allowing considerable democratic liberties'.

Finally the third prong, which was to tie together the other two: this aimed at ending the phenomenon of an antagonistic but complementary twosome, the post-liberation relationship between Gaulleism and Communism which had made them, to use a stock phrase, 'objective allies'. The aggressiveness they showed towards each other does not in fact give a correct idea of how much they really wanted to destroy each other: in 1947 De Gaulle was calling the Communists 'separatists' while the Communists were stigmatizing the RPF (Rassemblement du Peuple Français) as the 'American party', without any of this changing in the slightest the aim of the main assault which they intended to mount jointly on the Third Force. After the return to power of General De Gaulle, the Gaulleists might well demonstrate their ability to deprive the Communist Party of 1½ million votes with De Gaulle denouncing the 'totalitarian machine'; the Communists, for their part, might well anathemize 'personal power' or even 'monopoly power'; the truth was that both sides knew how far they could go without going too far: the 'positive aspects' of his foreign policy allowed the Head of State to think (with cynicism?) that, as he thus had power over those 'who placed service of a foreign state above all other considerations' he no longer had to worry about them. This calculation, in fact, proved correct for quite some time since the Communists, in accordance with the theoretical priority which they are obliged to give to the interests of the Socialist camp, behaved up to 1964 in such a way as not to cause ill-timed embarrassment to the Fifth Republic. They certainly had their reasons: at their 15th Congress in 1959, had they not blamed 'the class solidarity of French capitalism with world imperialism' for 'infeudation to the Atlantic Alliance, active participation in the cold war, maintenance of American bases in France, the setting up of the Common Market, the support for the Franco regime, participation in the intrigues of the aggressive middle-east agitators and the refusal to recognise the government of Popular China'? It must be recognised that the Gaulleist France of ten years later was innocent of most of these charges.

Now, this system of controlled reciprocal aggression was deliberately destroyed by Waldeck Rochet's decision to make 'unity of the left' the number one priority from then on. It is true that, even in December, 1962, the central committee, assembled at Malakoff, had indeed recalled that 'the highest duty of Communists is to do everything possible to prolong and consolidate reconciliations which have been achieved with socialists and other republicans'; but this time there was no question of reproaches: by adding the support of his party and its share of the electorate to the candidature of François Mitterand in autumn 1965, Waldeck Rochet was making a move against Gaulleism which was no longer merely part of the routine. The Russians were not fooled: even though they had been consulted, or at least informed of this development, they did not show tremendous enthusiasm, either in their press or through their diplomatic contacts, over the possibility that the united left might beat General De Gaulle, who was himself surprised by a battle-order which seemed ultimately to go completely against the strategic interests of the socialist camp as they had been imagined up to that moment.

Waldeck Rochet failed, as Krushchev had failed, as Dubcek failed more recently. The very differences between these three bold men show that it was not simply a matter of temperament: Rochet was neither a braggart like Krushchev, nor over-confident as Dubcek seems to have been. Prudent, reserved, subtle, ambiguous when it paid to be so, he was, of the three, the one who, by deft touches, got furthest, even though he managed it by concealing his master plan (to others or to himself?) to such a degree that someone could quite easily challenge my reading of his project by throwing at me a hundred quotations and a hundred actions which conclusively prove the opposite point of view.

Must one therefore blame Waldeck Rochet's failure on a fortuitous national incident like the May riots which, one might think, judging from the sequence of events, destroyed the delicate machinery conceived in 1962 and progressively installed since then? It is clear that the left wing uprising did not exactly make the operation in progress any easier: in view of the size of the stakes, both French and international, in the game that he was striving to win, one can appreciate that Waldeck Rochet did not view this elephantine explosion with any great enthusiasm but that, deeply grieved, he regarded these hare-brained left wing youths as the best collaborators —again, in the 'objective' sense—that French Gaulleism and international Stalinism could wish for; it is, moreover, obvious that on this subject Chairman Mao does not think differently from the Russians, as witness the favours being exchanged between China and France under Pompidou.

However, quite apart from the fact that one imagines that Waldeck Rochet would have managed to assimilate the embarrassing but probably ephemeral mess left behind by the May riots, one cannot logically explain in terms of a specifically French contingency a failure which forms part of an international sequence.

It was therefore another catastrophe, of a totally different dimension from the Parisian *revolutionspiel* which, in France as elsewhere, made 1968 into a turning point: the decisive counter-offensive against attacks from within the Soviet Union, from within the socialist camp, from within the world Communist movement, which were directed against Soviet supremacy and against its instrument, the Soviet Communist Party. Having absorbed a remarkable series of failures and knocks, the Russian Communists decided that the moment had arrived to deliver a free backstage warning, in the shape of a show of force, for which the venue happened to be Czechoslovakia.

It is here that we must assess the scale of what has come to be known as the Soviet crisis. This is an ambiguous expression: if one takes it to mean that, fifty years after the October Revolution, Soviet society is moving away from the Leninist dream, one is probably safe: Father Riquet is now the only Reverend Father capable of asserting angelically in 1970, 'that through all the errors, the faults and the imperfections that are common knowledge, the peoples of the Union of Soviet Socialist Republics are seeking and experimenting with a fraternal society where, in the words of Marx, "the development of every individual would be the condition for the development of all".' If one takes it to imply that Soviet society today no longer cherishes revolutionary projects on a world scale, nor even any revolutionary projects at all, or any world projects at all, that is probably also true. And if, finally, one were to suggest that it is an ossified, divided inegalitarian society—containing privileged persons but no *élites*—that would certainly also be correct. But the discrepancy between what has been accomplished and what was dreamed of achieving, the absence of clear purpose, and the almost total institutional inertia, do not for long suffice to prevent such an immense empire, affected in its most vital interests, from reacting. The exuberant energy radiating from the young Soviet Republic on the morrow of that October was of the sort needed to stimulate the revolutionary impetus of the world proletariat: but nevertheless the weak Russia of the period was hardly in a position to aid the bolshevik-inspired revolutions which, all across Europe, were being crushed one after the other. The Soviet Union is no longer the model for our hopes: but Russian power is capable of persuading those who wish to go their own way that separations must be agreed to by both sides. Only Maoist China has been able to escape from the brotherly embrace: but this particular case is an even better illustration of how force alone pays dividends. Even distance does not make separation any easier: Cuba and Latin America have discovered this for themselves.

Then, one might ask, what about the Italian Communist Party? This is indeed a strange case. For fifteen years already the Italian Communist Party has been moving steadily further away from a position of strict orthodoxy on major issues without provoking a clash of any significance, either for itself, for Italian politics, or for the international Communist movement. Of course, one must remember that the Italian Party was less specifically Stalinised than other sections of the International, the French party in particular: several factors contributed to this, firstly the personality of Togliatti, shaped by his long association with Bukharinite ideas; then, the origin of the party, which sprang from a 'leftist' base at its Leghorn congress, only to find itself swiftly uprooted under Mussolini—which at least enabled it to remain almost untouched by the ideological ups and downs to which more healthy sections were then being exposed; its long exposure to anti-fascist concepts, among which denunciation of 'charismatic authority' had central importance; and its dealings with the liberal movement in an Italy where a unitary state had been late in coming and was only weakly established. It must of course be acknowledged that the Italian political system favours convergence at the centre, rather than bipolarisation: the present shape of the governing majority, a coalition of the centre with slightly leftist leanings, which constantly succeeds itself in a self-perpetuating round of adjustments and alterations, downfalls and botched repairs, is putting the Italian Communist Party out of touch, as the PCF was under the 4th Republic. In short, the fact that the physical and verbal excesses of the Italian Communist Party seem regularly to expend themselves in a sea of indifference, that is, the feebleness of its impact upon reality, would seem to be the product both of the old tolerance shown towards its partial heterodoxy, considered as almost part of its nature, *and* of the limited hold which it seemed to have on the outside world, both nationally and internationally.

Within the sphere of obedience to the Soviet Union, the bastion which maintains and guarantees the unity and homogeneity of the system is thus still constituted by the Soviet Union itself and its Communist Party: it is still their calculations and their aims and, when all is said and done, their reserves of power, always crucial to their capacity for initiative and intervention, which assess the likelihood or otherwise of changes in the peripheral Communist Parties.

But the Soviet Union and its Party do not constitute a pure, almost abstract, force charged with maintaining a semi-formal structure, and available for any undertaking. The vigour of Soviet socialism stems also from its very nature, as it was conceived and cast in the mould of bolshevism; in other words, the vigour of Soviet socialism stems from its being a Stalinist socialism.

A brand of Stalinism which had been able to avoid all manner of corrective traps since the death of Stalin, notably the astute suggestion, made by Krushchev of a 'return to Lenin': the time-honoured manner of setting in motion processes of doctrinal cleavage is generally to dream of returning to the beginning, to look for the fork where the great adventure must unfortunately have split in two.

This notion of a 'return to Lenin', proclaimed on the morrow of the 20th Congress of the Soviet Communist Party, is still breeding quarrels and rifts fifteen years later. Not that, in the final analysis, the Stalinist yoke was lastingly smashed, so freeing national energies and cultural diversity, irritating the advocates of economic inequality and resuscitating the old political traditions. What was in fact smashed was the idea that one could so much as imagine a doctrinal alternative together with the capacity, whether individual or collective, for pursuing to its conclusion the analysis of the Stalinist phenomenon.

But very soon the 'return to Lenin' idea, apart from being a step towards a still more harrowing revision, was shown for what it was: a trick. The distance separating Lenin from Stalin is in fact too problematical for it to pass unnoticed. And the break, when artificially contrived in order to ensure the impunity of the former and crush the latter, merely subjects them both to the unending complications of bad faith.

Certainly it cannot be denied that Stalin introduced changes—whether these were successful or frighteningly negative is another question—even allowing for the difference between the situation facing the two men and their regimes. But did Stalin betray Lenin over *essential* points, that is, firstly, over the absolute priority which had to be given to the survival *of Soviet power* (nothing being possible without the basic assumption of bolshevism in power); then, over the nature of the Party and its need to play a dominating rôle in the revolutionary process and in the exercise of proletariat dictatorship? For all its brilliance and ferocity, the accusation which Trotsky lodged against the Stalin regime has the weakness of failing to demonstrate convincingly that the strategy of permanent revolution, in the form advocated by the 'armed Prophet', was anything but a wager in which the stake was Soviet power itself. Neither did he demonstrate any more conclusively that the methods of government were at all different under Lenin when, for instance, he, Trotsky, recommended 'militarization of the economy' as the overall solution to the reconstruction problem (spring 1920). Of course, at that time, the civil war was enough to justify these excesses: but, apart from the fact that the national war against the Fascists would seem to have provided at least the same extenuating circumstances, was any war, civil or national, their only source? Given that the physical liquidation of the Russian bourgeoisie was followed by that of the Kulaks and then by that of the 'old bolsheviks', is it certain that this persistent recourse to bloody violence was due only to Stalinist madness?

This 'return to Lenin' notion therefore prevented above all consideration of bolshevism in the form in which it had been established by a successful revolution: consideration which cannot be undertaken without recognising the striking consistency of the Leninist system. It would serve no great purpose here to give Vladimir Illitch a respectful polish in order to rid him of a few disagreeable little blemishes. As a system conceived to facilitate a particular method of winning power, in order to reach a certain stage of development, that of Lenin has proved its worth: it is workable. But it does include terrible 'disadvantages'. Is it possible to avoid the cost and the limits of the system without making the system itself break up? Is it enough simply to reshape it in depth, or are the pieces too interdependent for there to be any other solution but to abandon it in turn to 'the gnawing criticism of the mice'?

It was precisely this possibility of reducing the negative aspects of bolshevik power that, after Krushchev for the Soviet Union, and before Dubcek for Czechoslovakia, Waldeck Rochet undertook to examine in the plan which is, for France, easily accessible and experimental: the doctrinal plan. Now, it quickly became apparent, judging from the French Secretary General's tentative efforts in the domain of theory, that the corrections he was making to a questionable but coherent system of thought were making it scarcely less questionable but totally incoherent.

One can easily examine its mechanism in connection with the concept of the international Communist movement. As the 'World Party' of the revolutionary proletariat, the Communist movement had certainly, over forty years, experienced both changes on a practical level and refinements on the theoretical plane; but, until 1960, in spite of everything, it had duly remained a centralised advanced guard detachment under the direction of the Russian Communists. After the theme of the 'guiding rôle of the Soviet Communist Party' had been abandoned, the PCF, through a desire to preserve the essential, the very notion of a Socialist camp, put forward a formula which makes no sense in any system of geometry and just as little in any political sphere. One can well see the pitfall which the French delegate at the Budapest conference in March,

1968 is trying to avoid when he declares: 'There is not and cannot be *a* centre or even *several* centres of the international Communist movement'. Nevertheless, this idea is literally inconceivable: a structure is characterised by the fact that it has a centre, be it a centre of effort or a point of convergence at infinity of an infinite number of centres. The French proposal, dilatory to say the least, thus merely indicates the character of the moment: either a step towards general dislocation (or regional fragmentation) or else a period which is bound to end with the Soviet Communist Party, or a condominium of two or more leading parties, again establishing itself at the centre.

But perhaps Waldeck Rochet's bitterest experience of the difficulty of controlling the agitation communicated from theoretical zone to theoretical zone by the introduction even of limited correctives came over the question of pluralist democracy.

The discussion was made sufficiently public at the time for one to hope that the Communists no longer had in mind a pluralism of cowed, grovelling parties, as had been the case with the popular democracies, trembling beneath the rod of iron of the only party that counted, the Communist Party. The multipartism in question was theoretically a group of parties whose weight and respective influence allowed for real and reciprocal confrontation, collaboration and (the expression is Waldeck Rochet's) *competition*. Moreover, it really was to be a pluralism of actual *parties*: nothing in common, therefore, with the 1946 argument, revitalised in 1956, which caused Maurice Thorez to say: 'The restoration of France's fortunes is not a task for one party or for a handful of statesmen: it is the task of millions of French men and women, of the entire nation'. For it is clear that 'millions of Frenchmen', if they are not formed into distinct and structural parties, cannot offer serious resistance to a single organised party, just as the millions of Russians have never seriously resisted Stalin's Party.

From that time on were the Communists prepared to accept, during both the establishment and the running of a Socialist regime, the rival presence in the political arena of any party, whatever its doctrinal position, and even if it objected to the Socialist regime as much as the Communist Party today objects to that of the capitalists? The question was widely debated in 1966. It is true that Waldeck

Rochet maintained that even if one can 'envisage the possibility of a country like ours passing peacefully over to Socialism', that could not signify that 'Socialism would be established in France without a class struggle or without the mobilisation of all the forces of the working class and its allies'. But whereas he spoke at first of 're-cognition of the plurality of *democratic* parties' (January, 1964), he went on to suppress the adjective 'democratic', speaking merely of 'recognition of the plurality of parties' (March) and finally (April) putting forward a definitive amendment, 'Close and lasting co-operation between the Communist Party and the other demo-cratic parties can facilitate and speed up the move towards Socialism throughout the plurality of parties', which gave one to understand that power would be in the hands of a coalition of *democratic* parties, but that this coalition would allow the existence outside itself of other parties which would not necessarily be 'democratic' in the sense that the speaker meant.

The uncertainties of this exegesis suggest that the introduction of a plurality of parties into the classic Soviet blueprint of the Socialist regime disturbed at least three major theoretical areas: its central pillar, the notion of proletariat dictatorship, the concept of the class State and, finally, the very concept of seizing power, that is, the essence of the revolutionary act in the context of Leninist ideas.

If socialist democracy did indeed imply collaboration and lasting alliance, then one could not imagine a break as clean, a breach as easy to date, as the seizure of power in the young Russian Republic or . . . in Prague. It must be recognised that this seizing of political power remains at least the eschatological view of the PCF. 'The necessity for the working class to seize political power' is among the general principles of universal significance 'brought to light by the October Revolution'.

One is here approaching the supreme question, that of revolution. This had been well understood by Waldeck Rochet, whose most interesting theoretical work is actually entitled: 'What is a revolu-tionary in present-day France?' A legitimate and well-phrased question; what is more, the proposed reply begins promisingly. Waldeck Rochet writes in fact that 'the most fundamental in-gredient of the workers' new power is the continuing extension of socialist democracy with the ever-increasing participation of the workers and the entire people in the construction of socialism and in the administration, in different forms, of public affairs'. After such a preamble one expects more concrete analyses of the Italian type, and along the lines of Gramsci, of the conquest of civil society; of, for example, the role and the power of the unions, the defence, extension and general use of regional autonomies, rural co-operation, etc., in short, the whole range of stimulants which might allow the multiple incarnations of the body social to intervene at the very level of the decisions which concern them. But, alas, the train of thought suddenly withdraws to the familiar and banal and we fall back on the hazy distinction between reforms and revolution, on the tired assertion that 'Communists are struggling resolutely for immediate reforms that can be obtained within the framwork of the capitalist society, but without ever letting up on the struggle for the ultimate goal: socialism'.

In actual fact, questions like proletariat dictatorship, class State, seizure of power, all depend on the final question, the final, key question of Leninism, which transformed a momentary split into a lasting one and on which is based the indomitable originality of Communism: that of the Party.

One is here at the frontier where the PCF stops dead. In Italy, in Giorgio Amendola, a Party leader was found who was willing, at least once, to pose in public the major question: in order to establish socialism in a situation and country which have nothing in common with the bolshevik situation and country, is there still a need for a Party of the bolshevik type? But the French Party is still serenely ruled by the old taboos: 'The possibility of building and defending Socialism is linked with the Communist Party's capacity for acting as the vanguard of the working class in the Socialist society.' (*Propositions* (*Thèses*), point 17, 1970). As if the whole world had not heard what was said by Professor Svitak, one of the theorists of the Prague Spring: 'Ideology founded on the theory that the Party directs the working class and the people, and instils its own ideas into them, has nothing in common with Marx, but much in common with the ceaseless destruction of critical ideas and human liberty by the soporific monotony of the disciples of Stalin. If these are Marxists, then we are not; if we are Marxists, then they are not.'

What then is the Communist Party in the France of today? A

social democratic party, say some, modifying their statement by adding 'of a new type'; a revisionist party, say others; a party still bent on revolution, it says itself.

A social democratic party? What does the term mean? The unifying criterion of the various interpretations which have been and are given to the adjective 'social democratic' is that of integration: a social democratic party is one that both integrates and integrates itself into what one might call the national socio-political *structure* or the political system of a national state.

It was of course Georges Lavau who, basing himself on the conceptual framework of the systematic analysis elaborated by David Easton, made the most vigorous theoretical effort to give some formulation to the hypothesis according to which: 'progressively and in spite of its real intentions and tactical calculations, the net result of the actions and attitudes of the PCF has ultimately been to make an unusual contribution to the functioning of the French political system'.

And Georges Lavau tries on occasions to defend this hypothesis by means of historical references; based on a questionable conception of historical evolution, his reasoning is then unconvincing. When, for example, he considers that the Popular Front 'formed the decisive turning point in the transformation of the PCF' and that 'since 1936 (the PCF) has been following the same path (as the social democratic parties)', one cannot easily make out just where and when he found himself a social democratic party likely to approve the German-Soviet pact in 1939, to support Zdanov's strategic analysis in 1947, to proclaim in 1949 that it would never make war against the Soviet Union, to celebrate with ceremony Stalin's seventieth birthday in 1950, to go into deep mourning at the latter's death in 1953, to applaud the Soviet intervention in Budapest in 1956, to resign itself to the Czech 'normalisation' in 1968. All gestures which have nothing symbolic about them but which, besides outlining a definite foreign policy, have governed every aspect of the PCF's situation and activity within the exclusively French political universe.

Moreover, Georges Lavau is well aware of the difficulty, since he admits that the rules, the organisation and the structure of the PCF, the restraining power of its ideology, and its close association with the Soviet Communist Party constitute reasons why the 'Communist Party has not become a social democratic party "like the others".' How therefore can it be a social democratic party if it is not 'like the others'? And Georges Lavau is not alone in sensing that, now as yesterday, such a formula fails to grasp the essence of the Communist phenomenon. 'The Communist Party is a *new type* of social democratic party', suggest Denis Berger and Paul-Louis Thiraud, for one cannot 'place an equals sign between the present PCF and the Labour Party, the SFIO (Section Française de l'Internationale Ouvrière) or the Belgian workers' party of the thirties'. And always for the same reasons: organisational structures, and the almost organic liaison with the Soviet Union, with the result that, unlike the traditional social democracy, the PCF does not express 'the interests of modernising and rationalising elements within capitalism': it cannot be confused 'with the interests of the national State'. Thus, the *'new type* of social democratic party' would appear to resemble the 'mass social democratic parties which existed before 1914': it will be observed that, this being so, it is not a very new type. What, then, is the point of this comparison? It is that, like the German social democracy fo the period preceding the Great War, the PCF is 'representative of the working class—albeit a working class no longer engaging in extra-legal battles; opposed to the present government, it remains capable of conducting far-reaching offensives'. The analogy is valid: but it is simply going a long way round to discover that Lenin, when working out the theory and practice of a bolshevik party, had actually taken as one of his models the guiding party of the Second International, the German Social Democratic Party of which he long claimed to be an admirer and disciple.

Georges Lavau's reasoning is much more convincing when, thinking along functional lines, he analyses how the PCF, by carrying out certain of the functions for which it accepts, or seeks, responsibility, is contributing objectively to the overall working of the French political system.

It is in this way that Georges Lavau proposes to call the 'tribune function', that 'of organising and defending the plebeian social categories (that is, those that are excluded, or feel themselves to be excluded from the process of participation in the political system, and from the benefits of the economic and cultural systems), and giving them a feeling of strength and confidence'.

This is a very pretty name for what the Party, in a terser, more prosaic style, calls the defence of demands. It is true that the Party can be seen in the guise of a pressure group, a lobby, whose *clientèle* would be made up of workers and people of modest means. In the government (on occasion), in parliament, in the town halls, in the professional organisations, and by means of a whole flexible network of specialised groups, ministers, MPs, mayors, union representatives, staff delegates, and Communist militants in general devote themselves to defending the interests of the workers and those of modest means (farm workers, craftsmen, tradesmen, old age pensioners) and also— depending on circumstances—of nationalised industries, of social security, of peace, of home distillers, of republican liberty, of undenominational schools, of parent-teacher associations, of tenants' associations, and so on.

How does this *defensive* function help to integrate the PCF into the established system? The reply would seem to be quite straight-forward: the truth is that the PCF is tending more and more to limit itself to this function, to be satisfied with it, to wallow in it and, while remaining deeply reformist, is abandoning any attempt to take up revolutionary issues; in a word, it is a workers' Party, a good manager of the workers' interests.

Is this a satisfactory reply? One must first observe that, even if the Party has been working day after day to merit the reputation of being the best defender of workers' interests, it is not true, either in theory or in practice, that this is its first and exclusive concern: at what great moments of history, at what great national or inter-national emergency have its major decisions been dictated by a clamant need to win new devotees and please the old ones? How could it be electorally profitable to take up a position against the Common Market? To denounce 'the aggression of the reactionary governing circles in Israel'? Was it with votes in mind that, in May 1968, while the student movement was still very popular, the Party took the risk of denouncing the behaviour of the 'left' and, as it must have expected, of being itself accused of treachery in return?

It must then be observed that not only is the 'tribune function' quite outside the sphere of one of the Party's most important action groups, but it can actually become *totally incompatible* with decisions taken in fields which do not concern it: in such cases, it is jettisoned. In such an event, one may however assume that one is safe when the Party adds the adjective 'true' to its proposals: the *true* interests of the workers or the *true* French interests are always at least long-term interests.

Finally, it must be observed that the Party whose new 'reformist' tendency is widely lamented, is at the same time suspected of a lack of enthusiasm about reforms and accused of conservatism. It has, for example, been legitimately argued that the 'policies', both general and specific, which the Party is so fond of, are too often nothing but catalogues of obviously desirable objectives, presented in a confused order, without an order of priorities or any notion of how they might be financed. On the union front, the CGT (Con-féderation Générale du Travail) has been bitterly reproached for only concerning itself with outdated 'quantitative demands' and neglecting the 'qualitative demands', which are the only ones likely to modify in any lasting fashion the power structure within the companies. On the civic front, concern has also been shown over the fact the preoccupation with a 'social reform' likely to bear immediate and tangible fruit—housing, schools, leisure activities (sporting facilities, cultural centres, youth clubs), aid for the underprivileged (day nurseries, welfare centres, holiday camps for poor children, old peoples' homes)—had led the Communist municipal authorities:

1. To fail to recognize the true dimensions of the social problems of our age (the establishment of an educational system in which primary schools play a primary role; carefully coordinated town-planning, linked with a communication system taking into account such things as the demographic expansion and the drift to the towns; and the new questions of pollution and the environment).

2. To fail even more markedly to make an accurate allowance for the interaction between the social and economic spheres. The ill-considered increases in direct communal taxation, in special rates of taxation, and in taxes levied on the rateable value of commercial property, all of which hit without sufficient discrimination smaller firms as well as trusts and other monopolies, have speeded up the 'decentralisation' which the government was already encouraging, by means of removal subsidies and refusal of planning permission for new factory extensions. The uprooting of old firms

and the banning of new ones was finally shown to be a prejudicial exercise in boroughs with unemployment.

3. And finally, to delay, in the name of legitimate defence of municipal prerogatives, the inevitable evolution of local government structures (cooperation, fusion and strengthening of the boroughs) and the administrative and technical adaptation of a system confronted with increasingly complex tasks.

In short, I should be tempted to say of this celebrated 'tribune function' that the Party certainly fulfils it, but that it fulfils it neither as a priority nor in isolation; that it sometimes opposes it and that in any case it takes care not to fulfil it simply in order to canvass votes.

Were these limits born of chance or incompetence? Neither. They were engendered by the conception which the Party has of itself: that it is not a reformist party. Or, better still: an attentive examination of the emergence of social reforms in contemporary France shows that the Party and its sphere of influence are never, or hardly ever, their true place of origin. For the past fifty years, what are now fashionably known as the 'great social conquests': the establishment of shop stewards and staff representatives, statutory joint commissions, nationalisation of certain sectors, social security, works committees—all were at first subjected to unfavourable commentary on the part of the left wing of the CGT, revolutionary-syndicalist or Communist. Each structural modification of professional relations was viewed with distrust as being likely to feed that ever-renascent hydra, class collaboration. The Communists in particular tended to feel that such reforms were unlawfully encroaching upon the post-revolutionary construction of the 'perfect society' for which they alone had responsibility and competence. And so at each move their first step was to fight the new proposals—social insurance at the beginning of the thirties, nationalisation, etc.—explaining at one moment that they constituted a trap set by the employers and were designed to cause confusion among the workers, to spread the reformist illusions and to delay the revolutionary conflagration, and at another that they constituted a reactionary trap designed to cause confusion among the allies—the middle classes—which the working class then needed. Then, as soon as the reform had been secured, even though it was none of their doing, or, at least, not of their instigation, the Communists' central preoccupation was not so much to exploit its potential, as to win for themselves the new centres of power which it made available. For example, they were broadly in agreement, although for diametrically opposite reasons, with the most conservative section of the employers that the works committees would fail as centres for concerting social policy within the factories; but they did not fail to use to the full the functions, posts and free time which the works committees legally ensured for their elected members. And they were always prepared to defend them stubbornly when these 'conquests', drained of their substance and diverted from their object, in their turn appeared to be 'threatened'.

Even during the most recent period, the Communists have naturally been scoffing at the idea of the 'new society' outlined by the Chaban Delmas government. But what inter-union rivalry had not been able to obtain was obtained by the radical measures of the public authorities. The CGT, which had been sticking doggedly to wage demands and safeguards, in spite of the insistent concern of the CFDT (Confédération Française Démocratique du Travail) to integrate the structural demands into the inter-union programmes of unified action, progressively amended its list of claims, without however adopting a definite position on the basic issues, to correspond to all the projects and schemes for social action launched or instigated by the government; monthly wage payments, employee shareholdings, dividend contracts and multiannual growth contracts.

The formula, 'defence of working class interests', must therefore be understood in its most restricted sense: a 'defensive defence'. It is a defence which aims at *preserving* the status quo, at *forestalling* possible competition for the role of 'best defender' which the Communist Party is very anxious to monopolise, at *preventing* ultimately the gains promised or extorted from being weighed down with obligations which, at a future date, would transform the unions into organs of the 'establishment', make them play the capitalist game of economic 'rationality' and mortgage their freedom of expression and movement; in a word it aims at ensuring that, in return for a mess of pottage, they do not transform themselves from 'transmission belts' in the service of the Party into belts controlled by the State or the employers.

What therefore is the significance of the assertion that in carrying out such a function within such limits the PCF is 'contributing' to the general running of the French political system? Put in this way the question is not very satisfactory: for the notion of 'contribution' is too broad and vague and even bracketing with it the adjective 'positive' scarcely adds to its clarity. Revolution itself—seen as a means of destroying the established political system—might ultimately appear as a mere (albeit costly) ruse aimed at allowing the overall system to continue to pursue its historical destiny: from bureaucratic Holy Russia to Soviet Bureaucracy. . . . But, ultimately, is not everything a 'contribution'? Death alone dispenses one from 'contributing', except on the level of memory, and except, of course, when death itself is a 'contribution'.

This objection is valid too for the other functions the fulfillment of which, maintains Georges Lavau, leads the PCF to play its part, come what may, in the French political system. When, for example, it 'contributes' towards the legitimisation of the regime's values and principles by accepting responsibility for 'the symbols of the secular and revolutionary Republic', Democracy, Republic, Progress, Unity, National Sovereignty, has not the PCF then also accepted all the rules and norms of a republican regime: election by secret and universal suffrage, control of the government by parliament, independence of the judiciary, administration of local communities by elected councils and magistrates etc? Better still, it fights for the extension of these norms—seeking, for example, the suppression of the prefects and the transfer of their powers to the elected general councils. Moreover, it justified its initial opposition to the 5th Republic by reference to the respect which it entertained for the values, norms, rules and structures of the preceding regime.

But here we are at the heart of the mechanism which reveals that it would be premature to regard the PCF as having been victimized or corrupted or seduced by its surroundings. Once the regime of the 5th Republic had compelled recognition as the one with which it would henceforth have to deal, the PCF lost no time in demanding the return of the 4th Republic: at his press conference of February, 1957, Waldeck Rochet no longer demanded the convocation of the Constituent Assembly, nor the abolition of the referendum and presidential election by universal suffrage, nor proportional representation; and in their joint declaration of February, 1968, the

FGDS (Fédération Générale Démocrate et Socialiste) and the PCF no longer showed anything but a principled opposition towards the 1958 constitution. In these conditions, what does the fact of 'accepting' the established regime mean for the PCF? That it 'accepts' it to the point of being obliged to follow its precepts if it were to come to power? No, of course not.

The PCF sticks to the strategic pattern which consists of standing at the same time *inside* and *outside* the sphere of power. This pattern was fashioned by the international Communist movement at the time of the popular fronts and perfected after the war: it is a variant of the 'two powers' technique, on the lines of the 1917 Leninist model. Instead of wearing itself out fighting in vain the working class tendency to integrate, a tendency which has its roots in the social reality itself, it finds it more logical actually to rely on it and to participate in the power structure within the framework of the established society. In liberal democracies such participation takes the form of the Communists being admitted into the government, when the apparatus of the electoral and parliamentary chess-board allows, but it is also shown generally by the fact that Communists penetrate all the structures of the established civil society, securing a place there or even conquering the whole organism. Is that a concession to the social democratic thesis that 'internal' assistance is necessary for the accumulation of socio-economic modifications to give birth to a ripe, well-formed anticapitalist revolution? No, for this participation in the bourgeois power structure is necessarily accompanied by the stubborn maintenance of the radical alienation of the Communist Party as such. In fact, far from playing down the Party's strangeness it is on the contrary essential to define and strengthen it: the Party thus becomes the sole mustering point for that alienation which contains the seeds of the future socialist society. Moreover as it widens its range of intervention within the state and civil society it can progressively but systematically organise the transfer of power to its advantage.

Does this mean that Georges Lavau's observations are without foundation? No, because even if the Communist plan were finally to fail, the objective consequence of the lost battle would probably still have been an involuntary contribution towards making the workers and the popular classes as such into the social category which 'participated' most, albeit in opposition, and which were therefore most identified with the national situation. In the same way, bearing in mind the importance, compared with its real aims, which it has always attached to all categories of elections—municipal, local, parliamentary and presidential—the classes under its influence have acquired a very high degree of political coordination. In short, if, at the end of the historical progression which we are now in, it were the established political system which, in one form or another, had managed to wear down the PCF, the result would be that this system would have a greater chance not only of surviving but also of surviving with added support. For the PCF would have been working to reintroduce into the political community a working class capable of independent initiative and unlikely to dissolve or break up. From the original aim of radical disruption, the PCF would thus have transformed itself into a source of extra cohesion. But nothing yet allows one to decide which, the established political system or the PCF, has so far most worn down the other. The system is not doing badly, but then neither is the PCF.

In order to reach an understanding of the French Communist phenomenon one gains neither in clarity nor in scope by adapting it to a system of analysis to which it is just not suited. Theories formulated in order to give an account of political parties (especially when they are elaborated by American political pundits more accustomed to studying a system where revolutionary protest has never yet been known to crystallize into an enduring, concentrated, international structure), offer concepts which can certainly help in the examination of Communist parties, but only on those aspects which they have in common with every other party, that is, their least characteristic aspects. They do not excite one by their very 'strangeness'. And so their application to the French case leads more or less consciously to an initial mental reduction of the degree of strangeness, to a dissolution of this *residue* of which one nevertheless admits the existence in everyday language by saying that a Communist party is 'not like the other parties'. One has seen Communist parties collapse and disappear—the German Communist Party for example—or make changes of strategy, tactics, policy, size, language, leaders, or allegiance, but one has never seen them become social-democratic parties.

A party of bolshevik provenance and Stalinist temper: it is only from this standpoint that it seems to us appropriate to observe the PCF and to try to make out whether, having until now failed to cease being a Stalinist party, it is going to try once more to break out of the straightjacket and to turn itself into a party about which one knows virtually nothing—even though it has already received one, obviously polemical, epithet: a *revisionist* party—or whether it will resign itself to persevering with its present role: yesterday Stalinist, always Stalinist; or whether, even Stalinism being too ambitious for it, there is any alternative to its being a *degenerate Stalinist* party.

Every thought about the PCF is therefore a thought on two levels. They cannot be mixed without risking not only confusion, but also conceptual or political ineffectiveness; nevertheless one ought, in order firmly to grasp the unity of the phenomenon, to be aware of the liaison and relationship between the two levels; for it is here that in the final analysis, one can find the key to the overall diagnosis and to the future development of the process.

We are not here concerned with the classic distinctions between strategy and tactics, structure and contingency, or maximum and minimum policies. It is not simply a question of clothing the familiar dichotomies in new finery. The two levels in question are moreover only metaphorically placed one above the other: one of them being, as it were, exposed to the open air, the other buried in the political subsoil. But it is, in fact, much more a question of two states of the same phenomenon, or better still, its two poles.

A first level, not superficial but, let us say, unhidden, is that at which one seizes the Communist plan as it surfaces and pervades the day-to-day political scene. It is the point at which it confronts the outside world, the point at which one sees unfold the saga of its fight with established society: a fight which, although unceasing, can take many forms, at one moment that of a merciless battle, at another that of collaboration, of cooperation, of a more or less deep and prolonged integration, at yet another the intermediary form of a truce and the appearance of mutual disinterest.

Thus, the *class against class* strategy, at the turning point in the thirties, represents a sort of ill-tempered defiance of the world: the Communist Party hurling itself boldly to attack the citadel even though it has no chance, in view of the superior numbers of the opposing force. An aggressive spirit—in the context of a defensive situation—was justified by the fact that these raids and incursions into enemy territory have the advantage of carrying the war far from the sacred frontiers of the young Soviet Republic. They cannot, after all, end in total disaster because it is enough to retreat at the appropriate moment and rest out of harm's way in the sanctuary of the 'only country which is building socialism'.

The *antifascist* or *popular front* or *national front* strategy of the thirties and forties corresponds to a more subtle sort of defiance: it exploits a particularly serious rift in the capitalist universe—'a broken link in the imperialist chain'—in order to make an alliance with one side against the other. The choice of partner is not unimportant, but the Germano-Soviet pact shows that it is not fundamental. In this situation the PCF's policy presents a double aspect: very hostile towards the side which is now the common enemy, very conciliatory—exclusively—towards the side which is now its ally. The benefits of this double attitude are bound not only to accumulate but to snowball. The greatest possible hostility towards the common enemy and the greatest possible sacrifices for the common victory can only please and convince those elements who, within the alliance, believe sincerely in the the co-determined ideals; it then becomes easy to win them over definitively by passing through all the stages and displaying all the techniques of fraternization, participation, integration, collaboration and cooperation within civil society and the state, up to and including the established political authorities: if the alliance is in a majority position nationally, then the time has come for the Communists to gain a foothold in the government, or, if it is a minority position, in the Resistance Front. Here, one process can work miracles: the purge. Clamoured for as the proper punishment of the defeated, the purge has the triple advantage of permitting the setting-up of a police and parajudicial system of which the Communists naturally take possession, of transforming allies into embarrassed accomplices and then of placing them in turn in the position of virtual defendants as their decimated right flank remains exposed.

The *cold war* strategy, inaugurated in 1947, is a partial return to the past: but it is not to be confused with the old *class against class*

N

strategy. After the considerable gains of the preceding period it aims at classifying and exploiting the still fragile acquisitions and at ordering and organising the socialist camp. The Communist Parties of the capitalist countries have only a minor, diversionary role: to provide their governments with enough problems to distract them from taking an interest in the fates of countries and peoples within the sphere of Soviet allegiance. Apart from this, they have only to live quietly in isolation. It is a period when both worlds give the impression of drifting separately along, imprisoned within their mutual ignorance and isolation.

Those are the three strategies which have successively dictated concrete relationships between the Communist world and established French society. But a less cursory examination would enable one to make out an infinite number of positions ranging from the most radical alienation to overlapping and interpenetration, each one marked by the ambiguous dominant of hostility or cooperation.

The passage from one strategy to another—more or less direct and open, although that from cold war to peaceful coexistence resembles a slalom course—could not escape even an observer outside Communist affairs, as the change affects precisely the area of the contacts between the two worlds: this level is thus the one where the change is, by definition, *spectacular*.

Moreover this is the level, in so far as it is the level of confrontation, rivalry, and competition with the established world, at which operates that remarkable capacity for adaptation thanks to which, despite sectoral delays and temporary bouts of inflexibility, the Communist Party, *grosso modo*, had not yet been 'bypassed' for the fifty years since its foundation, even though its objective—to become in its turn the established world—has not been reached. In short, this level is, as it were, one pole of the reality in which the Communist movement has its roots and the one that gives it this 'grass-roots', sometimes limited, prudent and prosaic character.

But it is again at this level that the Party, mobile and flexible, fulfils, combines, and assigns priorities to the three principal functions of any political party in a liberal democracy: the *electoral* function, the function of *controlling and guiding* the political organs (by its parliamentary activity) and the function of *defining and expressing* political positions (by the elaboration and diffusion of its policies). It fulfils these functions by complying with the requirement that it should respond only to demands compatible with its true nature. Not desiring, for example, to make itself responsible for the whole range of national political culture, it makes a careful selection of those motives and values which it seeks to embody.

A point of spectacular change, and a source of the Communist phenomenon's capacity for adaptation and renewal, this first level is finally and correspondingly the one where the most pressing questions are dealt with, where the variables are emphasised. For the uncertainties about changes in the reciprocal relations between Communism and the established society initially concern their duration: it is only *a posteriori*, after a probationary period, that a modification can exchange its provisional, incidental, status for the more noble one of structural and principled permanence. For example, the rejection, in theory and in practice, of economic crises and war as classic methods of putting the revolutionary process into gear necessarily led to substantial revision in the field of strategy. But it was first necessary to ensure that the rejection was more than temporary.

Krushchevism as such was originally the result of a Soviet revision of the relationship between war and revolution after the uncertainties and gropings of the forties and early fifties. This was a revision which even the costly Chinese defiance could not persuade the Russians to reconsider; although they have of course carried out a few secondary modifications for Peking's benefit, aimed at drawing a clear distinction between problems and geographical sectors covered by atomic strategy and those which were not. But they remained inexorable on the essential point: on the fact that even the expansion of socialism is not worth the risk of war in the countries covered by atomic strategy.

It was this basic position which Waldeck Rochet was taking up again when he wrote 'As far as France is concerned, at this moment non-one can predict with certainty how socialism will be put into practice tomorrow. But the position and will of the PCF are quite clear: all its activities are orientated towards the creation of conditions favourable to a *peaceful* transition to socialism. . . .' These words, written in 1966, render unforgivable the illusion of those who were able to believe in May, 1968 that by imprisoning the Communist

Party within an impossible dilemma—revolution or betrayal—one could force it to take the risk of civil war, whose connection with the other sort of war, especially in Europe, is uncertain.

However reasonable the analysis of its presence in the 'real world', one could not reach a complete understanding of the Communist phenomenon if one stopped there. 'Beneath' this first level, or to one side, or in another 'state', or at a second 'pole', are concentrated all the elements which give it its fundamental *strangeness*. Strangeness in the original sense: is *party spirit* anything else but an awareness of the alienation of the Communist world from established society?

This second pole is the one which we have tried to describe throughout this essay, for it is the least known, in that it is hidden from those not directly or voluntarily concerned. It is the *hidden pole*.

It is also the *pole of the constant*: beyond circumstantial adaptations and modifications, it always maintains its own identity.

And, finally, it is a prefiguration of the future and something like a terrestrial paradise: it is the *pole of the imagination* where millenial aspirations for the 'perfect society' may be realised.

Hidden, constant, imaginary, is not this another way of saying that we are here at the *Absolute*? Hence the difficulty created by the PCF: it changes and changes and yet it never changes. Unalterable and intact, it remains itself: the setting, lighting and action may be transformed but the Party always re-emerges just as one had previously known it. Communists have a very simple way of summing up this permanence: 'Ask anything you like of us, they say, except that we should stop being Communists'.

For this reason also, the idea of being delighted or angry over the Party's ceasing to exist is totally without meaning: it is, from the very beginning, a different power from the established one. But one must avoid misunderstanding over the nature of the revolutionary phenomenon. A Leninist would say that *one* cannot create *the* revolution. One, that is, the oppressed, the masses, the people; the working class, a purely objective abstract political concept even if, at least in the advanced industrial nations, this concept has its roots deeply fixed in a specific social subsoil, cannot be the instigator of the historical initiative. The bearer of the initiative, of the conscience, the key to the historical rationality, is the Party. *One* can therefore occasionally create *a* (successful or unsuccessful) revolution, a mere anecdote, a ripple on the surface of time. But not *the* revolution, this *necessary* moment in which all the contradictions of capitalist society are resolved.

*The* revolution *creates itself*. It is no use wishing hard for it: it is not the moon of our childhood. It is a rational process which is obvious to the most myopic observer: one could not 'miss' it. The *contingency* is thus the *datum* without which it would be ridiculous for the Party to begin to play its game: a purely negative game initially since it is aimed at preventing well-intentioned people from hindering or slowing down the movement of social destruction which is under way. That is what Lenin grasped remarkably well in 1917. When the Russian system had broken down under the double blows of war and defeat (as had been universally predicted and without the wretched far-away exile playing any great part in it), he was especially careful that his forces should not commit the folly of helping Kerensky to restore the machine prematurely: this is the implication of the 'April Theses'. On the other hand, for a whole year (until six months after the October), he happily encouraged the antics of those elements possessing a powerful social corrosive. This was the period when he was reasonably friendly towards the anarchists, highly gifted in this field. Only when he considered the way sufficiently cleared did he decide to begin to design an order—his own, of course, not the Czar's—and with it the destiny of Russia; the anarchists were then dismissed without excessive gratitude.

That this 'revolution game' is the right one remains the firm conviction of the PCF. It therefore greeted with 'calm' disdain the paroxysms of those who, in May, 1968, decreed revolution. By the same token, it says nothing when others philosophize over the fact that in its 'softened' condition it could no longer in any way constitute a subversive power.

If this analysis is correct, it becomes fairly easy to envisage the functioning of the Communist system; change is introduced by means of the pole turned towards the outside world; but it is only assimilated if it is compatible with the invariable components concentrated at the other pole. The stability or, rather the staying power, of the system is thus based on its capacity for selecting those innovations which are found to correspond to its own essence.

Hence the present crisis. There are in fact three factors provoking these drastic changes.

Firstly, the more intangible character of the Soviet *model*. The October Revolution still claims to be the *way* towards socialism; in all but a few details this claim is still held to have universal validity. But it is admitted that Soviet society reveals imperfections which, although excusable in view of the conditions and difficulties peculiar to the experiment, nevertheless suggest that, in certain areas, there should be a return to the drawing-board.

Then there is the fact that peaceful co-existence is decidedly superior to cold war. The top priority accorded to solidarity with the socialist camp is easily justified if one can believe in the threat posed by 'revanchist' Germany or the dark aggressive plots of American imperialism. But when the two great powers are negotiating all round the compass—in Asia, in the Near East, in Vienna—when Moscow is also negotiating with Bonn and Peking, when the problems of war and peace and consequently of international relations, after dominating the fifties and sixties, are tending everywhere to give way to new and complex *domestic* problems, it is quite inevitable that PCF policy can no longer be more or less entirely dictated by its role as protector of socialist interests.

Finally, the third factor is the situation of the PCF *in France*. Under the 4th Republic, once the tripartite system had been abandoned, the only possible governmental majority—however ephemeral or unstable—was to the immediate left or immediate right of centre; the PCF, permanently cut off, was therefore somewhat justified in compensating for its exclusion from French affairs by developing its faculty of imagination. On the other hand, under the 5th Republic, the tendency of the Gaullist system towards bipolarisation at the same time reintegrates the PCF into the democratic game since it makes irrefutable the argument which says that any 'victory of the left' must come via an alliance with the Communists: in this respect no-one has made a greater contribution than General De Gaulle towards the unity of the left.

But the Gaullist 'present' contained poison: for although the unity of the left was indeed a product of the political system it was a sterile product, because it had been manufactured mechanically without those concerned contributing much to it, and without disagreements being settled between the various elements which had come together to form the union.

Now the two salient facts in the balance-sheet of the ostentatious blunder, which spring 1968 boils down to, have even more urgently forced the PCF openly to assume the leadership of any movement towards a 'democratic alternative', even if the CFDT is quite willing to do it the favour of relieving the FGDS as regrouping agent for the whole of the left. On the one hand, leftism, which might merely have been an intermittent explosion, a sort of episodically active geyser, has imposed itself as a stable political phenomenon: marginal, noisy, multiform, torn by irresistible fissiparous tendencies, cankered, delirious, but *stable*, that is, unlikely in the foreseeable future to be forced back and re-interred in the political substratum. On the other hand the non-Communist left is more moribund than ever. In these conditions the PCF naturally spreads itself to its right, where it meets neither resistance nor support, whereas on its left a displeasing accumulation of jointly held views tends to repel it. This arrangement of political forces has already registered gains, but of a suspect nature. For successes recorded in certain country areas on the occasion of elections to chambers of agriculture, and in certain student and university circles on the occasion of elections to management committees, are in fact situational successes (as, in economics, one talks of situational revenue) not necessarily born of conviction.

These three change-inducing factors exert such pressure that PCF policy tends almost mechanically to return to the course worked out by Waldeck Rochet and to pick up the threads of the interrupted plan.

One cannot, however, suspect Georges Marchais and Etienne Fajon of being drawn by talent and temperament towards theoretical analysis and adaptability: but, whatever one may say, psychology plays only a minor role in politics. Even if the Czech 'normalisation' does not crucify him as it crucified Waldeck Rochet, Georges Marchais is obliged to admit that he personally would not go about it like the normalisers. Even if the doctrinal dispute around the relationship between socialism and democracy has hitherto remained outside his personal preoccupations, he is now obliged to confront afresh the problem to which Waldeck Rochet had devoted so much

380 IMAGINATION AND PRECISION IN THE SOCIAL SCIENCES

thought; his article *Socialism and Democracy* (18th June, 1970) carries on from the 1966 texts and again runs up against the idea of *proletariat dictatorship*, naming without naming this ghost which the Communists seem unable to exorcize.

The force of the current filtering into the party's Stalinist substructure is shown by the fact that disagreements are no longer discreetly settled by means of hushed-up resignations or amicable arrangements: the Garaudy affair and the resurgence of the Tillon affair are, of course, not the result of an anticommunist plot but the expression of a process of *desacralisation* which the Party must put up with. How indeed can one appeal to the concept of Sacred Union —for the closing of ranks in the face of the enemy—at a time when, to say the least, the class struggle, nationally and internationally, is in abeyance?

Is that to say, when the memory of Prague has dimmed and the passage of time has revived the recurring illusions of the non-communist left, that, by carefully reknitting the 'unity of the left', by patiently diverting leftist impatience, by carefully training its troops through conventional skirmishes, the Party could readopt its interrupted course of de-Stalinisation and at the same time pick up the threads of its constant strategy of conquering power from the inside?

Of course, it will try. Will it succeed any better than before? That is doubtful.

One must truly admire the sturdiness of the three forces invented by Lenin to enable his bolshevism, after the 2nd International had foundered, to break down the hitherto unbreached and apparently invincible propensity of the working class and its organisations to identify itself with the social game and established power: the dimension of the revolutionary enterprise, the nature of post-revolutionary power, and the nature of the Party—or, in the words of Lenin: proletarian internationalism, proletarian dictatorship, and democratic centralism. These three flying buttresses still support the enterprise just as proudly, despite the knocks, aimed at weakening it, from those, both within and without, who desire to destroy the edifice which has become a prison.

But solidarity with the socialist camp, and the incompatibility between democracy (bourgeois and formal) and proletarian dictatorship, even in the eventuality of an 'advanced democracy' (a strange term: it suggests meat which is starting to go off) smoothing the transition, constitute formidable defences which cannot merely be softened, controlled, circumscribed, and dispersed in a verbal fog; one after the other politicians who take the plunge and speculate on an alliance with the Communists are forced to accept the wager that they will be able to lift the obstacles in time, or at least get round them, and not have to fall back at the cost of face, honour or life. This wager which has so far been lost: at every development, the allies having patiently cleared the way and reaped the first successes, giving everyone a sense of hopeful well-being, it has only needed some unfortunate, or apparently unfortunate, international situation in which the Soviet Union has felt an urgent need for a demonstration of solidarity in its favour.

But it is perhaps the very structure of the Party which constitutes the least flexible element. The extensive commentaries, occasioned by the 19th Congress, failed to consider on this subject the only really crucial symptom: the self-perpetuation of the leaders, this stifling drawing together of the group which, in a confined cultural space, tends to be debilitating. Out of 95 retiring central committee members and deputies 85 were re-elected, that is, 90 per cent. As for the group of newly elected deputy members of the Central Committee, not only does it have an *average age* of 39.7 years, which is an extremely high average for admission to the controlling organ of a party of militants, but, above all, 85 per cent (19 out of 22) of its members are made up of men and women who were party members *before 1953*, that is, before Stalin's death seventeen years ago. The one with the shortest *length of service* has nevertheless twelve years. The group's average length of service is 21 years. One could not wish for a clearer demonstration of the PCF's continuing tendency to recruit its senior officers from the purest Stalinist generation, the one educated *after* the Resistance and *before* the 20th Congress. The new Secretary General, Georges Marchais, belongs exactly to this generation, the new 'fundamental generation'.

To sum up, the conclusions which emerge from this analysis of the working of the PCF are not very new: it is still controlled by the unvarying pattern of external factors urging it to break with itself and internal pressures which prevent this; so that, but for the addition of some other element which would tilt the scales one way or the other, one can very easily imagine the PCF continuing unhindered for some considerable time its grey, sparkless career of confirmed neo-Stalinism.

What sort of element can one think of likely to bring the PCF out of itself?

The installation of a French political system different from the present one would be a first step. At the level of its partisan structures if not on the electoral plane (of secondary importance for it), the PCF burned itself up more under the 4th Republic than under the 5th. The manpower graph is quite clear on this point: it descends remorselessly throughout the fifties but begins to rise again at the start of the sixties. This was not—at least, not directly—a constitutional question: but a corollary of the regrouping of political tendencies from one regime to the other. The isolation into which the PCF had been driven prior to 1958 was slowly strangling it. On the other hand, it can only stand to gain when it contracts any alliance to its right. *Provided that* the policy of this alliance can be established within its sphere of preoccupations, it is not at all necessary that the alliance should adopt the *PCF's* own programme. The important thing is that its *manner of posing problems* be adopted, together with its long and short-term political outlook. That is why the PCF, as long as it continues to use its traditional system of reasoning, must fear above all a return to the previous situation which would result from reconstitution of a centre-left opposition offering a system of political logic indifferent and alien to the Communist sphere of preoccupations—a reformist logic based on the commands of an advanced industrial society, such as, for example, the degree, mode and nature of distribution between private and public consumption. And so it wastes no time in attacking without pity, as soon as they appear and, where possible, before they have had time to establish themselves, schemes like Gaston Deferre's Great Federation, Alain Poher's candidacy, or the more recent attempt by Servan-Schreiber.

A second, even more decisive factor would of course be created by an unforeseen development in the Soviet story. For the moment, the parallelism between the neo-Stalinism of Breznev's Russia and that of Marchais' Communist Party is exemplary: but it is well-known that any significant break in the smooth running of the Soviet Union would very soon have a considerable effect on the position of French Communism.

In view of the scope and complexity of the subject, this is not the place to analyse the various aspects of the crisis in the Soviet system, nor to formulate the resulting hypotheses regarding the two or three scenarios between which the next Soviet decade must make its choice. It is a crisis now recognised and admitted outside the narrow circle of specialists: an economic crisis in its most familiar, most banal, most calculable guise. But it is also a more generalised crisis which is affecting the system's most fundamental machinery. What is ultimately in question is, in fact, the possibility of maintaining a Stalinist system while depriving it of its classic regulating instrument: fear. The optimistic, soothing argument that purges, concentration camps, and the great trials had for more than thirty years been merely useless and regrettable excrescences of a tyrant's bloodthirsty madness is now recognised for what it is: unfounded.

One cannot say that fear has disappeared—it would be difficult to claim that the Soviet opposition is now assured of the same legal protection as in the West—but the abandonment of the more extreme methods of provoking fear has had the consequence of freezing the apparatus of the ruling political and social classes more or less at the level and in the state they were in at the death of Stalin.

Neither can one count any longer on the circulation of men and ideas, on the replacing of worn-out teams by new ones by the former 'natural' means of elimination, early illness and death. In the West, these things are guaranteed, on the political plane, by the changes brought about by electoral battles at various levels. In Soviet Russia they were, until the fifties, guaranteed by fear. Of course, although both methods entail a certain amount of human wastage (no wholly rational system has yet been devised which permits an economical use of manpower in any field), one can in many ways consider the western method, which only condemns one to an early and, moreover, reversible, retirement, superior to the old Soviet method which had too often condemned its opponents to death.

Nothing has yet appeared to compensate for the limitation in the use of fear: a restriction maintained even after the close of Krushchev's brief period of liberalisation and despite the return to rigorous neo-Stalinism in other fields. Hence the nervous clinging-on to power, in the Russia of the sixties, by a team which, otherwise, in a purely Stalinist course of events, would merely have served in the interval between two purges or two trials: it is all the more unfortunate since such a team is necessarily mediocre.

It is mediocre, firstly, because the men composing it are mere shavings from the efficient planing-down to which the political class was subjected, and secondly, because it was originally constituted in such a way that none of its members could possibly be in a position to compete with the dictator himself, the keystone, whose permanence and stability were as necessary to the functioning of the system as were the evanescence and instability of his collaborators.

That mediocrity which one can quite legitimately suspect of being a property necessary to elites in power in all contemporary systems has become dangerous in the present Soviet system because it is no longer corrected by its corollary: transience.

The type of stiffening vertebral arthritis which can be observed in the giant body of the Union of Soviet Socialist Republics serves as a stern warning. Are we beginning to see the same disease in the solid organism of French Communism? It is a chronic sickness, a long, long sickness, a painful interminable old age . . . and painful too for those around it?

# Eric Hobsbawm

# Some Reflections on Nationalism

Nationalism is probably the most powerful political phenomenon of our century, and one whose importance continues to grow, but analysis has found it remarkably hard to come to grips with it. The literature about it, other than the purely descriptive, is on the whole unsatisfactory and frustrating. Virtually everything that has been written by nationalists (at least about their own nations) is question-begging and therefore negligible. Until recently, most of what has been written by non-nationalists has considered nationalism in some sense intrusive and disturbing. Like that Roman soldier who threatened to blot out Archimedes' diagrams, it was there, real and powerful, and one had to come to terms with it. Also like him, it was fundamentally outside the analytic models of the students concerned. If it had not obtruded itself, they would have been happy to take no notice of it.

Moreover, a considerable proportion of all serious analytical writing on 'the national question' was inevitably concerned with problems of definition, and with the associated activity of de-mythologising conventional views about the subject. Criticism was tempting and easy. What nationalists said and say about nations and nationalism, especially their own, is generally so unconvincing to anyone who does not share their emotional commitments, and may be so inconsistent with rational enquiry, as inevitably to provoke extended expressions of scepticism, muffled only by politeness, diplomacy or caution. On the other hand, the difficulty of coming to analytical grips with the problem has meant that most definitions of 'nations' and 'nationalism' have been empirical, and all of them, as can readily be shown, partial or inadequate. The search for objective criteria of nationhood, singly or in combination, quickly breaks down. Is its basis territorial, linguistic, ethnic, historic, or something else—or a combination of these? Exceptions can always be found, if not today then tomorrow. As for the subjective definitions, these are tautological or a *posteriori*. To define a nation by the existence of 'national consciousness' or some analogous sense of solidarity between its members, merely amounts to saying that a nation is what behaves like a nation, or alternatively, that it cannot be predicted but only recognised. Able thinkers have found it difficult to escape from this frustrating predicament.

The most fruitful approach to 'the national question' has undoubtedly been historical. If nations and nationalism are seen as phenomena which develop within a specific historic situation and are determined by it, a good many of our difficulties disappear. We can abandon the search for permanent, let alone eternal, characteristics of either or both, and we shall not be surprised to find that phenomena which converge from different starting points and in different circumstances towards a single objective (let us say, for argument's sake, the 'nation-state'), show substantial variations, if we take a cross-section of them at any given moment. Historically oriented theories of nationalism have therefore been the most useful. Yet even the two most popular varieties of these, Marxism and the group of interpretations covered by the term 'modernisation', have their weaknesses.

Marxism has suffered, because, while recognising nationalism as a phenomenon arising in the 'bourgeois epoch' it has, largely because of a deep-seated lack of sympathy with it, underestimated its importance and persistence. It is true that since Lenin, Marxists have recognised and analysed its revolutionary historic significance, and have stressed its political force. Though grossly neglected in the academic literature, the writings of the Leninist tradition of Marxism constitute a major advance in our understanding of the problem, especially as regards the liberation movements of colonial and semi-colonial peoples, and the struggle of the European nations against Fascism. On the other hand it is plainly wrong to regard nationalism as a phenomenon *confined* to the bourgeois epoch, or to analyse phenomena powerful enough to have split the international communist movement in the past decades as mere (petty) bourgeois survivals.

The 'modernisation' theories, on the other hand, have suffered not merely from the extreme primitivism of their basically single-step model of history, but from their even more striking failure to predict. (I leave aside the question whether such models have any serious predictive value.) Marxism did indeed predict some very important matters, notably the fusion of social and national elements in the liberation struggles of the present century, and the historical importance of such movements in the non-European countries. It failed to analyse 'the national question' in certain situations, notably those following upon social revolutions. 'Modernisation', insofar as it considers 'national consciousness' as 'but one facet' of this process, which is in turn defined in such simple uni-directional terms as 'expanding control over nature through closer interaction among men', must naturally be puzzled by the characteristic current form of western nationalism, which is divisive rather than integrative.[1] 'Modernisation' has undoubtedly led political scientists to pay greater attention to the problem of 'nations' than anyone else, or perhaps it would be better to say that the great movements of the 'underdeveloped' countries since the second world war have led them to take an interest in the complex of problems of which 'nations' are one, unfortunately often with conceptually inadequate tools. Still, the historians are hardly in a position to feel superior, since they have, with few exceptions, neglected the subject shamefully.

The following notes will therefore not discuss the past analytical literature at length. Readers will recognise easily enough where it follows what has already been written and where it diverges from it.

## II

In defining 'the national question' it is more profitable to begin with the concept of 'the nation' (*i.e.* with 'nationalism') than with the reality it represents. This is not to deny that 'nations', whatever they are, are real, though often they are the products of nationalist movements or nation-states rather than their foundation. The 'nation' as conceived by nationalism, can be defined prospectively; the real 'nation' can only be recognised *a posteriori*. So it is convenient to begin with the first. We know what Mazzini thought a nation was or ought to be, and the objective datum for our in-

---

1    D. Rustow: *Nation* (in *International Encyclopedia of Social Science*, 1968).

vestigation is his programmatic idea, which need not, and in fact did not, correspond to the facts he supposed it to represent. We do not know what the 'nations' of his time were, or if they existed in the modern sense, and neither did Mazzini, whose own view of the future structure of a Europe of nations would be rejected by far more nationalist movements than would accept it.[2]

The following propositions about 'the nation' in this programmatic sense may be put forward. They represent not what nationalists actually thought, but the implicit socio-political content of their aspirations.

1. The 'nation' is an historically novel construct, characteristic of the period since the late eighteenth-century, though no doubt anticipations or a few earlier examples may be discovered by those who wish to. Its novelty consists in the combination of two main assumptions.

2. The first of these is that the bonds of loyalty to (or characteristic of) the 'nation' are not merely superior to all others, but in a sense replace them, so far as political obligation is concerned. A man is no longer definable as the locus of a complex of multiple, possibly overlapping, probably separable, loyalties, but overwhelmingly in terms of a single one, his 'nationality'.

3. The second of these is the belief that this single collectivity of 'the people' or 'the nation' must find its expression in an independent and sovereign 'nation-state', preferably containing a homogeneous population composed only of members of its 'nation' using a single language.

---

2　　He envisaged; (1) a united Iberian peninsula combining Spain and Portugal; (2) a united Scandinavian peninsula combining Norway, Sweden and Denmark; (3) a United Kingdom of England, Scotland and Ireland; (4) Italy; (5) an 'Alpine Confederation' uniting Switzerland with Savoy, German Tyrol, Carinthia and Slovenia (!!); (6) a confederation of the Balkan peoples under Greek presidency, with its capital in Constantinople, including Greece, Albania, Macedonia, Rumelia, Bosnia, Serbia and Bulgaria; (7) a Danubian federation of Hungary, the Rumanian race—among which he appeared to include the inhabitants of Hercegovina—and Bohemia; (8) Germany, including Holland and Flanders; (9) France, including Walloon Belgium; (10) Russia and (11) Poland dividing between themselves 'the rest' and associated with one another. (Mazzini 1857 in Mack Smith *Il Risorgimento*, 1968, 422).

4. 'The nation' is therefore a combination of elements which have at first sight no necessary or even probable connection: on the one hand those of structural 'modernisation', *i.e.* the territorial state and the transformation (or simplification) of socio-political relations within it; on the other, the appeal to a variety of means of asserting or symbolising group membership and solidarity in the most emotionally charged personal sense, most of which are deliberately archaic in form, reference or derivation. One might go further and say that before the 'national' era, which, as the very term United Nations demonstrates, has tended to identify the concepts of 'nation' and 'sovereign state', the various 'national' solidarities had only a casual connection, and were not supposed to have any special connection, with obligations to the state centre.[3]

5. The assumptions discussed under 2 and 3 above imply, as has often been noted, a strong democratic and egalitarian element, at least within each nation. Political nationalism is revolutionary in its origins. Nationality-citizenship is therefore particularly effective in disrupting traditional hierarchies and ties of dependence. It is, at least potentially, not merely a political device but a movement.

Since nationalisms characteristically define their 'nations' in terms of what they consider natural, permanent, traditional or even eternal, their revolutionary novelty as a political programme is obscured. 'Nations' are not so much invented as composed and developed out of pre-existing historical materials, generally with quite different

---

3    This may be illustrated by an actual example of conflict between them. In 1914 a Baltic baron, from a family settled in Courland since the 15th century, found himself, as a German, teaching at a German university. Since he was also a reserve officer in an Imperial Russian cavalry regiment, he returned without a moment's hesitation to St. Petersburg to fight and kill his co-nationals, on the ground that 'loyalty to lord comes before loyalty to kin'. The argument, entirely convincing to a feudal noble, seems shocking to a nationalist. What is significant about it is, that a man sufficiently 'national' to regard Germany and all Germans as his 'kin', simply did not accept that his nationality had the political implications which nationalism reads into it. By contrast the British government in 1940, in interning German immigrants (including Jews and political refugees) wholesale, acted on the purely 'nationalist' assumption that unless there was strong proof to the contrary, *any* German must be presumed to owe an overriding loyalty to 'his' nation-state.

socio-political functions. It is easy to demonstrate that such concepts as territory, language, history, culture, even ethnic unity, did not mean the same in the European fifteenth as in the twentieth-centuries, had quite different functions, if any, and were not necessarily connected with each other, and even less with a particular state. The novelty of nationalist procedures can be traced even through their most traditionalist rhetoric. Thus the most powerful appeal to group solidarity in modern nationalist movements and states, the metaphor of 'kinship' is at once the most ancient and operationally the least relevant to 'national' social and political systems, in which actual kinship plays only the most subordinate or marginal role, where it is not actually dysfunctional. Yet it is the persistent, one might almost say the basic, theme of nationalist rhetoric. The nation is the motherland or fatherland; its members are brothers. They are linked by ties of 'blood' and 'race' (*i.e.* by supposed biological ties) which exclude non-members, by a common 'home', with common physical and mental furniture whose full meaning cannot be understood by others; they possess common ancestors, and a common language which is, almost by definition, inaccessible to those not sharing the family heritage (*'traduttore-traditore'* is not merely a pun, but a deeply ambiguous phrase). But it may be observed that the kinship model adopted, at least in European nationalisms—there has been little research in this field, so we can only speak with great caution—seems to be the simple nuclear family, rather than extended kinship. 'Cousins' ('our American cousins') do not really belong; a 'family of nations', such as used to form part of the staple of British imperialist rhetoric, is very different from a fatherland. In a word, the 'family' of such rhetoric has little in common with the kind of kinship which actually produced and implied group loyalty and mutual aid in societies in which blood really was thicker than water. The conceptual framework of even the most archaising nationalist argument, tends to be very far from the real past.

### III

Is there a functional connection between the apparently so disparate sets of elements which make up the 'nation-state'? Nineteenth-century observers assumed so, without much thought, and the theorists of 'modernisation' have made their most useful contribution in attempting to demonstrate (though not always to explain) it. They have done so by making the nation a function of the development of the modern state (by which we may understand the state in the era of capitalist development, or, more broadly, of the development of all industrial economies). State-building, in modern terms, is 'nation-building'. The analysis rests on the undeniable 'great transformation' of states since the European middle ages.[4] Speaking generally, the 'territorial state' which has developed since then, at first without 'national' implications, later commonly with them, substitutes a unified territorial base for the previous political systems for which this was not essential (any more than it is essential today for units of economic ownership such as a corporation or an estate), a single set of standardised institutions and values for a multiplicity of unstandardised ones, and a single set of direct linkages between a central government (with growing, and eventually total, power) and the individual citizen for a complex of indirect linkages, which run parallel to, or replace, the direct relation between 'centre' and 'periphery'. The early versions of the territorial state may have been unable to realise this programme to the full—even France in 1789 had not quite achieved the sixteenth-century absolutist slogan 'Un roi, une loi, une foi', but that is another question.

Why this model of the state came to be adopted—probably for the first time in history, at least in polities of such size—in the period of developing capitalism, is a question which cannot be discussed here, though we may observe in passing that it has not been irrelevant to capitalist economic development. It may well be argued that something like this kind of territorial state was essential to it. However, granted that such a type of state was to be constructed, models requiring it to be infused with a 'national' content can be readily set up. A familiar ideological version of such a model is Rousseau's argument, taken up by the French Revolution. The 'nation', which is the sovereign people, cannot tolerate intermediate and sectional interests and corporations between itself and its members. But by

---

4       R. Bendix: *Nation-Building and Citizenship* (1964).

implication this very elimination of other centres of loyalty makes the relation of loyalty of citizen to 'nation' the only valid, and therefore the strongest, of his emotional-political commitments. It is the content of the 'civic religion' which the community needs. There is no difference between '*Gemeinschaft*' and '*Gesellschaft*', because the only valid *Gemeinschaft* is the *Gesellschaft*, organised as the polity. Free man equals citizen. It is irrelevant that Rousseau himself did not think in terms of modern nation-states, for such arguments were applied to them.

They can readily be translated into less ideological terms. A territorial state which functions through a direct linkage between the individual citizens and a strong centre must develop a set of motivations in the citizens which (a) give them a primary and overriding sense of obligation towards it and (b) eliminate or sidetrack the various other obligations which they feel towards other groups and centres within or outside it. The most obvious way to do this is to establish a sense of identity with it, and the most effective way is to transfer the strongest bonds which hold men together from other poles of attraction to the state. It then becomes not merely the emotional equivalent of family, local community, etc., but the family or community itself—and the elimination or demotion of the other centres leaves a void which the symbols of patriotism can fill. (It is probably no accident that the improvised slum communities of immigrants in Chilean cities, drawn from a variety of uprooted countrymen, establish their identity by hoisting the national flag.) The need to provide the citizen with this sense of obligation is obvious, and all the more urgent when the modern territorial state requires to mobilise many of its citizens directly and individually, rather than through the habitual pre-industrial mechanism of relatively autonomous intermediary bodies or superior authorities. Military conscription, for instance, raises the problem in an acute form. Recent research has demonstrated that the percentage of draft-evasion in the France of the 1820s was highest in Corsica, in the South, and in Brittany, and lowest in the relatively developed North East of the country, where identification with 'France' was traditionally greater than elsewhere. (It is no historical accident that Joan of Arc came from Lorraine and not from, say, the Gironde.)

In European history the process of making such transfers is

normally one of adapting and broadening (or changing) existing elements of loyalty, and this obscures the novelty of the phenomenon. There is a formal continuity between the 'France' or even the 'Italy' of nationalism and the political, cultural or other entities bearing this name in the past, so much so that we are struck by surprise at the information that in 1860 the percentage of citizens of the newly united kingdom who actually spoke Italian at home, and not merely (when they knew it at all) used it as a language of literate culture or a *lingua franca* for communicating with Italians from other regions, probably did not exceed 2.5 per cent. The case is much clearer in a country like the USA, where few of the traditional raw materials for nationalism were available at the time of its revolutionary creation, but where nevertheless the transfer has been made—and in part deliberately engineered (*e.g.* by the use of the flag as a ritual centre for the daily reaffirmation of national loyalty in schools). Such an example strengthens the argument that some kind of national loyalty is essential to make a modern territorial-centralised state function, and has to be constructed where the materials for adaptation are not available. Where there is no old wine to put into a new bottle, some new liquor must be brewed.

But need this consist of the familiar brew of 'patriotism'? And if so, what are the precise elements of this brew which actually produce the desired effect? The first question cannot at present be answered, except in the general term that any state of the type discussed requires some kind of 'civic religion'. So far none of the alternatives to national patriotism have worked for any length of time, but it ought to be added that, with the single exception of the Soviet Republic in its initial years, no alternative has been seriously tried on any large scale. One might also point out that, so long as the states, set up on whatever principles, have to coexist with other sovereign states, their 'civic religion' cannot but emphasise those things which distinguish their citizens from those of other states. To that extent they provide a natural breeding-ground for national patriotism, at least insofar as the common factors stressed are similar to those used to define, or rationalise, national loyalties in more orthodox cases.[5]

---

5    Federation does not invalidate this. Were western Europe to form a federal union, which is improbable, local nationalisms might be replaced by, or subordinated to, a wider 'Europeanism', as the powerful

This brings us to the second question—a remarkably difficult one, since, with the probable exception of common territory and political organisation, the actual content of nationalism *in existing states* may be almost wholly constructed *a posteriori*. None of the commonly accepted criteria are indispensable, or need exist prior to the state: language, common culture, religion, traditions or history, let alone 'race'; even the nation's common economy may follow rather than precede its state. It is by no means established that any combination of them need predate the establishment of the national state. Admittedly cases where some of the more obvious criteria are absent—*e.g.* multilingual nations such as Switzerland—are rare, and probably confined to certain geographical-historical situations.[6] The contemporary lability of old-established nation states, in which autonomist and even separatist movements emerge among groups long believed to have been integrated into a single 'nation' (*e.g.* France) or to have accepted a common economy and polity (*e.g.* Britain), illustrates the point.

Language is today the commonest *de facto* criterion of nationhood. At least it is hard to think of a nationalist movement which does not put it forward in some form. Yet there are numerous rival nations sharing the same language (*e.g.* Latin America), and there are speakers of the same literate idiom who may decide not to 'belong' to their co-linguists, as the Austrians have done since the second World War, having previously considered themselves German, at least in the opinion of all their political parties with the exception of the Communists in the later 1930s. Conversely, there are more cases than is usually realised, of 'nations' whose common language was the product rather than the precondition of nationalism. The extreme case is Israel, whose national language had virtually to be invented for purposes of modern secular use.[7]

---

*contd.*   regional loyalties of Texans have been to 'Americanism'. But this would cease to be really or potentially nationalist only if there were to be a global federation.

6        (Ed. S. Rokkan), *Centre Formation, Nation-Building and Cultural Diversity*, Report on a symposium organised by UNESCO.

7        It was first used for colloquial domestic intercourse by Bar Yehuda, who had recently invented the Hebrew term for 'nationalism' and was—characteristically—on his journey of emigration to Palestine.

Our question is therefore impossible to answer at present. All that can be said is that, even where the common criteria of belonging to a state are constructed on entirely non-traditional lines (and even when they may actually be deliberately ecumenical in their ideological content), the very fact of their being the possession of one state among several others, is likely to infuse them with a 'national' or 'nationalist' element. 'Americanism', whatever its present political connotation, was originally a universal programme as well as a definition of what the citizen of the USA ought to represent: an invitation to all men to become Americans if they so chose, as well as an ideal description of those who already were. This has not prevented it from turning into a strongly nationalist slogan.[8] It would therefore seem that the best way to avoid states generating their own nationalism is either to merge them all into a global federation, or to have a form of socio-political organisation quite different from the modern territorial-centralised one. There is no precedent for the former. As for the latter, there are plenty of precedents, though their circumstances were so different that they can prove nothing except that there are theoretical alternatives to the modern form of state. How likely humanity is to follow either or both these roads, is quite another question.

## IV

It is, as we have seen, not difficult to construct a model of the state which will generate nationalism. This model may well have a certain explanatory power, but it is unfortunately evident that it does not apply to a large part of the phenomena which are patently 'nationalist', namely those which are not functions of an already existing state, notably the movements of national self-assertion and liberation, especially those not linked to an existing or even a historically remembered polity (*i.e.* what nineteenth-century terminology called the 'unhistoric nations').

Such phenomena are, once again, extremely difficult to analyse,

---

8     That it lent itself with particular ease to imperialist or expansionist purposes because of its universality, should not mislead us. Even the most restrictionist criteria of nationalism and 'national destiny' have never prevented the generation of expansionist aspirations and slogans.

because we know so little about 'national consciousness', and even if we knew more, its social and ideological components would normally be very hard to disentangle. As soon as the phenomenon of 'nationalism' becomes politically so noticeable as to attract the attention of students it emerges—at least since the French Revolution—as a *programme*: in the increasingly common extreme case, as the programme of establishing a sovereign national state with certain conventional characteristics.

Now in the first place in the past century such a programme has been adopted almost automatically by all emerging nationalist movements, an example of what the economists call the demonstration effect. We do not know what programmes such movements would have formulated at any stage of their development, had the attraction of this prestigious model from the advanced world not been so great. Its standardised versions conceal many possible divergences between such movements, just as Roman Catholicism and Communism have in their time concealed substantial variations between the Catholicism and Communism of different regions. In the second place, such a programme is normally formulated and adopted by particular groups within a population, who provide the pioneers, ideologists, leaders, organisers and very often the political spokesmen of their 'nationalism'. The remainder of the population, in becoming 'nationalist', therefore buys a pre-selected package of miscellaneous goods. To acquire one is to acquire all. Support for any of nationalism therefore normally appears to imply support for one particular kind.

How great these masked divergences may be, is sometimes revealed by time. Thus before 1947 support for the expulsion of the British from India implied, for all except the followers of the Muslim League, support for a unified all-Indian state, which was the programme of the leading cadres of the national movement. It has since become clear (though this was actually anticipated earlier by some Marxist students) that this demand masked a powerful current in favour of linguistic states, which was neither envisaged nor accepted by the Indian National Congress. One need hardly add that even the all-Indian nationalism which emerged when the local and regional activists and bosses were revealed as an effective political force in politics, proved to be quite different from the ideology and programme of the small group of largely westernised *evolués* who

previously provided the programme and charismatic national
leadership of the movement. Gandhi, for instance, favoured Hindi
as the 'national language' of a free India because a nation needed a
common language, and it seemed hardly conceivable that English,
the imperial idiom, should be retained for this purpose, even sup-
posing that it had been spoken by more than a tiny minority of the
educated. Hindi, though admittedly not ideal—it was spoken by
less than half the population—was the least implausible candidate.
Coming from a native Gujerati speaker, who was pretty certainly far
more fluent in English than in Hindi, Gandhi's view was presumably
unbiased by linguistic loyalties. The briefest glance at the present
state of the movement in favour of Hindi reveals a very different
situation, carrying a much higher emotional charge, and implying
political consequences very different from those envisaged by Gandhi.

Even if we overcome such difficulties, sheer massive ignorance of
what actually happens when nationalist movements appear and
grow, still bedevils us, thanks to the gross neglect of the subject by
historians. (It has proved as disastrous to leave the history of
nationalism to nationalists as that of railways to railway enthusiasts.)
The social, economic, even the ideological, analysis of the pioneers
and early cadres and supporters of such movements has hardly been
begun for Europe; and there has been almost no comparative study
in this field. Even greater darkness encompasses mass nationalism,
especially when this meant the change of meaning of an existing
term rather than the formulation of a new one. So long as this is the
case, much about nationalism must remain a matter for speculation
rather than analysis.[9]

Fortunately one quite first-rate piece of comparative historical
analysis has been done recently by a Czech worker on a selection
of national movements among small European nationalities—
Czechs, Slovaks, Norwegians, Finns, Estonians, Lithuanians and
Flemings.[10] This throws much light on our problems, all the more so

---

9    Most of the useful European material comes from two regions:
     Scandinavia and Central-Southeastern Europe, *i.e.* the now mostly
     socialist succession states of the 19th-century multi-national empires
     of our continent.

10   M. Hroch: *Die Vorkaempfer der nationalen Bewegung bei den kleinen
     Voelkern Europas* (Acta Univ. Carol. Phil. & Hist. XXIV) Prague 1968.

as Hroch's results appear to converge with recent work on the apparently very different problem of peasant movements and revolutions.[11] In the following paragraphs I am greatly indebted to this excellent study.

Hroch divides the development of nationalist movements into three phases, of which he considers only phase A (when it is confined to a group of intellectuals without wider influence or even much ambition to mobilise mass support) and phase B (when a group of 'patriots' already attempt systematically to spread 'the national idea' but without as yet penetrating to any extent into the masses). Phase C begins when there is evidence of such mass penetration, as in Bohemia from 1848.

What is interesting about his work is not so much the excellent comparative analysis of the social, age, etc., composition and origins of both the 'patriots' and the circles directly affected by their agitation in phase B, as the geographical analysis, which seeks to define the areas of a 'national' territory within which the agitation is particularly intense or firmly established. National activity was of course rather unevenly distributed at this stage, but normally the zone of maximum nationalism formed (with some qualifications determined by the urban pattern) a fairly coherent and compact area.

Purely geographic, administrative, and linguistic factors and patterns of human settlement appeared to play no predominant role in determining the formation of such areas. (On the other hand education—especially the density of village schools—was significant, though not all well-schooled areas developed intense national activity.) Economic factors clearly played a highly significant role. However:[12]

(1) National zones were not areas in which industry or pre-industrial manufactures were of central importance. They were dominated by small scale artisan production for the local needs of towns and the peasant hinterland;

(2) they were situated in the most fertile part of the national territory (notably in regions of cereal production, sometimes combined with industrial crops);

---

11    E. Wolf: *Peasant Wars of the Twentieth Century* (London, 1971).
12    Hroch, *op. cit.*, 160.

(3) agrarian production, though no longer part of self-sufficient economies of the medieval type, was distributed through local markets and only through these linked with more distant markets.

(4) they consisted of areas whose economic activities and social structure were affected by the influence of the civilisation of a rising industrial society, but which were not themselves the main bearers of these processes of industrialisation.[13]

In brief, these European national movements emerged first in regions of *intermediate* social change: neither in the traditional peasant regions so remote from the 'new times' that the very concept of 'country' or 'nation' could hardly arise[14] nor in the areas already transformed. The growing suburbs of the Walloon towns, swelled by mass immigration from the Flemish countryside, remained notably uninterested in the Flemish nationalist movement. Similarly the national activists and supporters of phase B tended to be socially intermediate: weakest among the urban and rural poor and the workers, weak also among entrepreneurs and large merchants, not to mention the higher strata of the old regimes. One might say that such movements tended to take root first in areas (and perhaps strata) for whom 'modernisation' was sufficiently present to present problems—not necessarily problems of life or death—but not sufficiently advanced to offer solutions. The well-known phenomenon of an over-production of school and university graduates, whose possibilities of employment and upward social mobility were therefore inhibited, is a special case of such a situation. (With certain exceptions, the 'patriots' of the movements studied were predominantly the sons of parents from the lower ranks, who had risen just about as far as persons of such parentage could.[15]) More generally, as Hroch does not fail to point out, we may observe awareness of 'the difference between the old-style petty producer and modern industrial production, between the petty market and the great

---

13   As Hroch notes, all this implies a higher degree than the current one of 'social communication' in Deutsch's sense (Deutsch, *Nationalism and Social Communication*, 1953), both among 'national' activists and in 'national' regions; but, in my view rightly, he refuses to stop the analysis at this point. (Hroch: *ibid*. 167-70.)

14   Most of the inhabitants of the Pripet marshes answered the question about their nationality in the Polish censuses of 1919 and 1931 with the phrase 'from here' or 'local'.

15   This appears to apply least in Norway, Finland and perhaps Flanders.

market, between the petty-bourgeois idyll and the impersonal, harsh character of the rising civilisation of modernity'.[16]

There is an interesting analogy between these suggestions and Wolf's persuasive argument that the major force of peasant revolutionary movements lies in the 'middle peasants', the rural strata most firmly rooted in traditional agrarian society, fighting to maintain or re-establish the customary way of life—against a growing threat rather than an already accomplished disruption. Those already integrated into the new society (whether as its beneficiaries, like capitalist farmer-peasants, or as its victims, like the rural proletarians), or those who occupy marginal positions within it (like certain sections of the 'village poor'), are less likely to provide a sufficient force of negation.[17] Both early nationalist movements and peasant movements appear subjectively as defensive reactions against a process of (threatened rather than achieved) social transformation. Yet they cannot but be its vehicle. The 'programmes' of both are not merely impracticable but in a sense historically irrelevant, whether they are formulated with great precision, as among the peasants of Zapata's Morelos, or in terms of vague and barely defined aspirations, as among nationalists. Hence, insofar as such organised movements establish themselves firmly, it is by means of methods, ideas and leadership which belong to the new world, even when their object (like Gandhi's spinning wheels) may be to restore or preserve the old. Insofar as they are historically effective, their effect is at odds with their intentions. But here we are concerned not with results but with motivations.

The situation which stimulated the nationalist defence-reactions and is best known to historians, was that of the advancing capitalist market-economy and market-society. It may be that this provided an unusually favourable breeding-ground for 'nations', not only because the medium-sized 'nation-state' provided obvious advantages for 'progress' and the development of a middle class—or alternatively, because the states it replaced were more often than

---

16      Hroch, *op. cit.*

17      This does not prevent them from acting as channels for the dissemination of new political ideas and methods, which may influence such movements.

not backward, wrongly structured or both[18]—but also because
bourgeois society in the form of liberal capitalism destroyed the older
solidarities, communal bonds and structures of society continuously,
ruthlessly, and as a matter of principle, while deliberately putting
nothing in their place except the pursuit of self-interest. During the
time it did so, it provoked a defensive, sometimes a militant, nostalgia
for older collectivities, notably among the strata which found themselves unable to benefit adequately as individuals from the new
society (unlike the successful capitalist entrepreneurs and higher
professionals) or to evolve their own modern collectivities (as the
workers did through the labour movement). In Germany and
German-Austria we can trace the rise of nationalist, antisemitic,
potential mass movements among such strata in the last third of the
nineteenth-century as a double reaction against liberalism and
social democracy. After it had done so, it left a void which 'the
nation' could fill symbolically.

Yet it does not follow that reactions of this type are confined to
this particular historical situation. History does not come to a stop
when the state defined by some political scientists as 'modern' has
been reached. Social disruption continues, with occasional bouts of
particularly drastic change, such as that which has decimated those
resistant strata, the peasantry and the traditional small-shopkeeper-
type petty bourgeoisie in Western Europe since the 1950s. Whenever
it threatens the viability of institutions, values and practices within
existing social systems, even those formed to come to terms with
an earlier bout of change, the pattern of reaction may recur. All the
things which can be sheltered under the large conceptual umbrella of
'the community', the set of directly perceived primary social groups
and relationships, seem particularly vulnerable. They must be reinforced or replaced, if only symbolically, by something that purports
to perform the same function. It need not necessarily take the
form of a 'nation', though this has the advantage of an apparently
precise delimitation externally ('us' against 'the foreigners') and
almost total lack of precision in its internal definition, so that it can
simultaneously contain the most changing and contradictory

---

18    The three great multinational empires against which the bulk of
      European national movements were directed until 1918, were notorious
      anachronisms.

interests and aspirations. However, even if it did not have these advantages, once the stereotype of 'the nation' has been established and reinforced by prestige and a prevalent pattern of international political structure, it probably contains enough force to absorb and assimilate a variety of other expressions of communal nostalgia. Pakistan was clearly not the result of a 'national' movement, but both the original movement, the state, and doubtless the subsequent Pakistani patriotism have evidently been assimilated to the prevalent pattern.[19] Moreover, the very construction of internationally homogenous nation-states strengthens the 'nationalist' appeal among those groups which are being homogenised, or whose separate communal existence—often institutionally recognised—loses its function. Pluralist polities become monolithic nations with 'minorities', providing twentieth-century governments with headaches from which their pre-industrial ancestors rarely suffered.

The relation of nationalism to the social processes which provoke it, may thus differ widely, though the phenomenon itself appears to remain the same. Thus the characteristic 'nation-building' of the nineteenth-century tended to run parallel with the characteristic trend of economic and social development, the creation of larger homogeneous units out of (economically and administratively) smaller heterogeneous ones; so much so that quite a few examples of potential 'nationalism' which diverged from this trend tended to escape wider notice—like the Bretons or the Catalans. In the mid-twentieth-century the two trends run at an angle to each other, except insofar as the continuing tendency of economic and political units to grow further in size, power over their subjects or clients, and planned bureaucratisation may have taken them to a size beyond the optimal one for administration and management, or beyond that with which human beings can cope as participants, producing some movement towards decentralisation and devolution. Still, by and large the tendency towards gigantism continues (it is, by the way, no longer as closely linked with nation-states as before), while the

---

19    Generally 'the nation' replaces older communal structures symbolically. Where it genuinely fills the gap, it tends to do so at disproportionate social cost. As Fascism was aware, the most effective examples of a working *Volksgemeinschaft* occur when members of one 'nation' are mobilised in common hostility to foreigners, as in war.

tendency of nationalism has been increasingly to break up large units into smaller ones.

Where, for instance, are the contemporary equivalents of the unifying national movements of the period from 1815 to 1950—*e.g.* the German, Italian, Southern Slav, Indian or Chinese? Conversely we are today familiar with nationalisms which seek to disrupt established 'modern' economies, often of no great size, sometimes with a long history of national integration. Their success in doing so is evident: as witness the difference between the political problems raised by Flemish nationalism in Belgium before 1914 and since 1945. Subjectively their supporters of such movements may feel similar to those of earlier ones; objectively one cannot but conclude that the case for the small-size sovereign nation-state as a unit of economic or even cultural development is today considerably weaker than it was before 1914, especially in underdeveloped areas.[20]

But if the 'nationalist' reaction today lacks the built-in brake provided by the nineteenth-century aspiration to build viable nation-states—*i.e.* the assumption that there was something like a minimum size for such units—need they continue to be 'nationalist' in the established sense? It is true that they can still often borrow the concepts and symbols of historic nationalism. There are still enough 'suppressed nations' to make this easy, though one or two— at present politically insignificant—movements like the Cornish and the Occitan come close to actually having to invent their 'nations'. However, insofar as such movements are primarily re-actions against bigness (and they are not entirely this), it is not easy to set lower limits to their ideal units. Logically local patriotism might provide equally possible rallying-points, as was anticipated several years ago by the film *Passport to Pimlico*, and in practice in 1970 by the brief 'declaration of independence' of the Isle of Dogs against the rest of London. We need hardly as yet discuss at what point of such development an analysis in terms of 'nationalism' ceases to be realistic.

---

20  Whether such units become *de facto* dependent on a major capitalist economy ('neo-colonialism') or merge into some larger unit of economic activity, their sovereignty is likely to be infringed. The exceptions which occur, do not invalidate this generalisation.

## V

Nationalism is therefore a dual phenomenon, or rather an inter-action of two phenomena, each of which help to give shape to the other. It consists of a 'civic religion' for the modern territorial-centralised state, and of a mode of confronting social changes which appear to threaten and disrupt certain aspects of the complex of social relationships. The former reflects a specific historic situation, characteristic of Europe since the French Revolution, and of most of the non-European world in the twentieth-century: the combination of economic development, in the first instance capitalist (whether this is a necessary condition is not yet clear), with the mass partici-pation in politics of a mobilised population. It is possible that we may be approaching the end of this period, at least insofar as the medium-sized sovereign 'nation-state' seems to be losing its role as the necessary or optimal framework for economic development. The latter is in principle not confined to any particular historic period or society, though it only acquired the full features of 'nationalism' as we know it in the specific historical era since 1789, and would prob-ably not have done so in another setting.

Conversely, the state in this period tended to become a 'nation-state' whose civic religion took the form of national patriotism, largely because the elements from which such sentiments could be generated—territorial, linguistic, ethnic, etc.—lay ready to hand, being also those most likely to be used to formulate defensive group reactions. (An obvious weakness of most states of technically de-sirable size was, of course, that they were not 'nationally' homo-geneous, a state of affairs likely to lead to acute practical problems once 'national consciousness' ceased to be the property of only a few 'nations', as most nineteenth-century thinkers assumed it was and ought to be.)[21] A 'nationalist' civic ideology was convenient, moreover, not only inasmuch as a state required to mobilise its citizens *en masse* directly, but also insofar as they were already

---

21    Most of them assumed that the rest of the potential 'nations' would either be content to be assimilated to the state-nations, or with some-thing less than sovereign autonomy, or were destined by historical progress to fade away. The serious discussion of 'the national question' began, when it was clear that this did not generally happen.

mobilised for their own purposes (not necessarily only under 'national' banners) which conflicted with the interests of their rulers.

The characteristic nationalism of the past 150 years has been a constant interpenetration of these two elements. Hence the difficulty of analysing it. States have aspired to become 'nations', 'nations' to become states. Social movements (in the broadest sense of the term) have tended to become 'national' or to be split along 'national' lines, as the history of the most passionately and systematically internationalist among them demonstrates. 'National' movements have been imbued with a social and ideological content which has no necessary connection with their nationalism. Each tendency has reinforced the other, and given it a more self-conscious expression. The 'nation-state' has created its 'nation' and its 'nationalism' not to mention those of the other potential 'nations' with which it came into conflict. The 'national movement' in turn has forced both states and other political organisations with nationally unspecific aims, to adopt its ambiance and characteristics. (The Middle East provides illustrations for both these developments today.)

One error of older students of the subject was to seek for some entity, the 'people' or the 'nation' which, though doubtless subject to the processes of growth and evolution, had some sort of permanent objective characteristics. This is not the case, or rather, the search for human groups specifiable in such a manner throws no significant light on 'nations' and 'nationalism'. However, another error, which remains popular, is to assign only one specific historical function to nationalism—whether in the process of 'modernisation' or that of the development of bourgeois/capitalist society. It plainly has had such functions, though these require, as has been suggested, rather more complex analysis than they are often given. But it cannot be confined to such a role, and consequently the 'nationalisms' which fall outside it cannot merely be dismissed as troublesome 'bourgeois' or other survivals, though the establishment of the 'nation'-stereotype and of an international system which largely equates states and nations undoubtedly gives them a significant capacity to survive.

However, the capacity of nationalism to fit a wide variety of sociopolitical situations and to adopt new functions, need not lead us to abandon the view that it is not necessarily permanent. Nonnationalist students before 1914 assumed that it would eventually

o

disappear, to be absorbed into or replaced by, international forms of government, ideology, or even culture and language, reflecting the increasingly global character of the economy, of science, technology and communications. Such views were oversimplified, and as short-term forecasts were as wrong then as they are today. In spite of increasing evidence of globalisation, nationalism is on the increase, and the uneven character of historical change is likely to make it go on increasing, and above all multiplying. As a long-run forecast, on the other hand, the prediction that nationalism will decline may prove to be no more unrealistic than other mid-nineteenth-century predictions (e.g. the disappearance of the peasantry), which looked implausible enough even a century after they were made, but are far from implausible today. Such a prediction does not imply that the differences which nationalism uses to define 'nations' will disappear, that the self-identification of groups in such terms will cease, or that their relations with outsiders will become idyllic. It merely implies that their social, economic and political implications will become transformed to the point where terms like 'nation' and 'nationalism', in our sense, cease to be seriously applicable to them.[22] Still, since this is not a prospect of the politically foreseeable future, and in any case not one to which a timescale can be attached, it is hardly worth pursuing this line of analysis. Nevertheless, it may be worth concluding these reflections by stating the obvious, namely that nationalism is a historic phenomenon, the product of the fairly recent past, itself subject to change, and unlikely to persist indefinitely.

---

22    This already is the case with very broad classifications of colour (race), culture and history, such as pan-Africanism, Panslavism, pan-Latin-Americanism, which are real enough, but have not the political implications of traditional nationalisms. The attempts to use them as the base of state-formation have so far been uniformly unsuccessful.

T. J. Nossiter

# Shopkeeper Radicalism in the 19th Century

This discussion of the role of the shopkeeper in the politics of the North-east of England from 1832 to 1860 is a by-product of a long-term investigation of the social basis of voting in English boroughs between the first reform act and the ballot act of 1872, in which I was much encouraged by Peter Nettl. See also 'Voting Behaviour 1832-72', *Pol. Stud.* xviii (3), Sept. 1970.

The shopkeeper has had a raw deal from the historian—dismissed by the radical historian as one of the petty bourgeoisie and ignored by the 'aristocratic' historian as small fry of no significance. It is as if there had never been a nation of shopkeepers. Contemporaries were, however, well aware of the retailers' importance and freely used the term 'shopocracy' to describe the grocers and drapers of the Middlemarchs of England: as early as 1835 John Wilson was writing 'I cannot sit still, James, and hear you abuse the shopocracy'.[1] The retailer constituted a much more credible threat to the established order than the working man, for it was he who had the ability, motive and opportunity after 1832 to participate in and organise radical movements. This can be readily demonstrated from the history of Tyneside and County Durham—although there are some reasons for thinking that the north-east may not have been altogether typical, and these will be discussed at the end of the paper.[2]

We must begin with an attempt to define exactly who made up the 'shopocracy'. Victorians themselves understood it to mean a reasonably well-established grocer or draper with a shop on the

[1]  Christopher North (John Wilson), *Noctes Ambrosianae*, No. 39 (Feb., 1835).
[2]  See the fuller discussion in T. J. Nossiter, 'Elections and Political Behaviour in County Durham and Newcastle, 1832-74' (D.Phil. thesis, Oxford, 1968).

street corner or a pitch in the High Street. They normally thought of almost any retailer from butcher to tobacconist as likely to have distinctive values and attitudes, but the core of the class was the food and clothing trades both in terms of numbers and the unambiguous differences in work situation and political action.

The shopkeepers' social visibility was probably related to the decline of the stall in the market and the rise of the shop in the street, a process which was well under way before Marks moved from his Leeds stall in the seventies. Contemporary directories reflect this in the growing number of entries for grocers and tea merchants and the gradual appearance of a residential as well as a business address as the retailer left the upper rooms of his shop to the apprentices. By the fifties the newspapers were carrying shopping advertisements which quickly became a staple income for the new penny dailies of the sixties and seventies. But if we can readily grasp the meaning of 'shopocracy' on an intuitive basis we still need to know what the basis of the analytic distinction was for separating out a special shopkeeping class.

There is no problem about distinguishing the wholesalers from the retailers. The merchants were undeniably part of the commercial capitalist class whereas the retailers were actually or potentially members of the proletariat, owning little more than the product of their own labour. But the difference between retailers and craftsmen is less obvious and more revealing. Its essence lay in the three contrasts in their work situations: firstly, the shopkeeper was primarily concerned with the sale rather than the making of goods; secondly, his job called for a range of skills rather than one specific one; and finally, his orientation was to the customer not the craft. He might indeed be a provision merchant or butcher but he was significantly a 'high class' one. The smith, carpenter or engineer who were typical members of the craft trades worked with raw materials in a workshop, small factory or on a building site; their skill lay in their capacity to handle and fabricate one particular kind of material or machinery; and they had little call for the diffuse skills of personal relations, stock control or accountancy. Most craftsmen in a better way of business could no doubt read, write and add, but there was not the same need for literacy or numeracy as there was with the shopocracy. In the nature of their occupation the shopkeepers on the other hand required the ability to handle customers, to deal with the commercial traveller and, in many cases, the capacity to purchase, control and check stock. More successful shopkeepers might also have a good deal of practice in self-expression through their contact with middle and upper middle class clientèle. The shopkeepers thus developed clerical and organisational ability for which there was a natural political outlet after the first reform act in 1832. It was not surprising to find many shopkeepers on the reform committees of the 1830s or working at registration and the preparation of canvass books; and in the chartist period it was men like Blakey, mayor of Morpeth, and owner of an extensive mail-order business in hats, who helped to build up sizeable organisation, despite all the difficulties of lack of transport, long hours of work and inadequate media of communication. Could many of the Whig and Tory candidates, one asks, have achieved the sheer organisation of the chartist movement? Many, indeed, seem to have needed a lot of guidance in managing their own commercial affairs properly, never mind organising elections.

The shopocracy thus had the ability to organise radical and liberal movements. They also had the motivation and opportunity to do so. Far from being mere organisation men the shopkeepers often possessed an acute political consciousness, heightened by their marginal position in the social structure in the front line of class antagonism. It was this which George Eliot echoed in *Middlemarch* when she referred to the parcel-tying class;[3] and there is plenty of evidence of the scorn in which the shopocracy was held by their erstwhile allies of 1832, the Whigs. A quite typical illustration might be the unseemly clash between the well-connected Whig coalowner, William Hutt, and his nonconformist merchant rival Walters at Gateshead in 1852. The whole of this virulent and scurrilous campaign underlined the social implications of the Whig and Radical labels at this time. One of Hutt's men dismissed their opponent's committee as a beggarly one of petty traders and working men and later added for good measure that Walters would make a much better rent collector than MP.[4] Back came the highly significant

---

3      G. Eliot, *Middlemarch*.
4      *Sunderland Herald*, 20 March, 1857.

radical reply in the form of a satirical bill:[5] 'Gentlemen, only look at
them. What are they? Shopkeepers! Gentlemen, I AM NOT a
shopkeeper. I belong to a learned profession. I am a great Man . . .
I drive my own Dog-cart. . . . I AM a great Man, and therefore ought
to be consulted by the lower Orders of Electors, whose Intelligence is
fitting enough for the Counter, but quite inadequate to the task of
deciding upon a proper Person to represent them in Parliament . . .
Gentlemen, these Shopkeepers have outraged all propriety, by
selecting a Gentleman who pays some real Respect for Religion'.
This bill indicated the growing sense of class and exclusion among
shopkeepers and the 'labour aristocracy' and the dawning revolt
against influence and deference which spread through the urban
areas in the 1850s. All over the north-east the lesson the Whigs drew
—unlike their fathers—was that the franchise had been extended far
enough. The letters to Hutt's agents reflected this widespread
reaction: one correspondent wrote that it would be half a century
before 'that class of people' would be sufficiently educated to know
what a solemn trust had been placed in their hands;[6] while another—
himself an MP for one of the most corrupt constituencies in the
north—averred that if elections were to be as vitriolic as the 'Walters
family' had made them in Gateshead then no *gentleman* would stand.
This family, he added, had branches in every town in the country.[7]
Unfortunately for the Whigs they were closing the stable door after
the horse had bolted. The rising prosperity of the 1850s was accompanied by a rapid expansion of the parliamentary electorate
mainly among the working classes, over whom the lower middle
classes had considerable influence. The fifties were a critical decade
for the Whigs, with the lower middle class determined to bite the
hand that had failed to feed them.

Just as the Tories had failed to adjust to changing patterns of
social and economic power during their fifty-year hegemony before
1832, so the Whigs had dragged their feet after it. The shopocracy
were the most articulate of the disillusioned liberals of the thirties.
Prominent in the unions of 1831 and 1832, they had been the party

---

5        Bill. Brockett Mss. x, 289. Gateshead Public Library.
6        Midgeley to Brockett, 27 July, 1852. Brockett Mss. x, 537.
7        M. Forster to Clephan, editor of *Gateshead Observer*. Brockett Mss. x,
         379.

workers of municipal politics but were denied a share in the spoils; and at least in the north-east they had reacted by contributing to the chartist movement, and in the forties and fifties had been the body of the ratepayer and sanitary associations. It was the shopocracy rather than the working class—depressed or prosperous—which had the opportunity to sustain a radical movement in successive elections. Their social situation gave them more independence: the successful could leave the shop in the hands of the apprentice, while their clientèle was often sufficiently varied to offer protection against severe pressure from any one landowner, magnate or party. Certainly there were instances where undue influence was brought to bear— Lord Londonderry's list of tradesmen to be 'excommunicated' in the event of disobedience to his lordship's wishes in a local election (Durham 1843), or the tragic case of Mathison, stalwart supporter of the Northern Reform Union in that corrupt outpost Berwick, who was forced into taking a mean shop 'not one-fourth large enough' for his needs and into watching the Whig 'devils' drive off his customers —but these were exceptions from notorious constituencies.[8] On the whole the shopocracy enjoyed a considerable measure of political freedom; their capital at death, according to Vincent, three-quarters that of a professional and three times that of the craftsmen.[9] They rarely suffered from unemployment; and they were seldom exposed to the undue influence of one powerful magnate. It was usually possible to play off one social pressure against another—landlord against wholesaler, customer against customer. In the last resort a nation of shopkeepers was protected by the varied patronage of a nation of customers.

It could perhaps be argued that some of the tradesmen treated here as members of the shopocracy—for example, the butchers or the tailors—could just as plausibly be seen as élite craftsmen; and it is undoubtedly the case that some sections of the working class, particularly in the industrial centres, were radical. However, not only has Dr. Pelling shown that the politics of labour were much more complicated than some would like to suppose but the best contemporary estimate—a parliamentary return of 1865-66—by

8    Mathison to Reed, 29 Sept., 1859. Cowen Mss. C 763. Newcastle Public
     Library.
9    J. Vincent, *Poll Books* (1967).

implication treats such 'craftsmen' as middle rather than working class.[10] Certainly, the average constituency was said to be made up of only one-quarter working class and three-quarters middle and upper class on the eve of the second reform bill.

The provisions of the 1832 reform bill drastically altered the balance of the urban electorate in favour of the middle classes by the introduction of the ten-pound household franchise and the restriction of the freeman vote. Few of the working class could hope to be enfranchised by the ten-pound clause when the average terrace house outside London was rated at between £4 and £8 per year. The old freeman franchise was now hedged around with qualifications; and even more important, what working-class vote there was tended to be concentrated in the old freeman boroughs of the south. The industrial working class of the north was denied a voice, while the less politically-conscious artisans of the southern market towns voted in fairly large numbers. The importance of the latter can be gauged from the fact that in the eight most notoriously venal constituencies the average percentage of working men in 1865 was forty compared with the national average of twenty-five per cent.[11] On the other hand in the leading industrial centres of the north commonly associated with radicalism, the figure was very low indeed: eighteen per cent in Sunderland and as little as seven per cent in Leeds. These figures might have suffered from the erosion of the freedom vote with time but this has to be set against the effects of inflation in reducing the social significance of the ten-pound qualification. By contrast the house and the shop of the retail tradesman was generally rated between £10 and £20 and the shopkeeper formed in a very meaningful sense the 'class of '32', the voters who made up much of public opinion in the towns and were at the same time most conscious of their 'betrayal' by the Whiggish upper middle class.

Detailed analysis of the social composition of the electorate in the 'industrial' constituencies of the north-east, whether two or single-member constituencies, shows conclusively that the shopocracy was the biggest component in every case: the figures were Gateshead

---

10      H. Pelling, 'The Concept of the Labour Aristocracy', *Popular Politics and Society in Late Victorian Britain* (1968).

11      Boroughs. Electors (Working Classes) Return. Parl. Papers 1866, lvii, 47, 243.

34 per cent (1837), Newcastle 49 per cent (1860), Sunderland 29 per cent (1845), South Shields 37 per cent (1852) and Tynemouth 30 per cent (1852). Only Durham was different, an old freeman borough with an invidious record of corruption and influence, where the craftsmen heavily outnumbered the retailers. However, an investigation of 22 of the 56 largest constituencies over the country as a whole suggests that this might well have been a regional phenomenon, mainly confined to the north.[12] Nevertheless the shopocracy narrowly defined still constituted one-quarter of the electorate compared with thirty per cent for the craft trades. The gentry and professional classes made up seventeen per cent, manufacturers and merchants seven per cent and the drink trade—mainly licensees—another eight per cent. In nineteen cases the craftsmen were the biggest group and in ten the shopkeepers (including two in the north-east). In the light of what has been argued about the shopkeepers' abilities, motivation and opportunities, such findings even outside the north-east could well be important.

There is also some evidence on the actual voting behaviour of the different occupational groups from the same analysis of poll books. Full figures are not yet available for all the towns investigated but in the majority of cases the retailers and craftsmen were the most solidly advanced liberal. Examples from the north-east illustrated this: in Newcastle in 1835 as many as 55 per cent of the shopocracy supported the radical ticket and only 14 per cent the Whig ticket, compared with practically the reverse among the upper and professional classes, two-thirds of whom split for the 'right' and only 10 per cent for the 'left'. The craftsmen fell half way between the two, polling just under one-third for each. Both the retailers and the craftsmen were more inclined to vote radical if qualified on the ten-pound than the freeman franchise. The situation was much the same in Gateshead, on the other bank of the Tyne, and Sunderland, constituencies created in 1832; and outside the north-east, in places as far apart as Manchester and Brighton. It would be wrong to deny that the craftsmen played a considerable part in parliamentary and extra-parliamentary radicalism but almost everywhere the shopoc-

---

12    See the author's 'Voting Behaviour 1832-1872', *Political Studies*, September, 1970.

racy played at least a supportive role and in some areas, such as the
north-east, a leadership role. The retailers far more than the craftsmen had the ability as well as interest to keep up agitation and
channel it into formal political lines.

The history of radicalism in the north-east brings this out clearly.
Unfortunately there is only space to consider two cases, Newcastle
and Gateshead, chosen because, though both on the Tyne, they
represent contrasting types of constituency. Newcastle, centre of the
coal trade, was a long-established two-member borough with a
sizeable electorate including freemen. Gateshead on the other hand,
important for iron as well as coal, was a much smaller one-member
seat created in 1832. Yet despite their differences both show the
importance of the shopocracy in radical movements.

Newcastle for all its importance as an early industrial centre tends
to be a footnote in radical history. Only Schoyen's biography of the
extreme radical Harney deals with Tyneside in any depth;[13] and the
cumulative effect of the passing references has been to give the area
a not altogether justifiable reputation for radicalism and militancy,
in which the key groups were the miners and the pike-bearing ironworkers of Swalwell and Winlaton. In general, however, the ultra-
radicals were weaker in the north-east than in other industrial
districts; and the 'democratic' candidates of the thirties did badly in
elections. Not a single chartist went to the poll in Newcastle and
Gateshead in 1841 or 1847 and although chartism was strong in
early 1839 it virtually disappeared after the failure of the Sacred
Month of strike action in August. 1842 produced only slight ripples
and 1848 nothing. Ironically Bright, the one thorough-going radical
elected before the turn of the century, was returned for the notoriously corrupt Durham City in part at the instigation of Lord
Londonderry. Such men as William Hutt, Cuthbert Rippon and
W. A. Wawn, who were elected as liberals, turned out to be very
modest reformers in the Radical Jack (1st Lord Durham) mould
rather than popular radicals seeking household suffrage. A detailed
examination of Newcastle politics when radicalism was at its height
in the thirties demonstrates that the shopocracy gave as much
support and leadership as the working class.

---

13    A. R. Schoyen, *The Chartist Challenge* (1958).

The reform movement of 1831 and 1832 was led by the Northern Political Union—for the Whigs and moderates a 'front' organisation but for the radicals an independent body. Its legitimate leadership came from a group of well-known local radicals, Attwood, Doubleday, Fife and Larkin, aided and abetted by Whig fellow-travellers. Fife and Larkin were both doctors, Doubleday owned a small firm making soap and Attwood was a successful iron and glass manufacturer: none of them were men of great local influence at the time. Some, though by no means all, had nonconformist connections—but then so had the Whigs. Nonconformity was so widespread on Tyneside as not to be a defining characteristic of political partisanship. The radical leadership was a varied group; a few minor manufacturers, some medics, some prosperous shopkeepers and the inevitable printers, journalists and schoolmasters who made up the minor provincial intelligentsia.

Who were the radical voters exactly? Some of the union rank and file were indeed, as radical folklore has it, from the ironworks at Winlaton Mill and Swalwell and from the local collieries, but not many of these were entitled to vote under the new ten-pound franchise. Some were undoubtedly qualified as freemen in Newcastle but the support for the radical union candidate in 1832 was greater among householders than freemen. The precise composition of radical support can be seen from an analysis of the poll by occupation. In the following table each trade or profession is ranked in order according to its radical vote, together with the distribution of the remaining votes between Whig and Tory.

VOTING BY OCCUPATIONS, NEWCASTLE, 1832

|  | No. of Votes | % Rad. | % Whig | % Tory |
|---|---|---|---|---|
| Shoemakers | 75 | 42 | 33 | 25 |
| Shopkeepers | 93 | 39 | 43 | 18 |
| Coopers | 111 | 36 | 34 | 30 |
| Tailors | 122 | 33 | 38 | 29 |
| Drapers | 119 | 32 | 44 | 24 |
| Curriers | 80 | 30 | 36 | 34 |
| | | | | |
| Grocers | 200 | 28 | 46 | 26 |
| Butchers | 211 | 28 | 46 | 26 |
| Painters | 83 | 26 | 45 | 29 |

|             | No. of Votes | % Rad. | % Whig | % Tory |
|-------------|--------------|--------|--------|--------|
| Smiths      | 128          | 25     | 35     | 40     |
| Bricklayers | 159          | 22     | 40     | 38     |
| Joiners     | 373          | 21     | 39     | 40     |
| Cordwainers | 140          | 21     | 39     | 40     |
| Merchants   | 131          | 15     | 51     | 34     |
| Doctors     | 73           | 14     | 49     | 37     |
| Agents      | 141          | 14     | 48     | 38     |
| Gentlemen   | 240          | 10     | 51     | 39     |
| Solicitors  | 76           | 7      | 51     | 42     |
| All Votes*  | 2,555        | 22     | 43     | 35     |

* This analysis from the Newcastle Poll Book of 1832 refers to 1,502 voters (2,555 votes) out of a total of 2,856 voters. The overall percentage, however, refers to the total 2,856 voters.

At the top of the list were the shoemakers (42 per cent) and the 'shopkeepers' (39 per cent) while the champions of the existing order, the solicitors, were at the bottom (7 per cent). The real order is, however, somewhat obscured by the lumping together of freemen and ten-pounders in one list. The proportion of freemen (90 per cent living in sub-ten-pound property) and householders varied from trade to trade and so distorts the pattern. This is reflected in the fact that only 19 per cent of the freemen vote went to the radical compared with 26 per cent of the ten-pound vote. In those cases where there were enough to make meaningful comparisons the contrast is even more marked: 24 per cent of the freemen butchers voted radical compared with 41 per cent of the ten-pound butchers. Taking the total 'liberal' vote (tory-radical, liberal-radical and radical-plumper)[14] as many as 63 per cent of the shopocracy on the ten-pound register voted for the 'left' compared with 40 per cent on the freemen rolls. The comparable figures for craftsmen were 48 and 38 per cent, so from any standpoint there was a clear social division

---

14    In two-member constituencies the voter had the choice of voting for one candidate only (plumper) or two (split). There was often a sizeable cross-party split vote. For a discussion of this see the author's "Aspects of Electoral Behaviour in English Constituencies, 1832-1868" in E. Allardt & S. Rokkan, *Mass Politics* (Free Press, 1970).

discernible in Newcastle in 1832. The upper and professional classes backed the ruling Tory and Whig oligarchy and eschewed radicalism altogether. The rank and file of the union's support at the polls lay with the retail shopkeepers and especially those whose greater prosperity was reflected in their occupation of ten-pound property. The better-off members of the craft trades also gave above average support to radical or liberal positions but the poorer freemen were much less evident on Attwood's behalf at the polls.

Conditions could hardly have been more favourable for a radical in the industrial and political climate of 1832 but, devoid of influence and 'the necessary', the radicals knew their cause was hopeless at the poll and brought out their man, Charles Attwood, only on the eve of the election. Attwood took one-fifth of the votes, and the Tory and Whig influentials, splitting their votes on each other, easily returned their men. Nevertheless the election had revealed a new factor in Tyneside politics, the radical shopocracy, confirmed in the next election in 1835 when the radical took one-half of the votes cast by the shopocracy, one-third of the craftsmen's and only one-tenth of the upper class's.[15]

At first sight the fact that the radical leaders found more support among the middle classes and the utmost difficulty in mustering any permanent support among the working classes seems rather perplexing. But when one considers the difficulties facing radical politicians in those days the wonder is perhaps that they did so well among either class. It was not easy to convert the big crowds who attended major meetings into hard electoral support even where working men had the vote, as about one thousand did in Newcastle. The various means of communication open to a politician —the press, the 'union' and the public meeting—meant little at the polling booth when the chief thing was how much influence he commanded or how deep were his backer's purses. As one cost-conscious agent told his master in 1830, it was much cheaper to manufacture a few freemen at £2 5s. each (the price of making a man free) than to ship up the outvoters from London;[16] and this climate of assumptions on both sides survived long after the Reform Act.

---

15    Newcastle Poll, 1835.
16    Donkin to Ridley, 10 June, 1830. Ridley Mss. Blagdon, near Newcastle.

In any case radical means of communication had their drawbacks. Many who came to a public meeting would have had to walk miles to attend and so it was difficult to gather a big audience except at holiday times; and it was not everyone's choice to make a political rally into the site for a family picnic. Meetings held in the open air were always threatened with ruin by bad weather; and it was hard to adjourn to a hall with thousands to accommodate. In any case there were few halls in Newcastle capable of holding a big crowd. The Guildhall was the main venue and over this the mayor had a veto, should he dislike the objects of the meeting sufficiently. Even if he granted permission there was also the chance that rowdies might break the meeting up or opponents move wrecking amendments. In the light of such hurdles a successful public meeting was a real achievement.

The unions might hold public meetings but like their rivals they were dependent on the press for wider coverage; indeed one suspects that in an age before microphones many of the crowd waited till they got home to find out what was said. The radicals also depended more heavily than Whigs and Tories, with their greater influence on the press to rebut their opponent's hostile criticism and maintain their own continuous interpretation of events: only in this way could they become a serious political alternative. It was certainly one of the weaknesses of the first Northern Political Union that it lacked a newspaper until mid-1833, by which time it was too late. In any case the poorer classes could not efford the price of a paper, so to achieve any success the proprietor needed readership among the middle classes. The partial relief of the stamp duty in 1836 considerably helped the radical press and was followed by a wave of new liberal papers including the chartist *Northern Liberator*, organ of the second NPU, and the Durhamite *Gateshead Observer*.

The union itself was a broken reed by 1832. Not many of their paid-up members were to be found on the new parliamentary registers and few of those who were found themselves free to vote as they wished. One suspects that much of the NPUs success in 1832 depended on the patronage and influence of the local Whigs and moderate liberals who had joined it for as long as it suited their purpose. Although the union did not entirely disappear after their desertion its survival for another year was a struggle.

Public opinion in the north-east during the thirties grew increasingly hostile to the orthodox Whigs but strengthened the radical-liberals as much as the Tories. William Ord, one of Lord Durham's relatives, topped the poll in Newcastle in 1837 and the Whig hardly bettered the democratic outsider, Beaumont. Another local radical backed by the Lambtons came top in Sunderland; and the rakish but liberal Cuthbert Rippon beat off a Whig challenge in Gateshead. In the light of this movement of opinion the Whigs' outright rejection of further parliamentary reform on their return to office in the autumn of 1837 was bound to provoke a radical reaction; and it was against this background that the second Political Union was formed and chartism gained tremendous support.

The history of chartism in the north-east bears strongly on the theme of this paper for without the shopocracy it is impossible to understand its force or character. The standard view of Durham and Tyneside chartism is expressed by Maccoby and Schoyen, who both stress its militant and (with Monmouthshire and Staffordshire) its revolutionary tone. The most recent writer on the subject, Maehl, has been rather more cautious but even he sees a 'striking militancy' about the local movement.

The case for a revolutionary view of Tyneside chartism rests on three basic points: the character of the leadership, the mood of the working class and the local manufacture of pikes. Schoyen's view of events is manifestly coloured by the subject of his biography, J. J. Harney, who saw himself as some kind of latter-day Jacobin and so scared the chartist council that until his own arrest he was commonly thought to be a government agent-provocateur. Likewise Maccoby has fallen for the legend of the soldier-politician Augustus Beaumont, who briefly flitted across the scene in 1837 and 1838.[17]

Beaumont, born in 1800, and brought up as a plantation owner in Jamaica, was surely one of the most colourful characters thrown up even by by chartism. He had left the West Indies after being ostracised by colonial society for inviting a negro home to meet his family. His sense of honour in these situations was as keen as his

---

17    Schoyen *op. cit.* 92-93; Maccoby, Eng. Radicalism, 161 f. 6, 174; Maehl, 'Chartist Disturbances in North-eastern England, 1839', *Inter. Rev. of Social Hist.* 8; Maehl, 'A. H. Beaumont', *ibid.* 14.

principles were fine and during his brief life he fought no less than fifteen duels, killing one of his opponents and wounding several others. He had fought in the July revolution of 1830 in Paris and been presented with a sword for his services to the cause in Brussels in the same year. But what pistols and swords failed to do, the north-east climate succeeded in doing, and Beaumont spent only a few months in Tyneside before catching pneumonia and dying in January, 1838.

Beaumont originally came to Newcastle to stand in the 1837 election. A close friend of O'Connor, he had been active in the anti-poor law campaign as well as in the general agitation for parliamentary reform. He was an ideal recruit to the 'physical force' wing of the chartism movement; and contemporary opponents dismissed him as 'crazy' and fit to head 'any dangerous enterprise'. But, if he held some advanced views, including the duty of the state to provide employment, careful study of his speeches and the editorial columns of his newspaper, the *Northern Liberator*, founded in October, 1837, does not show him as wildly militant. His biggest contribution in fact was to have set up such a successful paper as the *Liberator* which became the best-selling journal on Tyneside at 4,000 copies, and as influential in the north-east as the *Northern Star* was in the West Riding. But the paper was owned not edited by Beaumont: this job was in the hands of Newcastle's two leading intellectuals, Thomas Doubleday and Robert Blakey; and these were the real leaders of local chartism, together with Binns and Williams on Wearside.

Blakey and Doubleday were extraordinary phenomena on the chartist scene: two middle-class moral-force intellectuals who managed to control the Newcastle chartist movement, influence the local council, and avoid the jail which was the fate of almost all the major chartist leaders for a time after 1839. Robert Blakey was a fashionable hatter and furrier who ran a profitable business from his shop in Morpeth, a few miles to the north of Newcastle. His trade extended over the whole country and the fact that he took over the proprietorship of the *Liberator* from Beaumont suggests he must have been in a fairly prosperous way of business. Doubleday was less commercially-minded and failed to succeed in his father's soap firm and gave it up to take a succession of salaried jobs beginning with the *Liberator*. Both men were Cobbettites and Blakey had indeed been a personal friend of Cobbett. Both were respected members of their local councils and Blakey was, in fact, first mayor of the reformed Morpeth Corporation. Blakey and Doubleday wrote a great deal of academic literature as well as political polemics, poems, plays and metaphysics. Blakey must have been the only old chartist to end up with a pension from the civil list as a reward for his tenure of the chair of Logic and Metaphysics at Queens College, Belfast.

Probably the most interesting aspect of their role on Tyneside was the charmed life they led in the eyes of the law. One of the wilder Irish spirits in the *Liberator* office, one Thomas Devyr, later wrote that 'it seemed as if the very purity and loftiness of their character enforced such respect on the Government that, whilst all other leaders were persecuted into prisons, no charge was preferred against either . . . if I expect one against Mr Blakey for publishing a fierce article . . . written by myself', on which incidentally the sentence was never executed.[18] There was a touch of Irish blarney here; the real reason for the leadership's immunity was their friends in high places. General Napier, one of the shrewdest men in the army and responsible for the Northern Command at this difficult time, confided to his diary that Newcastle Corporation was generally regarded as chartist.[19] Certainly there is evidence that while William Hutt, Lambtonite MP across the river at Gateshead, was lobbying for Fife's knighthood for handling a chartist mob in Newcastle, he was making sure the major local chartists got off the hook.

Were Blakey and Doubleday themselves typical of the revived NPU leadership? By and large the council members came from those classes more usually associated with moral-force than physical-force chartism: shoemakers, tailors, tobacconists, music dealers were not the stuff of which Jacobins were made. There were indeed some building workers—masons and bricklayers—and an Irish element from the Grainger and Dobson rebuilding programme, but not enough to change the fundamental lower middle class character of the executive.

The second argument for the revolutionary view of Tyneside chartism is the condition of the working class. But this is no more

---

18      T. Devyr, *Odd Book*, 69.
19      Sir Wm. Napier, *Life of General Napier*, ii, 74.

convincing than the leadership theory. Wherever chartism took a violent turn, one or more of three factors was present; severe depression in trade, the decline of old cottage industries such as hand-loom weaving, and the impact of the imposition of the new poor law. But in the north-east there were few signs of a slump before the second half of 1839. Both Newcastle and Sunderland were seething with activity: in Newcastle Grainger's scheme of reconstruction had given work not only to local people but also to upwards of two thousand migrant Irish workers; while in Sunderland more shipping was launched in 1840 than ever before; and the demand for coal in the London market was still fairly good as late as 1840.

The only group of workers in real difficulties was the iron workers of Winlaton on the southern outskirts of the Tyne. Weekly wages were down to less than ten shillings and there was considerable distress among the workers in a dying industry faced with more advanced modes of production. There can be no doubt that some of the violence of Newcastle chartism came from this village with its strong radical tradition.

Finally, although the poor law aroused local feeling, there was nothing like the steam behind the anti-poor law agitation on Tyneside that was found in the West Riding. There were perhaps two reasons for this. Firstly, the largest section of the work force was the miners, who enjoyed tied cottages and free heating as well as the indirect benefits of the owners' regulation of the market. The demand for coal in the London market was more buoyant than most, and it was with this section of the trade that the north-east was primarily connected. The coalowner rarely turned off men because times were bad, and granted credit at his 'tommy shop'. The second reason was the absence of any real fear that the middle class liberals, who would predominate on the new boards of guardians, would impose a vicious regimen on the poor. It was a faith which seems to have been justified, as Dr McCord has found little evidence that the Tyneside guardians changed poor law policy. Local custom and practice were too powerful for some distant bashaws in Somerset House to do very much about it.

The strongest argument in support of the Schoyen and Maccoby thesis is the extensive manufacture of weapons. Throughout 1839 and 1840 a pike market was held every Saturday above a shop in the

Side. Rough pikes retailed at 1s. 6d. and best quality ones at 2s. 6d. Devyr tells how one man was arrested for some minor offence while walking home and was discovered to be carrying two pikes under his coat.[20] On being cross-examined about it by the magistrates he pleaded that he was taking his weapons home to protect himself from burglars and got away with it. Of course, the sale of pikes was good for Winlaton business but it is quite another question whether there was ever any serious intention to use them in a militant rising. Devyr mentions the delivery of one case of fifty muskets but notes the failure of the Winlaton men, themselves, to produce fuses for the gunpowder stolen from some of the collieries. Pikes were widespread throughout industrial England in the summer of 1839, and there is no justification for taking them as necessarily an indicator of real danger to society. It is surely revealing that there was no great alarm on the part of informed magistrates and no reference by Napier to Tyneside as a danger spot.

The evidence of most reliable contemporaries seems virtually unanimous, whatever their own political standpoint. The Whig agent, Morton, who had dealt with a lifetime of strikes among the miners, denied that chartism was anything to worry about—not a patch on 1831 and 1832.[21] Doubleday from the other side startled the Newcastle town council later in 1839, when it was earnestly debating whether to retain the special constables or not, by informing it that he had good reason to know the local chartists were quiet and peaceable;[22] while Devyr, writing his story later from America, made light of the Tyneside part in the attempted nationwide rising of December, 1840, as well as the Sacred Month of strike action in August, 1839.[23] When the desperadoes—among them Devyr—gathered on the night of 12th December, 1840, there were only fifty ready to begin the revolution. There are some alarmist letters in the Home Office files from country JPs but, as Napier frequently reminded his superiors, these were common everywhere and not to be taken too seriously. The balance of evidence remains in favour of

20    Devyr, *Odd Book* quoted in *Newc. Chron.* 2 June 1882.
21    Morton to Durham, 26 July 1839; also 17, 18, 23, July, 1839. Lambton Mss. Lambton Estate, Durham.
22    *Northern Liberator*, 13 December, 1839.
23    *Newc. Chron.*, 2 June, 1882.

seeing Tyneside as a centre of moral rather than physical-force chartism; and explaining this in turn in terms of the strength of lower middle class support for the broad aims of the movement.

Unfortunately there is little or no decisive evidence of the social composition of the rank and file. The lists of contributors to the funds for the Glasgow Cotton Spinners and later Frost's Defence are unhelpful. The processions of the time were often said to contain a sizeable proportion of Winlaton ironworkers but on the whole mass meetings on abstract programmes lacked crowd appeal without the personal edge of deprivation. Meetings were relatively poorly attended; and even the so-called Battle of the Forth of July, 1839, has obviously gained a good deal in its passage through tradition by the efforts of Joseph Cowen's romantic journalism. Perhaps the best comment might be the independent *Newcastle Courant*'s that in the summer of 1839 the children of Newcastle had found a new game—playing at being chartists.[24]

The chartist scene in Sunderland was basically similar to that on Tyneside except for a still greater reliance on the middle class and a more marked role for dissent. Both the main leaders, Binns and Williams, were old dissenters, who had been involved with the Quakers at some time; both were from the lower middle class—Binns a draper and Williams a printer and stationer. The two became full-time chartist organisers, determined to make Sunderland the centre of a vital chartist movement in Durham; but, faced with the tremendous prosperity of the town in 1839 and 1840, they found it a pretty hopeless task. A Good Friday meeting in 1839 drew a mere 700 people; and only 4,000 out of a population of 45,000 signed the National Petition. There was a little more success among the local collieries but the tone of Wearside chartism remained essentially non-violent and touched with the language of the more fervent kinds of christianity which had recently swept the area. If Sunderland was, as it was said, the headquarters of Durham chartism, then it was a moral rather than a physical crusade in the county.

In the long term the most important development for radicalism in Newcastle during the thirties was not chartism but the creation of the reformed corporation. The unreformed corporation had been a

---

24        *Newc. Courant*, 20 July, 1839.

fairly typical self-electing oligarchy run by the Coal Trade with scant respect for party labels. The ordinary freemen had no real say, much less power. In theory the Municipal Reform Act should have rectified this: it was supposed to be a triumph for democracy with its franchise of *rated* household suffrage; but for a variety of reasons, from a three-year residence requirement to the rigging of the warding, the electorate turned out to be substantially the same as the parliamentary one minus the working-class freemen. As a result the Whiggish middle and upper classes found it easy to run the corporation in their own interests with little or no reference to the lower middle class support they had needed in the early thirties.

The change from unreformed Tory to reformed Whig was more apparent than real. On the key issues of the corporation's leasing policy and the river dues Whig and Tory policies were practically identical: as the big split vote in election after election showed (two-fifths in 1832, one-fifth thereafter) the Newcastle elector knew perfectly well that Whig and Tory were brand names for the same product. Witnesses to the Grey Committee of 1859,[25] which incidentally dealt with Newcastle politics, told their lordships how the 'new party' soon became the 'old party', forgetting all about reform in its haste to distribute the spoils. And very considerable spoils they were: a salary for the mayor of £800 a year, corporation property worth perhaps £20,000 a year let to friends at £1,500 a year, the proceeds of all river dues paid by shipping using the *whole* length of the Tyne, and free access to one of the best social sets in the north. Faced with such temptations it was understandable that 'reform' was marked more by its continuity with the old order than by change. Once more radicals were discovering that if you scratched a Whig, not far below the surface lurked a Tory.

The gradual penetration of the oil of patronage together with the attrition of the freemen vote and the movements of public opinion eventually gave the Whigs control of both seats in parliament as well as of the corporation but no sooner had this been achieved than the Whigs were forced on to the defensive. Their very success clearly exposed them for what they were, a corrupt jobbing clique, packing the aldermanic bench and the key council committees to insulate

---

25      Small Tenements Act. Select Committee H. Lord under Earl Grey. Parl. papers 1859 (56), vii.

themselves against the cold winds of elections, and exercising not only the corporation's own patronage but channeling that of the Government as well. This state of affairs did not escape the notice of the First Lord, but the Treasury's response was to instruct its officials 'not to injure Newcastle' if at all possible.[26] It was an answer which reflected the fundamental malaise of English politics in the fifties. Both nationally and locally Whig administrations were substituting means for ends, the rewards of government for government itself. And just as the Crimean War was to bring down Lord Aberdeen so the corruption and maladministration of the Whigs in Newcastle led to their defeat locally.

In the early thirties the Whigs had succeeded in part because they had mobilised hitherto neglected areas of social and economic power; but now the Whigs in turn were ignoring the new social forces around them—the dissenters, the manufacturers, the shopocracy and, on Tyneside, the estuary towns of North and South Shields. Increasingly they were to rely on 'illegitimate' influence and the purse to sustain them in power. The attack on the Whigs was greatly facilitated by changes in both the national and local political environments which helped agitation and hindered traditional influences. The first of these was the withdrawal of the upper classes into the countryside and the suburbs. On Tyneside this meant that the oligarchy played less and less part in municipal life. The second change was the reduction of social distance by technological advances, and the increasing 'nationalisation' of public life and opinion. For example, from 1849 it became possible to travel all the way from London by train. Equally, the telegraph and the penny post were having a considerable effect on the speed with which news circulated; and when stamp duties were finally abolished in 1856 the penny daily newspaper —locally the *Northern Daily Express*—quickly capitalised on the popular enthusiasm for news.

If the most difficult factor to pinpoint is the shift in values and attitudes that was imperceptibly taking place about the turn of the century, the process was none the less real. The new law of self-help was displacing the old law of patronage; the ethic of open competition of Trevelyan and Macaulay displacing purchase and connection;

---

26     Wm. Brockie, *Hist. of Shields* (Shields, 1851), 134.

and the Lives of the Engineers displacing those of the Chancellors as required bedside reading for ambitious young men. Put in another way, the men of '32 were yielding place to those of '52, electors whose starting point for change was what their father's destination had been. The new political generation of middle-aged voters of the fifties had minds moulded in the thirties and unthinkingly accepted the slogans and programmes their fathers had mouthed but rarely meant.

The trend of events nationally was against the Whigs but what finally precipitated their downfall in Newcastle was the little-known Small Tenements Act, which brought about the biggest change in Newcastle politics between 1832 and 1888 by drastically altering the social composition of the municipal electorate. The act's aim was to increase the efficiency with which revenue was collected by allowing parish officers to levy the rates for smaller property on the landlord rather than on the tenant. But to avoid disfranchising existing electors, a clause was introduced to protect their rights. This was an open invitation in a corrupt age to manufacture voters: what had been intended to defend existing rights had the unintended consequence of extending them and several towns were quickly converted to household suffrage in municipal elections. In Newcastle the constituency rose by 80 per cent to nearly 8,000 in the first year of operation (1852-53) and by 1858 the electorate was three times bigger than in 1850 in half the wards. The technique for increasing the electorate was a simple one: the overseer sent a letter to the landlord asking him to name those occupiers on whose behalf rates were paid and who satisfied the residential requirements. It was then a matter between the landlord and his conscience whether his answers bore any relationship to reality. Opponents could, of course, object to the list but to do so was to risk alienating the new claimants. It was much wiser to join in the fun; and in consequence politics rapidly hotted up on Tyneside. The Whigs recognised the thin end of a wedge when they saw one but by the time the Lords had set up its select committee under Earl Grey in 1859 to condemn the act—a nice historical irony which the second earl must have savoured from the top of his monument in Grey Street, Newcastle—it was too late, except to expose the sores of Tyneside politics.

The keys to the mobilisation of the new voters were the so-called Ratepayers' Association, founded in January, 1856, and the newly-established penny daily, the *Northern Daily Express*. The Ratepayers' Association was set up, according to one of its secretaries, 'to educate' the voter. Its opponents naturally thought this was a euphemism and certainly the association fought a very vigorous campaign in local elections. But there is little doubt that the Association's ultimate success rested on other factors besides the new electors: firstly, by concentrating on local affairs it avoided the frustrations of national agitations; it could vary the diet of vituperation by fighting local elections and lobbying the council with more tangible results than mere hot air. Secondly, because the only necessary condition of membership or support was the negative one of discontent with the Whig corporation, the Association could gather the strangest bed-fellows side by side. Finally, whatever the details, the opposition had the best possible case against a controlling party which had let property worth £20,000 a year for £1,500 with a loss to the ratepayers since 1836 of at least £100,000; squandered £10,000 a year from the river without spending a tithe of that to maintain and improve the capabilities of the Tyne in a competitive age; and wasting £20,000 on civic entertainment since reform. All this was daily hammered home in the *Express*, which, though not literally a mouthpiece of the Association, did for a critical time act as the organ of dissenting and ratepaying views. Its editorial line was the stock-in-trade of the Manchester School and the advanced liberal position of the fifties—economy, free trade, sanitation, national education and reform, but not manhood suffrage. From such papers public opinion was progressively acquiring a national dimension it had not previously had.

Press reports, the evidence given to the Grey Committee and finally the records of Newcastle elections show how central the shopkeeper class was to the radical ratepayers' movement, not only because of their own votes but by virtue of their influence over their working-class customers, who were in many cases also their tenants, for it was the corner shopkeeper who tended often to own the houses in the street as well. Both shopkeeper and working man were part of the same community, and influence was a two-way process: the shopocracy and the publican through 'the social glass' articulated their customers' and tenants' feelings as well as moulding them;[27] and in

27    *Northern Daily Express*, 31 October, 1855.

turn they themselves formed part of a wider network of influence and opinion stretching out to the chapel, the union, the sanitary association and the ratepayers' movement. How marked the social basis of the ratepayers' support was can be seen when the battle spilled over into the parliamentary arena. The following table shows the occupational composition of voters in one typical ward in the by-election of 1860 when the Whigs won 54 per cent of the ten-pound vote in a straight fight with the radicals.[28]

OCCUPATIONS OF WHIG AND RADICAL VOTERS
IN ELSWICK, NEWCASTLE 1860

| % | Whig | Radical |
|---|---|---|
| Upper and Professional | 29 | 16 |
| Retail | 30 | 64 |
| Craft | 20 | 12 |
| Shipping | — | 2 |
| Drink | 6 | 4 |
| Manufacturing | 15 | 2 |
| | 100 | 100 |

Clearly the Whigs were the party of the upper middle classes—the gentry, the professional men and the manufacturers and merchants—while the radicals were the party of the shopocracy: almost two-thirds of the radicals' votes came from the retail classes. It was a turning point for the Whigs—the Radicals had served notice that with a good candidate they could win, as they were to go on to do in 1865.

The significance of the shopocracy in the fifties can be underlined by contrasting this by-election with the failure of a defiantly working-class Northern Reform Union candidate the previous year. The Northern Reform Union was consciously designated as a successor to the earlier Northern Political Unions by Joseph Cowen junior—with the highly important difference that both its membership and its leadership were drawn from the working classes and trade unions

---

28   Newcastle Poll 1860; local directories.

—Cowen excepted[29]. In contrast to the ratepayers' movement it stood for manhood suffrage. The order of priorities of administrative and parliamentary reform was reversed. The latter was the panacea from which efficiency would flow. The union boasted 1,000 members but when it put its strength to the test in the general election of 1859, its candidate—later comfortably elected at Leicester—could only muster a derisory 462 votes. This could only be attributed to the failure of negotiations for shopkeeper and dissenting support and exposed the independent working class in all its powerlessness. Cowen was said to have lost a lot of face in radical circles in consequence.

The later history of radicalism on Tyneside is better known: Cowen's father was returned as MP in 1865 backed by Whigs, radicals and dissenters, and his son succeeded him in a by-election in 1874. Young Joseph then eliminated the Whigs altogether from Newcastle politics by withholding a liberal split from Headlam in the ensuing general election. Headlam, the defeated Whig, was said to have died of pique. But because the early history of radicalism on Tyneside was largely rewritten by Cowen in his *Chronicle* in later years, it should not necessarily be taken as gospel. His account of a great tradition of working class and collier militancy owed a good deal to selection of certain facts and suppression of others. The shopocracy of Tyneside deserve some small credit.

Neighbouring Gateshead illustrates the same basic points which form the two themes of this paper—the social tension between petty and upper bourgeoisie and the role of the shopocracy in radicalism. However, the retailers were not as successful in what was tantamount to a company town. Indeed single-member constituencies generally seem to have proved harder going for minorities.

Gateshead was a product of the industrial revolution and dominated by the great magnates of the coal and iron revolution—Bowes, Hutt, Hawks, Crawshay and Ellison. Economic power was converted directly into political power and although there was a superstructure of guided democracy Gateshead was really run by a small clique of agents and solicitors, led for twenty years by William

---

29    I am indebted to Mr. Harris of Rutherford College, Newcastle, for advice on Joseph Cowen, junior.

Brockett, one of the original Disraelian tadpoles. Brockett was, like Headlam and Phillipson of Newcastle, a political broker who took a small percentage cut on every transaction he handled and built up his own influence until no political manoeuvre was possible without him. In the end his control of the network of political communications gave him power over the outcomes despite his lack of personal social and economic power.

The only serious opposition to the clique in Gateshead came from the shopocracy. Indeed so cowed were the electors as a whole that when a chartist candidate was brought out in 1841 nobody could be found to second the nomination among six hundred electors; and during the period up to the second reform bill there were only two contests, in 1837 and 1852. 1837 has had rather more attention because it happened to produce the novelist Surtees as one of its candidates and so Gateshead was immortalised in *Hillingdon Hall*; but it was 1852 which was far more significant for the structure of politics in the constituency. The background to this three-sided contest between Tory, Radical and sitting Whig was a complex one but it boiled down to a conjunction of dissatisfaction with the existing member, William Hutt, and his omniscient agent, William Brockett, with more general social movements, mentioned earlier, which were altering the context of constituency politics during the fifties. *The Times* could not have been more wrong in describing the Gateshead contest as a 'miserable parochial quarrel'.[30] Its origins may have been trivial but it mirrored the new social basis of politics.

William Hutt had been suffering from poor health for some time and had, in fact, decided to retire at the next dissolution; but when a Tory candidate standing on protectionist principles was announced, Hutt decided to stand his ground as a leading free trade spokesman. He need not have worried, for though Liddell had local influence, protection was a rod to the Tory back in most of the north-east. In any case Liddell was from the same ruling caste, what one writer called 'one of the last specimens of a thorough *English Gentleman*' and hardly likely to constitute any threat to the established distribution of social power even if he won.[31] Although it was Liddell who

---

30    *The Times*, 13 March, 1852.
31    Brockett Mss. x, 171. 25 March, 1852. Gateshead Public Library.

came second in the poll it was the radical candidate, Ralph Walters, with whom the contest really lay. He was not an anglican gentleman from rural society but a dissenter—his brother a noted independent preacher—and his friends were the shopkeepers who made up one-third of the Gateshead electorate. A banker and a successful railway and property magnate, Walters had a deep purse which constituted an immeasurable danger, unlike landed influence which was fairly predictable. But in the last analysis Walters was seen as a real threat because he tried to mobilise voters on a programme, and campaign on an agitation.

As soon as Walters entered the lists the election took a new turn with a highly personalised attack on Hutt's sincerity as a reformer and a savage denunciation of his friend and agent Brockett's abuse of power in the town. The parallel with Newcastle was obvious. The political crimes of the sitting member ranged from voting for pensions to the ex-kings of Belgium and Hanover to voting against the ballot, a circumstance Hutt attributed to his failing sight but others hinted was due to insobriety. The case against Brockett was admirably summed up in one of the many broadsides emanating from the radical camp:[32]

'Who threw Attwood overboard because he would think for himself . . .
Who deceived the Parish by stating that the Corporation would not cost a farthing . . .
Who said no Working Man had a head to carry a Vote . . .
Who has monopolised all the Patronage of the Borough?'

Brockett, it concluded, had ruled over the town far too long. These sly innuendoes had some basis in fact but their real importance was as an expression of the frustrations of the shopkeeping middle class who had expected some small share in political power, an end to jobbery and the practice of economy. Walter's office as vice-president of the Parliamentary and Financial Reform Association symbolised these aspirations.

The vituperation that flew back and forth knew no bounds—the 'I am not a Shopkeeper, I drive my own dog cart' bill already cited was just one example—and Hutt, goaded beyond endurance, part blind though he was, sent a young officer to challenge Walters. The

---

32    *Ibid.* x, 167. 23 March, 1852.

duel never came off and Hutt was left fuming that Walters was unfit society for men of honour and Walters musing that he had no desire for such company anyway. Frightened by the momentum of the Walter's campaign, Hutt's side called on every influence they could muster and even resorted to personal canvassing which they had eschewed at the beginning of the campaign as political 'mendicancy'. Most important of all Hutt was forced to play Walters at his own game and answer argument with argument.

Walters easily won the war of words but it was another story at the polling booth, as it was for Newcastle's Attwood in 1832 and Carstairs in 1859. The basic strength of influence in a small constituency told heavily and Walters came bottom of the poll with only twenty-three per cent of the votes. But to have polled almost one-quarter of the electors in such a company town was a remarkable tribute to the growing power of 'the Walters' family'—the radical shopocracy—not only in neighbouring Newcastle but here in Gateshead. This interpretation can be confirmed by a close scrutiny of the basis of radical support in this election.[33]

ANALYSIS OF THE OCCUPATIONAL ORIGINS
OF GATESHEAD VOTERS IN 1852

| % | Whig | Radical | Tory | ALL |
|---|---|---|---|---|
| Upper and Professional | 30 | 11 | 19 | 22 |
| Manufacturers and Merchants | 25 | 12 | 22 | 21 |
| Retail | 25 | 47 | 32 | 32 |
| Craft | 11 | 12 | 6 | 9 |
| Drink | 6 | 14 | 14 | 11 |
| Other | 3 | 4 | 7 | 5 |
| | 100 | 100 | 100 | 100 |

The Tory voters were almost a mirror image of the social composition of the whole electorate; but the Whig and radical ones were biased towards specific groups: the Whig to the upper and professional classes and the radical to the shopkeepers. Nearly twice as many retailers voted for Walters as Hutt. Analyses of the Newcastle and

33    Gateshead Poll, 1852; local directories.

Sunderland electorates at the same time reveal the same picture. There was, however, in Gateshead no difference between their support among the craft tradesmen. Such crude occupational differences suggest the social basis of the political conflict but the best idea can be obtained from the examination of the indicators contained in the enumerators' originals of the 1851 census and the ratebooks for the town in 1852.[34]

SOME DATA RELEVANT TO SOCIAL STATUS IN GATESHEAD IN 1852

|  | Mean Rateable Value Voters | Mean Rateable Value retail Voters | Mean Rateable Value drink Voters | No. of Servants/ Voter | % of Voters no servants |
|---|---|---|---|---|---|
| Whig | £50 | £25 | £50 | 0·95 | 24% |
| Radical | £22 | £18 | £28 | 0·63 | 54% |
| Tory | £45 | £22 | £40 | 0·88 | 37% |

These results perhaps tend to confirm the common supposition that the successful voted Whig and the less so radical; but it is very interesting that this should hold true not only overall but when occupations are held constant.

Naturally as more Whigs and Tories were in better-paid occupations, they tended to live in better and more expensive housing. The average rateable value of Whig houses was £50, of Tory £45 and radical only £22. There were 19 Whigs in houses worth £100 or more per year, 21 Tories and only 3 radicals. Among shopkeepers Whig property was on average higher than Tory and Tory than radical. The social status of electors as measured by servants showed a similar trend to housing values. It is an exciting question whether these findings might be generalisable. Since this survey concentrates specifically on the north east we have to take the possibility into account that the north east was untypical; and there are some reasons for believing it was. An analysis of party support by counties (all seats) shows that nowhere was as loyal to the liberal party as Durham and Tyneside with the exception of the Metropolis; and only

34    Census Enumerators' Books, Gateshead, 1851. Public Record Office;
Gateshead Rate Book 1851, Gateshead Public Library.

Derbyshire was as consistent in its liberal affections. The liberals never held less than nine out of the total of thirteen seats between 1832 and 1867; and began on a high note by winning every seat bar one in 1832. Even the Tory revival of the thirties was heavily muted —for example by 1837 when the Tories had won three out of four county seats nationally, they had won only one in Durham. What they failed to do in the county, they naturally stood no chance of accomplishing in the towns.

This consistently liberal record made the area politically distinctive. What possible reasons were there? At least seven major factors could be suggested. Firstly, the north-east was socially and geographically isolated from the rest of the country: Leeds was 100 miles to the south, Edinburgh 120 miles to the north and London five days by coach. Secondly, the structure of land holding was untypical in two important respects: the aristocracy owned more than the average at the expense of the gentry and exercised considerable influence—often for the Whigs—and as a result of urbanisation and the coal trade an above average percentage of freeholders living in urban areas voted in the county constituency. The proportion of tenants at will in the county electorate was comparatively small.

Thirdly, there was the role of dissent. Nonconformity was powerful in all the big towns, partly by sheer weight of numbers and partly because of the preponderance of the older sorts of dissent—more prosperous and educated than many—the Quakers, Independents and Presbyterians. This was specially marked in Sunderland and the towns at the mouth of the Tyne and Tees. Dissenters were important in the two county divisions and in South Durham the Quakers returned one member for most of the period after 1832. It should be noted that Methodism was not politically powerful despite its large number of members. Fourthly the split between landed and industrial society which occurred in other regions did not appear in the north-east. In the early part of the period there were few factories and the dominant industry was the coal trade in which the landowners were themselves the capitalists. This helped to cushion the effects of the agricultural depression in corn and lessened the protectionist pull on landed society. Most of the gentry and aristocracy were as happy gathering coal as harvesting corn.

Fifthly, the north-east contained few small market towns with a large freeman electorate which could be bought by the purse. Tynemouth, South Shields, Sunderland and Gateshead were all electorally speaking middle-class householder boroughs, created in 1832 and likely to support the liberal party. This was moderated by the shipping industry, but even it was less conservative and protectionist than in other parts of the country. The only serious competition to the coastal trade was the domestic railway line. The ports were also strongly nonconformist, which influenced the character of politics. Sixth, the north-east enjoyed good liberal and bad Tory leadership. It was Radical Jack's Bailiwick and even though some considered his radicalism a bit bogus, the majority were impressed. His version of democracy stopped short at the working class. He was in favour of rated household suffrage—in the fashion of the Municipal Reform Bill—the ballot and shorter parliaments, and this was quite acceptable to the majority of the class of '32 who were no more genuine about manhood suffrage than the Whigs and moderate liberals. His platform echoed the feelings of most ten pounders in the north-east, as Durham's northern campaigns of 1833 and 1834 showed. By 1837 three of the towns were represented by a Lambtonite: Andrew White in Sunderland, William Ord in Newcastle and Cuthbert Rippon in Gateshead. On the other hand, the Tories had to live with Lord Londonderry who had several character traits in common with Durham but much less skill at hiding his other face of aristocratic arrogance.

Finally, the north-east was scarcely affected by three major agitations of the period—the poor law, factory reform and free trade. The old poor law does not seem to have been the burden it was elsewhere and in any case the administration of the new was quite humane, according to Dr McCord. The new poor law came to the north-east at a time of great prosperity, not of hardship as in the West Riding. Factory reform was not of great interest because of the absence of large workplaces in the twenties and thirties and forties, while conditions in the mines, though bad, were not perhaps as dreadful as in some other fields. The limited impact of Anti-Corn-Law League—notwithstanding Bright in Durham—was largely explicable in terms of the role of landowners in industrial life and the effect on agricultural demand of the towns and pit villages. The north also seems to have lacked at this early period the urban-based capitalists who were a feature of the scene in Lancashire and the West Riding. After 1832 the only big agitation in the north was chartism and throughout the early Victorian period the north-east was more interested in parliamentary reform than in any other reform. In sum, there seems to be some reason to be sceptical that the north-east was necessarily typical of the industrial and urban areas of the country.

In this paper I have argued that the usual interpretation of the origins of nineteenth-century radicalism is not enough to explain its course in the north-east. In particular it is striking that there was so little part played by a labour aristocracy. Existing explanations should be supplemented by an analysis of the role of the shopocracy. This class formed the rank and file of the reform movement in the 1830s but then soon ignored by the Whigs when they came to power, locally and nationally. But the fact that the shopkeepers were the biggest group in the reformed electorate even in freemen boroughs, and their tendency to vote more liberally than other groups, gave them a latent strength. The working class on the other hand were largely confined to the non-electorate and faced with the acute problem of sustaining an agitation without the means of communication to do so. In most of the bigger industrial towns the proportion of working-class electors was low and there seems to be less evidence than is desirable that any of them voted strongly radical. There is substantial evidence that contemporaries conceived of the shopocracy on the other hand as a distinct group and that there was a strong class consciousness about their situation in their own attitudes and those of the upper and professional classes above them. It was still inconceivable that the working class should come to play a significant role in political and social life but there was always the fear that the shopkeeper might become mayor. As a group the shopocracy enjoyed a certain freedom from social pressures influencing their vote unduly. Although they possessed little money and commanded little influence until the working class got the municipal vote in the north-east after 1850, their skills *were* appropriate to the task of mobilising public opinion by political means, whereas the strength of their enemies lay in influence and the purse. At first the appeal to individual political opinion, derived from but

P

not determined by its social context, stood little chance of success, but gradually the development of transport, the press, the government and public opinion gave this class more and more opportunity. It was a development which reached its zenith in the fifties, greatly facilitated by the passage of the Small Tenements Act and the introduction of the penny daily newspaper. From the assault on the Whig corporations it was a comparatively short step to the capture of a parliamentary seat, particularly as the Whigs opted for rural society and the urban electorate grew in the middle ranges.

That the Whig and Tory alliance did not in the end save the Whigs from rejection in the towns was the achievement of the shopocracy as much as anything else; and if perhaps there are certain special features in the character and history of the north-east which make the shopocracy more important and the labour aristocracy less important there than elsewhere the shopkeepers still deserve to be rescued from the dust of the stock-rooms.

Hannah Arendt

# Rosa Luxemburg

Reprinted from *New York Review of Books*, 6 Oct., 1966.

The definitive biography in the English style—lengthy, thoroughly documented, heavily annotated, and generously splashed with quotations—is among the most admirable genres of historiography, and it was a stroke of genius on the part of J. P. Nettl to choose the life of Rosa Luxemburg, the most unlikely candidate, as a proper subject. For this is the classical genre for the lives of great statesmen and other persons of the world, and Rosa Luxemburg was nothing of the kind. Even in her own world of the European socialist movement she was a rather marginal figure, with relatively brief moments of splendor and great brilliance, whose influence in deed and written word can hardly be compared to that of her contemporaries—to Plekhanov, Trotsky and Lenin, to Bebel and Kautsky, to Jaurès and Millerand.

How could Mr Nettl succeed with this woman who when very young had been swept into the German Social Democratic Party from her native Poland; who continued to play a key role in the little-known and neglected history of Polish socialism; and who then for about two decades, although never officially recognized, became the most controversial and least understood figure in the German Left movement? For the success and failure of English biography depend not merely on the chosen person's fame or the interest of his life story. In this genre, history is not treated as the inevitable background of a given life-span; rather it is as if the colorless light of historical time were forced through and refracted by the prism of a great character so that in the resulting spectrum a complete unity of life and world is achieved. In other words, success in the world seems almost a prerequisite for success in the genre. And it was precisely success—success even in her own world of revolutionaries—

which was withheld from Rosa Luxemburg in life, death, and after death. Can it be that the failure of all her efforts as far as official recognition is concerned is somehow connected with the dismal failure of revolution in our century? Will history look different if seen through the prism of her life and work?

However that may be, I know no book that sheds more light on the crucial period of European socialism from the last decades of the nineteenth century to the fateful day in January, 1919 when Rosa Luxemburg and Karl Liebknecht, the two leaders of Spartakus, the precursor of the German Communist Party, were murdered in Berlin —under the eyes and probably with the connivance of the Socialist regime then in power. The murderers were members of the ultra-nationalist and officially illegal *Freikorps*, a paramilitary organization from which Hitler's stormtroopers were soon to recruit their most promising killers. That the government at the time was practically in the hands of the *Freikorps* because it enjoyed 'the full support of Noske', the Socialists' expert on national defense, then in charge of military affairs, was confirmed only recently by Captain Pabst, the last surviving participant in the assassination. The Bonn government —in this as in other respects only too eager to revive the more sinister traits of the Weimar Republic—let it be known (through the *Bulletin des Presse- und Informationsamtes der Bundesregierung*) that the murder of Liebknecht and Luxemburg was entirely legal, 'an execution in accordance with martial law'. This was more than even the Weimar Republic had ever pretended, for it had 'punished' the murderers by meting out a sentence of two years and two weeks to the soldier Runge for '*attempted* manslaughter' (he had hit Rosa Luxemburg over the head in the corridors of the Hotel Eden), and four months to Lieutenant Vogel (he was the officer in charge when she was shot in the head inside a car and thrown into the Landwehr Canal) for 'failing to report a corpse and illegally disposing of it'. During the trial, a photograph showing Runge and his comrades cele-brating the assassination in the same Hotel on the following day was introduced as evidence, which caused the defendant great merriment. 'Accused Runge, you must behave properly. This is no laughing matter', said the presiding judge. Forty-five years later, during the Auschwitz trial in Frankfurt, a similar scene took place; the same words were spoken.

With the murder of Rosa Luxemburg and Liebknecht, the split of
the European Left into Socialist and Communist parties became
irrevocable; 'the abyss which the Communists had pictured in theory
had become . . . the abyss of the grave'. And since this early crime
had been aided and abetted by the government, it initiated a death-
dance in post-war Germany: The assassins of the extreme Right
started by liquidating prominent leaders of the extreme Left—Hugo
Haase and Gustav Landauer, Leo Jogiches and Eugene Leviné—and
quickly moved to the center and the right-of-center—to Walter
Rathenau, Matthias Erzberger, both members of the government at
the time of their murder. Thus Rosa Luxemburg's death became the
watershed between two eras in Germany; and it became the point of
no return for the German Left. All those who had drifted to the
Communists out of bitter disappointment with the Socialist party
were even more disappointed with the swift moral decline and
political disintegration of the Communist party, and yet they felt
that to return to the ranks of the Socialists would mean to condone
the murder of Rosa. Such personal reactions, which are seldom publicly admitted, are among the small, mosaic-like pieces that fall into
place in the large riddle of history. In the case of Rosa Luxemburg
they are part of the legend which soon surrounded her name.
Legends have a truth of their own, but Mr Nettl is entirely right to
have paid almost no attention to the Rosa myth. It was his task,
difficult enough, to restore her to historical life.

Shortly after her death, when all persuasions of the Left had already decided that she had always been 'mistaken' (a 'really hopeless
case', as George Lichtheim, the last in this long line, put in it
*Encounter*), a curious shift in her reputation took place. Two small
volumes of her letters were published, and these, entirely personal
and of a simple, touchingly humane, and often poetic beauty, were
enough to destroy the false image of blood-thirsty 'Red Rosa', at
least in all but the most obstinately anti-Semitic and reactionary
circles. However, what then grew up was another legend—the
sentimentalized image of the bird watcher and lover of flowers, a
woman whose guards said goodbye to her with tears in their eyes
when she left prison—as if they couldn't go on living without being
entertained by this strange prisoner who had insisted on treating
them as human beings. Nettl does not mention this story, faithfully

handed down to me when I was a child and later confirmed by Kurt Rosenfeld, her friend and lawyer, who claimed to have witnessed the scene. It is probably true enough, and its slightly embarrassing features are somehow offset by the survival of another anecdote, this one mentioned by Nettl. In 1907, she and her friend Clara Zetkin (later the 'grand old woman' of German Communism) had gone for a walk, lost count of time, and arrived late for an appointment with August Bebel, who had feared they were lost. Rosa then proposed their epitaph: 'Here lie the last two men of German Social Democracy'. Seven years later, in February, 1914, she had occasion to prove the truth of this cruel joke in a splendid address to the judges of the Criminal Court which had indicted her for 'inciting' the masses to civil disobedience in case of war. (Not bad, incidentally, for the woman who 'was always wrong' to stand trial on this charge five months before the outbreak of the First World War, which few 'serious' people had thought possible.) Mr Nettl with good sense has reprinted the address in its entirety; its 'manliness' is unparalleled in the history of German socialism.

It took a few more years and a few more catastrophes for the legend to turn into a symbol of nostalgia for the good old times of the movement, when hopes were green, the revolution around the corner, and, most important, the faith in the capacities of the masses and in the moral integrity of the Socialist or Communist leadership was still intact. It speaks not only for the person of Rosa Luxemburg, but also for the qualities of this older generation of the Left, that the legend—vague, confused, inaccurate in nearly all details—could spread throughout the world and come to life whenever a 'new Left' sprang into being. But side by side with this glamorized image, there survived also the old clichés of the 'quarrelsome female', a 'romantic' who was neither 'realistic' nor scientific (it is true that she was always out of step), and whose works, especially her great book on imperialism (*The Accumulation of Capital*, 1913), were shrugged off.

Every New Left movement, when its moment came to change into the Old Left—usually when its members reached the age of forty—promptly buried its early enthusiasm for Rosa Luxemburg together with the dreams of youth; and since they had usually not bothered to read, let alone to understand, what she had to say they found it easy to dismiss her with all the patronizing philistinism of their newly acquired status. 'Luxemburgism', invented posthumously by party hacks for polemical reasons, has never even achieved the honor of being denouced as 'treason'; it was treated as a harmless, infantile disease. Nothing Rosa Luxemburg wrote or said survived except her surprisingly accurate criticism of Bolshevik politics during the early stages of the Russian Revolution, and this only because those whom a 'god had failed' could use it as a convenient, though wholly inadequate weapon, against Stalin. ('There is something indecent in the use of Rosa's name and writings as a cold war missile', as the reviewer of this book pointed out in the *Times Literary Supplement*.) Her new admirers had no more in common with her than her detractors. Her highly developed sense for real differences and her infallible judgment, her personal likes and dislikes, would have prevented her lumping Lenin and Stalin together under all circumstances; quite apart from the fact that she had never been a 'believer', had never used politics as a substitute for religion, and had been careful, as Mr Nettl notes, not to attack religion when she opposed the church. In short, while 'revolution was as close and real to her as to Lenin', it was no more an article of faith with her than Marxism. Lenin was primarily a man of action and would have gone into politics in any event, but she, who, in her half-serious self-estimate, was born 'to mind the geese', might just as well have buried herself in botany and zoology or history and economics or mathematics, had not the circumstances of the world offended her sense of justice and freedom.

This is of course to admit that she was not an orthodox Marxist, so little orthodox indeed that it might be doubted that she was a Marxist at all. Mr Nettl rightly states that to her Marx was no more than 'the best interpreter of reality of them all', and it is revealing of her lack of personal commitment that she could write (to Hans Diefenbach on 8th March, 1917, in *Briefe an Freunde*, Zürich, 1950) 'I now have a horror of the much praised first volume of Marx's *Capital* because of its elaborate rococo ornaments à la Hegel'. What mattered most in her view was reality, in all its wonderful and all its frightful aspects, even more than revolution itself. Her unorthodoxy was innocent, non-polemical; she 'recommended her friends to read Marx for "the daring of his thoughts, the refusal to take anything for granted", rather than for the value of his conclusions. His mistakes . . . were self-evident . . .; that was why she never bothered to engage in any lengthy critique'. All this is most obvious in *The Accumulation of Capital*, which only Franz Mehring was unprejudiced enough to call a 'truly magnificent, fascinating achievement without its equal since Marx's death' (not quoted by Nettl, see *Briefe an Freunde*, p. 84).

The central thesis of this 'curious work of genius' is simple enough. Since capitalism didn't show any signs of collapse 'under the weight of its economic contradictions', she began to look for an outside cause to explain its continued existence and growth. She found it in the so-called third-man theory, that is, in the fact that the process of growth was not merely the consequence of innate laws ruling capitalist production but of the existence of pre-capitalist sectors in the country which 'capitalism' captured and brought into its sphere of influence. Once this process had spread to the whole country, capitalists were forced to look to other parts of the earth, to pre-capitalist territories, to draw them into the process of capital accumulation, which, as it were, fed on whatever was outside itself. In other words, Marx's 'original accumulation of capital' was not, like original sin, a single event, a unique deed of expropriation by the nascent bourgeoisie, setting off a process of accumulation that would then follow 'with iron necessity' its own inherent law up to the final collapse. On the contrary, expropriation had to be repeated time and again to keep the system in motion. Hence, capitalism was not a closed system that generated its own contradictions and was 'pregnant with revolution'; it fed on outside factors, and its *automatic* collapse could occur, if at all, only when the whole surface of the earth was conquered and had been devoured.

Lenin was quick to see that this description, whatever its merits or flaws, was essentially non-Marxist. It contradicted the very foundations of Marxian and Hegelian dialectics, which hold that bourgeois society creates its own anti-thesis, and the whole process is caused by the Hegelian law of historical motion. Lenin pointed out that from the viewpoint of materialist dialectics 'her thesis that enlarged capitalist reproduction was impossible within a closed economy and needed to cannibalize economies in order to function at all . . . (was) a "fundamental error".' The trouble was only that what was an error in abstract Marxian theory was an eminently sound analysis of things as they really were.

Historically, Mr Nettl's greatest and most original achievement is the discovery of the Polish-Jewish 'peer group' and Rosa Luxemburg's life-long, close, and carefully hidden attachment to the Polish party which sprang from it. This is indeed a highly significant and totally neglected source, not of the revolutions, but of the revolutionary spirit in the twentieth century. This milieu, which even in the twenties had lost all public relevance, has now completely disappeared. Its nucleus consisted of assimilated Jews from middle-class families whose cultural background was German (Rosa Luxemburg knew Goethe and Möricke by heart and her literary taste was impeccable, far superior to that of her German friends), whose political formation was Russian, and whose moral standards in both private and public life were uniquely their own. These Jews, an extremely small minority in the East, an even smaller percentage of assimilated Jewry in the West, stood outside all social ranks, Jewish or non-Jewish, hence had no conventional prejudices whatsoever, and had developed, in this truly splendid isolation, their own code of honor—which then attracted a number of non-Jews, among them Julian Marchlewski and Feliks Dzierzynski, both of whom later joined the Bolsheviks. It was precisely because of this unique background that Lenin appointed Dzierzynski as first head of the Cheka, someone, he hoped, no power could corrupt; hadn't he begged to be charged with the department of Children's Education and Welfare?

Nettl rightly stresses Rosa Luxemburg's excellent relations with her family, her parents, brothers, sister and niece, none of whom ever showed the slightest inclination to socialist convictions or revolutionary activities, yet who did everything they could for her when she had to hide from the police or was in prison. The point is worth making, for it gives us a glimpse of this unique Jewish family background without which the emergence of the ethical code of the peer group would be nearly incomprehensible. The hidden equalizer of those who always treated one another as equals—and hardly anybody else—was the essentially simple experience of a childhood world in which mutual respect and unconditional trust, a universal humanity and a genuine, almost naive contempt for social and ethnic distinctions were taken for granted. What the members of the peer group had in common was what can only be called moral taste, which is so different from 'moral principles'; the authenticity of their morality they owed to having grown up in a world that was not out of joint. This gave them their 'rare self-confidence', so unsettling to the world into which they then came, and so bitterly resented as arrogance and conceit. This milieu, and never the German party, was and remained Rosa Luxemburg's home. The home was movable up to a point, and since it was predominantly Jewish it did not coincide with any 'fatherland'.

It is of course highly suggestive that the SDKPiL, the party of this predominantly Jewish group, split from the official Socialist Polish Party, the PPS, because of the latter's stand for Polish independence (Pilsudski, the Fascist dictator of Poland after World War I, was its most famous and successful offspring); and that, after the split, the members of the group became ardent defenders of an often doctrinaire internationalism. It is even more suggestive that the national question is the only issue on which one could accuse Rosa Luxemburg of self-deception and unwillingness to face reality. That this had something to do with her Jewishness is undeniable, although it is of course 'lamentably absurd' to discover in her anti-nationalism 'a peculiarly Jewish quality'. Mr Nettl, while hiding nothing, is rather careful to avoid the 'Jewish question', and in view of the usually low level of debates on this issue one can only applaud his decision. Unfortunately, his understandable distaste has blinded him to the few important facts in this matter, which is all the more to be regretted since these facts, though of a simple, elementary nature, also escaped the otherwise so sensitive and alert mind of Rosa Luxemburg.

Only Nietzsche, as far as I know, has ever pointed out that the position and functions of the Jewish people in Europe predestined them to become the 'good Europeans' *par excellence*. The Jewish middle classes of Paris and London, Berlin and Vienna, Warsaw and Moscow, were in fact neither cosmopolitan nor international, though the intellectuals among them thought of themselves in these terms. They were European, something that could be said of no other groups. And this was not a matter of conviction; it was an objective fact. In other words, while the self-deception of assimilated Jews usually consisted in the mistaken belief that they were just as German as the Germans, just as French as the French, the self-deception of the intellectual Jews consisted in thinking that they had no 'fatherland', for their fatherland actually was Europe. This was especially true of the East-European intelligentsia, which was multi-lingual—Rosa Luxemburg herself spoke Polish, Russian, German and French fluently and knew English and Italian very well. They never quite understood why the slogan, 'the fatherland of the working class is the Socialist movement', should be so disastrously wrong precisely for the working classes. It is indeed more than a little disturbing that Rosa Luxemburg herself with her acute sense of reality and strict avoidance of clichés, should not have *heard* what was wrong with the slogan on principle. A fatherland, after all, is first of all a 'land', an organization is not a country, not even metaphorically. There is indeed grim justice in the later trans-formation of the slogan, 'the fatherland of the working class is Soviet Russia'—Russia was at least a 'land'—which put an end to the utopian internationalism of this generation.

One could adduce more such facts, and it still would be difficult to claim that Rosa Luxemburg was entirely wrong on the national question. What, after all, has more contributed to the catastrophic decline of Europe than the insane nationalism which accompanied the decline of the nation state in the era of imperialism? Those whom Nietzsche had called the 'good Europeans'—a very small minority even among Jews—might well have been the only ones to have a presentiment of the disastrous consequences ahead, although they were unable to gauge correctly the enormous force of nationalist feeling in a decaying body politic.

Closely connected with the discovery of the Polish 'peer group' and its continued importance for Rosa Luxemburg's public and private life is Mr Nettl's disclosure of hitherto inaccessible sources, which enabled him to piece together the facts of her life—'the exquisite business of love and living'. It now turns out we knew next to nothing about her private life for the simple reason that she had so carefully protected herself from notoriety. This is no mere matter of sources. It was fortunate indeed that the new material fell into Mr Nettl's hands and he has every right to dismiss his few predecessors who were less hampered by lack of access to the facts than by their inability to move, think, and feel on the same level as their subject. The ease with which Nettl handles his biographical material is astounding. His treatment is more than perceptive. His is the first plausible portrait of this extraordinary woman, drawn *con amore*, with tact and great delicacy. It is as though she had found her last admirer, and it is for this reason that one feels like quarrelling with some of his judgments.

He is certainly wrong in emphasizing her ambition, and sense of her career. Does he think that her violent contempt for the careerists and status-seekers in the German party—their delight in being admitted to the *Reichstag*—is mere cant? Does he believe that a really 'ambitious' person could have afforded to be as generous as she was? (Once, at an international congress, Jaurès finished an eloquent speech in which he 'ridiculed the misguided passions of Rosa Luxemburg [but] there was suddenly no one to translate him. Rosa jumped up and reproduced the moving oratory: from French into equally telling German'.) And how can he reconcile this, except by assuming dishonesty or self-deception, with her telling phrase in one of her letters to Jogiches: 'I have a cursed longing for happiness and am ready to haggle for my daily portion of happiness with all the stubbornness of a mule'. What he mistakes for ambition is the natural force of a temperament, capable, in her own laughing words, of 'setting a prairie on fire', which propelled her almost willy-nilly into public affairs, and even ruled over most of her purely intellectual enterprises. While he stresses repeatedly the high moral standards of the 'peer group', he still seems not to understand that such things as ambition, career, status, and even mere success were under the strictest taboo.

There is another aspect of her personality which Nettl stresses but whose implications he seems not to understand: that she was so 'self-consciously a woman'. This in itself put certain limitations on whatever her ambitions otherwise might have been—for Nettl does not ascribe to her more than what would have been natural in a man with her gifts and opportunities. Her distaste for the women's emancipation movement, to which all other women of her generation and political convictions were irresistibly drawn, was significant; in the face of suffragette equality, she might have been tempted to reply, *Vive la petite différence*. She was an outsider, not only because she was and remained a Polish Jewess in a country she disliked and a party she came soon to despise, but also because she was a woman. Mr Nettl must, of course, be pardoned for his masculine prejudices;

they would not matter much if they had not prevented him from understanding fully the role Leo Jogiches, her husband for all practical purposes, and her first, perhaps her only, lover, played in her life. Their deadly serious quarrel, caused by Jogiches's brief affair with another woman and endlessly complicated by Rosa's furious reaction, was typical of their time and milieu, as was the aftermath, his jealousy and her refusal for years to forgive him. This generation still believed firmly that love strikes only once, and its carelessness with marriage certificates should not be mistaken for any belief in free love. Mr Nettl's evidence shows that she had friends and admirers, and that she enjoyed this, but it hardly indicates that there was ever another man in her life. To believe in the party gossip about marriage plans with 'Hänschen' Diefenbach, whom she addressed as *Sie* and never dreamed of treating as an equal, strikes me as downright silly. Nettl calls the story of Leo Jogiches and Rosa Luxemburg 'one of the great and tragic love stories of Socialism', and there is no need to quarrel with this verdict if one understands that it was not 'blind and self-destructive jealousy' which caused an ultimate tragedy in their relations but war and the years in prison, the doomed German revolution, and the bloody end.

Leo Jogiches, whose name Nettl also has rescued from oblivion, was a very remarkable and yet typical figure among the professional revolutionists. To Rosa Luxemburg, he was definitely *masculini generis*, which was of considerable importance to her: She preferred Graf Westarp (the leader of the German Conservative party) to all the German Socialist luminaries 'because', she said, 'he is a *man*'. There were few people she respected, and Jogiches headed a list on which only the names of Lenin and Franz Mehring could be inscribed with certainty. He definitely was a man of action, he knew how to do and how to suffer. It is tempting to compare him with Lenin, whom he somewhat resembles, except in his passion for anonymity and for pulling strings behind the scenes. And this love of conspiracy and danger must have given him an additional erotic charm. He was indeed a Lenin *manqué*, even in his inability to write, 'total' in his case (as she observed in a shrewd and actually very loving portrait in one of her letters); and his mediocrity as a public speaker. Both men had great talent for action and leadership, but for nothing else, so that they felt impotent and superfluous when left to themselves.

This is less noticeable in Lenin's case because he was never completely isolated, but Jogiches had early fallen out with the Russian party because of a quarrel with Plekhanov, who regarded the self-assured Jewish youth newly arrived from Poland as 'a miniature version of Nechaieff'. The consequence was that he, according to Rosa Luxemburg, 'completely rootless, vegetated' for many years, until the revolution of 1905 gave him his first opportunity: 'Quite suddenly he not only achieved the position of leader of the Polish movement, but even in the Russian'. (The SDKPiL came into prominence during the Revolution and became more important in the years following. Jogiches, though he himself didn't 'write a single line', remained 'none the less the very soul' of its publications.) He had his last brief moment when 'completely unknown in the SPD', he organized a clandestine opposition in the German army during the First World War. 'Without him there would have been no *Spartakusbund*', which, unlike any other organized Leftist group in Germany, for a short time became a kind of 'ideal peer group'. (This, of course, is not to say that Jogiches made the German revolution; like all revolutions, it was made by no one. Spartakus too was 'following rather than making events', and the official notion that the 'Spartakus uprising' in January, 1918 was caused or inspired by its leaders—Rosa Luxemburg, Liebknecht, Jogiches—is a myth.)

We shall never know how many of Rosa Luxemburg's political ideas derived from Jogiches; in marriage, it is not always easy to tell each partner's thoughts apart. But that he failed where Lenin succeeded was at least as much a consequence of circumstances—he was a Jew and a Pole—as of lesser stature. In any event, Rosa Luxemburg would have been the last to hold this against him. The members of the peer group did not judge one another in these categories. Jogiches himself might have agreed with Eugene Leviné, also a Russian Jew though a younger man, 'We are dead men on furlough'. This mood is what set him apart from the others; for neither Lenin nor Trotsky nor Rosa Luxemburg herself are likely to have thought along such lines. After her death he refused to leave Berlin for safety: 'Somebody has to stay to write all our epitaphs'. He was arrested two months after the murder of Liebknecht and Luxemburg and shot in the back in the police station. The name of the murderer was known, but 'no attempt to punish him was ever made'; he killed another man in the same way, and then continued his 'career with promotion in the Prussian Police'. Such were the *mores* of the Weimar Republic.

Reading and remembering these old stories one becomes painfully aware of the difference between the German comrades and the members of Rosa Luxemburg's group. During the Russian revolution of 1905 she was arrested in Warsaw, and her friends collected the money for bail (probably provided by the German party). The payment was supplemented 'with an unofficial threat of reprisal; if anything happened to Rosa they would retaliate with action against prominent officials'. No such notion of 'action' ever entered her German friends' minds either before or after the wave of political murders when the impunity of such deeds had become notorious.

More troubling in retrospect, certainly more painful for herself, than her alleged 'errors' are the few crucial instances in which Rosa Luxemburg was not 'out of step', but appeared instead to be in agreement with the official powers in the German Socialist movement. These were her real mistakes, and there was none she did not finally recognize and bitterly regret. The least harmful among them concerned the national question. She had arrived in Germany in 1898 from Zurich, where she has passed her doctorate 'with a first class dissertation about the industrial development of Poland' (according to Professor Julius Wolf, who in his autobiography still remembered fondly 'the ablest of my pupils'), which achieved the unusual 'distinction of instant commercial publication' and is still used by students of Polish history. Her thesis was that the economic growth of Poland depended entirely upon the Russian market and that any attempt 'to form a national or linguistic state was a negation of all development and progress for the last fifty years'. (That she was economically right was more than demonstrated by the chronic malaise of Poland between the wars.) She then became the expert on Poland for the German party, its propagandist among the Polish population in the Eastern German provinces, and entered an uneasy alliance with people who wished to 'Germanize' the Poles out of existence and would 'gladly make you a present of all and every Pole including Polish Socialism', as an SPD secretary told her. Surely, 'the glow of official approval was for Rosa a false glow'.

Much more serious was her deceptive agreement with party

authorities in the revisionist controversy in which she played a
leading part. This famous debate had been touched off by Eduard
Bernstein (whose most important book is now available in English
under the title *Evolutionary Socialism*, Schocken Paperback, unfortunately lacking much-needed annotations and an introduction
for the American reader). Revisionism has gone down in history as
the alternative of reform against revolution. But this battle cry is
misleading for two reasons: It makes it appear as though the SPD at
the turn of the century still was committed to revolution, which was
not the case; and it conceals the objective soundness of much of what
Bernstein had to say. His criticism of Marx's economic theories was
indeed, as he claimed, in full 'agreement with reality'. He pointed
out that the 'enormous increase of social wealth (was) not accompanied by a decreasing number of large capitalists but by an
increasing number of capitalists of all degrees', that an 'increasing
narrowing of the circle of the well-to-do and an increasing misery of
the poor' had failed to materialize, and that Marx's slogan, 'the proletarian has no fatherland', was no longer true: Universal suffrage
had given him political rights, the trade unions a place in society,
and the new imperialist development a clear stake in the nation's
foreign policy. No doubt the reaction of the German party to these
unwelcome truths was chiefly inspired by a deep-seated reluctance to
re-examine critically its theoretical foundation. What was at stake
was the status of the SPD as a 'state within a state': the party had in
fact become a huge and well-organized bureaucracy that stood outside society and had every interest in things as they were. Revisionism
à la Bernstein would have led the party back into German society,
and such 'integration' was felt to be as dangerous to the party's
interests as a revolution.

Mr Nettl's brilliant analysis of the position of the SPD rests on an
interesting theory—which he has developed in an article 'The
German Social Democratic Party 1890-1914 as a Political Model', in
*Past and Present*, April, 1965—about the 'pariah position' of the
SPD within German society and its failure to participate in government. It seemed to its members that the party could 'provide within
itself a superior alternative to corrupt capitalism'. In fact, by
keeping the 'defenses against society on all fronts intact', it
generated that spurious feeling of 'togetherness' (as Nettl puts

it) which the French Socialists treated with great contempt.[1]

In any event, it was obvious that the more the party increased in numbers, the more surely was the radical élan 'organized out of existence'. One could live very comfortably in this 'state within a state' by avoiding friction with society at large, by enjoying feelings of moral superiority without any consequences. It was not even necessary to pay the price of serious alienation since this pariah society was in fact but a mirror image, a *'miniature reflection'* of German society at large. This blind alley of the German Socialist movement could be analyzed correctly from opposing points of view —either from the view of Bernstein's revisionism, which recognized the emancipation of the working classes within capitalist society as an accomplished fact and demanded a stop to the talk about a revolution nobody thought of anyhow; or from the viewpoint of those who were not merely 'alienated' from bourgeois society but actually wanted to change the world.

The latter was the standpoint of the revolutionists from the East who led the attack against Bernstein—Plekhanov, Parvus and Rosa Luxemburg—and whom Karl Kautsky, the German party's most eminent theoretician, supported, although he probably felt much more at ease with Bernstein than in the company of his new allies. The victory they won was a Pyrrhic one; it 'merely strengthened alienation by pushing reality away'. For the real issue was not theoretical and not economic. At stake was Bernstein's conviction, shamefully hidden in a footnote, that 'the middle class—not excepting the German—in their bulk (was) still fairly healthy, not only economically but also *morally*' (my italics). This was the reason that Plekhanov called him a 'philistine' and that Parvus and Rosa Luxemburg thought the fight so decisive for the future of the party. For the truth of the matter was that Bernstein and Kautsky had in

---

1   The situation bore very similar traits to the position of the French army during the Dreyfus crisis in France which Rosa Luxemburg so brilliantly analysed for *Die Neue Zeit* in 'Die Soziale Krise in Frankreich' (vol. 1, 1901). 'The reason the army was reluctant to make a move was that it wanted to show its opposition to the civil power of the republic, without at the same time losing the force of that opposition by committing itself', through a serious *coup d'état*, to another form of government.

common their aversion to revolution (the 'iron law of necessity' was for Kautsky the best possible excuse for doing nothing). The guests from Eastern Europe were the only ones who not merely 'believed' in revolution as a theoretical necessity but wished to do something about it, precisely because they considered society as it was to be unbearable on moral grounds, on the grounds of justice. Bernstein and Rosa Luxemburg, on the other hand, had in common that they were both honest (which may explain Bernstein's 'secret tenderness' for her), analyzed what they saw, were loyal to reality, and critical of Marx; Bernstein was aware of this and shrewdly remarks in his reply to Rosa Luxemburg's attacks that she too had questioned 'the whole Marxist predictions of the coming social evolution, so far as this is based on the theory of crises'.

Rosa Luxemburg's early triumphs in the German party rested on a double misunderstanding. At the turn of the century, the SPD was 'the envy and admiration of Socialists, throughout the world'. August Bebel, its 'grand old man', who from Bismarck's foundation of the German Reich to the outbreak of the First World War, 'dominated (its) policy and spirit', had always proclaimed, 'I am and always will be the mortal enemy of existing society'. Didn't that sound like the spirit of the Polish 'peer group'? Couldn't one assume from such proud defiance that the great German party was somehow the SDKPiL writ large? It took Rosa Luxemburg almost a decade—until she returned from the first Russian Revolution—to discover that the secret of this defiance was wilful non-involvement with the world at large and single-minded preoccupation with the growth of the party organization. Out of this experience she developed, after 1910, her program of constant 'friction' with society without which, as she then realized, the very source of the revolutionary spirit was doomed to dry up. She did not intend to spend her life in a sect, no matter how large; her commitment to revolution was primarily a moral matter, and this meant that she remained passionately engaged in public life and civil affairs, in the destinies of the world. Her involvement with European politics outside the immediate interests of the working class, and hence completely beyond the horizon of all Marxists, appears most convincingly in her repeated insistence on a 'republican program' for the German and Russian parties.

This was one of the main points of her famous *Juniusbroschüre*, written in prison during the war and then used as the platform for the Spartakus. Lenin, who was unaware of its authorship, immediately declared that to proclaim 'the program of a republic . . . (means) in practice to proclaim the revolution—with an *incorrect* revolutionary program'. Well, a year later the Russian Revolution broke out without any 'program' whatsoever, and its first achievement was the abolition of the monarchy and the establishment of a republic, while the same was to happen in Germany and Austria. Which, of course, has never prevented the Russian, Polish, or German comrades from violently disagreeing with her on this point. It is indeed the republican question rather than the national one which separated her most decisively from all others. Here she was completely alone, as she was alone, though less obviously so, in her stress on the absolute necessity of not only individual but public freedom under all circumstances.

A second misunderstanding is directly connected with the revisionist debate. Rosa Luxemburg mistook Kautsky's reluctance to accept Bernstein's analyses for an authentic commitment to revolution. After the first Russian revolution in 1905, for which she had hurried back to Warsaw with false papers, she could no longer deceive herself. To her, these months constituted not only a crucial experience, they were also 'the happiest of my life'. Upon her return, she tried to discuss the events with her friends in the German party. She learned quickly that the word revolution 'had only to come into contact with a real revolutionary situation to break down' into meaningless syllables. The German Socialists were convinced that such things could happen only in distant barbarian lands. This was the first shock, from which she never recovered. The second came in 1914 and brought her near to suicide.

Naturally, her first contact with a real revolution taught her more and better things than disillusion and the fine arts of disdain and mistrust. Out of it came her insight into the nature of political action, which Mr Nettl rightly calls her most important contribution to political theory. The main point is that she had learned from the revolutionary workers' councils (the later *soviets*) that 'good organization does not precede action but is the product of it', that 'the organization of revolutionary action can and must be learnt in revolution itself, as one can only learn swimming in the water', that revolutions are 'made' by nobody but break out 'spontaneously', and that 'the pressure for action' always comes 'from below'. A revolution is 'great and strong as long as the Social Democrats (at the time still the only revolutionary party) don't smash it up'.

There were, however, two aspects of the 1905 prelude which entirely escaped her. There was, after all, the surprising fact that the revolution had broken out not only in a non-industrialized, backward country, but in a territory where no strong Socialist movement with mass support existed at all. And there was, second, the equally undeniable fact that the revolution had been the consequence of the Russian defeat in the Russo-Japanese war. These were the two lessons Lenin learned from this event. One did not need a large organization: A small, tightly organized group with a leader who knew what he wanted was enough to pick up the power once the authority of the old regime had been swept away. And since revolutions were not 'made' but the result of circumstances and events beyond anybody's power, wars were welcome and large revolutionary organizations were only a nuisance. The first point was the source of her disagreements with Lenin during the First World War; the second of her criticism of Lenin's tactics in the Russian Revolution of 1918. For she refused categorically, from beginning to end, to see in the war anything but the most terrible disaster, no matter what its eventual outcome; the price in human lives, especially in proletarian lives, was too high in any event. Moreover, it would have gone against her grain to look upon revolution as the profiteer of war and massacre—something which didn't bother Lenin in the least. And with respect to the issue of organization, she did not believe in a victory in which the people at large had no part and no voice; so little, indeed, did she believe in holding power at any price that she 'was far more afraid of a deformed revolution than an unsuccessful one'—this was, in fact, 'the major difference between her' and the Bolsheviks.

And haven't events proved her right? Isn't the history of the Soviet Union one long demonstration of the frightful danger of 'deformed revolutions'? Hasn't the 'moral collapse' which she foresaw—without, of course, foreseeing the open criminality of Lenin's successor—done more harm to the cause of revolution as she understood it than 'any and every political defeat . . . in honest struggle

against superior forces and in the teeth of the historical situation'
could possibly have done? Wasn't she right that Lenin was 'completely mistaken' in the means he employed, that the only way to
salvation was the 'school of public life itself, the most unlimited, the
broadest democracy and public opinion', and that terror 'de-
moralized' everybody and destroyed everything?

She did not live long enough to see how right she had been and to
watch the terrible and terribly swift moral deterioration of the
Communist parties, the direct offsprings of the Russian Revolution,
throughout the world. Nor for that matter did Lenin, who despite
all his mistakes still had more in common with the original peer group
than with anybody who came after him. This became manifest when
Paul Levi, the successor of Leo Jogiches in the leadership of the
Spartakus, three years after Rosa Luxemburg's death, published
her remarks on the Russian Revolution just quoted, which she had
written in 1918 'only for you', that is without intending publication.
(It is not without irony that this pamphlet is the only work of hers
which is still known today, also, apparently, the only one ever to be
translated into English.) 'It was a moment of considerable embarrassment' for both the German and Russian parties, and Lenin could be
forgiven had he answered sharply and immoderately. Instead he
wrote: 'We answer with . . . a good old Russian fable: an eagle can
sometimes fly lower than a chicken, but a chicken can never rise to
the same heights as an eagle. Rosa Luxemburg . . . in spite of (her)
mistakes . . . was and is an eagle'. He then went on to demand
publication of 'her biography and the *complete* edition of her works',
unpurged of 'error', and chided the German comrades for their
'incredible' negligence in this duty. This was in 1922. Three years
later, Lenin's successors had decided to 'Bolshevize' the German
party and therefore ordered a 'specific onslaught on Rosa Luxemburg's whole legacy'. The task was accepted with joy by a young
member named Ruth Fischer, who had just arrived from Vienna.
She told the German comrades that Rosa Luxemburg and her
influence 'were nothing less than a syphilis bacillus'.

The gutter had opened, and out of it emerged what Rosa Luxemburg would have called 'another zoological species'. No 'agents of the
bourgeoisie' and no 'Socialist traitors' were needed any longer to
destroy the few survivors of the peer group and to bury in oblivion

the last remnants of their spirit. No complete edition of her works, needless to say, was ever published, and since the early twenties none of her major works has been reprinted in any language. After World War II, selections were published in East Berlin 'with careful annotations underlining her errors'. The two-volume edition was followed by a 'full-length analysis of the Luxemburgist system of errors. by Fred Oelssner, which quickly 'lapsed into obscurity' because it became 'too Stalinist'. This, most certainly, was not what Lenin had demanded, nor could it, as he had hoped, serve 'in the education of many generations of Communists'.

After Stalin's death, things began to change, though not in East Germany where, characteristically, revision of Stalinist history took the form of a 'Bebel cult'. (The only one to protest this new nonsense was poor old Hermann Duncker, the last distinguished survivor who still could 'recall the most wonderful period of my life, when as a young man I knew and worked with Rosa Luxemburg, Karl Liebknecht and Franz Mehring'.) The Poles, however, although their own two-volume edition of selected works in 1959 is 'partly overlapping with the German' one, 'took out her reputation almost unaltered from the casket in which it had been stored' ever since Lenin's death, and after 1956, a 'flood of Polish publications' on the subject appeared on the market. It is greatly to be regretted that Nettl does not mention this literature in his bibliography and does not discuss it in the text. One would like to believe that there is still hope for a belated recognition of who she was and what she did, as one would like to hope that she will finally find her place in the education of political scientists in the countries of the West. For Mr Nettl is right: 'Her ideas belong wherever the history of political ideas is seriously taught'.

A minor intriguing oddity of this splendid work should not go unnoticed. The jacket contains not a word about the author, who is practically unknown. Even his first name is withheld; according to 'research' it seems to be Peter. Was Rosa's passion for privacy that infectious for her biographer?

# Bibliography of the publications of J. P. Nettl

1. Inside Russia's Germany — Article — New Republic Aug. 2, 1948

2. Two Year Plan for the Russian Zone — Article — The Economist Aug. 8, 1948 pp.231-2

3. Rough Justice in Germany — Article — The Economist Oct. 23, 1948 p.665

4. Inside the Russian Zone 1945-1947 — Article — Pol. Quarterly XIX, 3, 1948 pp.201-233

5. The End of Military Government in Germany — Article — The Contemp. Review No. 1013 pp.265-270 May 1950

6. Fact and Fury (Basil Davidson 'Germany What Now? Potsdam to Partition') — Review — The Economist June 3, 1950 p.1216

7. 'Eastern Germany: A Survey of Soviet Policy' 1945-1950 — Article — The World Today (Chatham Hse. Review) pp.297-308, July 1950

8. The Eastern Zone and Soviet Policy in Germany — Book — O.U.P. London-N.Y. 1950

9. The Treaty-making power in Federal Constitutions — Article — Canadian Bar Review XXVIII, 10 pp.1051-70 December 1950

10. German Reparations in the Soviet Empire — Article — Foreign Affairs XXVIV, 2 pp.300-307 January 1951

11. Economic Checks on German Unity — Article — Foreign Affairs XXX, 2 pp.554-563 July 1952

12. Some Economic Aspects of the Wool Trade: Structure and Organisation of Distribution — Article — Oxford Econ. Papers IV, 2 pp.172-204 July 1952

| | | |
|---|---|---|
| 13. Untitled Review of Walter Ulbricht's 'Lehrbuch Fur Den Demokratisehen Staats—Und Wirtschaftsaufbau' | Review | Amer. Econ. Review Vol. XLII No. 5 December 1952 |
| 14. A Chapter in *Totalitarianism* Edit. Carl J. Friedrich | Contri- bution | Harvard U.P. 1953 pp.296-308 |
| 15. New Headaches for the Soviet Planners | Article | Problems of Communism III, p.22 ff 1954 |
| 16. L'Union Sovietique Etat Pouvoir et Culture | Article | Comprendre 12 pp.1-4 1954 |
| 17. A Decade of Post-War Germany | Article | Pol. Quarterly XXVII, 2, 1956 pp.162-175 |
| 18. A Note on Entrepreneurial Behaviour | Article | Review of Econ. Studies XXIV, 2, 64 pp.87-94, February 1957 |
| 19. Institutions versus Realities —a British Approach (with David Shapiro) | Article | Journal of Common Market Studies II, I, 1963 pp.24-37 |
| 20. Time to get tough with Europe (with David Shapiro) | Article | The Observer, p.10 21 April 1963 |
| 21. Untitled Review of Hugh Tinker's 'Ballot Box and Bayonet' | Review | New Society pp.26-7 6 August 1964 |
| 22. Rosa Luxemburg—A Sketch for a Portrait | Article | Survey 53 pp.48-59 October 1964 |
| 23. An Unknown Lenin Manuscript edited with notes | Article | International Review of Social History, Amsterdam, IX (1964) Part 3, pp.470-480 |
| 24. Consensus or Elite Domination: The case of Business | Article | Pol. Studies XII, I, Feb. 1965 pp.22-44 |
| 25. The German Social Democratic Party as a Political Model 1890-1914 | Article | Past and Present pp.65-95, 30 April 1965 |

26. Untitled Review of Wilfred   Review   Times Educ. Supple-
Hamson's 'Conflict and                ment, 14 May 1965
Compromise: a History of
British Political Thought,
1593-1900'

27. History, Biography and the   Review   Survey 57, pp.178-181
Russian Revolution. Review of      October 1965
'Merchant of Revolution': the
Life of Alexander Helphand
(Parvus) Z.A.B. Zeman and
W.B. Scharlan

28. 'Leeds West Constituency'   Contri-   London 1965
—a contribution to D.E. Butler bution
and Anthony King (Eds.). The
British General Election 1965

29. Rosa Luxemburg Today     Article   New Society
                                     7 April 1966

30. Rosa Luxemburg, 2 Vols.    Book     O.U.P. London/New
                                     York 1966

31. Are Two-Party Systems    Article   Parl. Affairs XIX, 2
Symmetrical?                       pp.218-224 Spring 1966

32. Comparative Political Studies  Comment Pol. Studies XIV, 2
a Cost-Benefit Analysis              pp.215-219 June 1966

33. Centre and Periphery in    Article   The American
Social Science                     Behavioural Scientist
                                   pp.39-46, June 1966

34. Europe's Laboratory: a     Article   New Statesman
Review of George Lichtheim's     pp.95-6, 15 July 1966
Marxism in Modern France

35. Presenting Politics: a Review  Review   Yorkshire Post
of Lord Windlesham's             21 July 1966
'Communication and Political
Power'

36. Industrialisation,       Article   Brit. Journal of
Development or Modernisation?    Sociology XVII, 3
(with R. Robertson)            pp.274-292, Sept. 1966

| | | |
|---|---|---|
| 37. The Concept of System in Political Science | Article | Pol. Studies xiv, 3 pp.305-338, Oct. 1966 |
| 38. Untitled Review of 'A Dictionary of the Social Sciences'. Editor: Julius Gould and William L. Kolb | Review | Pol. Studies xiv, 3 pp.404-405, 1966 |
| 39. Levi-Strauss: a Review of 'The Savage Mind' by Claude Levi-Strauss | Review | New Statesman pp.880-881, 9 Dec.1966 |
| 40. The Second International: a Review of three books by George Haupt | Review | Survey pp.180-183, Jan. 1967 |
| 41. Anniversary Offering: a Review of three books— Lionel Kochan, Russia in Revolution 1890-1918; George Katkov, Russia 1917, The February Revolution; Harold Shukman, Lenin and the Russian Revolution | Review | New Statesman 24 March 1967 |
| 42. Political Mobilization: A Sociological Analysis of Methods and Concepts | Book | Faber, London Basic Books, N.Y. 1967 |
| 43. Permanent Revolution | Article | New Society 15 June 1967 |
| 44. The Function of Opposition: a Review of The Politics of the European Communist States by Ghita Ionescu | Review | New Statesman 20 July 1967 |
| 45. Why Britain has a Brain Drain | Article | Yorkshire Post 8 August 1967 |
| 46. Return of the Intellectuals: a Review of 'The Social Origins of Democracy and Dictatorship' by J. Barrington Moore. 'Power and Privilege: a Theory of Social Stratification', by Gerhard E. Lenski | Review | New Statesman pp.435-436 6 October 1967 |

47. The Soviet Achievement — Book — Thames and Hudson
October 1967
Extract — Harpers Magazine
pp.90-98, Oct. 1967

48. The Problem of Equilibrium — Comment Pol. Studies
XV, 3 pp.357-358
October 1967

49. Alienation Anyone?—a — Review — Times Lit. Supp.
Review of Socialist Humanism — 7 December 1967
Editor Erich Fromm

50. Le 'Spectacle' de la Politique — Article — Analyse et Prevision,
S.E.D.E.I.S., v,
1 Jan. 1968 pp.47-45

51. Are Intellectuals Obsolete? — Article — The Nation
4 Mar. 1968 pp.300-306
The Listener
16 May 1968
New Society, April 1969

52. Untitled Review of 'The — Review — Labour History
Politics of Futility: the General — pp.307-9, Spring 1968
Jewish Workers Bund of
Poland, 1917-1943' by
Bernard K. Johnpoll

53. Rosa Luxemburg (revised — Book — Kiepenheuer & Witsch
and enlarged German edition) — Cologne 1968

54. International Systems and the — Book — Faber London 1968
Modernisation of Societies: the — Basic Books N.Y. 1968
Formation of National Goals
and Attitudes (with
R. Robertson)

55. Marx Substitutes. A Review — Review — New Statesman
of The Open Philosophy and — 5 July 1968
the Open Society by Maurice
Cornforth and Social and
Political Thought of Karl Marx
by Schlomo Avineri

56. The Politics of Development    Article    Commentary
    (with Karl Von Vorys)                    Vol. 46, 1 pp.52-59
                                             July 1968
57. The State as a Conceptual      Article    World Pol. xx, 4
    Variable                                 pp.559-592, July 1968

---

Published Posthumously:

58. Untitled Review of Gunnar      Review    Commentary
    Myrdal's Asian Drama: An                 December 1968
    Inquiry into the Poverty of
    Nations
59. The Leadership Analysed         Article    Purnell's History of
    (Section on the                          the 20th Century
    2nd International)                        1, Chap. 10, pp.262
                                             & 270-277
60. Savvy Savant: a review article Review    N.Y. Times Review of
    on the writings of Raymond               Books, Jan. 16 1969
    Aron
61. Rosa Luxemburg (revised         Book      O.U.P. London/New
    paperback edition with new               York 1969
    preface)
62. Ideas, Intellectuals and        Long      Forthcoming
    Structures of Dissent           Essay
    (A contribution to 'Intellectuals'
    Edited by Phillip Rieff)
63. Power and the Intellectuals     Contri-   Forthcoming
    (A Contribution to Power and    bution
    Consciousness, Edited by
    C. C. O'Brien)
64. The Early Works of Karl         Article    Forthcoming
    Marx and their significance for
    the Social Sciences
65. German Social Democracy         Contri-   Forthcoming
    and Marxist Revisionism         bution
    (A Contribution to 'The
    Dictionary of the History
    of Ideas')